COMPANION TO NARNIA

Eustace, Edmund, and Lucy bid farewell to Reepicheep, the courageous mouse, as his coracle skims the smooth green current and he rides the wave of eternity into Aslan's country. (VDT 213, 207.)

Companion to Narnia

PAUL F. FORD

Illustrated by Lorinda Bryan Cauley

1817

Harper & Row, Publishers, San Francisco

Cambridge, Hagerstown, Philadelphia, New York, London, Mexico City, São Paulo, Sydney

FIRST EDITION

Designed by Jim Mennick

Library of Congress Cataloging in Publication Data

Ford, Paul F

    COMPANION TO NARNIA.

    Includes index.

    1. Lewis, Clive Staples, 1898–1963. Chronicles of Narnia. I. Cauley, Lorinda Bryan. II. Title.

PR6023.E926C533   1980   823'.912   80–7734

ISBN 0–06–250340–5

80 81 82 83 84   10 9 8 7 6 5 4 3 2 1

In memory of
JAMES D. O'REILLY
(1916–1978)
who was C. S. Lewis to me

to
GEORGE L. CRAIN
GEORGE H. NIEDERAUER
JOHN BORGERDING
ANDRÉE EMERY
my living spiritual guides

and to
JOHN F. C. RYAN
VINCENT MARTIN
in gratitude for their priestly lives

Contents

List of Illustrations
and Maps

MAPS

Foreword

It is a great pleasure to write a foreword to Paul Ford's *Companion to Narnia* —and how my children would have loved such a rich compendium when they were "middle aged children" and the Narnia books were coming out. We used to keep a dictionary and a few other handy reference works in the dining room, in case we needed to look something up during meals—which usually happened.

My own first encounter with the worlds of fantasy came when I was a solitary only child in New York, and my grandfather, who was living in London, sent me books for my birthday and for Christmas—books by George MacDonald and E. Nesbitt (that remarkably liberated lady of the nineteenth century), and the *English Children's Annuals,* which were filled with fantasy. Perhaps my own loneliness contributed to the fact that the world of imagination was as real for me as the everyday world—in fact, more real.

I was not aware, until I began to read the MacDonald tales to my children, that he was occasionally preachy during his stories. He was, after all, a Congregational minister, even if he had been asked to leave his church, and preaching came naturally to him. And I would guess that it comes naturally to the child.

I looked at a contemporary copy of *The Water Babies* in a bookshop recently, and saw that it had been radically cut. I am glad that I read it all, sermons as well as story. Again, when I was a child, I didn't even notice that there were sermons in the book, and that I was being taught as well as amused. Perhaps as children we are more willing to be taught than we are as adults? We are aware that there is an infinite amount to learn, and if we are drawn into a "real" world of fantasy while we are learning, then the learning becomes a pleasure instead of the pain it often is in school.

And here I discover that I am enmeshed in paradox. Being instructed while I was reading seemed perfectly natural to me as a child, and yet I do not, by and large, like didactic stories. *Pilgrim's Progress* never had much attraction for me, and I would guess that this was because it teaches in a different way than the fantasy-spinning of MacDonald, Kingsley, Nesbitt—and C. S. Lewis. It is deliberate allegory, whereas the others are inadvertent allegory, and that makes all the difference in the world.

When I took a course in the techniques of fiction with Dr. Caroline Gordon, she taught us that Dante's great work of fantasy, *The Divine Comedy,* could be read on four levels,

> the literal level
> the moral level
> the allegorical level
> the anagogical[1] level

and these four levels are to be found in all true fantasy. The literal level is the story itself. The moral level is what the story has to say. It is impossible for a writer of fantasy to say nothing, and if he manages to do so, that in itself says something. But the impulse behind the writing of fantasy is usually an attempt on the part of the writer to express something, a particular personal concern. It is very obvious in MacDonald and Kingsley; they tell us exactly what their concern is at the moment of writing. E. Nesbitt is more subtle, perhaps because the world of intuition has, for many centuries, been more available to women than to men, who are taught from early childhood on to live in a restricted, rational world. If they delve into the realms of the intuition it must be apologized for, or explained.

For quite a while I struggled to understand the difference between the allegorical level and the anagogical level. Finally it came to me that allegory is simile; this is *like* this. But an anagogue is metaphor; this *is* this; it contains within it something of that which it is trying to express.

I do not believe that allegory is always conscious, and perhaps it is best when it is not; perhaps I've never much cared for Bunyan because I feel that he is beating me over the head with his allegory. And—despite the sermonizing—MacDonald and Kingsley do not. They are not objective teachers, but subjective ones; the sermon is as much for their own personal benefit as for the reader's.

The anagogical level, I am convinced, is never conscious when it is there, it is sheer gift of grace; the writer cannot strive for it deliberately for that would be to ensure failure.

So I understand Lewis's protestations that he is not writing allegory; of course he isn't. Nevertheless, there is an allegorical level to his stories, and, when he is at his best, an anagogical level. A writer who has grown up on

---

[1] The religious or mystical sense. Dante's theologian, St. Thomas Aquinas, recognized two senses of scripture: the literal (which the author intends, and the author is God) and the spiritual. This second sense is divided three ways: allegorical, moral, and anagogical. "So far as the things of the Old Law signify the things of the New Law, there is the allegorical sense; so far as the things in Christ . . . are types of what we ought to do, there is the moral sense; but so far as they signify what relates to eternal glory, there is the anagogical sense" (*Summa Theologica*, First Part, question one, article ten). William Tyndale, three centuries later, rightly complained that theologians had lost sight of the literal sense in favor of the spiritual sense; but enough of the tradition had survived for him to acknowledge that the allegorical sense appealed to the virtue of faith, while the anagogical sense appealed to the virtue of hope. See his *Obedience of a Christian Man*, Collected Works, I, 303. —P. F.

E. Nesbitt and Beatrix Potter, who encounters MacDonald as a teenager, in one of the most sensitive periods of life, cannot help having learned from these masters, even if the learning is intuitive and subconscious rather than the rational kind of learning that comes from a struggle with spelling or with the multiplication table or memorizing the imports and exports of Brazil.

I first encountered the work of C. S. Lewis when I was in my twenties, and in a period of confused agnosticism. Ten years of female institutions, six of them Anglican, is enough to confuse the hardiest psyche. I turned to Lewis for help, and unfortunately the first book of his I read was *The Problem of Pain*. I probably should go back to it again, now that the shepherd has called me back into the flock, for all I remember from it is outrage: he showed a total lack of sensitivity toward the pain of animals. It would seem that to him it did not matter whether or not animals were hurt—his most unEnglish trait! This is not the place to get into whether or not animals have souls, but if we return to Genesis, it was only man, Adam and Eve, who was expelled from the garden. And the pain of any kind does matter. I held in my arms an old collie who was dying, in great pain, from a heart attack. That pain is part of the pain of the world; if it doesn't matter then nothing matters. I put Lewis aside.

Then someone gave me *Out of the Silent Planet*. No longer was I being preached *at*, coldly and unlovingly (as I then felt), but I was given a story. Here was a world where I, too, could live; characters with whom I could identify. I was already into my own worlds of fantasy in my writing, and there was a wonderful sense of recognition: after all, we were taught by the same teachers! It is, obviously, not a matter of comparisons, but of kinship.

Slowly my reading friendship with Lewis strengthened. I was growing and changing. So was he. He did things he would probably have thought impossible at the time that he wrote *The Problem of Pain*—such as marrying a divorced woman while her husband was still alive. How strange it is that we grow more in doing the things we think we cannot do than in the things we think are possible or permissible! Lewis's theology lost its academic quality after he married Joy Davidman, and became infused with love. We have a tendency today to want people to be consistent; we change; we dwindle or we grow, and Lewis grew. His theology became more human as he grew through his surprises with joy and his battles with pain.

It doesn't bother me at all that Lewis was convinced that he did not allegorize at all in the *Chronicles of Narnia*. When a writer opens up to a fantasy world, a world which has more depths of reality to it than the daily world, all kinds of things happen in his stories that he does not realize; often the fantasy writer, if he is listening well, writes far more than he knows, and I believe that when Lewis was his best he did exactly that: he listened and he looked and he set down what he heard and what he saw. If grace comes during the writing of fantasy, the writer writes beyond himself, and may not discover all that he has written until long after it is published, if at all. The Narnia stories do instruct, and that is all right, for they are also story, they are also real. If they teach the reader, of any age, what Lewis himself was struggling to learn, that is an added benefit, not a detraction. Probably, as an adult, I am far more aware of the *teaching* in the *Chronicles* than I would have been if I had read them as a child. I don't think that my children noticed it, any more than I, as a child, noticed the teaching in *At the Back of the North Wind* or *The Water Babies* But I believe that if a writer is writing out of his own truth, then the reader is going to learn from that truth; it need not and should not be didactic, but it is nevertheless teaching, and I am grateful for it. We all have an infinite amount to learn, still, as adults; the learning period should never end; and the best way for me to learn has always been in coming across a writer's shared truth in story.

Now my granddaughters are eleven and twelve years old—those wonderful years for appreciating story. Again we rush to the dictionary in the middle of dinner. Now we have a new reference book to have fun with, and we are all—big and little—delighted.

MADELEINE L'ENGLE

Crosswicks
July, 1980

Acknowledgments

"The test of all happiness is gratitude," said G. K. Chesterton. And I am a very happy man because I have this chance to thank all the people who helped me complete this *Companion to Narnia*.

My single greatest benefactor of the past two years has been Mrs. Edith M. Keese who welcomed me into her home with the hospitality and the practical faith of a Mrs. Beaver.

I am very grateful to my superiors and coworkers at Franciscan Communications who have generously let me have three different leaves-of-absence in which to finish the book. A special word of thanks to my colleague, Dr. Corinne Hart, who (in addition to her heavy responsibilities there as associate producer) worked two months with me to turn my notes into entries. She helped me to break through to insights that otherwise I would not have had.

My friends in the Southern California C. S. Lewis Society, especially Marilyn Peppin, Dr. George Musacchio, and Dr. Ken Futch, formed a circle of encouragement around me. The Learning Church at Pasadena Covenant Church and the Women's Institute at Fuller Theological Seminary gave me a chance to uncork whatever vintage scholarship I had laid down these past years and I trust my classes were satisfying, and even sometimes sparkling. Dr. Robert Meye, Dean of the School of Theology at Fuller Theological Seminary, gave me the special privilege of developing and teaching with him a course in New Testament spirituality for the past three years. Two things have nourished me deeply during these years: learning along with my students the ways of the Lord; and growing in friendship with this man of earnest faith. His colleague and my mentor, Dr. Jack B. Rogers, professor of philosophical theology, has fostered me throughout my doctoral program at Fuller. Many others at Fuller have been paracletes in my writing process but three must have their praises sung: Vera Wils and Dolores Loeding, without whom the seminary would not be the happy and well-run place it is, typed much of the first draft and all of the second draft; and Wendy Bernhard, who was in on this project from the beginning and who was much more than the transcriber of my notes and Evangelical respondent to the draft.

I have succeeded in involving nearly all of my dearest friends in this book: Kerry and Jeremy Bell, who helped me greatly in the research; Patrick Dooling, my oldest friend, who researched Latin and Greek etymologies; Bridie and Charles Franich, Sr., whose loan of their beach-house allowed me to do a little more writing and to renew the friendship with my schoolmate, Charles Jr.; Roger and Sue Newell, who researched for me in Scotland and England; John Schiavone, who took me to a cabin in the mountains for a week to write; and Dr. Aune Strom, and her friends Keith Brandt and Kathy Olson, who read the American and British editions aloud to one another to compile a list of variants in the texts. Jim Bordenave and George Sullivan assisted me financially when I was on my various leaves from my job. Such friends!

I am especially grateful to my Dad and my sisters and brothers and, indeed, to all who have tolerated my absence from holiday celebrations and other occasions in the two years I worked on this book. I am also grateful to my monastic family, the Benedictine monks of St. Andrew's Priory at Valyermo, California, who helped make me the person I am today, and for their hospitality and prayer support.

The following scholars taught me that the fellowship of letters really exists: Dr. Jeanette Bakke, whose dissertation and correspondence was so helpful; Pauline Baynes, Lewis's own illustrator, whose vision of Narnia will always delight us; Dr. Bruno Bettelheim, whose insights into the importance of fairy tales helped me to understand Lewis's own growth to maturity; Fred and Antoinette Brenion, who were the first to make me aware of differences in the editions of the *Chronicles;* Dr. H. E. Ellis Davidson, author of *Gods and Myths of Northern Europe,* for her help with mythological allusions; Roger Lancelyn Green, Lewis's co-biographer and an authority on and author of children's literature; Father Walter Hooper, manager of C. S. Lewis's literary estate and my friend of seven years, upon whose own editing of Lewis's works every volume of scholarship gratefully depends; Dr. Thomas Howard, whose enthusiasm for Lewis is a "good infection"; Dr. Clyde S. Kilby, dean of American Lewis scholarship, founder of that *sanctum sanctorum,* the Wade Collection, and the all-helpful and ever-gracious seraph there; Dr. Peter Kreeft, who shares with me the joy Lewis gives the world; Dr. Jenijoy LaBelle, the Blake scholar at California Institute of Technology; Kathryn Lindskoog, who has been a constant encouragement to me in Lewis study; Dr. Gilbert Meilaender, whose book *The Taste for the Other* is the best philosophical and theological study of Lewis I have read; Mr. George Sayer, lifelong friend of Lewis and now, I am pleased to say, my friend; and Dr. Peter Schakel, who sets the standard for scholarship and courtesy where Narnia is concerned.

Two scholars need to be singled out from this list: Professor Thomas W. Craik, Department of English, the University of Durham, England, who in response to my request for help with the medieval and renaissance allusions made a special study of Narnia of his own and poured forth four lengthy letters packed with references. My debt to him is acknowledged throughout this volume. Dr. Robert Hurd, Department of Philosophy, Loyola Marymount University, drafted four of the philosophical entries—this work, and months of encouragement, and years of friendship, are part of the gift from God he is to me.

I am grateful for the patience and encouragement of everyone at Harper & Row in San Francisco. No author could hope for a more nurturing group of people to work with. Although, like Niggle painting his leaves, I would have liked to pause to perfect every entry, my editor and friend, Roy M. Carlisle, pushed me beyond my concern with perfection, and on to communication. Besides, he was the one who came up with the idea for this *Companion.* Max Perkins would see a reflection of his own editorial fostering in the attention Roy has paid to me and to this book. Roy encouraged me to find an artist who would try to do in our generation what Pauline Baynes did in hers: I found this artist in Lorinda Bryan Cauley (and Baynes agrees). Roy introduced me to his wonderful friend, Madeleine L'Engle; I am so grateful that this premier writer would pen a foreword to my book. Perhaps Roy's greatest find was my collaborator, Naomi Lucks. She made the labor and even the terror of writing this *Companion* an exhilarating experience. With incredible energy, she waded into this project, organized it, and got us both working at top efficiency. Her own good sense and good cheer can be seen in many entries: *Stories, Schools, Adventure, Books, Talking Beasts, Horses, White Witch,* and many more. In short, without Naomi, this book could not have been finished. A hearty word of thanks must also be said to Jessie Wood, Naomi's friend and a fine copy editor, who stepped in at a crucial time to help bring the project to completion.

And I am grateful in advance to the reviewers and readers who will show me how and what to improve in this *Companion* for future editions.

Finally, I am like Chesterton in his poem "Eternities," in which he wondered if eternity would be long enough to thank God even for the grass, when I think of how much I owe the seven people—six priests and one wise woman —to whom I have dedicated this fruit of the life of learning they inspired and encouraged. May our Lord give us time and words enough to begin to tell our gratitude to Him and to one another.

Introduction

The test of a good story, said C. S. Lewis, is whether it is often re-read. His own stories, *The Chronicles of Narnia,* have surpassed that test for hundreds of thousands of readers. Most of those who have fallen under the spell of *The Lion, the Witch and the Wardrobe* have not only stayed to hear or read the story of Narnia from its beginning to its second beginning, but they find themselves returning again and again, perhaps every few years, to savor anew its real beauties. Each reader brings to the *Chronicles* his or her own story and comes away with expanded horizons and renewed vision. This *Companion to Narnia* has been written for those who know the *Chronicles* to be good stories and who want to take a friend back with them to point out sights they haven't seen or want to see again through another pair of eyes.

If you have ever read the *Chronicles* aloud to a child or group of children, you know that they raise questions you haven't even considered. This volume does not intend to give final answers (because no final meaning can ever be put to a work of the imagination), but to suggest the direction in which answers and deeper meanings can be sought. Thus *Companion to Narnia* means to help you explore the various strands that Lewis weaves into the fabric of the *Chronicles*—literary, religious, philosophical, mythopoeic, homely, and personal images—the same fabric out of which our own stories are woven.

An encyclopedic format was chosen for *Companion to Narnia* because with it you may explore whatever angle you wish to take on the book. Beginning anywhere, with a character, an object, or a theme, you may go as far as you wish in pursuing a thread of curiosity. But no guide to Narnia can ever take the place of the seven books themselves. This book has been written for young people and adults who have read the *Chronicles* at least once, and who now want to explore what one critic has called the "allusive sub-text" that Lewis, as scholar and Christian, delighted in providing older readers of his fairy tales.

Lewis himself was very careful not to decode the *Chronicles* for the children who wrote him about their meaning. Typical of his response is the answer he made to the girl Hila Newman (June 3, 1953):

As to Aslan's other name, well I want you to guess. Has there never been anyone in this world who (1) Arrived at the same time as Father Christmas (2) Said he was the son of the Great Emperor (3) Gave himself up for someone else's fault to be jeered at and killed by wicked people (4) Came to life again (5) Is sometimes spoken of as a Lamb (see the end of The Dawn Treader). Don't you really know His name in this world? Think it over and let me know your answer![1]

Lewis would agree that the best way to appreciate a story is to step into it and enjoy it. One hazard in an encyclopedic study such as this is the ever-present risk of analyzing the life right out of a story. Stories are living things; and the result of any vivisection is only data about the thing and not the thing itself. The information and analyses in this book are meant to guide a person to a deeper experience of the open-ended nature of the *Chronicles* and not to close off all debate. Another hazard to be avoided is the desire to look for allegories, one-to-one correspondences between philosophical or religious concepts and the characters or events or objects in a story. Lewis was adamant that he was not writing allegory when he wrote the *Chronicles*.[2]

---

[1] Jeanette Anderson Bakke, *The Lion and the Lamb and the Children: Christian Childhood Education through "The Chronicles of Narnia"* Doctoral Dissertation, University of Minnesota, 1975 (Ann Arbor: University Microfilms, 76–4021), p. 341. Dr. Bakke transcribes many of these delightful letters in her text and in Appendix B. She also transcribes the entire correspondence that Lewis had with a nine-year-old American boy, Laurence Krieg, whose mother had written Lewis about her son's fear that he had committed idol-worship by loving Aslan more than Christ. Lewis responded immediately and with great sensitivity that when the boy thinks he is loving Aslan, he is really loving Jesus: and perhaps loving him more than he ever did before. "The things he loves Aslan for doing or saying are simply the things Jesus really did and said." The boy shouldn't worry about preferring the lion-body to a man-body because that's how a little boy's imagination works. But if he continues to worry, Lewis recommends the following prayer:

> Dear God, if the things I've been thinking and feeling about these books are things You don't like and are bad for me, please take away those thoughts and feelings. But if they are not bad, then please stop me from worrying about them. And help me every day to love You more in the way that really matters far more than any feelings or imaginations, by doing what You want and growing more like You. (May 6, 1955.)

Lewis adds a postscript to the prayer:

> And if Mr. Lewis has worried any other children by his books or done them any harm, then please forgive him and help him never to do it again. (Bakke, pp. 110–111.)

The Lewis-Krieg correspondence also preserves clues as to the meaning of Lewis's own writing for himself. In a letter just after his marriage to Joy Davidman, he writes Laurence (April 22, 1957):

> Well, I can't say I have had a happy Easter, for I have lately got married and my wife is very, very ill. I am sure Aslan knows best and whether He leaves her with me or takes her to His own country, He will do what is right. But of course it makes me very sad. I am sure you and your mother will pray for us.

Eight months later Lewis writes (December 23, 1957):

> . . . Aslan has done great things for us, and she is now walking about again, showing the doctors how wrong they were, and making me very happy. I was also ill myself but am now better. Good wishes to you all. (Bakke, pp. 110 ff.)

[2] Lewis was not trying to take these abstract ideas and personify them; this would be to allegorize. He was instead writing "supposals," as he called them. In a letter to a Mrs. Hook (December 29, 1958) Lewis explains the difference:

> If Aslan represented the immaterial Deity in the same way in which [in Bunyan's *The Pilgrim's Progress*] the Giant Despair represents Despair, he would be an allegorical figure.

The question remains, then, what *was* Lewis writing and why? A partial answer may be found in another story. A fictional C. S. Lewis and Dr. Elwin Ransom, hero of Lewis's Space Trilogy, are strategizing together in the last chapter of *Out of the Silent Planet.* Their problem: how to expose to the world the cosmic danger and the eternal consequences of the interplanetary activities of the deranged physicist Dr. Weston and the amoral opportunist Mr. Devine *without* risking "universal incredulity" and "a libel action." Their solution is "to publish in the form of *fiction* what would certainly not be listened to as fact." This plan would also reach a wider audience as fiction than would any detailed report. Ransom concludes, "What we need for the moment is not so much a body of belief as a body of people familiarized with certain ideas."

Nowhere does Lewis say as clearly that this is his chief concern in writing the *Chronicles* as he does in *The Voyage of the Dawn Treader* itself. In the last scene of the last chapter, Edmund and Lucy are disconsolate at Aslan's revelation that they will never come back to Narnia:

> "You are too old, children" said Aslan, "and you must begin to come close to your own world now."
> "It isn't Narnia, you know," sobbed Lucy. "It's *you*. We shan't meet *you* there. And how can we leave, never meeting you?"
> "But you shall meet me, dear one," said Aslan.
> "Are—are you there too, Sir?" said Edmund.
> "I am," said Aslan. "But there I have another name. You must learn to know me by that name. This was the very reason why you were brought to Narnia, that by knowing me here for a little, you may know me better there." (VDT 215–216, 209–210.)

But it is only partly true, as many have noted, that the *Chronicles of Narnia* have been written to familiarize a body of people, especially children, with certain ideas, namely the Christian faith and the way of life that goes with that faith. Lewis would insist that what he intends to teach is *mere* Christianity, "that which has been believed everywhere, always, by all," in the famous phrase of the fifth-century French theologian, Vincent of Lerins. There were, in fact, two Lewises, the one we might call the Augustine and the other the Aesop. Like

---

In reality, he is an invention giving an imaginary answer to the question, "What might Christ become like, if there really were a world like Narnia and He chose to be incarnate and die and rise again in *that* world as He actually has done in ours?" This is not an allegory at all. . . . Allegory and such supposals differ because they mix the real and the unreal in different ways. Bunyan's picture of Giant Despair does not start from a supposal at all. It is not a supposition but a *fact* that despair can capture and imprison a human soul. What is unreal (fictional) is the giant, the castle, and the dungeon. The Incarnation of Christ in another world is more supposal; but *granted* the supposition, He would really have been a physical object in that world as He was in Palestine and His death on the Stone Table would have been a physical event no less than His death on Calvary.

The distinctions are these: (1) In the *Chronicles* Lewis is beginning with the supposition that there *is* a world like Narnia (where some of the animals talk and where mythological creatures are real), that this world needs redemption, and that the king of beasts is to carry out the roles of creator, redeemer, and judge, as he does in our world; and (2) for Bunyan the giant is unreal but the despair is real; for Lewis in the *Chronicles* giants and talking beasts and the like *are* real and their spiritual situation is also real.

Augustine, Lewis came to Christianity in midlife, a man well-trained in the ancient tongues and a philosopher to his fingertips. He changed to become "the most converted man I ever knew," as a friend once wrote of him; and he put the full forces of his intellect and his gifts for communication to do battle for the truth. And like Augustine, Lewis's heart was fired with a sometimes ecstatic love for the world and its Creator. Unlike the North African bishop, however, Lewis hid his feelings and let his characters reveal in the stories he told the emotions he could not directly share.

The Aesop in Lewis is the older of the two. He learned his Irish folk tales on the knee of his nurse, Lizzie Endicott (who serves as model for Caspian's unnamed nurse in *Prince Caspian*), and was swept away by the newly published Beatrix Potter stories. Soggy Irish days kept him housebound; but this caused him, with his brother, to discover the joys of inventing one's own imaginary worlds. Lewis peopled his worlds with dressed animals and knights in armor: he was nearly born a storyteller. But Aesop was not the pure storyteller. The Greek slave was also a moral educator. And Lewis believed that talking animals and mythological creatures like giants and dwarfs could serve in children's books as picture-writing—hieroglyphs—which could communicate by the very fact of being well-drawn.[3]

Lewis offers much help to those who would read his stories as to how and why he wrote them. He complains that the heart of any story is often undetected by the most earnest critic thereof. A story is a "series of imagined events," "a net of successive moments." Yet the critic concentrates on style, order, and character delineation, the "everything else" which ought to exist *in fantasy* for the sake of the story. Lewis says[4] that in a certain sense he has never really "made" a story, that his stories began with pictures in his imagination, which—if the process happened perfectly—linked themselves together into a narrative. He only deliberately invented connections where the images didn't provide them on their own. (This may explain the episodic quality of *The Voyage of the Dawn Treader*.) He explains that he wrote stories for children because it was just the form for what he, the author, had to say.[5]

[3] In "On Three Ways of Writing for Children" (OOW, p. 27) Lewis says, "[the hieroglyphic] conveys psychology, types of character, more briefly than novelistic presentation and to readers whom novelistic presentation could not yet reach. Consider Mr. Badger in *The Wind in the Willows* —that extraordinary amalgam of high rank, coarse manners, gruffness, shyness, and goodness. The child who has once met Mr. Badger has ever afterwards, in its bones, a knowledge of humanity and of English social history which it could not get in any other way."

In his poem "Impenitence" in *Poems*, Walter Hooper, ed. (New York: Harcourt Brace Jovanovich, 1964) p. 2, Lewis writes again about animals as hieroglyphs:

Why! [the animals] all cry out to be used as symbols,
Masks for Man, cartoons, parodies by Nature
  Formed to reveal us

Each to each, not fiercely but in her gentlest
Vein of household laughter. . . .

[4] C. S. Lewis, "On Three Ways of Writing for Children," in OOW, p. 32.

[5] For Lewis, the purpose of a story is to set "before our imagination something that has always baffled the intellect." If, as defined above, a story is a "net whereby to catch something else," that "something else" is "much more like a state or quality." "The internal tension at the heart of every

As a child, Lewis had been told *how* to feel about God and religious realities. And this obligation to feel froze his feelings. Night after night in his school dormitory, he tried to muster all the proper feelings attendant upon saying the Lord's Prayer with devotion. His scrupulosity wearied him and he gladly gave all of this up when he left the practice of his religion in his early teens. There were "watchful dragons" at the Sunday school door, and these fostered a schism in his personality that lasted into his late forties. On the one hand, he was a deeply feeling person ("All my deepest, and certainly all my earliest, experiences seem to be of sheer quality"[6]); and on the other, his culture, his upbringing (an overly emotional father and an emotionally distant mother whose death, when Lewis was nine, was nevertheless his greatest loss), his education in stern logic, and his early religious training conspired to put his heart in a strait jacket. After his re-conversion to Christianity, he discovered he could pray from his emotions in a long process that was enabled by his writing of, first, *The Pilgrim's Regress,* and then the Space Trilogy, followed by the immensely liberating *Chronicles,* and completed by the greatest of his works, *Till We Have Faces.*

Essentially, Lewis saw the story as the bridge between the two ways of knowing reality: thinking about it and experiencing it. Thinking is incurably abstract; experiencing is always concrete. The human dilemma is that "as thinkers we are cut off from what we think about; [as experiencers] we do not clearly understand [what we are experiencing]. The more lucidly we think, the more we are cut off: the more deeply we enter into reality, the less we can think. You cannot study Pleasure in the moment of the nuptial embrace, nor repentance while repenting. . . ."[7] The thinking and the experiencing come together in only one place: a good story. A good story gives a concrete experience of a universal. As a work of the imagination, it helps people both to *contemplate* and to *enjoy* either an aspect of reality they already know or

story between the theme and the plot constitutes . . . its chief resemblance to life" in that "we grasp at a state and find only a succession of events in which the state is never quite embodied." To the extent that this incarnation takes place, however, to that extent the story can be called good. (OOW, pp. 20–21.)

[6] What is this state or quality that Lewis is talking about? He describes it best in Letter XVI of *Letters to Malcolm: Chiefly on Prayer* (New York: Harcourt Brace Jovanovich, 1964) p. 86:

> Yet mental images play an important part in my prayers. I doubt if any act of will or thought or emotion occurs in me without them. . . . In their total effect, they . . . mediate to me something very important. It is always something qualitative—more like an adjective than a noun. That, for me, gives it the impact of reality. For I think we respect nouns (and what we think they stand for) too much. All my deepest, and certainly all my earliest experiences seem to be of sheer quality. The terrible and the lovely are older and solider than terrible and lovely things. If a musical phrase could be translated into words at all it would become an adjective. A great lyric is very like a long, utterly adequate, adjective. Plato was not so silly as the Moderns think when he elevated abstract nouns—that is, adjectives disguised as nouns—into the supreme realities—the Forms.

Applied to God himself, Lewis states that *what* God is (the quality) cannot be abstracted from the person himself. "Our whole distinction between 'things' and 'qualities,' 'substances' and 'attitudes,' has no application to Him."

[7] C. S. Lewis, "Myth Became Fact," in *God in the Dock,* Walter Hooper, ed. (Grand Rapids: Wm. B. Eerdmans Publishing Co., 1970) p. 65.

something that they don't know and that the author of the story thinks would be good for them to know.

Lewis says in an early essay: "Reason is the natural organ of truth; but imagination is the organ of meaning."[8] One can reason about or *look at* another's experience all day and be able only to abstract about it; it is only when we *look along* that person's experience (if not actually, at least in imagination) that we can see, touch, taste what that person is experiencing. In this sense it can be said of theologians and many ordinary people that they contemplate Christianity but they do not enjoy it. In the *Chronicles of Narnia*, Lewis reverses this trend: he allows people, especially children, to look along Christianity without, perhaps, knowing Christ explicitly. He wants people to experience the meaning of the Christian facts first, to have their own feelings spontaneously, and then to become aware that this meaning is fact. But when well-meaning Christians short-circuit this process by decoding the *Chronicles* for their children, the watchful dragons resume their sentry posts outside the Sunday school door. As Gilbert Meilaender says:[9]

> Moral education . . . does not look much like teaching. One cannot have classes in it. It involves the inculcation of proper emotional responses and is as much a "knowing how" as a "knowing that." . . . The picture we get when we think of "knowing how" is the apprentice working with the master. And the inculcation of right emotional responses will take place only if the youth has around him examples of men and women for whom such responses have become natural. . . . Lewis, like Aristotle, believes that moral principles are learned indirectly from others around us, who serve as exemplars. . . . This is also the clue to understanding the place of the *Chronicles of Narnia* within Lewis's thought. They are not just good stories. Neither are they primarily Christian allegories (in fact, they are not allegories at all). Rather, they serve to enhance moral education, to build character. . . . To overlook the function of the *Chronicles of Narnia* in communicating images of proper emotional responses is to miss their connection to Lewis's moral thought.

Lewis took his storytelling seriously and his audience seriously.[10] In fact, his *Chronicles* have succeeded in restoring storytelling to the sharing of faith from one generation to the next. They reveal a writer at the apex of his art, in which his Christianity naturally effervesces. Yet many people inside and outside the Christian Church suspect him of having concocted his stories as a seven-part, subtle vehicle for converting children. Much as a soft-drink manufacturer adds carbonation to various syrups, so Lewis is accused or praised for selecting the central Christian doctrines and adding allegories to them. This

---

[8] C. S. Lewis, "Bluspells and Flalansferes: A Semantic Nightmare," in *Selected Literary Essays*, Walter Hooper, ed. (London: Cambridge University Press, 1969) p. 265.

[9] *The Taste for the Other* (Grand Rapids: Wm. B. Eerdmans Publishing Co., 1978) pp. 212–213.

[10] Lewis's affinity for children is apparent in this story he told about himself:

> Once in a hotel dining-room I said, rather too loudly, "I loathe prunes." "So do I," came an unexpected six-year-old voice from another table. Sympathy was instantaneous. Neither of us thought it funny. We both knew that prunes are far too nasty to be funny. That is the proper meeting between man and child as independent personalities. (OOW, p. 34.)

is not the case at all! The stories, in fact the pictures, came first and the ⦿ effervescence is natural.

Although Tolkien, like Lewis, began his storytelling spontaneously, he polished his stories like gems, revising time and again for inconsistencies. So thorough was his subcreation that he was able to devise whole histories and languages, and to people his novels with characters whose roots went deep into Middle Earth. Lewis, however, was less of a subcreator than he was a story-teller. He let the pictures of Narnia flow from his mind through his pen, and didn't bother about explaining inconsistencies until after the first three books had been published. Thus as pure subcreation, [11] Lewis begins his storytelling at perhaps a less exalted and intricate place than did Tolkien,[12] yet his first three books are alive with inventiveness and fun. *The Lion, the Witch and the Wardrobe* is caught up in describing the new world of Narnia, its enchantment by the White Witch, the lot of the Talking Beasts and the mythological creatures under her rule, the transformation of the country by the intervention of the Great Lion, and its subsequent rule by the four English children. *Prince Caspian* concentrates even more on the geography and astronomy and history of Narnia and adds considerably to the cast of characters; the dual plot seems to embellish the more essential story of the second liberation of Narnia with the gratuitous tale of Aslan's bacchanal. But this second plot is *not* superfluous, for the reasons cited in the text of this *Companion*. Then, in almost an excess of imaginative energy, *The Voyage of the Dawn Treader* takes the reader from the slave-trading intrigues on islands close to Narnia to the very threshhold of Aslan's country in a crescendo of what we would have to call mysticism. After a pause of at least two months, Lewis, like a portraitist finished with his subject, begins *The Horse and His Boy* to fill in the background by telling a story that takes place in Calormen and Archenland. But along the way, much as Shasta encountered Aslan in the fog, Lewis is overwhelmed with the possibilities of moral education through his long-cherished form of the fairy tale. So, after a second pause of at least four months, Lewis plunges into the creation of the last three *Chronicles*.

The tone has changed when we enter the world of *The Silver Chair*. The scene is Experiment House, the progressive school that Eustace Scrubb attends. In this fifth *Chronicle* (published fourth), Lewis shows how aware he is of the two senses of the word "spell." Tolkien had written, "Small wonder that *spell* means both a story told, and a formula of power over living men."[13] Since

---

[11] See J. R. R. Tolkien, "On Fairy Stories," in *Essays Presented to Charles Williams*, C. S. Lewis, ed. (Grand Rapids: Wm. B. Eerdmans Publishing Co., 1968) pp. 66–67.

[12] See *Appendix One* for a chart of the chronology of the composition of the *Chronicles*. It is important to be aware of the fact that Lewis did not begin with any plan to write seven *Chronicles of Narnia*. He seems to have worked out of three separate spurts of energy. The first produced LWW and a rough draft of MN. The second resulted in PC and VDT. The third was responsible for HHB. And the final impulse saw SC, LB, and MN. The series was christened *The Chronicles of Narnia* in 1952 by Lewis's dear friend, Roger Lancelyn Green, on analogy with Andrew Lang's *Chronicles of Pantouflia*. See *C. S. Lewis: a Biography*, Roger Lancelyn Green and Walter Hooper (New York: Harcourt Brace Jovanovich, 1974; London: Collins, 1974) p. 245, *245*.

[13] *Essays Presented to Charles Williams*, p. 56.

INTRODUCTION

the time he wrote *The Pilgrim's Regress,* Lewis was alive to the paralyzing hold the enchantment of the spirit of the age has on the minds and hearts of living men and women. He often refers in addresses and sermons to his desire to weave a counter-spell. And it is this tone we detect very strongly in *The Silver Chair.* The emphasis is on discipline ("Remember, remember the Signs"), on the power of fear and of the desire for pleasure, and on obstinacy in belief (the very title of an address he gave to the Socratic Club during the same time he was finishing this *Chronicle*).

In *The Magician's Nephew,* Lewis returns to the threads of a story about the creation of Narnia that he had begun and almost immediately abandoned after he had finished *The Lion, the Witch and the Wardrobe.* Less a sub-creator than simply alive to his own memories of the turn of the century, he recreates those times as the background for a discussion of the consequences of the unbridled desire for knowledge and power in Andrew Ketterley and his nephew Digory. Lewis's ability to create real characters doesn't fail him, of course, and his Jadis is menacingly real; but she is also the logical outcome of what exists in its beginning stages in the boy and well-advanced in the uncle. A certain balance between the subcreator and the moral educator is re-achieved in the Narnian creation scenes. But the pull is in the direction of the moral educator.

The Last Battle has all the quality of the "twilight of the gods" (one of Lewis's earliest experiences) transformed, though not right away, by the Christian hope of *eucatastrophe,* Tolkien's term for the "joyous sudden turn" of a fairy tale.[14] A sense of invention is lacking, but its absence is scarcely noticed because Lewis is working in the white heat of his artistry within the world he has already created. The story has a life of its own and it moves easily through the eschatological themes of death, judgment, hell, and heaven. It is not only the fitting conclusion to the *Chronicles:* given Lewis's Christian faith, it is their only possible conclusion.

Thus we are left with a crucial question: In which order should the *Chronicles* be read? *Companion to Narnia* studies them in the order of their publication: *The Lion, the Witch and the Wardrobe; Prince Caspian; The Voyage of the Dawn Treader; The Silver Chair; The Horse and His Boy; The Magician's Nephew;* and *The Last Battle.* This is the order that Lewis and his publishers first settled upon. However, at the very end of his life, Lewis suggested that they might be read in the order of their internal chronology: *The Magician's Nephew; The Lion, the Witch and the Wardrobe; The Horse and His Boy; Prince Caspian; The Voyage of the Dawn Treader; The Silver Chair;* and *The Last Battle.* [15] If Lewis had been able to complete his intended revision, perhaps this second enumeration would be the better. But for several reasons, the order of publication is to be preferred. First, in order to avoid the ever present danger of decoding the *Chronicles,* the publication order carries the reader along in a less logical, less factual mode, and presents the pictures and the meanings of Lewis's stories in the way he first decided to tell them and in the way the first readers of the

---

[14] *Essays Presented to Charles Williams,* p. 81.
[15] See PWD, p. 32.

Chronicles enjoyed them. And though at least two other possible reading orders exist (the order in which they were begun and the order in which they were completed), there is at least one other reason for reading them in the order of publication.

Many modern Christian theologians,[16] basing their thinking on the best of modern biblical scholarship, have discerned that the Hebrews first knew themselves as a people as the result of their having been miraculously rescued from slavery in Egypt. Their first experience was one of redemption. Only later, when they came into contact with the Babylonian culture in which an elaborate explanation of the creation of the world was given, did they gather their own creation stories together and write, under inspiration, their own origins and the origins of the universe. If, as Charles Huttar suggests,[17] the only adequate literary classification for the *Chronicles* is biblical; if the *Chronicles,* as genre, find their closest analogue in the Judaeo-Christian Scriptures themselves; if the *Chronicles* are a supposal of salvation history (creation, redemption, and completion) in Narnian terms—then reading them in the order of publication has one additional reason to recommend itself. Lewis began by writing a redemption story in *The Lion, the Witch and the Wardrobe.* He then tried to write a Narnian creation story but was unable to complete it at the time. It was only after he had involved himself in the transformation stories of several characters that he was able to tell the story not only of Narnia's beginnings but also of its consummation. I submit that reading the *Chronicles of Narnia* in the order in which they were published enables the reader to experience something truer even than Lewis intended: the primordial necessity of passing first through redemption, then into a reinterpretation of one's own story, and finally allowing the future to take its provident course.

When I first read the *Chronicles* as a college student, I knew that I had crossed a frontier. I found in them a world in which I was welcome, in which I was at home. At first they made a strong appeal to my more apologetic side: they gave explanations of all that I held most dear. But as the years and the re-readings went on, I found myself returning to Narnia at times of crisis, and recommending them to everyone I cared about.

My mentor, Monsignor James D. O'Reilly, who is the principle dedicatee of this *Companion,* suffered a stroke in the early 1970s. I most readily accepted the task of assisting him during his weeks of recovery. It was then that I persuaded him to read the *Chronicles.* He found the stories wonderful and I cherish my copies with the pages he dog-eared.

But it was in the winter of 1978, when I was making the difficult transition from life as a Benedictine monk to life "in the world," that the meaning beneath the apologetic of the *Chronicles* overtook me. During this time I fell ill for a week and took up these books for perhaps the fifteenth time. Little

---

[16] For example, John Courtney Murray, *The Problem of God* (New Haven: Yale University Press, 1962).

[17] "The Grand Design" in *The Longing for a Form,* Peter Schakel, ed. (Kent, Ohio: Kent State University Press, 1977; Minneapolis: Baker Book Publishing Co., 1979).

did I know that I was not only being nourished in the depletion I was then feeling, but I was also being prepared for a loss greater even than my temporary loss of vocational direction: Monsignor died suddenly in the spring of 1978. On the day, weeks later, when we cleared out his rooms completely, I could not rest for the abandoned feeling I felt. As I lay down to what I thought would be another fruitless nap, I remembered Shasta's experience with Aslan at the ancient tombs in *The Horse and His Boy*. The only prayer I could manage was, "Aslan, lie at *my* back. The desert is ahead of me, the tombs behind. Help me rest." For the first time in months I rested.

So only those who have looked at the world of Narnia from the outside conclude that Lewis is didactic. Those of us who return to the *Chronicles* year after year, sensing in them the "Grand Design" of the Scriptures themselves and deriving from them the courage to go on through the deserts and the underlands of life, the conviction to pass by the luxurious enticements of Tashbaan or Harfang, and contentment with the splendor hidden in the ordinary fare and fidelities of our existence, know Lewis to be our spiritual pilgrim-companion.

To assist him in this role of service is the aim of *Companion to Narnia*.

PAUL F. FORD

Arcadia, California
August 15, 1980

Using the Companion

How To Find An Entry   Entries are in alphabetical order. Characters are listed by first name (e.g., Andrew Ketterley is listed under "A" for Andrew), and honorifics or titles are left off (e.g., Prince Caspian is listed under "C" for Caspian, and Mr. Beaver is listed under "B" for Beaver, Mr.).

How To Read An Entry

> **ENTRY TITLE**   Perhaps the first element you will notice when reading the text of an entry is the asterisk.* It is there to alert you that the word or phrase it follows is also an entry.[1] Singular and plural forms of the entry title will both be asterisked (e.g., animal* and animals*). Some longer titles, such as Seven Friends of Narnia* and Castle of the White Witch* are listed under the first word of that phrase, not the last (e.g., "Seven . . ." and "Castle . . ."). Listed at the end of most entries you will find the critical apparatus: the pages on which the referenced material can be found are listed parenthetically (when pages are not given after certain entries, it is because these pages have already been given in cross-referenced entries). Cross references not specifically mentioned in the text are listed in [*brackets*] below the page numbers. The book title will always be abbreviated (as it will be when discussed in the text), and a list of abbreviations is included at the end of this section. The first page number following the book title refers to the American edition of that book, and the second—*italicized*—number refers to the British edition. Thus LWW 1, *11* means you will find the same information on page 1 of the American edition and page 11 of the British edition of *The Lion, the Witch and the Wardrobe*. Whenever books other than the *Chronicles* are cited in American and British editions, the *italicized* number always refers to the British edition. The letters "ff." following a page number mean the reference can be found on at least four pages following that number; and the word "passim" following a page or chapter number means the reference can be found throughout the rest of the chapter or book.
>
> (LWW 1, *11*; 23, *34*. PC 36, *45*; 43–44, *66–67*. HHB passim. MN 34 ff., *43 ff.* LB Chapter 11 passim.)
> [*Astronomy, Narnian; Owls; Providence.*]

---

[1] Footnotes are listed following the entry.

Major Characters and Themes   The following entries are major characters and themes and are therefore not referenced or asterisked in the text of other entries:

Aravis, Aslan, Bree, Cair Paravel, Caspian X (Prince Caspian), *Chronicles of Narnia, Dawn Treader,* Digory Kirke, Edmund Pevensie, Eustace Clarence Scrubb, Hwin, Jill Pole, Lucy Pevensie, Narnia, Peter Pevensie, Polly Plummer, Puddleglum, Reepicheep, Shasta, Susan Pevensie, White Witch.

List of Abbreviations   The books of the *Chronicles of Narnia* are abbreviated as follows:

LWW   *The Lion, the Witch and the Wardrobe*
PC   *Prince Caspian*
VDT   *The Voyage of the Dawn Treader*
HHB   *The Horse and His Boy*
SC   *The Silver Chair*
MN   *The Magician's Nephew*
LB   *The Last Battle*

Frequently used references are abbreviated as follows:

OOW   *Of Other Worlds,* Walter Hooper, ed. (New York: Harcourt Brace Jovanovich, 1966).
PWD   *Past Watchful Dragons,* Walter Hooper, ed. (New York: Macmillan Publishing Co., 1979).

The abbreviation "N.Y." following a date means "Narnian Years"; thus 1014 N.Y. is Narnian time.

The Companion from A to Z

ADAM   See *Son of Adam, Daughter of Eve.*

ADELA PENNYFATHER   See *Gang, the.*

ADULTS   Throughout the *Chronicles,* Lewis uses "grown-up" as a synonym for wrong thinking: Lucy identifies as "grown-up" the skepticism she sees in Susan's question, "Where do you think you saw Aslan?"; Lewis as omniscient author comments that ". . . it is the stupidest grown-ups who are the most grown-up"; and Shasta "has the fixed habit of never telling grown-ups anything if he [can] help it." Perhaps the main complaint children have against grownups is that they have lost their imaginations.* One short conversation between Polly and Digory illustrates this quite well. When they propose to explore the long-unoccupied house beyond Digory's, he says, "It's all rot to say a house would be empty all those years unless there was some mystery." "Daddy thought it must be the drains," replies Polly. Digory comments, "Pooh! Grown-ups are always thinking of uninteresting explanations."

The good grown-ups of the *Chronicles* are few: Professor Kirke, King Caspian, Puddleglum, the High King Peter, Ramandu,* the Hermit of the Southern March,* King Lune,* Mabel Kirke,* Letitia Ketterley,* Mr. and Mrs. Pevensie,* and Erlian.* Of these, three are really child characters, two are not human, and one is dead. These characters have in common their honesty and goodness, and are generally not as interesting as the more wicked adults, who have in common their total contempt for things childish. In fact, it is a dead giveaway of wickedness in the *Chronicles* for an adult character to identify things children hold dear as "fairy tales," "old wives' tales," or "impractical"; and they usually pay for their nonbelief in the end. Miraz* does not believe in the old stories,* and instructs Caspian never to talk or think about them; eventually (and almost as a direct result) he loses his life and his kingdom. Digory recognizes right away that Uncle Andrew* is an evil* magician,* and he knows from stories that magicians always come to a bad end. The implication is that if Andrew had believed these "old wives' tales," he might never have gotten started in the business. For Lewis, adults in general are narrow-minded, disbelieving, and concerned only with practicality. It is their world that spawned Experiment House.* The children of the *Chronicles* have very few good relationships with adults,[1] and their parents, guardians, and elders often mean them harm. Uncle Andrew is ready to sacrifice Polly for science, and he doesn't really care at all about his nephew Digory unless the boy can serve him in some way; Miraz* is ready and willing to kill his nephew Caspian; the White Witch is driven to kill the Pevensie children; the Queen of Underland* murders Rilian's mother. The only good parent-child relationship is that between King Lune and his sons; even the emotional reconciliation between Erlian and Tirian* takes place after death. The Tisroc* is ready to kill his son Rabadash* for his cowardice; Arsheesh* has never treated Shasta well and is willing to sell him into slavery; and Aravis has a stepmother who hates her and a father who wants to marry her off. The very old characters fare somewhat better, but they do not enter a contented old age and spend much of their time being rejuvenated. The problem of adulthood is finally reconciled in Aslan's country,* where those who have grown old become young and lose their gray hair and wrinkles, and the very young mature only to the flower of their manhood and womanhood.

---

[1] This is very close to Lewis's own experience with his parents. Like the parents of many of the children in the *Chronicles*, his mother died when he was young, and he didn't get along well with his father, who was uncontrollably emotional and unable to listen to his son. Tirian's reconciliation with Erlian is in fact Lewis's own literary reconciliation with his father, and the scene is full of images from his own life. See *Autobiographical allusions.*

ADVENTURE   In the *Chronicles,* adventure is a metaphor for life in its highest realization. There is no turning away from the adventure, for it is only in leaving the known for the unknown that honor* may truly be found. The meaning of adventure is perhaps made most clear to the two characters who have hardly an inkling of its meaning: Jill and Eustace, the two victims of modern education at Experiment House.* Both are unprepared to deal with the adventures they meet in Narnia, but it is precisely in taking adventures as they come that they learn what adventure is; indeed, by recapturing this lost sense of adventure they are able to bring it back with them and infuse Narnian life into the pale shadow of England.* Queen Susan is the first to use the word adventure, and notes that people who have had similar adventures share a special speech and look. Reepicheep is perhaps the greatest adventurer in all the *Chronicles.* He is the first to leap into adventure, and considers turning away to be cowardice.* He proclaims the entire purpose of the *Dawn Treader's* voyage to be the search for honor and adventure, and takes his own final adventure, alone and valiant, into the Utter East.* But his love of adventure does not prevent him from ignoring the inexorable law, and he reminds Caspian that the king* "shall not please himself with adventures as if he were a private person," thus reminding Caspian of his vocation. Caspian himself appeals to the crew's sense of adventure when he asks them to continue on to the East.

In SC, Rilian underscores Reepicheep's belief that adventure is not to be taken lightly. When the children* and Puddleglum are trying to guess the meaning of the fireworks, he says, ". . . when once a man is launched on such an adventure as this, he must bid farewell to hopes and fears,* otherwise death or deliverance will both come too late to save his honor and his reason."[1] Rilian gives adventure another meaning. His faith in the truth of Aslan gives him confidence to say, ". . . let us descend into the City and *take the adventure that is sent to us*" (my emphasis). This passive acceptance of the necessity of adventure is echoed three times in LB: once by Tirian,* after Jewel's* reiteration that Aslan is not a tame lion*; once again by Jewel himself, when he announces they should return to Stable* Hill; and again by Tirian when he accepts the fact that Jill and Eustace will stay with him for the inevitable Last Battle.* Just as HHB is an adventure for Shasta and Aravis and Bree and Hwin; and as the adventure of exploring the attic leads Digory and Polly to greater adventures in Narnia; and as Narnia is an adventure for all of the Seven Friends of Narnia*; the *Chronicles of Narnia* are an adventure for the reader, which Lewis hoped they would keep with them for the rest of their lives.

(LWW 184, *169;* 186, *170–171.* VDT 152, *152;* 169, *166–167;* 172, *169;* 168, *165;* 183, *180;* 209, *203.* SC 19, *29;* 36, *43;* 168–169, *164–165;* 181, *176.* MN 5, *12.* LB 20, *24;* 92, *85;* 94, *87;* 135, *124.*)
[*Imagination.*]

---

[1] This recalls Reepicheep's response to the Dark Island.* His special quality consists of having no hopes or fears,* so that he is able to see the voyage into the darkness as pure adventure. Alone of all the crew he is untouched by the island's horror. But Lord Rhoop* and the Dawn Treaders enter the darkness, bringing their hopes and fears with them: They do not *take the adventure;* rather, the adventure *takes them.* Lost in their illusions, they almost lose their hope and their reason. Rhoop, indeed, is only restored by Aslan's gift of dreamless sleep.*

AHOSHTA TARKAAN   The Tisroc* of Calormen's* Grand Vizier, and the man to whom Aravis has been promised in marriage. Originally of the lowest class in Calormen, he has intrigued and flattered his way into the highest circles of power. He owns three palaces, and an especially expensive one at the lake at Ilkeen.* He is described as a "little, hump-backed, wizened old man," and he is most often seen in a pose of prostration at the feet of the Tisroc. In Aravis's perception, he is a "hideous grovelling slave" who pretends to be obsequious but is really trying to manipulate the Tisroc to his own ends.

(HHB 34 ff., *36 ff.*)
[*Axartha Tarkaan.*]

ALAMBIL   One of two planets in the Narnian night sky (the other is Tarva*), it is surnamed "The Lady of Peace" by Glenstorm* the Centaur.*

(PC 43, *47;* 74, *72.*)
[*Astronomy, Narnian.*]

ALBATROSS   A large sea-bird, and a symbol of good luck to sailors, who believed that to shoot one is to court bad luck.[1] It is a likely symbol for Christ in the *Chronicles.* As the *Dawn Treader* seems hopelessly caught in the spell of the Dark Island,* Lucy calls on Aslan for help. Soon a broad beam of light cuts the darkness. Looking first like a cross, the source of the light is seen to be an albatross, who through his words and voice* reveals himself to Lucy to be

Aslan (or at least a messenger from Aslan) and tells her to take courage.* The ship is soon out of the blackness, and the albatross disappears, unnoticed.

(VDT 159 ff., *158 ff.*)
[*Aslan's voice; Birds; Dreams; Literary allusions; Providence.*]

ALBERTA SCRUBB   The mother of Eustace and the aunt of Edmund and Lucy. The children dread spending their summer holiday at "Aunt Alberta's home," where even the one picture they like is banished to a small back room. A nonconformist in many ways, Alberta furnishes her home very sparsely; bed covers are few and the windows are always open. Along with her husband Harold,* she is a vegetarian, teetotaler, and nonsmoker; both she and Harold wear "a special kind of underclothes." She is apparently something of a feminist, as indicated by Eustace's remark that she would consider Caspian's giving Lucy his cabin because she is a girl to be demeaning of girls. When the children return from the experience of the *Dawn Treader* and remark how changed for the better Eustace is, Alberta only finds him commonplace and boring, and blames his changed demeanor on the influence of "those Pevensie children."

(VDT 25, *32;* 216, *210.*)
[*Adults; Sexism.*]

ALCOHOLIC BEVERAGES   See *Wine.*

ALIMASH   A Calormene* nobleman, captain of the chariots, cousin of Aravis, and comrade-in-arms of Bree. He is among the victors in the conquest of Teebeth.*

(HHB 41, *43.*)

AMORALITY   See *Right and wrong.*

ANDREW KETTERLEY   The mad magician* of MN. Andrew is Digory Kirke's uncle, the older brother of Digory's mother, Mabel Kirke,* and resident in his sister Letitia Ketterley's* London house, where he lives on the top floor.[1] He is a pale shadow of his Narnian counterpart Jadis,[2] but through him Lewis provides a frightening suggestion of the destruction that can occur in our world if power is given over to the hands of immoral experimenters. Completely without conscience, he is only out for himself: he has no scruples about sending Polly unwittingly into an unknown world—one into which he does not himself dare to venture; he shows the depths of his despicableness when he silences Digory's protests by suggesting that any further noise might frighten his seriously ill mother to death; and he thinks nothing about his godmother, Mrs. Lefay,* and his deathbed promise not to open her Atlantean* box. He shows himself to be the very antithesis of stock responses* to human values at every step of the conversation he has with his nephew in

Chapter 2. Rules are for children,* servants, women, and ordinary people—not for "geniuses" such as himself.[3] He has toiled his entire life to learn magic, at great cost to himself, so that he could open the forbidden box—and all it contained was dust (Lewis expects his readers to agree that this is the natural reward for a life devoted to magic). At the reminder in Digory's speech that he is just another in a long line of evil* magicians from the fairy tales, and that justice is always done, Andrew seems for a second to realize the horror of his perfidy. But his choice for evil takes over again and he attributes Digory's "warped" moral sense to his having been "brought up among women . . . on old wives' tales." In their experimenting with the rings,* Digory and Polly discover that Uncle Andrew does not really know how the rings work; like most magicians, Lewis says, "Uncle Andrew . . . was working with things he did not really understand." At the arrival of Queen Jadis into his study, his chaotic speech is quite similar to Dr. Wither's in *That Hideous Strength.*[4] He has obviously met a magician of greater power, and tries to piece together the shreds of his dignity by boasting that he comes from an old Dorsetshire family —a boast that is all the more pitiful for his lack of the more fundamental virtues. As MN progresses, Uncle Andrew becomes more and more a figure of fun. A combination of his best clothes and brandy turn his head to the grown-up kind of silliness called imagining one is in love. He looks even sillier when he stumbles out of the crashed hansom cab; and when he is swept into the Wood between the Worlds* by Digory's magic ring his troubles really begin. Thinking he is dead, he claims he never wanted to be a magician and it's all his godmother's fault. His total removal from the world of the spirit is evident during Aslan's creation* song, of which Andrew has no comprehension. His mouth falls open, but not in joy.* His chief desire is to hide from the sound.* He calls Narnia "completely uncivilized," because he thinks technology* is the mark of civilization. His primary reaction to the wildness of the Lion is a desire to shoot him, especially as he presents an obstacle to Andrew's dreams of commercial possibilities in this land where everything grows.

Andrew's extreme selfishness is most tellingly expressed in his inability to understand anything that doesn't directly relate to his own needs.[5] He and the newly created Talking Beasts* watch one another, the animals* out of curiosity and Andrew out of fear. Here he shows himself to be not a true scientist, but only "dreadfully practical." Andrew sees the animals* only as potential threats, and cannot understand their intelligent speech. For their part, they can't figure out whether he is animal, vegetable, or mineral, and their ensuing conversation about Andrew's nature is one of the funniest in all of the *Chronicles.* The miserable Andrew is eventually released by Aslan from the cage in which the animals have kept him, and he spends the rest of his days living at the Kirke's country house.

(MN passim.)
[*Elephants; Golden Tree; House of Professor Kirke; Humor; Jackdaw; Right and wrong; Silver Tree.*]

[1] Polly's suggestion that Andrew is keeping a mad wife upstairs is a literary allusion* to Rochester's action in *Jane Eyre*.

[2] See *White Witch* for a discussion of the parellels between Andrew and Jadis.

[3] This appeal is similar to that of the Grand Inquisitor in Dostoevski's *The Brothers Karamazov*.

[4] C. S. Lewis, *That Hideous Strength* (New York: Macmillan Publishing Co., 1965, and London: Pan Books, 1955).

[5] This is also true of another remarkable character, Peggy, in Lewis's short story "The Shoddy Lands."

ANIMALS   Animals of all sorts play a large part in the *Chronicles,* and are present in all the books. Two types of animals inhabit Narnia: Dumb Beasts* and Talking Beasts.*[1] Although most animals are good and helpful, several are outstandingly bad. Thus giant bats are in the Witch's army, and wolves are present for Aslan's sacrifice. Fenris Ulf* (Maugrim) is one of the Witch's chief lieutenants. Apes assist in binding Aslan for sacrifice, and Shift* is perhaps the most despicable animal of all.

Each animal acts according to its stereotype. Moles* dig the apple* orchard at Cair Paravel; Mr. Beaver* builds Beaversdam*; horses* carry smaller creatures into battle with the Witch; Glimfeather* is a wise owl.* Distinct from this, Lewis uses animals as hieroglyphs or "pictures" of certain human attributes; Reepicheep, for instance, is a hieroglyph of courage.[2]

According to Trufflehunter,* beasts (unlike humans and dwarfs*) "hold on"—they do not change and they do not forget. For this reason he is able to recall that Narnia was only "right" when a Son of Adam* sat on the throne. Also, unlike humans, animals do not have nightmares, and cannot understand why men fear* things.

Finally, the regard in which animals are held is a good barometer of moral health. In PC, when Narnia is under the rule of the Telmarines* and the old stories* are almost forgotten, it is observed that many more beasts are dumb than was the case in the Golden Age.* The Witch, who hated beavers, stamped out all but Mr. and Mrs. Beaver so that there are none left in Narnia by the time of Prince Caspian. Uncle Andrew* uses guinea pigs in his experiment with the magic* dust, and—because he owns them[3]—is not troubled that he has to kill them. And the fact that the giants* of Harfang* would eat Talking Stag—not to mention Men and Marsh-Wiggles*—shows that they are far from being good giants.

(LWW 149, *132;* 148, *138;* 154, *143;* 171, *158.* PC 18, *24;* 65, *64;* 67, *66;* 164, *145.* VDT 157, *156.* HHB 163, *143.*)

---

[1] Animals from various world mythologies* (such as the Kraken,* the Phoenix,* and the Unicorn*) are also present in Narnia; however, they seem to be a variety distinct from either Dumb Beasts or Talking Beasts.

[2] For a fuller discussion of Lewis's use of hieroglyphs, see *Introduction.*

[3] As exemplified by the title of *The Horse and His Boy,* Lewis does not—at least in Narnia—recognize ownership of animals. In fact, they are presented as another sort of people. Hwin is spoken of as a gentle person (HHB 131, *117*), and the Hermit* calls the horses and goats his cousins (HHB 141, *125*). See also the unnamed hedgehog* in HHB (163, *143*), "a small prickly person."

ANNE FEATHERSTONE   A schoolmate of Lucy Pevensie. Lucy is not fond of Anne, and Anne is jealous of Lucy's relationship with Marjorie Preston.* Lucy magically overhears a conversation in which Anne shames Marjorie into pretending she does not care for Lucy at all.

(VDT 131 ff, *133 ff.*)
[*Magic; Privacy; Vanity.*]

ANRADIN   A Tarkaan,* remarkable for his scrupulously kept crimson beard. He visits the hut of Arsheesh* and, in an act typical of an insensitive Calormene* overlord, offers to buy his "son" Shasta. He is the master of Bree and thus by inference a veteran of the battle at Zalindreh.* Later he is part of Rabadash's* insurgents and a participant in the battle of Anvard.* His fate is unknown.

(HHB 3–6, *12–15;* 181, *159.*)

ANVARD   The name of the King of Archenland's* castle. Very old, it is built of warm reddish-brown stone and sits amid green lawns with a high, wooded ridge in back. It has many towers, but no moat. In his plot to take over Archenland and Narnia, Rabadash* intends to hold Anvard and gather his forces there. It is the site of the battle of Anvard.

(HHB 110–111, *99–100;* 163, *144;* 165, *145;* Chapter 13 passim; 203, *178.*)

APPLES, APPLE TREES   Apples and apple trees are a recurring motif in the *Chronicles,* and are connected with good things and salvation. In PC, the apple orchard helps the Pevensie children remember the days long ago when they were Kings and Queens,* and it helps them to remember that they are once again at Cair Paravel; and the apples are their first source of food on that journey. In the very center of the garden* of the west is a tree with silver apples, one of which Digory picks and brings back to Aslan. Digory plants the silver apple, and from it grows the Tree of Protection.* The smell of this tree is loathsome to the witch, who had eaten one of its apples, and so—at least for a time—she is prevented from entering Narnia. Digory brings an apple from this new tree to his mother, Mabel Kirke,* back in London. The color and smell of this apple of youth are scarcely describable, and like all Narnian things it is even more glorious against the drabness of London. It restores life to his mother, and sends her off into her first real sleep* since her illness. Digory buries the apple core in the back garden, and an apple tree grows from its seeds. Eventually this tree is knocked down in a storm, and from its wood is made the wardrobe* through which Lucy first enters Narnia.

(PC 10, *17–18.* MN 158, *147;* 181, *167–168.*)

ARAVIR   Narnia's morning star.* It is phonetically similar to Tarva,* another heavenly body.

(PC 150, *135*.)
[*Aravis; Astronomy, Narnian.*]

ARAVIS   A Calormene* noblewoman, in her early teens, who is one of the four main characters in HHB (the others are Shasta, Bree, and Hwin). The story details her flight from the cruel, stifling world of southern Calormen to freedom in the north, specifically Archenland.* More important, HHB is the chronicle of her transformation from arrogance and self-centeredness into an example of true Narnian nobility; that is, the exercise of humble and compassionate leadership. She becomes Queen of Archenland (the wife of King Cor) and the mother of King Ram* the Great. She is last seen in the assembly of famous Narnians in the Great Reunion* in Aslan's country.*

She is the only daughter of Kidrash Tarkaan,* a Calormene nobleman. As is the case for many characters in the *Chronicles,* her mother is dead and her stepmother is cruel. Her one older brother was killed in one of Calormen's innumerable wars; her one younger brother is still living, but only because he is still too young for battle. Her already difficult homelife is rendered absolutely unlivable by her father's decision to marry her to Ahoshta Tarkaan,* an ugly, loathsome ladderclimber in the country's labyrinthine civil service. This circumstance precipitates her desire to flee; first through a suicide attempt, and that foiled, to a new life in the North. She is small and slender enough to be mistaken for a boy, and has in fact been raised as something of a tomboy.

That she is an equestrienne of great competence is a clue to more than her athletic ability. For Lewis, horsemanship* is a symbol for the relationship between spirit and body and between humankind and nature. But as a Calormene horsewoman, Aravis is perhaps too much the one in control. In her interaction with the talking Narnian horses, she learns to respect all Narnian Talking Beasts* as fellow rational beings who are never to be exploited.

To her credit she is an efficient, intensely loyal, and brave person: she doesn't lose her head in the confusion at the gates of Tashbaan*; despite Shasta's fears to the contrary, she would never even think of abandoning her promised rendezvous with him; and while hidden during the Tisroc's* secret meeting with Rabadash* and Ahoshta, she conquers her terror and keeps Lasaraleen* quiet. She despises her former fiancé all the more for his spineless obsequiousness, and she is revolted by the Tisroc's cool heartlessness and his son's savagery. These are some of her good stock responses.* But some of the Calormene ruthlessness is also in her character. Thus she is able to exert great pressure on her father's scribe to forge a letter for her, and to drug her stepmother's maid to facilitate her own escape, without regard to either servant's fate.[1]

Her arrogance is especially revealed in her attitude toward Shasta, whom she initially takes to be a common horsethief. Learning otherwise, she nevertheless shows her ignobility by resenting his inclusion on the journey to Narnia. Furthermore, his sensitivity to her maidservant's fate offends her. Thus she speaks to him only when necessary.

Lewis depicts her transformation by a succession of lessons, which she (like Eustace) masters with uneven progress. Bree gives Aravis her first lesson in the meaning of Narnian freedom* (so far as he understands it) by speaking with her horse before addressing her. When Aravis is offended by this, he tells her that all talking creatures are equal in Narnia (this is not exactly the case): "Hwin isn't *your* horse any longer. One might just as well say you're *her* human." She shows that the lesson has, for the moment, passed over her head, by holding exclusive conversation with Bree for the next several days. Her second lesson comes at the gates of Tashbaan when she has to make a humble entrance into the capital city. She doesn't do too well here, either, because she compensates for the humiliation by picturing in her imagination* the royal treatment she ought to be receiving from the unknowing citizenry. But a model of the stifling reality of such royal treatment is presented to Aravis by the arrival on scene of her friend, Lasaraleen Tarkheena. The sight of what Aravis could turn out to be, all aflutter about fashions, foods, and *affaires-de-coeur,* drives the lesson home. For the first time she is convinced that she would rather endure the "impropriety" of journeying with a peasant boy to "horrible" Narnia, there to be a free "nobody," than to stay and be a petted and petty "somebody" in Calormen. Confirmed in her rejection of the luxurious exterior of Calormene life, Aravis witnesses the treachery at the heart of her country when she overhears the secret council of the Tisroc. She leaves Tashbaan with relief, a feeling* she was heretofore incapable of experiencing.

Lewis juxtaposes an advance and a retreat of Aravis's transformation in the desert journey, to underscore his belief in the nature of conversion as a process. Aravis wears a prim expression on her face as she walks beside Hwin, almost as though she thinks herself better than Shasta, who (having scorched his bare feet on the burning sand) has to ride Bree. On the other hand her strong sense of duty, aided by her nascent humility,* causes her to accept the blame for the four travelers falling asleep after their grueling day on the desert, and to make excuses for the horse and for Shasta.

The crisis of this process is reached in the days of her recuperation from the Lion's attack. She first learns that providence,* not luck, has spared her more serious hurt. Shasta's bravery in the face of the Lion has moved Aravis deeply; and she is now more concerned about him than about herself. In fact, she wants to apologize to him before she can feel worthy to enter free Narnia: she feels the need for confession. This in turn disposes her to appreciate the beauty of the Lion when he finally comes to her. He completes her transformation by calling her to himself and revealing that it was he who scratched her in order that she might feel the consequences of her cruelty to her stepmother's maid. Her contrition moves her to ask about the slave girl (this is the final sign of the process), but here Aslan invokes the doctrine of privacy.* In order to absorb this whole experience, she withdraws for a period of silent meditation.

At last a true Narnian, Aravis is ready to meet Shasta, now Prince Cor of Archenland. The goodness of her character combines with her new virtues in several different scenes that illustrate her transformation: her grateful courtesy to the new prince, her invoking of the doctrine of privacy when he expresses the desire to know more about the knight who died to save him, and her refusal to let him apologize for his poor manners. A remnant of hauteur shows itself in her reaction to the sight of King Lune* in his old clothes; but the bow he gives her, "stately enough for an emperor," moves her further beyond her old ways of thinking. A final sign of her new generosity and sensitivity comes out when she volunteers the story of Cor's bravery against the Lion. When she greets with instant friendship* the model ruler, Queen Lucy, and delightedly goes off with her to discuss clothes and other womanly things (her inward nobility is ready to wear royal robes,* in contrast to the fashions of Calormen that disguise empty or treacherous hearts), Aravis is ready to reign as a queen in a northern country.

(HHB passim. LB 179, *161*.)
[*Animals; Autobiographical allusions; Centaur; Government; Horses, Horsemanship; Sexism.*]

---

[1] This quality is reminiscent of the character Orual in C. S. Lewis's *Till We Have Faces* (New York: Harcourt Brace Jovanovich, 1980) in her treatment of the Fox, Bardia, and others of her subjects.

ARCHENLAND   The smaller and more southern of the two northern kingdoms, the other being Narnia. It is bordered to the south by the Southern Marches (where the Hermit* lives), and to the north by the Northern Mountains (which are, of course, Narnia's Southern Mountains). Archenland is a lovely country of gentle hills, snow-clad, blue-peaked mountains, and narrow gorges. The slopes are covered with pine, and all varieties of trees grow in the park-like portions of the country. Archenland and Narnia have been friends since before memory,* and the High King Peter intends to make Corin* a Knight* at Cair Paravel. The wine* of Archenland is so strong that it must be mixed with water before drinking. In MN, Aslan foretells that some of the descendents of King Frank* and Queen Helen* will be kings* of Archenland.[1]

(PC 57, 58. VDT 67, 74. SC 171, *166*. HHB 58, *57;* 72, *68;* 133–135, *118–199*. MN 140, *130*.)
[*Geography, Narnian.*]

---

[1] According to Lewis's outline of Narnian history (PWD, p. 41) Prince Col,* the younger son of King Frank V, founds Archenland in 180 N.Y.

ARDEEB TISROC   Paternal great-great-great-grandfather of Aravis.

(HHB 33, *37*.)
[*Ilsombreh Tisroc; Tarkaan; Tisroc.*]

ARGOZ   One of the Seven Noble Lords,* and one of the four Telmarine* visitors to the Land of the Duffers* in the years 2299–2300 N.Y. At Aslan's Table* he is one of the Three Sleepers.* When the Lord Rhoop* is rescued from the Dark Island,* he is seated beside Argoz to begin his rest.

(VDT 16, *23;* 149, *149;* 168, *165;* 186, *182.*)
[*Sleep; Time.*]

ARLIAN   See *Erimon.*

ARSHEESH   A poor fisherman who lives in the far south of Calormen* on a little creek of the sea[1] with his "son" Shasta. The awkward expression "with him there lived a boy who called him father" is indicative of something irregular in their relationship. Silent and distant, Arsheesh is constantly finding fault with the boy and sometimes beats him. His practical mind and limited vision make him unable to answer Shasta's questions about the North, the land of freedom. As a result, the boy becomes wary and uncommunicative towards grown-ups in general. There may be an intended similarity between the name "Arsheesh" and the word that best describes him, "harsh."

(HHB Chapter 1 passim; 70, *67;* 157, *138.*)
[*Adults.*]

---

[1] Note Lewis's use of the British meaning of "creek" as a small inlet or bay that is narrower and extends farther inland than a cove. Confusion with the American meaning has caused some misunderstanding of the picture Lewis has in his mind of Glasswater Creek.*

ASLAN[1]   [1]The Lion King of the land of Narnia and of all its creatures, the son of the Emperor-beyond-the-Sea,* true beast and the king* of beasts, the highest king over all high kings, and the as-yet-unrecognized good and compassionate Lord of all, beginning with the children* from England.* The very hearing of his name is an experience of the numinous* for all who are destined to live in his country, but for those who are for a time or for ever under the spell of evil* magic* his name is filled only with horror. The beholding of his beautiful face sustains one all one's days; and the recognition of that face with love and awe at the end of time* opens out onto an eternity of joy.* To be addressed by him as "dear heart" or "little one" or by name is a lasting, cherished blessing; to be rebuked by him is an everlasting shame. Whom he praises with an earthshaking "Well done" remains forever favored; whom he blames or punishes is humbled in the hope of an enduring change of heart. Though he is wild—that is, all-powerful and free—he delights to be at the center of the dance* of those whom he has made; he welcomes the help of others, both beast and human, to accomplish his plans; and he is the very often unnoticed storyteller behind every person's story, guarding the privacy* of each, keeping faith with all. Lucy and Caspian and Reepicheep seem the English woman and the Narnian man and the Narnian Talking Beast* most beloved of Aslan in the *Chronicles* only because more of their stories* is told.

But the apex of C. S. Lewis's literary, mythopoeic, and apologetic gifts is the character of Aslan, because this Lion comes straight from the heart of Lewis's contemplation and enjoyment of God and of the world God made.

Physical appearance   Aslan is towering in size, larger than a horse,* as large as a young elephant,* and always growing bigger with respect to the person who sees him; in this respect he is the very figure of the greatness of God.* In overall aspect, he is "so bright and real and strong" that all else pales in comparison. His coat is a "soft roughness of golden fur" (to quote Lewis's paradoxical description). During Aslan's ecstatic romp with Susan and Lucy on the morning of his resurrection, his tail lashes back and forth in the Lion's intense joy. His paws are beautifully velveted in friendship and terrible in battle; he walks noiselessly, as do all his feline relatives. His legs, haunches, shoulders, chest, and back are powerfully muscled. His mane is a beautiful sea of rich, silky, golden fur, scented with a solemn, strengthening perfume. He uses his long whiskers to prove his lion-ness to the doubting Bree. His golden face reveals his regal personality in all of its emotions. This is especially true of his "great, royal, solemn, overwhelming eyes," which reflect the full range of his feelings,* from happiness and mirth to scorn and anger. If it weren't for the calming quality of his deep voice, no one could stand in his awesomely beautiful presence.

(The following page references are not in the customary order of publication, but are keyed to the phrases in the above paragraph on Aslan's physical appearance: VDT 215, *209*. SC 215, *205*. VDT 107–108, *111–112*. HHB 192, *168*. HHB 159, *140*. PC 136–138, *124–126*. SC 210, *200*. LWW 162, *149*. PC 148, *133*. HHB 192, *168*. LWW 160, *148*; 125, *118*. PC 144, *130*. VDT 134, *135*. MN 108, *100*. PC 136, *124*; 209, *183*. PC 138, *125–126*. HHB 160, *140*. LWW 138, *128*. HHB 193, *168*. LWW 123, *117*. LWW 124, *117*.)

The Lion, the Witch and the Wardrobe   Aslan is talked about in two of the seventeen chapters of this first of the *Chronicles* (Chapters 7 and 8) and he is present for five chapters: from near the beginning of Chapter 12 to near the beginning of Chapter 17. (Only in MN is he more on the scene than in this book.) His chief activities are bringing spring to Narnia after the Hundred Years of Winter,* dying in Edmund's stead to fulfil the demands of the Deep Magic,* restoring to life the creatures turned to stone in the Castle of the White Witch,* killing the White Witch, and installing the four Kings and Queens* at Cair Paravel.

Mr. Beaver* is the first person to use Aslan's name, the sound of which occasions the first of the children's many numinous experiences connected with Aslan. Using the battle-imagery that has been a chief ingredient in the background of Lewis's writing since his first Christian book,[2] Mr. Beaver says that the Lion is "on the move," that indeed he may have "already landed." Once in Narnia, he is expected to "put all to rights," that is, to bring justice. Similar expectations are made of the Messiah in the Old Testament (for

As Mr. Tumnus, the faun, serves tea, Lucy looks over the curious books on the shelves. (LWW 12, 19.)

example, Isaiah 42:1–4, the first of the four Servant Songs in which the prophet pictures Israel's redeemer as one who will suffer on behalf of the whole nation in order to bring the long-awaited Kingdom of God on earth). Mr. Beaver emphatically rejects any thought that Aslan is human because he (and Lewis at the time of writing LWW) understands Narnia is inhabited by Talking Beasts* (even the term is not used until PC) and mythological creatures and not by humans; therefore, for him to be truly their king, he must be the king of beasts, that is, a lion.* Lewis is not writing a christology in the *Chronicles;* if he were, then he would have to indicate somewhere that Aslan is the pre-existent son of the Emperor and became a lion through a miraculous and at the same time natural birth. But there is no precise analogue of the Incarnation of Jesus Christ, as Christian theology understands it, in the figure of Aslan: he comes on the Narnian scene already and always a lion; he did not become lion to save Narnia.

Aslan is first seen in the *Chronicles* in a heraldic setting, a tableau of mythological creatures seated in a half-circle around the splendid lion. It is very important to let this picture sink into the imagination*: Dryads* and Naiads* are playing music*; four magnificent Centaurs* are standing at attention; the Unicorn,* the pelican, and the eagle (all symbols of Christ) are present; a man-headed bull,* a great dog,* and two leopards sit at either side of Aslan, one with Aslan's crown and the other with the Lion's standard. Aslan here is *seen* (before he is known) as the center of the best pagan and Christian intuition.[3] He is "good and terrible at the same time," yet another reference to the numinous. Addressing the three children as Sons of Adam* and Daughters of Eve, the Lion underscores the fact that this phrase almost single-handedly raises these books to a theological power for the older reader. In his silent gaze, Edmund's absence and Peter's partial guilt need only acknowledgment, not explanation. In Lewis's understanding of judgment, we are the agents, God is the witness; he accepts our confession or allows us to condemn ourselves.[4] Fully aware of the cost of helping Edmund, Aslan looks sad; but he attends to the business of maturing Peter for the boy's role as High King.[5] He holds back any who would assist the future ruler in his lonely, necessary confrontation with fear*: obedience* to the reality of his sisters' need should be and is his only consideration. Aslan rewards this tested courage* with the honor* of being a knight.

Edmund is rescued; and after a private conversation with Aslan (the detail of "dewy grass" suggests that the restoration the boy is experiencing is refreshing), he is returned by the Lion to the fellowship of his brother and sisters with a word to them that his past is his "own story"—though these words are not actually used, this is the first mention of a major motif in the *Chronicles:* Lewis's "doctrine" of privacy.*

In Aslan's parlay with the Witch, Lewis intends to contrast his serenity with her villainy: his golden face, her death-white face; his calm strength, her agitation; his looking her in the face, her avoiding eye contact. Her outrage at his feigned forgetting of the meaning of the Deep Magic* is complemented by his roar at her suggestion that he won't keep his promises. Her look of fierce joy at the arrangement to exchange Aslan's life for Edmund's is contrasted with Aslan's look of sternness so strong as to forbid conversation.

The fact that the Lion makes two plans with Peter for the course of the coming battle with the Witch and her forces and that he cannot guarantee to Peter that he will assist Peter in the battle is an allusion to the "humanness" of the Lion. Lewis is aligning Aslan with what some Christian theologians believe of Christ in his earthly life: that he did not, as man, know the future, that he did not see the resurrection on the other side of his death, and that, therefore, he had to suffer and die like all of his fellow humans, trusting that his Father had a plan even for dying. Lewis goes on to accentuate the parallels between the passion of Christ[6] and the passion of Aslan: both seek the comfort of a few close friends, both suffer ridicule and torture at the hands of their enemies, both are cruelly tied down and savagely executed, the bodies of both are ministered to by friends (the mice* who nibble away Aslan's ropes work silently, so it is not clear[7] until the end of PC that they were Dumb Beasts* until Aslan rewarded their kindness with the gift of speech*); and, rising out of sight of anyone (the empty table suggests the empty tomb), both must reassure their loved ones that they are indeed alive, and alive in a new way.[8] First Aslan explains the meaning of the Deep Magic and the Deeper Magic* to the girls, and then a most remarkable scene takes place. The ecstatic romp of the Lion and the girls has no equal in Lewis and perhaps none in any works of Christian imagination. None tires or gets thirsty (an anticipation of the glory communicated to the Dawn Treaders by the sweet waters of the Last Sea,* and of the run of the Seven Friends of Narnia* and the blessed Narnians to the garden* of the west in LB).

Aslan's roar, his run to the Witch's castle, and his leap over its walls are all Narnian supposals of what Christ's ascension would look like in this imaginary world. Particularly significant is the harrowing of Narnia's "Hell*" and the release of the creatures who had been turned to stone by the witch's wand. Aslan revives them by his breath, here most assuredly an image of the Holy Spirit.* His encouragement of the now-revived lion with the phrase "us lions" and his employment of the giant* to break down the castle walls and the sheep-dog to organize the creatures into a force that will be helpful in what will later be called the First Battle of Beruna* are all instances of Lewis's profound belief that one of the consequences of the incarnation (God's desire to identify with us by becoming one of us)[9] is that he wants our help in the process of transforming the world.[10] As if to emphasize another aspect of the incarnation, Lewis describes the killing of the Witch by saying, "The great *beast* flung himself upon the White Witch" (my emphasis).

There is an intended contrast between the two ways Aslan addresses Lucy in the scene where she aids the wounded Edmund with her cordial.* The Lion calls her by name when he reminds her to use her gift; but when she stays to see the results rather than to go on to help others,[11] he calls her "Daughter of Eve," that is, one who shows her sinful ancestry in her sinful actions. (A similar differentiation in how Aslan addresses people occurs throughout the *Chronicles,* especially in the Lion's dialogue with Digory in MN.) After breathing on the creatures turned to stone by the Witch in battle, Aslan miraculously provides a splendid high tea for the combatants, an echo of Father Christmas's* breakfast tea two days before and a foretaste of the delights at Aslan's Table.*

The next day Aslan solemnly crowns the four children and enthrones them at Cair Paravel. His words of commission, "Once a king or queen in Narnia, always a king or queen. Bear it well, Sons of Adam! Bear it well, Daughters of Eve!" is Lewis's way of restating the ancient dictum of Pope St. Leo the Great: *Agnosce, Christiane, dignitatem tuam,* "Recognize, O Christian, your dignity."[12]

Then, during the course of the coronation celebration, Aslan slips away. His withdrawal does not surprise the children because Mr. Beaver had instructed them in Aslan's ways: "he has other countries to attend to" (the first hint of the other worlds, including ours, over which he is Lord); and he comes and goes at his own discretion, because "he's wild . . . Not like a *tame* lion" (Lewis's emphasis). This is the first enunciation of what, after one mention in VDT (by Coriakin*), will become a major motif in LB.

Prince Caspian   Aslan is on scene for three and a half chapters of this fifteen chapter book (for a brief instant toward the end of Chapter 9, from the middle of Chapter 10 and all of 11, and from the middle of Chapter 14 to the end). He is also present in Narnia, though not talked about, for Chapters 12 and 13 to the middle of 14. His chief activity is to deliver Narnia for a second time with a two-fold battle plan: by inspiring Caspian in his fight against his usurping uncle, Miraz,* and by rekindling the joy of Narnia by working miracles of revitalization. In both strategies Aslan demonstrates his dependence on people or beings besides himself: Caspian and his army of dwarfs,* giants, Centaurs, and animals are reinforced by Peter and Edmund and the Tree-People*; and Aslan is assisted by Bacchus,* Silenus,* and the Maenads* in releasing the shackled spirits of Narnia. A theme that runs through the book is the faith-suspicion spectrum, from the mystical faith of Lucy on one extreme to the agnosticism of Trumpkin,* the atheism of Nikabrik,* and the pragmatism of Miraz. The attitude that each character takes toward Aslan is crucial to knowing what Lewis understands by faith.

In the midst of the discussion among the children and the dwarf about which route they should take to Aslan's How,* the Lion appears for an instant to Lucy, the one most attuned to his will. If the others had the gift of discernment that Edmund has, they would have agreed with him that Lucy is the one to follow. But after a vote,[13] they go off in another direction. In a second and longer appearance to Lucy, a most extraordinary scene takes place. Aslan calls her by name and rolls over on his side in order to allow her to repose between his front paws.[14] He reveals to her his continued growth in greatness and they share together the silence* of that revelation. But this is only a respite[15] from the task ahead of them. Lucy has become so sensitive to him that he has but to growl faintly and she knows she must cease to criticize the others. He has but to look at her and she takes responsibility for following him by herself, realizing that he would have been with her. When he tells her that what *would* have happened is irrelevant and that only what will happen is under anyone's control, he announces another theme that is elemental in Narnia, the positivity* or the givenness of reality. The others *will* see, depending on their faith.[16] The fragrance of his mane fills her with the courage to confront the others with the message that she will go on alone. Aslan is impatient enough to stamp his paw as a signal to hurry. Each sees Aslan in proportion to the faith each has, first as "a something" and then as himself. When all see him, he stops and gives them a look so majestic that they have yet another experience of the numinous. "My dear son" is Aslan's reply to Peter's greeting and repentance. His "well done" to Edmund foreshadows the larger praise Aslan will give to Digory and Tirian. The Lion calls Susan by name and "child" to indicate his understanding of the power of fear* in human life. Though the children can tell by Aslan's look that he loves Trumpkin, the Lion subjects the dwarf to a welcome guaranteed to remove the dwarf's doubts about Aslan's visibility and vitality. At this point the narrative divides into two strands:[17] the direct confrontation of Caspian's reinforced troops with Miraz's army and the flanking action of Aslan's own efforts to call Narnia forth from its second relapse into coldness, this time a chilling of its heart. His roar inaugurates this reliberation and the first of the five dances* in PC begins. If Lewis wanted to disguise the divinity of Aslan, he would not have used such terms as "gaze on," "stood still and adored," and "bowed" to describe the activity of the Dryads* and Tree-People* as they come into the presence of the Lion.[18] Onto the scene rush Bacchus,* Silenus,* and the Maenads* with their ecstatic cry right out of the heart of classical Latin literature, *Euan, Euan, euoi-oi-oi-oi.* This release of the passionate frightens Lucy and Susan until they realize who these personages are and to whom they answer: Aslan.[19] This theme continues through to the morning after the third dance when Aslan announces that all in his company will make holiday together. As if to stress the significance of this event, Aslan allows the girls (whom he calls "children") the privilege of a second ride on his back.

They dance their way to Beruna, which is the very picture of the pent-up lifestyle imposed by the Telmarines. The bridge at the fords—the oppression of the River-god*—is destroyed by Bacchus and his followers.[20] In every instance Aslan's revelry* is itself the sword of division[21] which separates those who will permit themselves to be happy from those who are horrified at the thought. Most flee, but a few join in, especially from the ranks of the oppressed.[22] To Aslan, Gwendolen* is "sweetheart"; the weary schoolmistress* is "Dear Heart" (a greeting later given to the distraught Lucy at the Dark Island* by the albatross*); the crying child at the door of the nurse's* house in Beaversdam* is "my love"; and the nurse herself is called "dearest." Aslan receives this woman's profession of faith and restores her health. For her and the rest, Bacchus brings water turned to wine,* a "miracle of the old creation."[23] In a lovely scene, the girls dismount Aslan and the nurse takes their place. All dance* off to the scene of the struggle between the Old Narnians and the New.

At this point, the two narrative strands are woven back together. Aslan, coming to the battlefield, strikes an unqualified fear into the ranks of the Telmarines, renders the Red Dwarfs awed and speechless, and causes the Black Dwarfs to edge away. But, like the Dumb Beasts who greeted him from Beruna to Beaversdam, the Talking Beasts on the battlefield receive Aslan with joy. He interrogates Caspian on his fitness to be king and applauds the boy's humility. He confers with Reepicheep* about the mouse's lost dignity —his severed tail—and he restores it on account of the magnanimity of the mice, their love of their leader, and their ancient kindness to him at the Stone Table. All celebrate their victory with the feast that Aslan provides through the "agency" of the dance of plenty. This scene closes with the complex symbolism of the Lion and the Moon gazing upon one another lovingly throughout the night.[24]

In the final scene, Aslan sets Narnia on a new course by returning the Telmarines to earth and enthroning Caspian as king over a restored land. That Aslan knows of earth is another hint at his divine identity. He dismisses the fears of one group of Telmarines and disabuses the royal pretentions of the other. He reveals to Caspian that the boy is legitimate ruler of Narnia only because he is a Son of Adam, albeit in the line of earthly pirates, and makes one of the most important statements in the *Chronicles* about the dignity and humility of the human race. He rewards the courage of the Telmarine man who volunteers to be the first to return to earth through the miraculous door* with his blessing and his breath. His deep eyes are the last sight the Pevensie children have of Narnia, for Peter until he sees the Lion again in Aslan's own country in LB and for Susan seemingly forever (or until she has a complete change of heart).

The Voyage of the Dawn Treader   Significantly, only in LB is Aslan less on scene than in VDT—in parts of little more than two chapters in the entire sixteen chapters of the voyage narrative.[25] He is active with Eustace offstage at Dragon Island,* in an apparition on Deathwater Island,* with Lucy during her reading of Coriakin's* Book* in the Land of the Duffers,* as an albatross* near the Dark Island,* with Caspian offstage during the king's attempted abdication on the Silver Sea,* and as the Lamb* at World's End.* The voyage is undertaken only because Caspian sought and received Aslan's approval to swear a solemn oath* to search for the Seven Noble Lords.* Aslan's image in beaten gold is hung above the door of Caspian's cabin, a sign that this quest* is made under the Lion's patronage.

In Aslan's appearance to Eustace, a halo or aura of moonlight surrounds the Lion, even though it is a moonless night. The sight of the Lion excites in the boy-turned-dragon* the fear of the holy. In silence* Aslan leads Eustace to a well in the middle of a garden on a mysterious mountain top. And, again wordlessly, he instructs the boy to shed his skin. When Eustace tries three times and fails to really remove his dragonishness, Aslan asks permission to intervene to do the job and the boy submits out of his desperate desire to end the pain of his arm and to doff his dragon appearance.[26] The pain (paradoxically a pleasure) that Eustace experiences as Aslan pierces through with his claws to his boyhood is a sign that this time the shedding will be complete. The Lion throws the freshly peeled boy into the well and he emerges Eustace again. Aslan dresses him and returns him to the king's beach camp, and to the fellowship of the Dawn Treaders. The wonderful dreamlike quality of this scene, coupled with the reality that Eustace is changed back into a boy to begin trying to be a better human being, is perhaps the most beautiful visualization of the meaning of conversion and baptism in children's literature.

When Eustace asks Edmund who Aslan is and whether Edmund knows him, Eustace recites what might be considered the first adequate Narnian creed; most significantly, he reverses Eustace's phrasing to the proper biblical order: "Aslan knows me."[27]

In the crisis of greed* on Deathwater Island, Aslan appears on the other side of the pool, "shining as if he were in bright sunlight though the sun had in fact gone in" (a picture of his divine radiance paralleling his nighttime appearance to Eustace). This vision seems to erase the memory* of the explorers in a manner similar to the way in which the sight of Aslan seems to stay with people all their days (as in the case of Digory and Polly).

When the beautifying spell in the Magician's book becomes a temptation to vanity* for Lucy, an illumination of Aslan's growling countenance appears in bright gold on the very page at which she is looking. When she recites the spell that makes everything invisible visible, Aslan appears, standing in the doorway. From his willingness to receive her embrace and kisses and the purring sound he makes, it is obvious he is glad to see her. He explains that he had been there all the time[28] but that he has now become visible because he obeys his own rules.[29] He declares that she has been eavesdropping, overrules her silence, deflects her avoidance in her attempt to shift the blame to the technique (magic*), calls invasion of privacy* an evil, whatever the technique, and explains that she misjudged her friend by failing to understand the pressure of human respect. In response to Lucy's lament about what could have been, Aslan again reminds her of the positivity* of reality. He knows how difficult this confrontation with him must be for her because he calls her "dear heart" and asks her to speak her deep desire. He promises to tell her the story* of refreshment "for years and years."[30]

The feeling of solemnity diminishes for the reader as the next scene unfolds. Aslan is called "sir" by Coriakin; and during the course of their conversation, the reader discovers that the Duffers* were given to the care of Coriakin by Aslan. The Lion promises the retired star* that in good time the Duffers will be able to be ruled with wisdom rather than with magic. Aslan laughs at the thought of showing himself to the easily frightened Duffers. The Lion hastens away to speak with Trumpkin in Cair Paravel but not before he promises Lucy, saddened by his departure, that he will see her soon. When she asks what "soon" means to him, he replies that all times are soon, implying that he has a perspective on time* that she doesn't understand now. Coriakin's colophon to this conversation is his recapitulation of the "not a tame lion" motif already mentioned.

It is in answer to the first explicit prayer in the *Chronicles,* offered by Lucy in the terrifying darkness near the land where nightmares come true, that Aslan comes in the form of an albatross to lead the *Dawn Treader* to the open, sunlit sea. This is no ordinary albatross,[31] because he sheds a broad beam of daylight on the ship, he calls to everyone on board in a "strong sweet voice" in words beyond understanding, and to Lucy he whispers "Courage, dear heart" with his fragrant breath.[32]

When Caspian attempts to abdicate his kingship and thus renounce his vocation, Aslan appears to him in his cabin. The golden icon of the Lion becomes the head of Aslan himself, who at first speaks quite sternly to the king about his responsibilities. He ends by consoling the king, while making it clear that Reepicheep and the English children are to be allowed to sail East.

Finally (in a scene too reminiscent for the older Christian reader of the breakfast the risen Christ prepares for his apostles in the Gospel of John, chapter 20, for Lewis not to have intended the association), Lucy, Edmund, and Eustace meet a beautiful Lamb at the World's End.* From the fact that the Lamb is almost too bright to look at, even for eyes strengthened by the sweet waters of the Last Sea,* it must be inferred that he is a divine figure. He bids them eat of the breakfast of fish roasting over a fire (if the fish aren't miraculous in origin, the fire certainly is; consider the utter flatness and the utter freshness of the grass at World's End: no wood or peat could have been procured). The Lamb, in the course of answering the children's questions about the way to Aslan's country, is transfigured into Aslan himself. He reveals that there is a way into his country from earth, that they must enter through that way,[33] that he will always be showing them this way; he does not say how long it will be, but it always goes across the river of death.* He tells them not to fear death because he is the *Pontifex Maximus,* one of the earliest christological titles: he has bridged the gap—death*—between life and life. Lucy, out of her real love but showing she needs to grow in hope, wants the assurance that she will see him again; and she thinks she needs to be in Narnia to see him. With great gentleness, Aslan explains to them that they will not be returning to Narnia but will find him in their world under another name. At this point in the narrative it is clear that Lewis intended to end the *Chronicles* with VDT.[34] And, just as Jesus refused to tell Peter what John's fate would be,[35] Aslan does not answer Lucy's question about whether Eustace will come back to Narnia. He tears open a door in the sky (the tear reveals for only an instant the "terrible light" of the heaven of heavens where dwells the Emperor-beyond-the-Sea) and kisses the children goodbye.

The Silver Chair   Aslan is least present in SC, of all the *Chronicles.* He appears at the very end of Chapter 1 and the beginning of Chapter 2, in Jill's dream in the middle of Chapter 8, and at the very end of Chapter 16—scarcely one chapter in all the sixteen. Even so, major themes in Lewis's theology—vocation, prayer, and especially faith and providence*—find their meaning expressed in the story of Eustace and Jill in their quest to rescue Prince Rilian.

Aslan bounds into the story to the edge of the cliff in order to blow Eustace safely into Narnia. He turns to begin his education of Jill in his way of doing things. First he looks directly at her and then looks away, as if in disdain. After the longest silence,* he invites her to drink from the stream that flows beyond them.[36] Terribly thirsty yet terribly afraid of him, Jill wishes that he would go away,[37] a desire that only moves him to stare the harder at her and to growl in a low voice. He refuses to promise not to do anything to her; and, in answer to her question about whether he eats children, he states plainly, "I have swallowed up girls and boys, women and men, kings and emperors, cities and realms," a declaration of his inexorability and his omnipotence. He does promise Jill that she will die of thirst if she does not drink and that, contrary to her wish for another stream, "there is no other stream."[38] His stern demeanor is one that would not permit disbelief of this point. After her drink, he calls her to himself. She tries looking into his eyes but she is not ready for long looks yet. He addresses her five times as "Human Child," a term equal in seriousness to "Son of Adam" or "Daughter of Eve." In the strong light of his straightforward questioning, Jill faces the truth about herself without evasion. She accepts responsibility for Eustace's fall and even realizes the motive for her action: "I was showing off, Sir." After telling her to behave this way no longer,[39] Aslan immediately goes on to talk about the task he has assigned Eustace and her. She is correct to question whether the Lion has confused her with someone else he seems to know. But it is she he knows and has called. In one short line, Aslan explains one of the meanings of grace and prayer, namely that he is behind every effort of ours, even the desire to pray.[40] He identifies himself as the Somebody Eustace had spoken to her of and immediately gives her and Eustace the task of finding the lost prince. A hint at Aslan's omniscience can be seen in the fact that, though everyone in Narnia presumes Rilian is dead, the Lion knows that he is alive. When Jill asks how she and Eustace are to carry out this quest, Aslan gives her the four signs* by which he will continue to guide them. When Jill responds out of courteous reflex that she "sees," the Lion is very quick (but also gentle) to point out that she doesn't see quite as well as she thinks she does.[41] So he very patiently teaches her the importance of memory* by making her recite the signs as a pupil would before a teacher. On the glorious wave of his breath, she is blown into Narnia.

In a scene which is true to the surrealism of dreams,* Jill, asleep in the castle of the giants at Harfang,* imagines that the large wooden horse in her bedroom becomes Aslan. In her dream, the "smell* of all sweet-smelling things there are" fills the room, another indication of the reality of Aslan's presence though still true to the nature of sense-experience in dreams. Her conscience smites her so that she cries: She cannot remember the signs. Like a mother cat picking up a kitten,[42] Aslan picks her up and takes her to the window and points out one of the missed signs. The dream ends; but not its effect, for it has anticipated her experience the next day when she sees the missed sign in reality and the quest is taken up again.

Though Aslan doesn't come into the picture again until the end of the book, several important observations about his nature are made by Puddleglum that need to be mentioned here. First, in Chapter 8, Puddleglum makes a profession of faith in Aslan's providence, the sum of which is: "Aslan's instructions always work; there are no exceptions." The Marsh-Wiggle* seems to forget the Lion's mercy, however, in the dreadful scene when he and the children discover they have been eating Talking Stag. Here Puddleglum reflects what some ethicists call a taboo mentality whereby, discounting any intention to do wrong, the mere fact of having broken a rule incurs a curse. The Marsh-Wiggle actually speaks of a curse having fallen upon them as the result of their inadvertent crime. Puddleglum rules out suicide as a method for atonement only because there are laws against it. This proposal can perhaps be attributed to his propensity to make the darkest possible interpretation of reality; nevertheless, this scene might be open to misinterpretation.[43]

In Chapter 10, Puddleglum makes his second affirmation of the Lion's providence: there are no accidents[44] because Aslan, present at the beginning of everything, foresaw every event and the reaction people would have to each event.[45]

When the Queen of Underland* tries to weave a new spell over the freed Rilian and his liberators, Jill fights the enchantment long enough to declare that if nothing else exists, at least Aslan does. At the sound of his name, the witch is perceptively moved but she tries to cover her anxiety by reducing Jill's assertion to psychological projection.[46] But it is only Puddleglum's obstinate belief in the meaningfulness of Aslan and Narnia apart from the fact that they exist, combined with the smell of burnt Marsh-Wiggle, that breaks the new spell.[47]

The restored Rilian shows the depth of his faith and his discernment in the way that he interprets his miraculously changed shield as a sign that "Aslan will be our good lord, whether he means us to live or die. And all's one, for that." His sense of the continuity of life and death can also be seen in his decision that they will fight to the death if they are ambushed and that if they die, Jill must "commend [herself] to the Lion."[48] (Meanwhile, at about this time, Aslan has appeared to King Caspian X, Rilian's father, who had gone on a voyage to the east in hope of meeting the Lion, visions of whom had been seen in the islands.)

Finally, immediately after Eustace and Jill express a desire to return home, Aslan appears, saying, "I have come." The very beholding of him in his leonine glory makes all else pale in comparison.[49] In the silence, Aslan knows of Jill's contrition and beckons both children to him and kisses their sorrows away. He tells them not to brood on the past and that he will not always be scolding them; indeed, he congratulates them for accomplishing what he brought them to Narnia for.[50] He announces that he has come to bring them Home, that is, to his own country, before he sends them back to earth. Reversing the process by which they came to Narnia (and also revealing how insubstantial every other world is compared to his own), he blows wintry Narnia away "like wreaths of smoke" and they find themselves on Aslan's Mountain in midsummer splendor beside the stream mentioned in the second chapter.[51] As he leads them along this stream, he grows so beautiful to Jill that she cries with joy as she had cried with sadness over Caspian's funeral music. They walk to the place where the dead Caspian lies in the stream bed. Like Jesus over the death of his friend Lazarus,[52] Aslan is weeping "great Lion-tears, each tear more precious than the Earth would be if it was a single solid diamond." He commands Eustace to fetch a huge thorn and to drive it into his right front paw; he will not allow Eustace not to do this. A drop of his blood,[53] "redder than all redness that you have ever seen or imagined," splashes into the stream flowing over the body of the dead king. The funeral music stops and Caspian is transfigured before their eyes.

His first act is to rush to embrace and to kiss Aslan, receiving the "wild kisses of a Lion" in exchange for the "strong kisses of a King." Aslan quips to Eustace, awed at the thought that Caspian is a ghost, that since most people do die,[54] Caspian has died and so has he, the Lion. Aslan addressed Eustace and Jill as "dear hearts" as he explains to them that now is not yet the time for them to stay in his country. They must return to England until the day when they will meet him in this place again.[55] On that day—that is, the day of their deaths—they will be able to stay.

When Caspian hesitantly asks if it is wrong for him to desire to visit England, Aslan calls him "my son" and assures him that now that he has died, he is incapable of wanting anything wrong.[56] He promises Caspian five earth-minutes to bring justice to the Gang* at Experiment House.* Jill and Eustace are surprised to learn that Aslan knows all about their situation. He turns the switch he orders Jill to take from a nearby bush into a new whip, tells her that he intends to show only his back to the earthlings,[57] and walks them to the edge of his country where the wall around Experiment House is seen.[58] He roars a section of the wall down, breathes on the two children and touches his tongue to their foreheads to give them strength, and sits down in the wall's breach. When the punishment is over, he seals the wall up again; and, we can assume, he walks with Caspian in his own country.

The Horse and His Boy   In this story about Narnia's two neighbors to the south, Archenland* and Calormen,* Aslan is present for most of four of the fifteen chapters. Besides adding insights to an understanding of providence, HHB also focuses on freedom, justice, and humility. There is, too, the profoundly moving and revelatory scene in the eleventh chapter in which the Large Voice discloses a part of the meaning behind the doctrine of the Trinity.*

It is the roaring of what sounds like two lions* that unites the two horses and their riders in a common quest* for freedom in the North, away from the stifling stratification of Calormen society. Bree and Hwin, Aravis and Shasta, all have different pictures of what this freedom is, and it is the Lion's purpose to help all four and the reader understand it. He is seen on the shore of the unnamed creek:[59] "a great, shaggy, and terrible shape crouched on the water's edge."

Interestingly, when Queen Susan and Tumnus* use Aslan's name* in Shasta's presence, the boy has no feeling of awe. Lewis has, by this point in the writing of the *Chronicles,* abandoned the theme of the numinous excited by the very sound of the name.

Shasta meets the Lion in the form of a cat at the ancient tombs on the edge of the Great Desert.* This is no ordinary cat as Lewis makes clear when he describes the ancient, mysterious, and commanding look in the cat's eyes. The cat's presence is profoundly reassuring to the otherwise terribly lonely boy. When Shasta is frightened awake, he notices that the cat is gone. The black shape of a lion bounds onto the scene and roars the jackals away. But to Shasta's great surprise and mortal relief, the lion becomes the cat again at his feet. The boy thinks he is in a dream* but gladly welcomes the spreading warmth of the cat. As if to anticipate the greater instance of retribution in Aravis's wounding by the Lion, the cat scratches Shasta when the boy confesses his previous cruelty to animals.* The cat is gone in the morning.

In passing, a view of Aslan through Calormene eyes is seen in the Tisroc's* remark that the Kings and Queens of Narnia did not liberate Narnia on their own from the Hundred Years of Winter,* but had the help of a "demon of hideous aspect and irresistible maleficence who appears in the shape of a Lion."[60] This could, of course, be more truly said of Calormen's god Tash,* a demon of hideous aspect and irresistible (an adjective used of Tash frequently) maleficence who appears in the shape of a vulture.

In Chapter 10, Aslan's roar behind the fleeing horses spurs them into an all-out gallop;[61] and Shasta recognizes the Lion as the one who brought Bree and Hwin together in their flight from lower Calormen in Chapter 2. The Lion jabs at Aravis's shoulders with his right paw. With courage* that he didn't know existed in him, Shasta confronts the Lion and "stare[s] into his wide-opened, raging mouth." Aslan turns a somersault and runs away.

Chapter 11, "The Unwelcome Fellow Traveller," is significant for more than its remytholigization of the Trinity. It reflects both Lewis's own experience of life and his meditation on life's meaning. The shock that Shasta feels at the presence breathing "on a very large scale" mirrors the shock Lewis experienced when, as a professor of philosophy, the vague, undemanding God of the Absolute Idealism he taught turned out to be the very disconcerting God of Abraham and Sarah and of Jesus; the myth of a dying and rising God which so nourished his spirit has actually become fact in the uncompromising and compassionate historical figure, Jesus of Nazareth. Lewis often spoke of himself as a "reluctant convert"[62] because he knew that he would have to learn not only to tolerate but even to welcome an Interferer into the core of his personality, that spot which he would rather have all to himself.[63] What Shasta is unaware of is that this Presence is walking between him and the edge of a cliff. As in the scene with Jill at the beginning of SC, Aslan demonstrates his great patience* with the boy and his respect for the boy's freedom. It is only when Shasta can pretend to ignore the Presence no longer that Aslan replies to his question "Who are you?" with "One who has waited long for you to speak." The Lion explains that in a sense he is like the giants Shasta is fearing: this is another figure of the greatness of God.* When Shasta has the even greater fear that this Presence might be a ghost, the Lion breathes on him[64] and thus reassures him with both his warm breath and his invitation to the boy to tell his sorrows. Shasta does unburden himself but calls all his sorrows "misfortunes." Aslan differs: "I do not call you unfortunate." By this he means to slowly reveal to the boy the difference between fate (where all that happens in the universe and in individuals is haphazard and meaningless) and providence* (where everything, down to the smallest detail, is known and guided by a Person who is completely good).

The Lion then discloses to the boy that he has been present at all the most recent crucial turns in the boy's life, going back to when Shasta was an infant. He was the Lion who pushed the boat carrying the sick child ashore where Arsheesh* (whom, it is implied, Aslan kept awake that night) rescued him. This revelation moves Shasta to conclude that the Lion also wounded Aravis, a fact which the Lion acknowledges but upon which he does not elaborate, out of his desire to preserve the girl's privacy. This so perplexes Shasta that he asks a final time "Who are you?" and he receives in answer the revelation of the Trinity.

This scene is radiant with almost the same light that came forth from the fiery bush from which Moses received the name of God in the Book of Exodus, chapter 3. A golden light, a "fiery brightness," comes from Aslan, walking to the left of Shasta, a light brighter than the rising sun on the boy's right. "No one ever saw anything more terrible or beautiful" is yet another description of what it is to have a true experience of the numinous. When Shasta falls silently to Aslan's feet, the Lion stoops toward him in splendid condescension, buries the boy's head in his fragrant mane, touches Shasta's forehead with his tongue, and then looks directly into the boy's eyes. The Lion disappears in a swirl of glory, leaving behind a deep footprint out of which begins to flow a stream of ice-cold, clear water,[65] from which Shasta takes a refreshing drink. Later, when Shasta returns to Archenland with the Narnian cohort, he realizes that during the foggy night the Lion walked between him and the edge, a picture of the reality that even in opaque situations where God seems quite uncomforting, he is probably keeping the uncomfortable person from still greater dangers.

Aslan enters into Bree's conversion process just when the horse has been trying to explain away the reality of the Lion by whom he has been swearing oaths.* The sight of the Lion is a numinous experience for Aravis and Hwin. Lewis sets up a contrast between the way the two horses respond to the Lion. Hwin, fearful though she is, surrenders to Aslan absolutely.[66] Bree, like the doubting Thomas,[67] must be persuaded of Aslan's reality and beastliness. And Aravis is told something of the explanation the Lion gave to Shasta, that Aslan was the Lion of their journey north and the one who scratched her in retribution for the abuse that Aravis's stepmother's maidservant received in the girl's stead. The Lion does not tell her any more of this servant's story because, again, this would go against the principle of privacy.

When Shasta, now Prince Cor, relates his story to Aravis and reaches the point where Lord Bar's* knight is too weak to row himself and the boy ashore, he sums up the meaning of HHB (and, indeed, of the *Chronicles* to this moment) by saying that Aslan, in pushing him to shore, "seems to be in back of all the stories."

Aslan's final appearance in HHB is in the discussion of Rabadash's* fate.[68] He asks him to forget his pride and anger and to accept the mercy of Lune and Edmund. He interrupts the bragging prince with one more quiet warning[69] and then, when Rabadash persists, he turns him into an ass. Aslan makes the pronouncement[70] that Rabadash will be healed in the temple of the god to whom he has appealed, Tash. But he promises no second chance if Rabadash disobeys the Lion's restrictions. Then he vanishes, leaving "a brightness in the air and on the grass, and joy in their hearts, which [assures] them that he [has] been no dream."

The Magician's Nephew   Aslan makes his longest appearance since LWW and PC in the six and one-half chapters of the fifteen chapters of MN. In this book Lewis returns to the theme he more obliquely remythologized in PC, namely, that Aslan is the Lord of Creation in Narnia. There he rejuvenated the land through the agency of the English children and the gods; here he creates the land and is revealed more clearly as the maker of the gods and other mythological creatures that inhabit Narnia. In addition, Lewis attempts a second and better explanation of the necessity for human rulers in Narnia and of many Narnian details, such as the ever-shining Lamp-post* in Lantern Waste.* More significantly, he comments on knowledge* and curiosity,* especially of the scientific kind, while explaining the meaning of magic.* These concerns are illustrated by the way the Lion trains Digory, neutralizes Andrew Ketterley,* and protects against Jadis. Finally, in writing about Digory and his mother, Lewis exorcises some of the pain he experienced as a boy when his mother was dying of cancer.[71]

Aslan comes on scene as the Singer in Chapter 8, a Lion "huge, shaggy, and bright." The sight of him entrances Frank,* Digory, and Polly, terrifies Andrew, and fills Jadis with hate. From the fact that the grass grows out from him in waves, the Lion is seen as the center of this creative activity.[72] Frank and Digory comment about the Lion's apparent invulnerability when the witch's blow with the cross-bar from the lamp-post doesn't seem to slow his deliberate approach or stop his song.[73] When Aslan creates the animals, he goes among them selecting pairs from each kind; these follow him, while the rest disperse. The elected ones form a solemnly silent circle around him, similar to the half-circle of creatures around the Lion in LWW. With wonderful detail, Aslan confers the gift of speech* upon them. He gives them and their land the name of Narnia and they respond to this naming with the first use of his name (to speak from the viewpoint of internal chronology).

The shock of hearing him speak is "lovely and terrible" to Frank and the two children.[74] He covenants with the Talking Beasts, assigning the Dumb Beasts to their care. At the Jackdaw's* gaffe, he explains the meaning of humor* and even seems to join in the subsequent laughter. But then he calls the First Council* to discuss how Narnia should be protected against the evil that Digory introduced into the land in the person of Jadis. The boy chooses

The stare of the White Witch makes Edmund uncomfortable: she is tall and beautiful, proud and stern; her red lips are the only spot of color in a face pale as ice. (LWW 27-28, 32-33.)

this moment to come forward to ask Aslan's aid in obtaining help for his mother. Digory discovers the Lion to be much more of an experience than he suspected and can't look Aslan in the face. Aslan resumes the use of the "Son of Adam" form of address three times in his probing of Digory's motives. Aslan promises the council that there will be ultimate deliverance from this evil but that beforehand it will have its time of triumph. He calls Frank and Polly into the council, addresses Frank as "son," reveals that he has known him better than the cabby realizes, and promises that he will know him even more intimately in Narnia.[75] Aslan brings to Narnia Frank's only stipulation: his wife Helen. He names them the King and Queen of Narnia in terms that evoke God's covenant with Adam and Eve in the Book of Genesis 1:26–31 and 2:18–25. When Frank demurs on the grounds that he is uneducated, Aslan leads him by way of five questions to understand his readiness to assume this vocation. He then calls Polly forward to complete the process of reconciliation between her and Digory. Finally he commissions Digory to repair the damage he has done. He doesn't allow the boy to evade this assignment, and he seems a little severe with him. But when Digory breaks down over his disappointed hopes for his mother's recovery, Aslan reveals the depths of his compassion by crying more fervently over Mrs. Kirke than even Digory. In a great shift of mood, Aslan calls Digory "my son, my son."[76] He tells the boy that he knows how enormous grief can be. "Only you and I know that yet. Let us be good to one another." Thus he indicates his solidarity with the boy and reaches out to *him* for *his* compassion, a startling statement.[77] Aslan's plan to protect Narnia with a tree depends upon the success of Digory's journey to the garden* of the west to obtain an apple from the tree at the garden's center. Aslan grows more deeply sympathetic to Digory, moving from calling him "dear son" to "little son of Adam" when the boy modestly suggests he might be a long while accomplishing this task. Aslan calls to Strawberry and asks if he wants to become a winged horse. Sensing the horse's desire, he commands the change and renames Strawberry Fledge, calling him father of his kind. Always respectful of free beings, Aslan asks Fledge if he will fly Digory to the garden. At Queen Helen's request, Aslan permits Polly to accompany Digory. When the winged horse agrees, he instructs him as to the route and promises that "there will always be a way through" (this is an echo of Puddleglum's profession of faith in SC). Later, when Digory ponders the momentous decision he has made in the crucible of the witch's temptation to keep his promise to Aslan, the memory* of Aslan's tears reassures him that he has made the right choice. This scene culminates in Aslan's earthshaking "Well done" over Digory's success. The Lion designates the boy as the one who deserves to plant the Tree of Protection.* The coronation of the first King and Queen of Narnia can take place.[78]

When it comes to dealing with Andrew Ketterley ("that creature" as Aslan significantly calls him), it is plain that Lewis wishes to show what God can and cannot do to save a person if that person does not want to be saved. Fittingly, the old magician is released from his pen and brought before the Lion. Polly, a figure of compassion, pleads with Aslan to remove the old man's fear and to prevent his ever returning personally or by proxy to Narnia for the purpose of commercial exploitation. Aslan explains that the gift of original fertility will diminish quickly and thus no such venture will be feasible. As for comforting or confronting Andrew, Aslan reveals that he is helpless even to communicate with "this old sinner."[79] In a lament heavily reminiscent of Jesus' lament of Jerusalem,[80] Aslan says that Andrew is able to receive only one gift: sleep,* the temporary surcease of care. Aslan's bowed head is a sign of the hopelessness of Andrew's case.

He draws the attention of all the Narnians present to the Tree of Protection, commanding them to care well for this guardian against the witch's ever-increasing power.[81] It is in answer to Digory's question about the consequences of the witch's having eaten of the Tree that Aslan explains the meaning of pleasure and the meaning of right and wrong.* Significantly, Aslan tells Digory what would have happened if he had taken the Apple of Youth back to his mother without first returning to Aslan—this is the only instance in the *Chronicles* when the principle of positivity* is abrogated. It is in this connection that Digory learns "there might be things more terrible even than losing someone you love by death."[82] He now permits Digory to take an apple to heal his mother. The Lion immediately knows the boy's desire to return home and his implicit "thank you."

In the blink of an eye, Aslan transports the two children and the sleeping magician back to the Wood between the Worlds.* His warning about the earth going the way of Charn* in its search for a Deplorable Word* strikes up allegorical overtones with the older reader; but this should not be allowed to interfere with the larger meaning Lewis intends: it is not only the atom bomb and genetic engineering in our age we must fear, but in every age the human inclination is to let curiosity and desire for control threaten the moral and natural order of things. Aslan commands them to bury the magic rings* so that they cannot be used again. Finally, like the vision of whirling glory given Shasta after his midnight walk with Aslan, Digory and Polly see a vision of the Lion that stays with them all their lives.[83]

The Last Battle   The Lion is present for one and one-half chapters of the sixteen of LB, and he is just offstage for one chapter more. But he is talked about and lied about for nearly all of the rest of this last of the *Chronicles.*[84] His chief activities are bringing justice to the renegade dwarfs* and to Emeth,* the true believer; ending Narnia; judging its inhabitants; and inaugurating the new Narnia. Aslan is the welcomer, the forerunner, and the transfigured lord of his own country and of all real countries.[85]

The chief crisis of LB stems from the distance all the characters feel from the events in which Aslan took an immediate part during and soon after the Golden Age.* Lewis takes this fictional stance because people today experience the same sort of psychological separation. Only fragments of an entire faith-picture are remembered, the most prominent being the "Aslan is not a tame Lion" motif.[86] Some characters, the villains, take refuge in this phrase to perpetrate their fraud and take advantage of the distance sensed by the other characters, the heroes, in whom the phrase arouses doubt that their history and theology are true accounts of the Lion's behavior. The modern equivalent to this crisis is the debate about whether objective moral values exist and what relationship belief in God has to moral systems. What was in LWW and VDT a way for Mr. Beaver and Coriakin to explain to Lucy and the other children Aslan's freedom has now become a subterfuge for immoral activity (the re-enslavement of Narnia) and the destruction of the sense of Aslan's goodness. That Aslan is subject to both the good magic (the Deep and Deeper Magic of LWW) and to his own rules (for example, the spell of invisibility* and the spell of making hidden things visible in VDT) has been forgotten.[87]

Each character can be defined with respect to this crisis. Shift* is the archetypical conniver; unlike Puzzle—the archetypical dupe whose heart is nevertheless in the right place—Shift is not afraid of Aslan's return. He uses the not-a-tame-lion motif to cow the other animals into doing his bidding. Some creatures remember other fragments of the Aslan story. The boar, for example, recalls that the Lion was accustomed to see his people face-to-face. And Roonwit* contradicts the hope of Jewel* and Tirian* that Aslan has returned because the Centaur* is a student of the heavens and the stars* have predicted only disaster. Jewel, disagreeing with Roonwit, tries to connect the fact that Aslan is the maker of the stars with the not-a-tame-lion motif and Tirian echoes this sentiment. Neither is remembering the essential goodness of the Lion and both are unaware that they are driving a wedge between Aslan and creation and lending credence to the belief that Aslan is above the law. Later, when it appears that, under Aslan's orders, the ancient forest at Lantern Waste is being cleared with the forced labor of talking horses for Calormene trade, Tirian explains this contradiction by using the not-a-tame-lion motif. This doesn't wash with the dwarfs, however, who have already been enslaved at Shift's orders under the rubric of the motif. There is no relief from this confusion until the principal characters find themselves on the other side of the Stable* Door.*[88] The one course remaining is to take the adventure* Aslan sends them by fighting the Last Battle.*

On the other side of the door Aslan appears, accompanied by earthquake,* sweet air, and brightness. He kisses the Seven Friends of Narnia* and then Tirian, to whom he gives the second great "Well done" of the *Chronicles.*[89] In answer to Lucy's tearful request,[90] the Lion shows what he is able and unable to do for the dwarfs. His low growl doesn't impress them; and the splendid meal he shakes from his mane doesn't get through to the dwarfs' jaded palates. Aslan pronounces their fate: eternal helplessness. Next he steps to the Door and awakens the giant Time* with an enormous roar. He calls for the end of Narnia.* The stars, called home, stand behind and to the right of the Lion, causing the Lion's shadow to be cast to the left into the devastated country. In one of the finest pictures of the judgment in Christian fantasy, Aslan looks into the eyes of every creature; the ones who look upon him with hate or fear pass into his shadow and into oblivion and the ones who love him, even though they are awed, pass through the door into his country. It is at the Lion's bidding that the giant makes an end of the sun and that Peter locks the door on that old world. He has laughter in his eyes as he shouts the new motif,[91] "Come farther in! Come farther up!" He returns ahead of them, off to the west.

When the Seven Friends and the blessed Narnians meet Emeth, he tells them the story (much as Eustace explained his de-dragoning to the people he had opposed) of how Aslan met him. Emeth uses extravagant Calormene similes to describe the Lion. Aslan addresses him as "son," "child," and "beloved"; he explains to him how all the desires and good deeds of Emeth's life have really been focused on Aslan though they were done in Tash's name.[92] He breathes on Emeth and the young man's fears fall away. Then, in a swirl of glory,[93] the Lion disappears.

In the final scene of the *Chronicles,* the Lion bounds down the cliffs west of the garden as though they were so many treads of a giant staircase. To Lucy, he seems as glorious as a living waterfall.[94] He calls Puzzle to himself and both confronts and comforts the donkey. Then he turns to the children, asking why they are not as happy as he means them to be. Lucy speaks for them all when she tells her fear* that he will again send them away. He reveals to them that they have died and that their real life is just beginning.

With the last paragraph of LB, Lewis turns the very *Chronicles* themselves into a metaphor for the meaning he has been trying to communicate through all his books. Even the finest story* written or told by the finest storyteller is the barest prelude ("cover" and "title page" are the terms Lewis uses) to the archetypical Story being told through the lives of every person who has ever lived or will ever live. This story will always be told by the Lion, now transformed into Jesus the Christ whom Lewis believes is the Person behind these stories of every person in every world. Shasta is right: Aslan is behind every story. And the Lion keeps his promise to Lucy: I will tell you the story for refreshment of spirit not only for years and years but for ever.

---

[1] The plan of this entry is to summarize Aslan's identity and his physical characteristics and then to proceed to a book-by-book analysis of Aslan's activities and attributes. More detailed information can be found under related entries: Aslan's country,* Aslan's How,* Aslan's name,* Aslan's Table,* and Aslan's voice.* For Aslan's breath, see *Holy Spirit.* For commentary on the theological significance of Aslan, see *Credal elements.*

[2] In the last paragraph of the 1943 preface that Lewis wrote for his 1933 allegory, *The Pilgrim's Regress* (Grand Rapids: Wm. B. Eerdmans Publishing Co., 1958) p. 14, he explains that on the map of the "Holy War" the two railways, one from the north (the region of the mind) and one from the south (the region of the body), are the devil's routes into "the country of Man's Soul." This battle motif is prominent in *The Screwtape Letters* and the Space Trilogy.

[3] Lewis was only a little more than a year beyond the exhilaration of completing one of his finest theological works, *Miracles: A Preliminary Study* (New York: Macmillan Publishing Co., 1978; London: Collins Fontana, 1960) when he resumed his long-stalled work on LWW. *Miracles* sparkles with many anticipations of the images Lewis will develop in the *Chronicles.* In the former, Lewis speculates on a springtime coming to the whole cosmos as the result of Christ's incarnation on earth (123–124, *127–128*). Earlier, in a passage significant for our study of the *Chronicles,* Lewis explained the Incarnation thus:

> Christians are not claiming that simply "God" was incarnate in Jesus. They are claiming that the one true God is He whom the Jews worshipped as Jahweh, and that it is He who has descended. Now the double character of Jahweh is this. On the one hand He is the God of Nature, her glad Creator. . . . He is the God of wheat and wine and oil. In that respect He is constantly doing all the things that Nature Gods do: He is Bacchus, Venus, Ceres all rolled into one. . . .

On the other hand, Jahweh is clearly *not* a Nature-God. He does not die and come to life each year as the true Corn-king should. He may give wine and fertility, but must not be worshipped with Bacchanalian or aphrodisiac rites. He is not the soul of Nature nor any part of Nature. . . . (114–115, *118–119*).

Aslan, the Incarnation of Christ in Narnian terms, represents in Narnia what Christ represents on earth: the God of the Chosen People, the "glad Creator" of Nature and her activities. Thus the integration of pagan and Christian representatives surrounding Aslan.

4 See, for example, Lewis's *Great Divorce* (New York: Macmillan Publishing Company, 1946) p. 69:

There are only two kinds of people in the end: those who say to God, "Thy will be done," and those to whom God says, *"Thy* will be done." All that are in Hell, choose it. Without that self-choice there could be no Hell. No soul that seriously and consciously desires joy will ever miss it.

See *Eschatology.*

5 Reminding Peter to clean his sword after every fight is the first in a whole series of practical notes* that the avuncular Lewis adds throughout the *Chronicles.*

6 Meditation on the Passion of Christ was at the heart of Lewis's own spiritual life and his spiritual direction of others. Consider the sterling example of this in his fictional *Letters to Malcolm: Chiefly on Prayer* (New York: Harcourt Brace Jovanovich, 1963/64) pp. 41–45, esp. p. 43.

7 Nor, it seems, was it clear to Lewis. This is another instance of the ongoing evolution of the *Chronicles* from the wellsprings of Lewis's imagination.

8 Lewis was well aware of the discussion among theologians about the nature of the resurrection of Christ and knew that this mystery must be connected with the ascension of Christ to be true to the biblical and patristic understanding of the events that took place after Christ's death. See *Credal elements.* See also Lewis's *Miracles,* pp. 143–149, *147–153.*

9 Again, see *Credal elements.*

10 Though Lewis was decidedly Protestant on the question of faith and works, he nevertheless stressed the need for the person saved by Christ to *appropriate* that salvation by responding with works that will mirror Christ, or carry the "good infection" (to use Lewis's term) of Christ to others. See *Mere Christianity* (New York: Macmillan Publishing Co., 1960; London: Collins Fount, 1977) pp. 156–164, pp. *153–161.*

11 Detachment from the outcome of one's Christian activity is one hallmark of true discipleship. See the Gospel of John 3:29–30 and 4:36–38; Gospel of Luke 10:17–20.

12 "Sermon for Christmas Day," *The Liturgy of the Hours* (New York: Catholic Book Publishing, 1975) vol. 1, p. 405.

13 There seems to be an implicit indictment of the democratic method here. Lewis felt that democracy is perhaps the best form of government* in a fallen world, but that patriarchal monarchy would be the best in an unfallen world.

14 This suggests both nuptial intimacy and the intimacy between friends. The Old and New Testaments are filled with the promise that our union with God will be like the union between spouses and between friends. For an example of the first, see Psalm 63:1–8; for the second, see the Gospel of John 13:23 (the Apostle John reposing on the breast of the Lord during the Last Supper).

15 For Lewis, even ecstasy is only an inn along the journey to heaven. See *Comfort,* note 1.

16 This is a very primitive meaning of the analogy of faith as found in Paul's Letter to the Romans 12:3: "By the grace given to me I bid every one among you not to think of himself more highly than he ought to think, but to think with sober judgment, each *according to the measure of faith* which God has assigned him" (my emphasis). Lewis carefully differentiates among the three children: Edmund is on Lucy's side but wants to sulk over his loss of sleep; Peter's motivations are close to Edmund's but he cannot yet believe Lucy is right; Susan is quite self-centered and out-of-sorts.

17 The only serious flaw in Janet Schulman's otherwise excellent abridgement of the *Chronicles* for the fine Caedmon recordings (what awful choices she must have faced!) is the loss of the entire Dionysian strand in PC and similar descriptions which, to someone who has to condense seven long stories to two sides of an LP or two sides of a sixty-minute cassette, have to seem superfluous.

18 Younger readers would not be troubled by this obviousness; they worship naturally, as Chesterton reminds us. They might wonder, however, why Lewis is not getting on with the story, by which they mean the battle against the Telmarines. What they and some older readers miss is the significance of ecstasy in life, which, as Lewis tells us throughout this section of PC, comes to full fruition when it takes place in the presence and with the approval of the God of joy. See Lewis, *The Four Loves* (New York: Harcourt Brace Jovanovich, 1960) p. 166.

[19] In line with what Bruno Bettelheim has to say in *The Uses of Enchantment* (New York: Random House Vintage, 1977) about fairy tales being vital to helping children mature, the fact that Susan is the more frightened of the two girls is perhaps because (as she is thirteen years old in PC and Lucy only nine) Susan is growing into womanhood, never an easy process, but one that can be aided in Narnia by Aslan. But see what happens to her at *Susan*.

[20] This is a scene remarkably similar to the destruction of the Lydian ship in Ovid's *Metamorphoses*, Book III, lines 600–690 (Mary M. Innes, tr., Harmondsworth: Penguin Classics, 1955) pp. 90–92.

[21] See note 4.

[22] Recall the "He who is not with me is against me" and the "Many are called but few are chosen" passages of the gospels (Mark 9:40; 10:31. Matthew 12:30; 19:30; 22:14. Luke 11:23).

[23] This is the term Lewis uses in *Miracles* (pp. 132–141, *136–145*) to cover the New Testament miracles of fertility, healing, destruction, and dominion over the inorganic. When something happens on a small scale that actually happens on a large scale throughout nature, this is a miracle of the old creation. When something happens on a small scale that anticipates God's future activity on a large scale, this is a miracle of the new creation (some miracles of dominion over the inorganic, and every miracle of reversal and glorification are miracles of the new creation). A Narnian example of the first kind is the water turning to wine in Bacchus's hand; this is a fertility miracle, belonging to the old creation where God changes water into wine every day through the growth of grape vines, the work of human hands, and the process of fermentation. Aslan's return to life after his death on the Stone Table and his run to the Witch's castle and leap over its walls are Narnian examples of miracles of glorification or miracles of the new creation. For more examples of this second type, see *Miracles*, pp. 141–163, *145–167*.

[24] It is difficult to determine Lewis's intention or the meaning of this beautiful image. If the overall meaning of PC is the liberation of nature from the fetters of fear and technology,* then this image suggests the ultimate reconciliation of the rival principles of creation, symbolized by the Lion or Sun or masculinity, and the Moon or femininity. Some great communion is going on in this scene.

[25] This is significant because VDT can profitably be studied as the conclusion of one phase of Lewis's composition of the *Chronicles* (see *Introduction*). LB is truly the end of the *Narniad* (a term mentioned in Marion Lockhead's fine book, *Renaissance of Wonder: The Fantasy Worlds of J. R. R. Tolkien, C. S. Lewis, George MacDonald, E. Nesbit and Others* [San Francisco: Harper & Row, 1980] p. 83), but both books have the quality of distance that our own age feels with respect to the biblical events.

[26] Aslan respects Eustace's freedom; "He cannot ravish. He can only woo," says Screwtape rightly to his nephew Wormwood (*The Screwtape Letters*, p. 38).

[27] God's knowledge of us is primary, Lewis believed. Consider this excerpt from perhaps his single most important address, "The Weight of Glory":

> I read in a periodical the other day that the fundamental thing is how we think of God. By God Himself, it is not! How God thinks of us is not only more important, but infinitely more important. (p. 10, *103*)

Lewis here is in line with the biblical doctrine of God's knowledge. "To know" in Hebrew thought is "To be on the most intimate terms with." Thus, for that first Christian theologian, St. Paul, "Now I know in part; then I shall know fully, even as I have fully been understood" is the summary statement of our present condition, as well as of our possible future (I Corinthians 13:12). The other possible future is summarized by Jesus himself: "I never knew you; depart from me" (Gospel of Matthew 7:23). Of all the characters in Narnia, Eustace has perhaps the deepest experience of being known. He has begun the process of learning to like the nakedness that God will eventually demand of all of us. Says Lewis:

> No possible complexity which we can give to our picture of the universe can hide us from God: there is no copse, no forest, no jungle thick enough to provide cover. . . . All that seems to divide us from God can flee away, vanish leaving us naked before Him, like the first man, like the only man, as if nothing but He and I existed. And since that contact cannot be avoided for long, and since it means either bliss or horror, the business of life is to learn to like it. That is the first and greatest commandment. ("Dogma and the Universe" in *God in the Dock*, Walter Hooper, ed. [Grand Rapids: Wm. B. Eerdmans Publishing Co., 1970] p. 47, and [London: Collins Fount, 1979] p. 38).

[28] It is not clear from the narrative whether Lewis intends for us to understand that he is trying to give us a picture of the omnipresence and the providence* of God, or whether the Lion is present for the purpose of this story only.

[29] See *Invisibility*, note 2.

---

³⁰ And readers of the *Chronicles* can return to this section of VDT for themselves when they need heartening.

³¹ It is difficult (again, for Christians of a more literalistic stripe) to avoid an allegorical interpretation of the cross-like appearance of the speck in the beam that Lucy first notices when she looks along the beam. Such an interpretation, however, seems to obscure rather than enhance the experience of the scene: the rescue from whatever darkness haunts us all. It is impossible to determine whether Lewis *intended* such a connection; but a book will *mean* whatever it stirs up in a reader's powers of association. More tantalizing, perhaps, is the suggestion that Lucy's looking *along* the beam might be connected to Lewis's "Meditation in a Toolshed" in *God in the Dock,* Walter Hooper, ed. (Grand Rapids: Wm. B. Eerdmans Publishing Co., 1970) pp. 212–215. This 1945 essay is perhaps too distant to form immediate background for VDT, but the distinction between looking at and looking along is too elemental to Lewis's epistemology to go unremarked upon here. For more on this subject, see *Introduction* and *Knowledge.*

³² For an extended commentary on the meaning of this scene, see *Dreams.*

³³ Lewis, like his friend Charles Williams, did not allow for escaping from reality. "The cross comes before the crown," preached Lewis in "The Weight of Glory" (p. 14, *108*); and he goes into this matter at great length in *The Problem of Pain* (New York: Macmillan Publishing Co., 1967; London: Collins Fountain, 1977) pp. 148–149, *136–137.*

³⁴ See *Introduction.*

³⁵ Gospel of John 21:21–22.

³⁶ Those in the Judaeo-Christian tradition will find strong echoes of the Psalms and the Prophets in this scene. See, for example, Psalm 42:2, 63:1, 143:6, and Isaiah 55:1. For Christians, the evocation of the Gospel of John, Chapter 4 (Jesus with the woman at Jacob's Well) and Chapter 7 (Jesus in the Temple at Jerusalem for *Succoth,* the Feast of Tabernacles). On the last day of the latter, Jesus stood up and proclaimed, "If anyone thirst, let that one come to me and drink" (John 7:37).

³⁷ Fortunately for the apostle Peter, Jesus also refuses to go away when the man desires him to depart from him (Luke 5:8).

³⁸ Aslan is not saying there is only one stream in his country—this is contradicted by other pictures given in the *Chronicles*—but that he is the source of the life she desires, of which water and thirst are only the natural symbols. See the Gospel of John, 4:13–15.

³⁹ The Narnian equivalent of Jesus' command, "Go and sin no more" (Gospel of John 5:14 and 8:11).

⁴⁰ Lewis seems to be alluding to Isaiah 45:4–5 and John 15:16. With respect to grace, Protestant theology of the more Evangelical orientation distinguishes between prevenient grace, the strength and insight that moves a person in the direction of God, and redemptive grace, the gift of faith in which a person is carried over the chasm that divides the human race from God and by which this person is so attached to God that he or she lives by a new principle of life. This distinction roughly corresponds to what Roman Catholicism means by actual grace and sanctifying grace. But since the understanding of grace is the key controversy that caused the Reformation, further consideration of this question is not appropriate here. Prayer, being the heart of a life lived out in the presence of God, must be inspired by grace. Learning this distinction between "religion" as she thought of it and the work of God as it actually is marks the turning point in the conversion of Jane Studdock in Lewis's *That Hideous Strength* (New York: Macmillan Publishing Co., 1965, pp. 317–319, and London: Pan Books Ltd., 1955, pp. 195–197). This is a key theme not only in Lewis's theology but in Christian theology as well.

⁴¹ This is a reference to the qualitative difference between the atmosphere of Aslan's country* and Narnia and any other created world.

⁴² A noteworthy passage for the fact that Lewis uses a feminine image for Aslan, as rare for Lewis as it is in Judaeo-Christian scriptures. See Isaiah 49:15 and 66:13. See also *Sexism.*

⁴³ For one formulation of a tri-level approach to morality—the taboo, the philosophical/ethical, and the Christian/religious levels—see Louis Monden, *Sin, Liberty, and Law* (New York: Sheed and Ward, 1965) pp. 4–13. Of course, the crime of eating Talking Beast has been committed, objective guilt has been incurred, and the order of nature needs to be restored. But talk of the "anger of Aslan," of being "under a curse," and of suicide is very serious language. The fact that this event is mentioned only once more in SC, in the context of another scene in which Puddleglum's black humor is also prominent, may serve to mitigate the seriousness of Lewis's potential carelessness in handling this ethical matter. The second scene is when, upon Jill's "disappearance" in the tunnel leading up to Narnia, Puddleglum complains that his fate must be entirely bad: he has caused Jill's death in the same way that he was responsible for eating Talking Stag (190–191, *184*).

⁴⁴ "For a Christian, there are, strictly speaking, no chances," says Lewis in *The Four Loves,* p.

126. That is, there is no fate, fortune, chance, or accident for the Christian; there is only providence.*

45 Again, see *Providence.*

46 For a discussion of this matter, see *Knowledge.* Two enormous themes are being developed in this scene, one philosophical (concerning the meaningfulness of religious language) and the other theological (concerning the nature of proof [demonstration] and assent before and after conversion to faith). The witch is arguing on the first level and Puddleglum is responding on the second. See *Puddleglum* and *Queen of Underland.*

47 Pain is very disenchanting. It breaks through all sorts of rationalizations. There are two kinds of pain in this scene: the burning that the Marsh-Wiggle feels on his webbed foot, and the acrid odor of his burnt flesh that the children smell. Both kinds serve to clear the air and three heads. For this benefit of pain, see *The Problem of Pain,* pp. 92–93, 80–81.

48 The sexism* here is regrettable and obvious. The biblical allusion is Acts 20:32.

49 For the significance of this beholding or looking at Aslan, see *Biblical allusions.*

50 Isaiah 65:16, Psalm 103:9, and Matthew 25:21 and 23 are alluded to here.

51 See *Aslan's country,* note 1.

52 Gospel of John 11:1–44, esp. verse 35.

53 Lewis discusses the significance of being "washed in the blood of the Lamb" in *Mere Christianity,* p. 157, 154.

54 Lewis takes the same humorous tack in his sermon, "Learning in War-Time," *The Weight of Glory,* pp. 43–54, esp. p. 53, and *Fern-seed and Elephants: and Other Essays on Christianity* (London: Collins Fontana, 1975) pp. 26–38, esp. p. 37.

55 It is impossible to determine whether Lewis knew that Eustace and Jill would return in LB, since SC was finished a year and a half before LB was begun, or if he was only generalizing about the need to die as the way into Aslan's country.

56 See *Right and wrong.*

57 An allusion to Exodus 33:23.

58 This is a picture of the spiritual belief that every scene of tribulation is secretly connected with glory.

59 See *Glasswater Creek* for the British meaning of this word.

60 Supernaturalism and naturalism, a major theme in Lewis's apologetics, is hinted at in conversation between the Tisroc, the Grand Vizier, and Rabadash. The older men offer a supernatural explanation of the Hundred Years of Winter; they attribute it to the struggle between an enchantress and a lion-shaped demon. The younger, more modern man offers a more naturalistic explanation based on the positions of the stars.* See *Reductionism.*

61 Lewis gives the reader a striking picture of how we often don't know our true strength until it is tested. This is the message of St. James 1:2–3: "Count it all joy when you meet various trials, for you know that the testing of your faith produces steadfastness." See also 1 Peter 1:6–7; 4:12–19 and Hebrews 12:1–17.

62 *Surprised by Joy* (New York: Harcourt Brace Jovanovich, 1955; London: Collins Fontana, 1959) pp. 228–229, 182.

63 While Lewis's autobiography, *Surprised by Joy,* gives a fairly candid portrayal of his own conversion, it hides the emotional depths of the man. This discrepancy is noted by Owen Barfield (Lewis's friend from 1923 on) in Barfield's Introduction to *Light on C. S. Lewis* (New York: Harcourt Brace Jovanovich, 1965) pp. ix–xvi, and in subsequent biographies, especially Humphrey Carpenter's *Inklings* (Boston: Houghton Mifflin Co., 1979) pp. 59–64. Light begins to dawn on the private Lewis only through his later fiction, especially the *Chronicles* and *Till We Have Faces* (New York: Harcourt Brace Jovanovich, 1980). One of the reasons why Lewis can write so convincingly from the point of view of Jane Studdock, disappointed in her marriage with Mark in *That Hideous Strength,* and of Orual, Queen of Glome, disappointed in her love for her sister in *Till We Have Faces,* is because Lewis had a sense that, before God, humankind is feminine (*That Hideous Strength,* 315–316, 194) and—because of the Fall of Adam and Eve—resents God's interference in our affairs, in our very persons. It is against this background that the adjective "Unwelcome" in the chapter title should be understood.

64 A gesture analogous to that of the Risen Lord in the Gospel of Luke 24:37–43, and another image of the Holy Spirit.*

65 There are many legends from the Middle Ages about visions of Christ or of a saint after which a miraculous spring gushes forth to mark the spot of the event.

66 Through Hwin, Lewis can write more successfully about this height of mystical surrender than he could even through Lucy. Lewis is finally able to put his meaning into words through the twin stories of Psyche and Orual in *Till We Have Faces.*

67 This whole scene is modeled on the Gospel of John 20:26 ff.

[68] That no one sees him coming among the discussants suggests the appearances of the Risen Lord among the disciples in the Upper Room, Gospel of John 20:19 and 26.

[69] The phrase he uses suggests the Gospel of Mark 13:29, and Daniel 4.

[70] This may be hard to understand, especially for older Christian readers who have heard much preaching against a certain kind of universalism,* that is, a belief that one god is as good as the next and that it doesn't matter what you believe in as long as you're sincere. Lewis is not a universalist in this sense (nor perhaps in any sense) because he shows clearly in this scene that Rabadash understands only his god Tash and that Aslan, always in charge, has arranged for this form of punishment and for this form of release.

[71] See *Autobiographical allusions.*

[72] For more detailed comment about this activity see *Aslan's name, Aslan's voice,* and *Creation of Narnia.*

[73] At his own discretion, Aslan can be very vulnerable: He submits to death at the Witch's hand in LWW. This conforms with the Gospel of John 10:18, "No one takes [my life] from me, but I lay it down of my own accord. I have power to lay it down and I have power to take it again; this charge I have received from my Father."

[74] This is similar to the shock Shasta experienced when he discovered he was not walking alone in the fog. Those who have read Lewis's *Miracles: A Preliminary Study,* may remember the end of Chapter 11, "Christianity and 'Religion,' " (pp. 93–94, 97–98), which describes the shock that the Pantheist has when the God who does nothing and demands nothing becomes the God of Judaeo-Christian revelation, the "hunter, king, husband":

> There comes a moment when the children who have been playing at burglars hush suddenly: was that a *real* footstep in the hall? There comes a moment when people who have been dabbling in religion ("Man's Search for God"!) suddenly draw back. Supposing we really found Him? We never meant it to come to that! Worse still, supposing He had found us?

[75] Aslan, as Jesus in earthly experience, knows the faith of the London cabman Frank.

[76] Recall the pathos of King David's lament over his son Absalom in the Second Book of Samuel 19:1–5.

[77] Lewis attempts to explain this mystery of God's suffering and needing human comfort in his *Letters to Malcolm: Chiefly on Prayer:* " . . . God, besides being the Great Creator, is the Tragic Redeemer. Perhaps the Tragic Creator too. For I am not sure that the great canyon of anguish which lies across our lives is *solely* due to some pre-historic catastrophe. Something tragic may . . . be inherent in the very act of creation" (p. 91). See Gerald Vann's *The Pain of Christ and the Sorrow of God* (London: Templegate, 1945).

[78] From what Lewis believed about the symbolism of horse and rider (see *Horses, Horsemanship* and *Centaurs*) it is possible to interpret the meaning of this entire scene as the transformation of Digory from one who has the potential for the unbridled curiosity that is his uncle's dissolution, to one who in harmony with Nature faces the stern test to disobedience to God's laws and to selfishness and passes the test.

[79] Lewis is not trying to disguise the theological import of this scene (or any other, for that matter). But he seems to hope that young readers will store away the meaning of these events for the day when the facts of their relationship with God come into their lives. See the discussion of the "adjectival quality of reality" in the *Introduction.*

[80] Gospel of Luke 19:41.

[81] The implication here is that because Jadis was later able to reign for the Hundred Years of Winter, the Narnians somehow neglected their care for the Tree. This story is not told. The only hint that we have of what took place is from Lewis's outline chronology where he records that the Witch came out of the North in 898 N.Y. and was two years in perpetrating the treachery that placed her in power over Narnia (PWD, 42).

[82] The autobiographical implications of this passage are enormous. If the thesis is accepted that telling the story of Digory is partly a way for Lewis to work out his own agony over his mother's sickness and death, then this is the conclusion he reached: God knows what would have happened if his prayers for her life had been answered and He must be trusted to have known why it was necessary (in the awesome sense of that word) for her to die when she did. Lewis's theology of providence and the compassion of God are not worked out in the antiseptic atmosphere of an academic laboratory but in the crucible of his own heart.

[83] This mystical passage is one of the finest in all of Lewis's writings (which are notable for many such). Lewis intends to weave a spell here that will be with his readers all their days for their having been in Narnia and met the Lion. He means for them to be more awake and alive for having read the *Chronicles;* and if later they become members of the Judaeo-Christian tradition, the vision of the Lord they have come to believe in ought to sustain them throughout life.

[84] For the substance of this conversation and these lies, see *Tash, Tashlan,* and *Eschatology.*

[85] See *Aslan's country.*

[86] This motif is used eight times in LB, once in LWW, and once in VDT.

[87] The final three paragraphs of Lewis's 1943 essay, "The Poison of Subjectivism" in *Christian Reflections,* Walter Hooper, ed. (Grand Rapids: Wm. B. Eerdmans Publishing Co., 1967) pp. 72–81 are crucial for understanding this motif and, indeed, the central issues behind LB. The heart of Lewis's conclusion is:

> A Christianity which does not see moral and religious experience converging to meet at infinity, not at a negative infinity, but in the positive infinity of the living yet superpersonal God, has nothing, in the long run, to divide it from devil worship; and a philosophy which does not accept value as eternal and objective can lead us only to ruin. (pp. 80–81)

The "devil worship" he mentions is pictured in the worship of Tash. The loss of the sense of the connection between God and the moral law ("God neither *obeys* nor *creates* the moral law" is Lewis's guiding principle) in the "Christians" in LB—Shift* and Puzzle,* many of the Talking Beasts, and even Jewel* and Tirian—leads to the ruin of Narnia. See *Invisibility,* especially note 2.

[88] Lewis does not intend to imply through the hopelessness of the situation in LB that there is also no hope of reversing the valueblindness of our own Western culture. The feeling of hopelessness comes from the great Norse theme of the Last Battle,* the Twilight of the Gods, a feeling for which Lewis is trying to create in his readers through LB.

[89] Recall the one he gave Digory when the boy returned with the apple. These two scenes evoke the Gospel of Matthew 25:21 and 23.

[90] Recall Polly's plea for Uncle Andrew.

[91] Anticipated by Roonwit when he first comes into Aslan's country. The British editions print "farther" and the American print "further." Since Lewis intended a platonic theme here, he probably intended to use farther, the comparative of *far,* a spacial reference. The phrase "farther up and farther in" is used seven times in LB, a book noted for two other motifs: "Not a tame Lion" and "The Dwarfs are for the Dwarfs." The reason why Lewis might have devised such motifs may be found in his essay "Historicism" in *Christian Reflections* and *Fern-seed and Elephants:* "In Norse theology cosmic history is neither a cycle nor a flux; it is a tragic epic marching deathward to the drum-beat of omens and prophecies" (p. 103, 49).

[92] For a discussion of the implications of this encounter, see *Universalism.*

[93] Recall Shasta, and Digory and Polly, and their visions of Aslan.

[94] One of Lewis's favorite images. See *Great Waterfall.*

ASLAN'S BREATH   See *Holy Spirit.*

ASLAN'S COUNTRY   The land that is home to Aslan and to all creatures who recognize Aslan with joy.* It is a range of incredibly high yet snow-free mountains, bathed in late-spring/midsummer[1] warm breezes and freshness, alive with the sounds of running water, waterfalls, and birdsong against a "background of immense silence,"* and covered with orchards of autumn-ripe fruit, forests of mighty trees,* and flower-decked meadows. It is not connected with any created country but every real country is connected with it, as peninsula to mainland.[2] It lies beyond the edge and beyond the sun of every world and can only be reached by magic* or through the door* of a noble death.* No one is any particular age there: all come into the full flower of their manhood or womanhood. It is also known as Aslan's Land and as Aslan's Mountain.

Aslan's country is not mentioned in LWW, in HHB, or in MN; and its single mention in PC is in Doctor Cornelius's* story* to the young prince Caspian. In VDT it is the object of Reepicheep's quest* and part of Edmund's profession of faith. The sight of it at the World's End* fades for Edmund, Eustace, and Lucy, as Narnia's sun rises. SC's transitions* between England* and Narnia take place through Aslan's country; it is in this book that we

---

discover that the air there is clearer than in Narnia or in other worlds. So too minds are clearer in Aslan's country—down in Narnia and other countries the air is thicker and minds more confused and confusable.[3]

The most significant observations about the nature of Aslan's country are made in LB. Jewel's* hope is that the Door of the Stable* may lead to Aslan's country and to Aslan's Table.* Tirian,* having ushered Rishda* into the arms of Tash* through the door, discovers himself refreshed, cooled, cleaned, and dressed for a feast. The pleasures attendant on eating the wonderful fruit there are not only not wrong (and therefore forbidden), but are entirely right* and lawful and encouraged. And when Lucy, Peter, and Edmund have their power of vision magnified immeasurably, they see that the mountains of the Utter East* ring Narnia round to become the Western Wilds* at the heart of which is the garden* in which they are standing.[4] In addition, they see the real England and their parents, Mr. and Mrs. Pevensie,* waving to them. Tumnus* explains the heart of each good culture survives because it has always been a part of Aslan's country. Finally, all are welcomed to go farther up[5] into these mountains and farther in this land—the real adventures* have only begun.

(PC 51, 53. VDT 16, 23; 92, 93; 211 ff., 205 ff. SC 9 ff., 18 ff.; 211 ff., 201 ff. LB 128, 118; 131 ff., 120 ff.; 157 passim, 143 passim, esp. 181–182, 163–164.) [Biblical allusions; Credal elements; Plato; Time.]

---

[1] As winter is a natural metaphor for death* and lifelessness, so summer is a metaphor for life and festivity. Lewis was alive to this significance and uses the metaphor often. Two vivid instances are the final paragraph of his 1945 sermon essay, "The Grand Miracle," in *God in the Dock* (Grand Rapids: Wm. B. Eerdmans Publishing Co., 1970) pp. 80–88, and the penultimate paragraph of Chapter 15 of *Miracles* (New York: Macmillan Publishing Co., 1978; London: Collins Fontana, 1960) p. 142, 146. The former closes thus:

> We have the power either of withstanding the spring, and sinking back into the cosmic winter, or of going on into those "high mid-summer pomps" in which our Leader, the Son of man [sic], already dwells, and to which He is calling us.

(Lewis is quoting Matthew Arnold's "Thyrsis," line 62.) The latter concludes:

> . . . the Miracles of Perfecting or of Glory, the Transfiguration, the Resurrection, and the Ascension . . . are the true spring, or even the summer, of the world's new year. The Captain, the forerunner, is already in May or June, though His followers on earth are still living in the frosts and east winds of Old Nature . . .

[2] This echoes Dr. Dimble's speech in the final chapter of Lewis's *That Hideous Strength* (New York: Macmillan Publishing Co., 1965, pp. 370–371, and London: Pan Books, 1955, p. 242):

> [God] doesn't make two blades of grass the same: how much less two saints, two nations, two angels. The whole work of healing [Earth] depends on nursing that little spark . . . which is alive in every real people, and different in each. When Logres really dominates Britain, when the goddess Reason, the divine clearness, is really enthroned in France, when the order of Heaven is really followed in China—why, then it will be spring.

And Lewis says that the real Narnia and the real England* will always exist in the spring of Aslan's country.

[3] It is not clear whether the thorn-bush (from which Eustace plucks the foot-long thorn that he will drive into Aslan's paw to obtain the drop of blood needed to rejuvenate Caspian) exists in Aslan's country forever as a reminder of the sorrows of other worlds, or only for the convenience of the author in obtaining the rejuvenating blood of the Lion.

[4] This vision of the "coincidence of opposites" (to use Nicholas of Cusa's phrase), of the ultimate unity of the two foci of humankind's longing,* is one of the oldest themes in Lewis, one which he surely met in Chesterton's *Orthodoxy* (New York: Doubleday Image, 1959, pp. 9–12).

Susan, Lucy, and Edmund help Mrs. Beaver prepare dinner as Peter and Mr. Beaver come in with the main course, fresh-caught trout. (LWW 70, 70.)

The final reconciliation of the Landlord's Country and the Island of the West is a fundamental motif in Lewis's earliest Christian work, *The Pilgrim's Regress* (Grand Rapids: Wm. B. Eerdmans Publishing Co., 1958).

⁵ See *Aslan*, note 91.

ASLAN'S HOW In LWW, it is the round, high, open hilltop south of the Great River* and west of the River Rush* on the edge of the Great Woods.* From its brow, a person can look down upon all the forests of Narnia and the Eastern Sea* in the distance. Its other name is the Hill of the Stone Table* because this ancient place of sacrifice is in the very center of the hilltop. Lewis chooses this sacred site as the place where the three English children, Peter, Susan, and Lucy, first[1] meet Aslan in a magnificent heraldic tableau.

In PC, whose story takes place thirteen hundred Narnian Years after the events of LWW, this hill has gotten the name Aslan's How (from the Old Norse and Old Teutonic name for mound or cairn). A second huge round hill has been raised by ancient Narnians over the broken Stone Table, which is now referred to simply as "the Stone." The mound is hollowed into mazelike tunnels, galleries, and caves, all lined and roofed with smooth stones, and carved with ancient writing, snaking patterns, and—everywhere—stone reliefs of Aslan. (The suggestion of similar Celtic shrines and burial places is inescapable.) At this point, the place is also known as the Great Mound, or simply the Mound. Prince Caspian's army makes its headquarters here during the War of Deliverance.* And though heretofore perhaps the most hallowed place in Narnia, it is not mentioned again in the *Chronicles,* except once, in passing, in HHB.

(LWW 121, *114;* 142, *132;* 146, *135.* PC 85–86, *81–82;* 147, *132;* 150, *134.* HHB 168, *148.*)
[*Geography, Narnian.*]

---

[1] Since LWW is the first of the *Chronicles* to be written, this fact is especially significant. See *Introduction* and *Appendix One.*

ASLAN'S NAME It is the tradition among the Centaurs* that Aslan has nine names; but we are given only four and these may not be among the nine the Centaurs know. They are: Aslan, the great Lion, the son of the Emperor-beyond-the-Sea,* and the King above all High Kings.[1] From the first time Mr. Beaver* pronounces the name of Aslan[2] in LWW to the scene of the Great Reunion* in the garden* of the west in LB when Reepicheep welcomes the Seven Friends of Narnia* and the blessed Narnians "in the Lion's name," Lewis intends to ring the changes on the themes of the power of Christ's name, especially in prayer, and of the proper awe one ought to feel in a genuine experience of the numinous,* that is, the reverential fear* and joy* which always accompany a true meeting between God and the human being.

True to his own principles about good writing,[3] Lewis, in his first several uses of the name of Aslan, does not throw descriptive adjectives and adverbs at his readers but tries to elicit from their imaginations* and memories* the experience of the "enormous meaning" some names have in dreams.* Everyone has experienced a dream turn into a nightmare or a dream become so beautiful that it becomes a lifelong memory and kindles the desire always to live in that beauty. It is *this* terror and *this* delight that the name of Aslan evokes in each of the Pevensie children (though for Edmund, given his addiction to the black magic* of the Turkish Delight,* it occasions only horror until he undergoes his conversion).

This theme, and indeed any significant use of Aslan's name, recedes altogether in PC. In VDT, the power of Aslan's name, especially prayer in his name, is highlighted. Caspian undertakes the voyage into the darkness surrounding the Dark Island* only after invoking the name of Aslan. It is in answer to Lucy's prayer to Aslan that the albatross* comes to lead the *Dawn Treader* out of that same darkness. Caspian demonstrates the urgency of his desire to help the Three Sleepers* and to express his growing love for the Star's Daughter* by asking Ramandu* in Aslan's name how to disenchant them. Then, in a closing scene which suggests a major reason why Lewis wrote the *Chronicles,* Aslan reveals to Lucy that he has another name in our world and that the reason the children were brought to Narnia was to know him by his Narnian name in order to be able to recognize him by his earthly name.[4]

Perhaps still under the spell of his own ending to VDT, Lewis intensifies his own fictional exploration of the "theology" of Aslan's name in SC. Jill and Eustace, having refused to force their way into Narnia by the use of magic, have time enough only to invoke Aslan's name three times before they are interrupted by members of the Gang.* This is quite sufficient, however, for their transition* into Aslan's country.* And, as part of Jill's quest* (her temporary vocation), she is given four signs,* the last of which is that she will know who Prince Rilian is because he will be the first person to ask her something in Aslan's name. Here the reference to the Gospel of Mark, 10:42, is clearly intended, because later in the crisis of the Silver Chair,* Puddleglum is able to distinguish between Aslan's command to Jill and their fear* of the consequences of their obedience* to this command. The deranged man has solemnly entreated them for assistance (the meaning of "adjure") in the Lion's name; and help they must. Summoning all their faith and hope, they invoke the Lion's name as they sever Rilian's bonds. When the Queen of Underland* seeks to weave the tightest chains of her spell over the freed prince and his three rescuers, she masks her inner disturbance at hearing the name of Aslan by shifting the conversation again to the meaning of religious language: "What a pretty name! What does it mean?" Good reductionist* that she is, she tries to distract their attention from the fact that in that name they have just set the Prince free with a discussion about how all their beliefs are nothing but glorified metaphors, merely childish ways of speaking about something whose nature they really don't understand.

No new ground about the numinous* quality of Aslan's name is broken in HHB. The fact that Shasta does not experience any feelings* of awe and joy at the two times he hears the Lion's name mentioned in the Narnians' conversation indicates less that Shasta lacks the proper stock response* to an experience of God than that Lewis, two years distant from the original impulse that sparked his completion of LWW, has forgotten this theme. He is more concerned with the implications of Bree's invocation of the name of Aslan without the sufficient knowledge* and faith in what he is actually doing (for contrast, Lewis has Aravis swear once "by Tash*"). Oaths* are a serious matter, as the reader will soon see in LB. In his vision of Aslan, Shasta experiences the terror and delight of the Lion; and Lewis adds, as omniscient author, the four names of Aslan that we do know in the *Chronicles.*

MN contains both the most exalted insight about the meaning of Aslan's name and the most trivial (or at least the most gratuitously allegorical) use of the name. In the great scene in which the gift of speech* and thus reasoning is conferred upon the animals,* Aslan's first use of the name "Narnia" in his command for the land and its creatures to awaken is reciprocated by the very first word *they* speak: his name.[5] This is an awesome hint at and a beautiful picture of what Lewis believed to be the deepest meaning of creation itself: Whatever the comprehensive meaning of God's desire to create other rational beings beside himself, humankind realizes the apex of its vocation when it becomes the priest for dumb creation and speaks the name of God back to him.[6] But only a few pages later, the He-Beaver asks aloud, "What in the name of Aslan are [Digory, Polly, and Frank]?" To some readers, this is a lapse in style, although Lewis may have been attempting to add a touch of humor to a rather heady chapter.

LB adds little to the development of the themes suggested by the name of Aslan. One of the Seven Friends of Narnia* (probably the High King Peter, given his other roles during the end of Narnia*) dismisses Tash* to take his prey and himself back to his "own place" (hell*) in the name of the Lion and of the Emperor. It is possible that Lewis alludes to the actual power of exorcism, casting out devils, by the use of the name of Christ; but it is more likely that he is suggesting that Aslan's is the power and the prerogative for consigning evil* to its place.

Lewis's "theology" of the name of Aslan is deeply imbedded in the Judaeo-Christian tradition (and, indeed, in the North American Indian and other cultures), in which the name profoundly reflects the reputation and the experience of the person. God's name among the Chosen People, *Yahweh,* is not only the metaphysical "I am Who Am" but, to use John Courtney Murray's much more suggestive translation, "I shall be there as who I am shall I be there."[7] His name is his reputation for having been behind his people's history* from the beginning; it is also a promise to care for them as well or even better in the future. For Christians this future has arrived definitively in Jesus the Christ, whose own name, *Yeshua,* means "Yahweh saves." Thus the scope of God's salvation is seen both in the continuous theological reflection on the meaning of God's name[8] and also in the life stories of the people who respond to his call.

(LWW 64, *65;* 74, *74;* 85, *82.* VDT 153, *153;* 159, *158;* 174, *171;* 216, *209.* SC 7, *16;* 145–146, *144–145;* 156, *154;* 207, *198.* HHB 62, *60;* 72, *78;* 122, *109;* 135, *120;* 160, *140;* 181, *159;* 191, *167.* MN 116–117, *108–109;* 120, *113.* LB 133, *121;* 177, *160.*)

[1] Later in this scene, Aslan is also named "High King above all Kings"; but this name does not differ substantially from "King above all High Kings."

[2] In Turkish, *aslan* is the word for "lion." It is not clear whether Lewis made up the name because he liked its sound and then later discovered its meaning, or if he made a deliberate search. Those who have speculated that he might have seen or used a Turkish brand of pipe tobacco or cigarette sporting the silhouette of a lion or even the name "Aslan" will be disappointed to learn that the Turkish Consul in Los Angeles conducted a survey among his colleagues for this author and none remembers such a brand. *As* is also an old Scandinavian word meaning "god," as in *Asgard,* the home of the gods in Norse mythology.*

[3] Lewis received many letters from would-be writers, even children, asking his counsel on the writing craft; and true to his generous nature, he answered every one. In almost every answer, he included the following advice:

> Never use adjectives or adverbs which are mere appeals to the reader to feel as you want him to feel. He won't do it just because you ask him: you've got to *make* him. No use telling us a battle was "exciting". If *you* succeed in exciting us the adjective will be unnecessary; if you don't, it will be useless. Don't tell us the jewels had an "emotional" glitter; make us feel the emotion. I can hardly tell you how important this is. (*Letters of C.S. Lewis,* ed. W.H. Lewis [New York: Harcourt Brace Jovanovich, 1966] p. 279)

For a detailed analysis of Lewis's advice on writing, see Dr. Ken Futch's essay, "C. S. Lewis on the Art of Writing" in *The Lamp-post* of the Southern California C.S. Lewis Society, vol. 1, nos. 2 and 3 (April and July, 1977).

[4] See *Introduction.*

[5] These "first usages" are first only with respect to the internal chronology of the *Chronicles.* This entry, as well as this entire *Companion to Narnia,* tries to deal with themes in the order of the publication of the books, as explained in the *Introduction.*

[6] The most striking picture of this truth comes in the song of Nature (modelled on Psalm 110) in Lewis's *The Great Divorce* (New York: Macmillan Publishing Co., 1946, pp. 105–106) which concludes: "Master, your Master has appointed you for ever: to be our King of Justice and our high Priest." The first "master" is the man who has overcome his lust; the second "master" is God; and the lust, converted, is now a magnificent horse.

[7] For a full discussion of the meaning of the name of God, see John Courtney Murray, *The Problem of God* (New Haven: Yale University Press, 1964) pp. 5–14, esp. p. 6.

[8] See, as only one striking instance among many similar, the *Treatise on Christian Perfection* by Saint Gregory of Nyssa, a fourth century bishop and theologian, on the names of Christ in the writings of St. Paul (found in *The Liturgy of the Hours* [New York: Catholic Book Publishing Co., 1975] vol. 4, pp. 391–392).

ASLAN'S TABLE   Located on Ramandu's Island,* the table is surrounded by richly carved stone chairs with silk cushions. It runs the length of a clearing, which is paved by smooth stones and surrounded by large pillars, but open to the sky. A crimson cloth covers the table nearly to the ground, and the stone dagger rests upon it at all times, almost as if enshrined. When the Daughter of Ramandu* (who first calls it "Aslan's Table") sets her candlesticks upon it, all the gold and silver accoutrements glow richly in the light. By Aslan's decree, each evening at sunset the table is magically laden with a banquet far grander than any ever set in the Golden Age of Narnia.* If this food is not eaten by travelers before daybreak, it is consumed by the Birds of Morning*; and so the table remains empty until the next sunset. A place of magical renewal, the table—with its medieval setting and grail-like knife— suggests the spirituality of the ancient Arthurian legends; and being Aslan's table, it also suggests the eternal refreshment of the Eucharist as the heavenly banquet.

(VDT 165 ff., *163 ff.* LB 128, *118.*)

ASLAN'S VOICE   One of the greatest advantages in the choice of a talking lion* to be the hero of the *Chronicles* is the addition of a whole repertory of roarings, growlings, and purrings to the ordinary range of human speech expression. Beyond understanding what Aslan actually says, the reader's chief way of gauging the Lion's thoughts and feelings* is through the quality of his voice. The fact that Digory's tree* in London does not grow up to be fully magical since it is far away from the sound of Aslan's voice is an instance of the Lion's voice being an integral part of the atmosphere of Narnia. It is "deeper, wilder, and stronger" than a man's voice; "a sort of heavy, golden voice."

Aslan's roar is reserved for celebrating his chief exultations (most notably his resurrection in LWW), expressing his greatest displeasure (for example, at the White Witch's suggestion that he might go back on his promise in LWW[1]), announcing his victory (as when he kills the Witch in LWW and when he returns to Narnia in PC), and issuing his most momentous commands (such as calling Father Time* to begin the end of Narnia* in LB).

Aslan's growl is usually probing, more tentative, as when he compels Digory to take responsibility for his actions or when he attempts to draw the renegade dwarfs* into the joys* of Aslan's country.* He also growls at his loved ones when they would misunderstand him or his ways, as when Lucy suggests that he not follow his own laws in VDT. But it is only with his loved ones that he also purrs, one of his rarer expressions in the *Chronicles;* Aslan purrs his love for Lucy with a low, earthquake*-like sound (also in VDT) and at the sound of Susan's horn* in LWW.

In a performance reminiscent of Tolkien's Music of the Ainur,[2] Aslan sings Narnia and its creatures into existence. Beginning wordlessly and nearly tunelessly, the Lion's song grows in strength and glory until the sun* rises, becomes gentle and lilting for the growing of grasses and trees,* and, after a wildly passionate section, lapses into a solemn silence.* But Aslan's "deepest, wildest voice" is used only for the bestowing of the gift of speech* upon the chosen Narnian animals.*

Aslan's shouts are set aside for approvals and encouragements*; note his earthshaking "Well done" to Digory and his invitation to the Seven Friends of Narnia* and the blessed Narnians: "Come farther in! Come farther up!"[3] In contrast, his somberest moods are reflected in his "dull voice," as on the evening of his death.*

Finally, his voice alone communicates the profoundest mystery of the Trinity* to Shasta. Aslan *is* his voice, the "Large Voice," to the boy surrounded in the night fog; and the threefold distinction of voices (the first, very deep, low, and earthshaking; the second, "loud and clear and gay"; and the third, the almost inaudible but all-encompassing whisper) is one of the singular achievements of Lewis as a remythologizer.

(LWW 124, *117;* 126, *119;* 141, *131;* 144, *133;* 174, *160.* PC 150, *135.* VDT 135, *136.* SC 16, *26;* 121, *122;* 214, *204.* HHB 157, *139.* MN 98 passim, *93 passim;* 118, *109;* 135, *125–126;* 166, *154;* 184, *170.* LB 147–148, *134–135;* 158, *144.*)

[1] The American editions substitute an inane "Wow" for the much more descriptive "Haa-a-arrh" of the British editions, which suggests that Aslan found the Witch's question surprising, laughable, and outrageous.

[2] J. R. R. Tolkien, *The Silmarillion* (Boston: Houghton Mifflin Co., 1977; London: George Allen & Unwin, 1977) pp. 15–17, *15–17.*

[3] See Aslan, note 91.

ASTROLABE   See *Coriakin.*

ASTRONOMY, NARNIAN   In the *Chronicles,* Lewis recovers a medieval worldview of a Narnia-centered universe.[1] Narnia itself is flat—Caspian has heard stories* about worlds that are round, like balls, but he never believed they were true.[2] The planets are great lords and ladies, the stars* are wondrous, silvery beings. As befits a medieval universe, the portents of astrology are taken seriously, and Centaurs* are especially good at reading these omens in the heavens. In many ways, the Narnian planetary system is very much like our own: the day is twenty-four hours long (Orruns* immediately recognizes the reference when Eustace says it's after 10 o'clock); the sun* rises in the east and sets in the west and has a companion moon;[3] many constellations can be seen in the night sky, among them the summer constellations of the Ship, the Hammer, and the Leopard.* There is apparently some scientific study of the night sky, as a number of astronomical instruments are found in the House of the Magician.*

(PC 45–46, *49;* 73, *71;* 111, *102;* 133, *120;* 150, *135;* 207, *181.* VDT 110, *113;* 138, *138;* 141, *141;* 163, *161;* 170, *167;* 171, *168;* 177, *173.* SC 207, *198.* HHB 85, *78;* 109, *98.* LB 15, *19–20;* 58–59, *58;* 150–151, *136–137;* 156–157, *142–143.*)

[1] See *Emperor-beyond-the-Sea,* note 2.

[2] See *Imagination* for a discussion of Lewis's deliberate inversions of reality in the *Chronicles.*

[3] The Narnian moon is larger than ours. After it has set, Aravir,* the morning star, gleams like a little moon in the east. In HHB, the moon is said to be behind Aslan as he bounds on the scene between Shasta and the desert. This suggests that Calormen is far to the south of Narnia and Archenland. For a discussion of the lovely image of Aslan and the moon gazing upon one another, see *Aslan,* note 24.

ATLANTEAN, ATLANTIS   Andrew Ketterley surmises that his godmother's box is Atlantean; that is, a remnant of one of the oldest civilizations on earth. Whether or not Atlantis really existed has never been proven, but traditionally it is thought to have been an island west of the Strait of Gibraltar that long ago vanished into the sea.

(MN 19, *24.*)
[*Fairy; Mrs. Lefay.*]

AUTOBIOGRAPHICAL ALLUSIONS   The pattern of parentlessness in the *Chronicles*—and the consequent dependence on peer approval—is the deepest and most constant allusion to Lewis's own childhood, which was marked by the death of his mother when he was nine and his troubled relationship with his father.[1] Thus Aravis's father is heartless; Shasta's "father" is sullen and mean (the boy has lost his mother and does not know his real father); Caspian is an orphan and his father figure, Miraz,* is a tyrant; and the Pevensie children's father is absent. Digory's desperate desire to help his seriously ill mother reflects Lewis's crisis over his own mother's illness. Other patterns that emerge in the stories from Lewis's life are his love of the sea and his love of nature and walking and his loathing of insects* and schools.* Eustace's fall over the cliff and Jill's vertigo in SC reflect Lewis's own fear of cliffs. These themes and specific incidences are highlighted and commented upon in the appropriate entries.

[*Adults.*]

---

[1] Only in the fleeting scenes of Digory's mother's recovery of her health and her playing with Polly and Digory and of Tirian's* meeting his father Erlian* does the reader catch a glimpse of the kind of healthy relationship of parent and child that is so notable in the works of Lewis's mentor, George MacDonald.

AUTUMN FEAST   Two Autumn Feasts are mentioned in the *Chronicles:* the feast of the "gentle giants*" of Harfang,* in which Jill and Eustace are to *be* the feast; and the feast of the Calormenes* at which the ass Rabadash,* stepping into the temple of Tash,* returns to human form. The Autumn feast of *Samain,* which took place in November, was one of the four main feasts of the Celtic year in ancient Britain. The year began on this day for the Celts; much ritual, of which human sacrifice was quite probably a part, was associated with it. This was a time of great tension for the ancient Celts, in which the supernatural and material worlds drew close to one another as the earth moved into the darkness of winter.[1] Thus the trek of the three travelers across Ettinsmoor,* during which they meet the Queen of Underland* and the Black Knight, is quite appropriate; they do enter into the darkness of Underland, the spell of which is only broken by the death of the Queen.

(SC 76, *81;* 95, *98;* 114, *115.* HHB 211, *184.*)

---

[1] *New Larousse Encyclopedia of Mythology* (London: The Hamlyn Publishing Group Ltd., 1978) p. 236.

AVRA   One of the three Lone Islands.* It is the site of Bernstead,* the estate of Lord Bern,* and noted for a good harbor on its southern shore.

(VDT 30, *36;* 32, *39;* 39–40, *47–48.*)
[*Geography, Narnian.*]

AXARTHA TARKAAN   Grand Vizier of Calormen* before Ahoshta Tarkaan.*

(HHB 96, *87.*)
[*Tarkaan.*]

AZAROTH   A Calormene* goddess, otherwise undescribed, named by Aravis in her oath to Hwin.

(HHB 36, *39.*)
[*Gods.*]

AZIM BALDA   A major Calormene* city southwest of Tashbaan.* Located at the crossing of many important trade routes, it is the site of the House of Imperial Posts, the post office of Calormen.

(HHB 38, *40.*)

AZROOH   See *Rabadash.*

BACCHUS   In Roman mythology,* the god* of wine* and ecstasy[1] (in Greek mythology, he is named Dionysus). He is a youth dressed only in a fawn-skin, and vine leaves wreath his curly hair. His face is wild, and almost too pretty for a boy. Edmund thinks he looks capable of doing absolutely anything. He is often accompanied by Silenus* and the Maenads,* with whom he dances the wild dance* of plenty. He is the very spirit of Dionysian revelry.*[2]

(LWW 13, *21.* PC 152, *137;* 192, *168;* 196, *173.*)

---

[1] The cry *Euan, Euan, euoi-oi-oi-oi* is the traditional ecstatic utterance at the rites and feasting of Bacchus. *Euhan* or *Euan* is a Greek surname of Bacchus and *euhoi* or *euoi* is an interjection, a shout of joy heard throughout a bacchanal. (PC 152, *137;* 154, *138;* 196, *173.*)
[2] Lewis believed that the God of Israel, Jahweh (Lewis's transliteration), was truly the God of Nature hinted at in mythology under the names of Bacchus, Venus, Ceres, and Genius. For a discussion of this matter, see *Mythology* and *Aslan,* note 3. See also C. S. Lewis, *Miracles* (New York: Macmillan Co., 1978; London: Collins Fontana 1960) p.136, *140.*

BANNER, STANDARD, CROWN, CORONET   Mentioned throughout the *Chronicles,* these emblems of royal office help lend a medieval flavor to the adventures.*

Banners, Standards   The Narnian flag is a rampant lion* (Aslan, of course) on a green field. In LWW the lion Lucy sees is red, as is the lion that graces the banner carried by Lord Peridan.* However, the great banner that flies at half-mast above the castle at Cair Paravel* in SC bears a gold lion. Whether the color of the lion varied, or whether Lewis simply forgot what color the lion was, is a matter for speculation.

Crowns, coronets   Narnian crowns are "light, delicate, beautifully shaped circlets," especially in contrast to modern European crowns. People actually look better when wearing Narnian crowns. Dwarfs* made the gold circlets worn by King Frank* and Queen Helen,* his covered with rubies and hers with emeralds. In VDT Lucy can tell that the group of Sea People she is seeing is lordly and noble, because they are wearing coronets.

(LWW 122–123, *115.* VDT 41, *49;* 194, *189.* SC 209–210, *200.* HHB 169, *149.* MN 172, *159.*)
[*Kings and Queens; Kings, queens; Orders, chivalric.*]

BANNISTER   See *Gang, the.*

BAPTISM   See *Credal elements.*

BAR   Former Lord Chancellor of Archenland,* he was dismissed by King Lune* for embezzling royal monies and spying for the Tisroc.* When the Centaur* predicts that Prince Cor will some day save Archenland from great danger, Bar kidnaps the boy and flees to Calormen. However, before he can reach his destination, his galleon is overtaken and Lord Bar is killed.

(HHB 198–199, *173–174.*)
[*Prophecies; Shasta.*]

BASTABLES   The famous fictional children created by Edith Nesbit (1858–1924), one of C. S. Lewis's favorite writers. They are mentioned in the same context as Sherlock Holmes,* to give further support to Lewis's sense that fictional characters "really" exist in the world of fiction. The Bastable children are the heroes of *The Story of the Treasure Seekers* (1899), *The Would-Be-Goods* (1901), and *The New Treasure Seekers* (1904). These were collected in 1928 as *The Bastable Children.* Lewis often recommended Nesbit's other cycle of stories about four children and their baby brother (Cyril, Robert, Anthea, Jane, and the Lamb), *The Five Children.*

(MN 1, *9.*)
[*Wardrobe.*]

BATTLE IMAGERY   See *Violence.*

BEAUTY   See *Vanity.*

BEAVER, MR.   A cordial, hardworking creature, proud of his dam-building skills and lovingly content with his domestic situation. He seems to be a prototype of the sturdy working-class Englishman. He befriends the four children in the Narnian wood, proving to Lucy that he is trustworthy by showing her the handkerchief she had left with Tumnus.* He invites the children to dinner at his cozy home. There he becomes the expository vehicle by which Lewis introduces them and his readers to some Narnian history and characters.

Mr. Beaver tells of the wickedness and power of the White Witch, revealing that she has turned Tumnus into stone because he did not betray Lucy. He introduces the character of the great Aslan and informs the children that they are to meet him. A creature of deep and simple faith, Mr. Beaver recites the three ancient prophecies* that tell of Aslan's triumph and the end of the Hundred Years of Winter* as well as foretelling that the coming of four human beings is to figure in the future of Narnia.

An astute judge of character, Mr. Beaver knows immediately where Edmund has gone and why. He tells the children that only Aslan is capable of rescuing Edmund and overcoming the White Witch. Then, in keeping with this faith, he and his wife lead the group on the journey to escape the Witch and to meet Aslan at the Stone Table.* His basic practicality is evident in his act of locking the door to delay the Witch's pursuit, and in his delight with his workaday gift* from Father Christmas*—a refurbished dam and new sluice gate. His loyalty to Aslan, always apparent, erupts into anger when he hears the Witch hailed as Queen of Narnia and into anxiety and prayer as he holds Mrs. Beaver's* paw during Aslan's private talk with the Witch. True to Aslan and those whom Aslan loves, he shares in the rewards and honors at the children's coronation and is among the blessed at the Great Reunion.*

(LWW 60 ff., *61 ff.;* 95 ff., *93 ff.;* 119 ff., *113 ff.;* 135 ff., *126 ff.;* 179, *165.* LB 179, *162.*)
[*Beaversdam; Feelings; Talking Beasts.*]

BEAVER, MRS.   A kind old she-beaver devoted to her husband, Mr. Beaver,* she is happily busy at her sewing machine most of the time. She keeps a snug home, which is decorated in a sea motif. When the children arrive, she greets them with a Simeon-like, "To think that I should see this day." In speaking of Aslan, she says that anyone who does not fear him is either very brave or very foolish. She is both intuitive and practical: intuitive in sensing that the Witch will try to use Edmund as bait to catch the other children; practical in taking pains to determine just how much Edmund knows to tell the Witch and how long it will take her to catch them.

Good provider that she is, she insists on packing dinner and a cordial for the journey to the Stone Table,* much to everyone's annoyance at first, though they later come to appreciate her foresight. Her gift* from Father Christmas,* a new and better sewing machine, evokes the practical concern about how it can be delivered since the door to their house is locked. Eager to be of comfort, she is first to tell the children that Edmund has been rescued, and she later nurses him when he is wounded. At the meeting of the Witch and Aslan, she intuits a hidden weakness in the Witch's failure to look Aslan in the eye. And during the private talk of the two leaders, she holds Mr. Beaver's paw, both giving and receiving comfort.

Beloved by the children, she receives many gifts and honors at their crowning. Finally, along with Mr. Beaver, she is part of the happy company at the Great Reunion.*

(LWW 67 ff., 67 ff.; 95 ff., 93 ff.; 119 ff., 113 ff.; 135, 126; 138, 128; 140, 130; 179, 165. LB 179, 162.)
[Beaversdam; Talking Beasts.]

BEAVERSDAM   The dam of which Mr. Beaver* is so proud in LWW later becomes a historic site. As a town, it is bordered to the north by lush grasslands. Its waterfall can be heard at a mile's distance on very quiet nights. Beaversdam has a marketplace; and two great Telmarine* Lords, known as the Brothers of Beaversdam,* live and rule there under Caspian IX.*

(LWW 66–68, 66–67. PC 45, 48; 56, 56. VDT 103, 107. HHB 32, 36.)

BELISAR   See Uvilas.

BERN   A fine-looking man with a beard, this Lord is first seen on the island Felimath,* where he buys Caspian's freedom from the slave trader, Pug.* When he learns Caspian's identity, he immediately acknowledges him as King* and explains that he disapproves of the piracy and slave trade* on the island and has petitioned Gumpas* that they be stopped. He entertains Caspian at his home, Bernstead* (a prototype of the prosperous English estate), on the island of Avra.* An ideal nobleman, he has a gracious wife and merry daughters; and his people are free. He tells Caspian that he came to the islands weary of travel, fell in love, and settled down. His favors to the King—suggesting a ruse to outwit Gumpas and arranging for his friends on Doorn* to greet Caspian when he arrives at Narrowhaven*—earn him the gratitude of the Crown and the dukedom of the Lone Islands.* He takes the oath of office by placing his hands between Caspian's—a gesture of fealty from the time of chivalry and indicative of the noble and courteous class that Bern represents. When the *Dawn Treader* leaves the Islands, Bern is half-ashamed that he does not go on with his new friends.

(VDT 35 ff., 42 ff.)
[Government; Orders, chivalric.]

BERNSTEAD   The estate where Lord Bern* lives in "a low pillared house" and where his people, all freemen, enjoy happiness and prosperity.

(VDT 39–40, 47–48.)

BERUNA   A town—complete with walls, gates, and marketplace—located in central Narnia a half-day's march from the Stone Table,* at the confluence of the Great River* and the River Rush.* Because most of the inhabitants are Telmarines* or under their influence, they flee from Aslan's company when the revelers visit Beruna. The few Old Narnians that live there join in the celebration of the deliverance of Narnia from Telmarine rule. The name of the town is also identified with a bridge, the fords, and two battles fought there.

(PC 191, *168;* 195, *171.* VDT 103, *107.*)

Bridge of Beruna   Built sometime since the Golden Age of Narnia,* it is a barrier to the freedom of the River-god,* who begs Aslan to remove it. Aslan delegates this task to Bacchus,* whose vines destroy the bridge in a scene reminiscent of Bacchus's destruction of the Lydian ship in Ovid's *Meta-morphoses.* [1]

(PC 104, *97;* 128, *116.*)

Fords of Beruna   The fords mark a broad and shallow place where the River Rush joins the Great River. It is the scene of the final surrender of the Telmarines in the War of Deliverance.*

(LWW 142, *132.* PC 114, *105.*)

First Battle of Beruna   The scene of the defeat of the White Witch and her army. It is first mentioned by this title in PC though the battle took place in LWW.

(PC 128, *117* [referring to LWW 173 ff., *159 ff.*])

Second Battle of Beruna   The closing battle of the War of Deliverance,* this title is first used in VDT though the battle took place in PC.

(VDT 11, *19* [referring to PC 198 ff., *166 ff.*])
[*Mythology; Violence.*]

---

[1]Book III, lines 600–690. Mary Innes, tr. (Harmondsworth: Penguin Classics, 1955) pp. 90–92).

BETTY   One of three servants to Professor Digory Kirke. The other two are Ivy* and Margaret.*

(LWW 1, *2.*)

BIBLICAL ALLUSIONS   Lewis had a lifelong appreciation of the Bible, which is a collection of various kinds of literature—history, poetry (both religious and secular), proverb, myth, gospel, prophecy, and letters—considered to be the revelation of God and God's will for us by people within the Judaeo-Christian tradition. In grammar school, he read the Bible as a devout Christian; only when he had become an atheist in his early teens did he leave off his Bible reading. As a student of Classical and English literature, he became a student of biblical content and style, but rejected its claim to be inspired by God. When he recovered his Christian faith in his early thirties, he resumed his prayerful reading of the Bible, prayed the Psalms daily for the rest of his life, and wrote in praise of the literary qualities of the Authorized Version (also known as the King James Version) and of modern translations (such as J.B. Phillip's *New Testament* and the Grail Psalter). He also attempted to help people read the Bible with more spiritual understanding. (His *Reflections on the Psalms* [New York: Harcourt Brace Jovanovich, 1958] is the best of these works.)

The *Chronicles of Narnia* are filled with biblical allusions. In contrast to direct or explicit scriptural references, which are extremely rare, the numerous allusions are indirect hints of actual biblical phraseology or suggestions of biblical themes or scenes. The following list is arranged in the order in which they appear in each of the *Chronicles* in their publication order. The suggested allusion or reference is first abbreviated, the page numbers are given, and then the biblical parallel is cited.

The Lion, the Witch and the Wardrobe

Daughter of Eve (8, *16*)	Romans 5:12
I should live to see this day (68, *68*)	Luke 2:30
Wrong will be right when . . . (74, *75*)	Matthew 12:18–20
At the sound of his roar . . . (74, *75*)	Hosea 11:10–11
Sorrows will be no more (74, *75*)	Isaiah 65:19
When Adam's flesh and Adam's bone (76, *76*)	Genesis 2:23
They are tools, not toys (104, *99*)	Ephesians 6:11–17
Deep Magic (138, *128*)	I Corinthians 2:5–8
No need to talk about what is past (136, *126*)	Isaiah 65:16
He just went on looking at Aslan (138, *128*)	Hebrews 12:2
I should be glad of company tonight (147, *135*)	Matthew 26:38
I am sad and lonely (147, *136*)	Matthew 26:38
Let him first be shaved (150, *139*)	Matthew 27:28
Jeering at him saying (150, *140*)	Matthew 27:29
In that knowledge, despair and die (152, *141*)	Matthew 27:46
Warmth of his breath . . . came all over her (159, *147*)	John 20:22

Susan and Lucy watch in awe as Aslan's gentle face grows terrible to behold and the very trees bend before the power of his roar. (LWW 161, 149.)

A magic deeper still (159, *148*)   I Corinthians 2:7–8

Wondering if the cordial would have any result (176, *163*)   John 4:36–38

Aslan provided food (178, *164*)   John 6:1–14

He has other countries to attend to (180, *166*)   John 10:16

Prince Caspian

The People That Lived in Hiding (68, *67*)   Isaiah 9:1

Help may be even now at the door (158, *141*)   Mark 13:29

A few join his company (195, *171*)   Matthew 22:14

Not water but the richest wine (198, *174*)   John 2:9

You shall have your tail again (203, *178*)   Mark 3:5

The Voyage of the Dawn Treader

Lucy gives . . . of her water (62, *68*)   Galatians 6:1

Well—he knows me (92, *98*)   I Corinthians 13:12

As bad as I was (91, *97*)   James 5:16

Beautiful . . . beyond the lot of mortals (129, *132*)   James 3:16

Caspian obeyed (173, *170*)   Ephesians 6:21

A little live coal (178, *174*)   Isaiah 6:5

Come and have breakfast (214, *208*)   John 21:12

The Silver Chair

I have swallowed up . . . (17, *27*)   Hebrews 1:8

There is no other stream (17, *27*)   John 4:14

Do so no more (18, *28*)   John 8:11

Remember the signs (21, *30*)   Deuteronomy 6:7

Aslan will be our good Lord (168, *164*)   Romans 14:8

I will not always be scolding (210, *201*)   Psalms 103:9

A great drop of blood (212, *202*)   Matthew 27:49

It turned into a fine new riding crop (214, *204*)   Exodus 4:4

His golden back (215, *204*)   Exodus 33:23

The Horse and His Boy

Not the breath of a ghost (157, *138*)   Luke 24:39

Tell me your sorrows (157, *138*)   Luke 24:38

Joy shall be yours (193, *169*)   Matthew 25:21

Happy the horse (193, *169*)   Psalms 1:1

Touch me (193, *169*)   John 21:27

Aslan was among them (208, *182*)   John 20:19

Not a Donkey! (210, *183*)   Daniel 4

The Magician's Nephew

Stars themselves . . . singing (99, *93*)   Job 38:7

It laughed for joy (101, *95*)   Psalms 19:5

Land bubbling like water (113, *105*)   Genesis 1:24

For out of them you were taken (118, *109*)   Genesis 3:19

Adam's race has done the harm (136, *126*)   I Corinthians 15:21

Name all these creatures (138, *128*)   Genesis 2:19

My son, my son (142, *131*)   II Samuel 18:33

Well done (166, *154*)   Matthew 25:21

Oh, Adam's sons . . . good (171, *158*)   Luke 19:42

It does not work happily (175, *162*)   Genesis 3:3

The Last Battle

There came a great thunderclap (10, *16*)   Mark 13:8

Worst thing in the world (20, *24*)   Psalms 77:10

Is not like the Aslan (25, *28–29*)   Psalms 77:10

They kill Men on his altar (31, *34*)   II Chronicles 33:3–6

By whose blood (33, *36*)   Ephesians 1:7

Send me helpers (41, *44*)   Hebrews 1:14

Seeing is believing (104, 97) John 20:25–29

Courage, child . . . (107, 99) John 14:27

Sup at his table (128, 118) Luke 13:29

Lovely fruit trees (135–137, 124–125) Revelation 22:2

A Stable once . . . inside (140–141, 128) Luke 2:7

Well done (146, 134) Matthew 25:21

Stars will fall from heaven (150–151, 136–137) Mark 13:25

Moon . . . looked red (156, 142) Joel 2:31

Though he should slay me (163, 148) Job 13:15

No one got hot or tired (171, 155) Isaiah 40:31

One can't feel afraid (173, 156) I John 4:18

[*Aslan.*]

BIRDS   The air of Narnia is alive with birds of all sorts. The first bird mentioned in the *Chronicles* (and the first encountered in Narnia by the Pevensie children*) is appropriately a red-breasted robin, the first bird of spring. It acts as their guide. The next bird is a messenger—one of the chief jobs of birds in Narnia—who tells Mr. Beaver* of Tumnus's* arrest. A pelican and an eagle are in Aslan's court; eagles are sent to rescue Edmund, and they also bear smaller creatures into battle with the White Witch. Vultures—carrion birds— are in the Witch's army. Perhaps the most thrilling birds in the *Chronicles* are the Birds of Morning* in VDT, which flock each day to Ramandu's Island* to eat their breakfast at Aslan's Table.* In HHB, Sallowpad* the Raven is quite informed about routes across the Great Desert*; and in PC, the Old Raven of Ravenscaur* is present at Caspian's council. Glimfeather* and the other owls* are prime movers in the eventual overthrow of Miraz.* Eagles appear once again in HHB, in a passing reference to the three eagles who survey the battle against Rabadash,* including the oldest of the eagles (an evocation of Tolkien's *Lord of the Rings*). The creation* of the birds is not described in detail, but they seem to come out of the trees, rather than the ground like the other animals.* The He-Owl and the Raven are summoned to Aslan's First Council* to discuss the evil* that has already entered into the newly created world.

(LWW 57–60, 58–61; 72, 73; 122, 115; 134, 125; 154, 143; 171, 158. HHB 180, 158. MN 114, 106; 119, 111.)

BIRDS OF MORNING   Large white birds* that come each morning by the thousands to Ramandu's Island.* Flying out of the sun,* they sing the same song voiced by the Old Man and his Daughter,* but it is wilder and in an unknown language. They bring a rejuvenating fire-berry* to Ramandu,* and pick clean the leavings from Aslan's Table* before they return to the realms of the sun.

(VDT 177–178, *174–175;* 188, *184;* 189, *185.*)

BISM   See *Underland.*

BLACK KNIGHT   See *Rilian.*

BLACK WOODS   The Telmarine* name for the Great Woods.* The Telmarines allow the wood to grow in order to cut their people off from the Narnian coast, gateway to the sea and the realm of Aslan, whom they fear and hate. However, the Telmarines quarrel with the trees,* and begin to fear the very woods they had intended to be their protection, calling them "black" and peopling them with imaginary ghosts.* Thus the Telmarines are caught in a circle of fear centered on Aslan and extending outward to his realm beyond the sea, to the coasts that border the sea, and to the woods that line the coast. In one sense, they resemble contemporary technocrats, attempting to exploit and control nature for their own ends.

(PC 50, *53;* 85, *81.*)
[*Ecology; Technology.*]

BOGGLES   Evil spirits summoned by the White Witch to the Stone Table* for the slaying of Aslan. *Boggles,* a dialectal variant of the word *bogles,* probably does not refer to specific entities, but can refer generically to phantoms causing fright, goblins, bogeys, specters of the night, or undefined creatures of superstitious dread. Lewis uses the north England spelling to evoke the Scottish origin of the term as well as the Scottish experience. Lewis's inclination to use Norse and Celtic images in his writing is well known.

(LWW 132, *123.*)

BOOKS   In the *Chronicles,* Lewis maintains that there are two types of books: the right books and the wrong books.[1] The right books teach children about adventure,* honor,* and the world of the imagination*; the wrong books have useless information about grain elevators and governments* and drains. These latter are the staple of "progressive" schools* like Experiment House,* and reading them has left Eustace completely unprepared for life in Narnia. Thus he has never read about dragons,* and doesn't recognize the dragon when he sees it. But Lucy, who has read *Androcles and the Lion,* knows to come to the aid of the dragonized Eustace. Edmund has read *Robinson Crusoe,* and when the children are "shipwrecked" in Narnia, he knows that they should look for a source of fresh water. He has also read detective stories, and on Deathwater Island* he is able to deduce that the dead Lord was not killed in a fight. Jill observes that books about hunting never mention how messy it is to clean the kill and prepare it for eating. She recognizes the various mythological creatures at Cair Paravel* because she has seen pictures of them. Shasta, who can't even read, doesn't know what lions* or jackals are, or how treacherous desert journeys can be.

Two libraries are mentioned in the *Chronicles*. Tumnus's shelf of books includes *The Life and Letters of Silenus,* * Nymphs* *and Their Ways, Men, Monks and Gamekeepers; a Study in Popular Legend,* and *Is Man a Myth?* Coriakin's* library has books of every shape and size from floor to ceiling, and Lewis's description of their wonderful smell (and that of the Magician's Book) makes it apparent that he is a true book lover. The Book itself is fastened by two leaden clasps, and the beautifully written manuscript is vividly illuminated. Prince Caspian learns grammar from the *Grammatical Garden or the Arbour of Accidence pleasantlie open'd to Tender Wits* by Pulverulentus Siccus.[2]

(LWW 12, *19*. PC 5, *14;* 9, *17;* 39, *43;* 43, 47. VDT 2, *10;* 61, 67; 69, 75; 71, *78;* 80, *86;* 82, *89;* 103, *108;* 127, *129;* 169, *167.* SC 29, *36;* 63, 69; 71–72, 76. HHB 89, *81.*)
[*Autobiographical allusions; Mythology; Imagination; Stories.*]

---

[1] Compare this with Lewis's *An Experiment in Criticism* (London: Cambridge University Press, 1961) pp 1–4, in which he says that it is readers rather than books who should be judged good or bad.

[2] Lewis's opinion of pedants can be deduced from his choice of name for this fictitious grammarian: the Latin *pulver* (dust), *lentus* (slow), and *siccus* (dry) paint a picture of a plodding pedant, dry as dust. Dr. Jonas Dryasdust is the fictitious dedicatee of Sir Walter Scott's novels *Ivanhoe* and *The Fortunes of Nigel.* See *Literary allusions.*

BRAMANDIN   See *Charn.*

BRAVERY   See *Courage.*

BREE   The strong, dappled stallion who carries Shasta to Archenland* in HHB, his full name is Breehy-hinny-brinny-hoohy-hah, which sounds like a horse's neigh. A talking Narnian horse,* he was (like Hwin) captured at an early age and taken to Calormen.* To survive, he has had to hide his true nature and be reckoned as a "dumb and witless" Calormen horse; this has chafed him, but he is not so foolish as to give himself away. He longs for "Narnia and the North," his standard cry on the journey, and he despises the Calormenes. He refuses to add the obligatory "may-he-live-forever" to the Tisroc's* title, and when he calls Aravis "Tarkheena" he cannot help putting his ears back in an instinctive horse's expression of anger. It is from Bree that we learn the most about Narnian Talking Beasts,* and he is an interesting combination of horsey attributes and human weaknesses.

He sees everything from the perspective of a horse: he remarks about the absurdity of human legs; he only begins to understand Shasta when he can perceive him as a human "foal" in need of riding lessons; and his sharp horse's hearing tells him immediately that the sound of hooves in the distance belongs to a thoroughbred mare being ridden by a competent rider. His greatest weaknesses, his pride and his vanity,* are human. He is continually plagued by the question of whether or not Narnian horses can, with dignity, roll in the grass. His horse-nature tells him to enjoy the roll, but his questioning nature wonders if this is too much like a Dumb Beast.* He has been away from his own kind for so long that he is riddled with doubt. He thinks a great deal of himself, and considers himself a great war-horse—which he is. When Hwin suggests timidly that they may be able to do what they feel they cannot do by thinking of what freedom from spurs and whips and their destination might mean, he lords it over the shy Hwin, claiming superior knowledge of the capabilities of horses. Ironically, it is Hwin who sets a faster pace and keeps the group going, although they are all exhausted. For all of his much-touted war experience, Bree identifies as a sandstorm what Hwin correctly identifies as soldiers; she takes off, leaving Bree to follow. He thinks he is galloping flat out, but discovers motivation to really move only at the sound of the Lion's roar. When Shasta orders Bree to stop, he doesn't, and later claims that he never heard or understood the order. Lewis comments that since Bree is "in general a very truthful horse we must accept his word."[1] Bree has his lowest moment at the Hermit's* enclosure; he feels remorseful for what he thinks is his disgraceful behavior of fleeing from the Lion and not returning to help Aravis and Hwin. He refuses to be consoled and says that all he's fit for is a life of Calormene slavery. Of course, this very humility is what saves him from that supposed fate. When he says in self-pity that he has "lost everything," the Hermit replies that he has "lost nothing but [his] self-conceit." Still completely demoralized, his shredded vanity is centered on his unkempt tail and he is reluctant to move on into Narnia. He is suspiciously over-enthusiastic about taking the time to apologize to Shasta, a plan Aravis suggests; and she asks him to explain his habit of swearing by the Lion. He replies that every Narnian does so, but that Aslan is not really a lion. With his old condescension, he patronizes Aravis's inability to understand this contradiction by calling her too young, although he does admit that, when he left Narnia, he, too, was too young to understand. As he begins to demythologize the lion-ness and beastli-ness of Aslan, the Lion touches his ear with a whisker and startles him thoroughly. He addresses Bree in a loud voice and calls him near to touch and smell* him.[2] Bree confesses that he has been a fool, an admission Aslan praises. The Lion calls him poor, proud, and frightened; and Bree meditates on this for two hours. On the final stretch into Anvard,* he is still gloomy and preoccupied with proper manners, and takes his last roll in the dust privately. But once in Anvard, he is addressed courteously by King Lune* and is present at the great feast that night, where he tells the story of the fight at Zalindreh.* Contrary to his fears, he marries and lives a long and happy life in Narnia, visiting his friends in Archenland often.

(HHB passim.)
[*Animals; Fledge.*]

---

[1] This is an indication of Bree's compunction, and is also true to his horse-nature—a horse galloping for its life from a pursuing lion* is not likely to hear, feel, or understand any order from its rider.

[2] This scene is modeled on Jesus and doubting Thomas, John 20:26 ff.

BRENN   The second of the Seven Isles.* Its main city is Redhaven.*

(VDT 18, *25*. HHB 180, *158*.)

BRICKLETHUMB   See *Duffle.*

BUFFIN   One of the most respected of the giant* clans of Narnia. An old family, it is not known for its cleverness but is rich in traditions.

(LWW 171, *158*.)
[*Rumblebuffin.*]

BULLYING   See *Gang, the; Schools.*

BULVERISM   To impune another person's reasoning by calling attention to that person's motivations (for example, "You say that because you're a woman"). Bulverism is Lewis's coined term to describe such a process.[1]

---

[1] For a further explanation see his very humorous essay, " 'Bulverism': or, The Foundation of 20th Century Thought" in *God in the Dock,* Walter Hooper, ed. (Grand Rapids: Wm. B. Eerdmans Publishing Co., 1970) pp. 271–277. See also *Reductionism.*

BURNT ISLAND[1]   This low green island, one day's sailing out of Dragon Island,* has only rabbits and a few goats as inhabitants. Ruins of stone huts, blackened fire pits, bones, and broken weapons give evidence that it was once inhabited by people. But the island has since been made desolate by pirates or dragons.* The small coracle[2] found there is given to Reepicheep because it is just his size.

(VDT 94, *100*.)
[*Geography, Narnian.*]

---

[1] Burntisland is an island off the Fife coast, south of the fishing village Pittenweem, the source of the name Pittencream.* (Professor Thomas W. Craik, letter to author July 31, 1979.)
[2] This is the British form of the Gaelic word *curach,* any wicker, skin-clad fishing boat.

CAIR PARAVEL   The castle of the Kings and Queens* in the Golden Age of Narnia,* and the city in which it is located.[1] The castle sits high on a hill, overlooking the Great River* valley, on a seacoast peninsula near the mouth of the river. The chief mole,* Lilygloves,* planted an apple* orchard for King Peter outside the north gate. In its prime, the Great Hall has an ivory roof, colored pavement floor, and tapestry-covered walls. The west door is hung with peacock feathers and the east door is open to the sea (and, symbolically, to Aslan who comes from over the sea). It is not clear who, if anyone, lived in the castle before the Pevensie children; Mr. Beaver* recites an old rhyme that predicts the evil time will end when Adam's flesh and blood sits on the throne at Cair Paravel. There are in fact four thrones already waiting at the castle, and it is there that the Kings and Queens are crowned by Aslan.

By the time of Prince Caspian, however, the castle and its surrounding city are greatly changed. Telmarines* are apparently responsible for having dug a channel across the penninsula; and the hill on which the castle sits is now a densely forested island. These are the Great Woods* (the Black Woods* to the Telmarines, who think the woods are haunted by ghosts*). The apple orchard has grown wild—right up to the north gate—but still bears delicious fruit. The castle itself is in ruins, and ivy has overgrown the door at one end of the dais that leads to the treasure chamber.

In SC, the castle and town are inhabited once again. Jill sees the river, a smooth green lawn, and towers and battlements with banners* flying. A crowd is gathered, people are dressed in bright clothes and shining armor. Music fills the air. An orchard—undoubtedly the apple orchard planted so long ago—is still outside the north gate, and the courtyard is covered with grass. Jill's homey room looks to the west, and the window has a glass pane.

In LB, twenty Calormene ships bring soldiers by night, who take over the city and kill all the citizens who don't escape in time. However, the real* Cair Paravel remains into the time of the new Narnia, and Lucy sees it from her place in the garden* above that world.

(LWW 10, *17;* 17, *24;* 32, *38;* 76, *76;* 78, *77;* 126, *119;* 178, *164.* PC 17 ff., *21 ff.;* 18, *24;* 172, *151.* SC 25, *34;* 36, *43.* LB 12, *17;* 91, *85;* 181, *163.* [*Aslan's country; Prophecies.*]

---

[1] The etymological derivation of Cair Paravel is probably from *kaer,* which according to Lewis is an old British word for "city" (see *They Stand Together,* Walter Hooper, ed. (New York: Macmillan Publishing Co., 1979; London: Collins, 1979) p. 263, *263;* and *paravail,* from the Old French *par aval,* meaning "down," and Latin *ad vallem,* "to the valley." Thus, Cair Paravel is a "city in the valley," and gives its name to its castle.

CALAVAR   The only province of Calormen* named in the *Chronicles.* It is ruled by Kidrash Tarkaan,* the father of Aravis.

(HHB 33, *37.*)

CALDRON POOL   The source of the Great River* in Western Narnia. It is created by the Great Waterfall,* which churns the waters like a boiling pot, hence its name.

(LB 2–3, *8;* 88, *82.*)
[*Geography, Narnian; Puzzle; Shift.*]

CALENDAR, NARNIAN   The Narnian calendar seems to parallel the earthly calendar, although Lewis does not seem to have thought this topic completely through. Thus he mentions summer, winter, January, February, March, and May, but also includes Greenroof,* a summer month known only in Narnia. New Year is mentioned twice in VDT, as is Christmas in LWW. The only interruption in the regular flow of seasons is the Hundred Years of Winter.*

(PC 173, *152*. VDT 109, *112;* 183, *179*. SC 49, *55*.)
[*Father Christmas.*]

CALORMEN   The empire to the south of Archenland* and Narnia, from which it is separated by the Great Desert.* Tashbaan* is the capital city and the seat of power of the Tisroc* and his prime minister, the Grand Vizier. The lords and ladies of the realm are called Tarkaans* and Tarkheenas, and live in perfumed splendor. Lewis probably fashioned the name "Calormen" from the Latin *calor,* meaning "heat, warmth," and the English *men;* thus Calormenes are "men from a warm land." Indeed, the culture is modeled on the desert cultures of the Near and Middle East.[1] Lewis describes the Calormenes as a "wise, wealthy, courteous, cruel, and ancient" people. They worship the bloodthirsty god* Tash,* and hold life to be cheap: slavery is common, war is a way of life, and citizens as well as slaves may be put to death* for minor offenses. Truly imperial, the Calormenes are determined that the free Narnians and Archenlanders shall someday submit to their rule, and from the Golden Age* to the Last Battle* they do not give up their fanatical obsession with tyranny. The only named Calormenes to enter Aslan's country* are Emeth* (who loved Tash with the love that was really Aslan's) and Aravis (who sought freedom* in the North). From Aslan's country Lucy can see the real Tashbaan, which suggests that something in Calormen culture is good enough to allow it to survive into eternity. Most Calormenes, however, are the archenemies of the free Narnians, and Lewis has given them qualities diametrically opposed to those of the Narnians.

Animals   There are no native Talking Beasts* in Calormen. When such animals are kidnapped (notably the talking horses* Bree and Hwin) they are treated badly. Ownership of animals is common practice in Calormen, and the Calormenes think nothing of over-riding their mounts, whipping and harnessing horses for hard work, and selling worn-out horses to be rendered into dog-meat. In Narnia, respect for life extends even to dumb animals. Talking horses are never mounted, except in battle, and are certainly not used as slaves.

Art and poetry   The statues of gods and heroes that line the finer streets of Tashbaan are "impressive rather than agreeable to look at." In Narnia, craftsmanship is valued; and although its art is not specifically described, carved woodwork and medieval-style tapestries are mentioned. Calormene poetry is aphoristic in nature and extravagant in expression. Northern poetry is, by contrast, enchanting. When Aravis and Shasta hear that poetry will be sung at the Archenland feast, they prepare themselves to be bored, thinking northern verse consists of dull maxim after dull maxim. But when they hear the first bit of music, "a rocket seemed to go up inside their heads." When the song is over, they want to have this fireworks experience again.

Cities   Tashbaan is crowded with slaves, disorder, and filth. By comparison, the streets of Cair Paravel are clean, bright, and full of happy people. Green lawns gleam in the sunlight.

Class system   The line between the classes in Calormen is clear and abrupt, and the authority structure is rigid. The Tarkaans and Tarkheenas live in extreme comfort, take perfumed baths, and vacation at seaside resorts. They dress fabulously and lord it over the peasants who live in filthy cities, dress poorly, and are generally dull and practical. They are impersonal and even cruel to their servants, to whose fates they are indifferent. That there are classes in Narnian society is indisputable (given the monarchy and the existence of lords and ladies), but the differences are not highlighted. The peasant class of Narnia is made up of simple, hard-working folk—animals, dwarfs,* and human beings alike. The assumed dignity of all Narnians eliminates the possibility of the condescending behavior toward assumed inferiors that permeates Calormene society. The class system can also be seen in formalized words of address: Calormene soldiers call their officers "My Master," and junior officers call senior officers "My Father." The Calormene tendency toward superlatives ("Tash the inexorable, the irresistible," "The Tisroc, may-he-live-for-ever") also indicates the clearly drawn line between classes. There are no such Narnian forms of address except the polite "sir," which is part of Narnian courtesy.*

Clothing   Calormene clothing is based on Middle Eastern–style dress. The wealthy Tarkaans and Tarkheenas wear turbans and robes* that are embroidered, bejewelled, and dripping with tassels and ornaments. Calormene peasants wear dirty clothes, turbans, and shoes that curl up at the toe. Narnian clothing is simple; it not only looks good, but it also feels good and smells* good. It is designed for freedom of movement and colored in earth tones.[2] Calormene battle-dress is also more opulent: Tarkaans wear chain-mail shirts (which Tirian calls "outlandish gear"), spiked helmets that poke through their turbans, and carry curving scimitars, embossed shields, and lances. The Narnian chain-mail is apparently lighter weight, and Narnian soldiers carry straight swords.

Food   The food of Calormen is the food of desert feasts, and the Calormenes eat well and heartily to the point of overeating. They cook with oil, onions, and garlic, while the Narnians use butter. Shasta's two meals in HHB succinctly point out the differences between Calormene and Narnian meals. His Calormen-style meal consists of lobsters, salad, snipe stuffed with almonds and truffles, rice with nuts and raisins, melons, desserts, and ices, all washed down with wine.* His Narnian meal in the dwarfs' house is typical English fare: eggs, bacon, toast, milk, and coffee. Although Lewis is clearly partial to the Narnian food, the hungry Shasta enjoys both meals.

Hospitality   In Calormen hospitality* is demanded; in Narnia it is willingly extended.

Physical appearance   The Calormenes are a southern, desert race, dark and swarthy; they wear long beards, which may be perfumed, oiled, and dyed. The Narnians are very definitely northerners. They are mostly fair, pale-skinned people, and beards are mostly worn by older men and dwarfs.

Religion   The Calormene religion is pantheistic. Three gods* are mentioned (although more can be assumed): Tash,* Azaroth,* and Zardeenah.* The Narnians are monotheistic and follow Aslan. Although nature gods abound in Narnia, they are alive, equal to the other Narnians, and are not worshipped.

Slavery   The slave trade* is common in Calormen, and is probably one reason for the wealth of the Tarkaans. Slaves are treated as badly as the animals, and may be put to death for any assumed offense. In LB, the treachery of Calormene slavery is in full force, and even dwarfs and Talking Beasts are intended for labor in the Tisroc's mines. Slavery is abhorrent to the Narnians. When Caspian encounters the Lone Islands'* thriving slave trade (which was allowed to flourish only because the islands were isolated from Narnian influence for so many years), he abolishes it immediately.

Storytelling   The Calormenes are consummate storytellers. Young Calormene school children learn storytelling as we learn essay-writing, and their stories are much more interesting than our essays. Both Aravis and Emeth tell their stories in the grand Calormene fashion. Narnians also love stories, but apparently—like the Narnians themselves—these stories tend to be more truthful and less filled with embellishment.

Women   Calormene women are chattels of their husbands and parents. Their marriages are arranged and their own feelings* are immaterial. They do not know how to write. Narnian women seem to be equal to men, and to enjoy the same rights and privileges.[3]

(HHB passim. VDT 50, 58. LB passim.)

---

[1]Like many Englishmen of his era (sadly, even G. K. Chesterton), Lewis was unconsciously unsympathetic to things and people Middle-Eastern. That Lewis opts into this cultural blindness is regrettable.

[2] See *Robes, royal.*

[3] See *Sexism.*

CAMILLO   A talking hare who leads a contingent to the Great Council.* Just before the council begins, he warns of a man nearby, who turns out to be Doctor Cornelius.*

(PC 76, 73; 81, 77.)
[*Talking Beasts.*]

While Nikabrik and Trumpkin argue about his fate, Caspian awakes to the smell of a sweet, hot drink being offered him by Trufflehunter, the Talking Badger. (PC 62, 62.)

CARTER   One of the students in power (likely a member of the Gang*) at Experiment House,* he seems to have delighted in torturing animals.* Eustace confronts him in a matter concerning a rabbit.

(SC 3, *12.*)
[*Vivisection.*]

CASPIAN I   The first Telmarine* King of Narnia, also known as the Conqueror. He brings the Telmarine nation into Narnia, and fights against the Nine Classes of Narnian Creatures.* His armies silence them, kill them, drive them away, and try to erase their memory from the land because they are the subjects of Aslan, whom the Telmarines fear.

(PC 41–42, *45; 47,* 50.)

CASPIAN VIII   A Telmarine King of Narnia, father of Caspian IX* and Miraz.*

(PC 172, *151.*)

CASPIAN IX   A Telmarine* King* of Narnia, son of Caspian VIII,* brother of Miraz,* and father of Caspian X. He is murdered by Miraz in 2290 N.Y.[1]

---

[1]PWD, p. 43.

CASPIAN X   Telmarine* King of Narnia (born 2290 N.Y., reigned 2303–2356 N.Y., died 2356 N.Y.) called "The Seafarer." He is the orphaned son of Caspian IX,* raised by the usurper Miraz* and his wife Prunaprismia,* husband of the Daughter of Ramandu,* father of Rilian* the Disenchanted. Caspian is the hero of the great War of Deliverance* in which Old Narnia is freed from the tyranny of its Telmarine conquerors, who style themselves New Narnians. Caspian is also leader of the voyage of the *Dawn Treader,* * a quest* which he undertakes with Aslan's permission in order to discover the fates of the Seven Noble Lords* who stood faithfully by his assassinated father, as well as to explore the islands of the Eastern Sea.* Caspian's years as king are marred by the horrible death of his beloved wife and the disappearance of his only son and heir. But these hurts are mended by the mercy of Aslan. His story is one of the most complete that Lewis tells in the *Chronicles;* and his is the best developed character of all the Narnians.

From the first pages of his story the seeds of his potential greatness and his possible downfall are apparent. On the one hand, he would rather live in the old days when the stories* (especially about Aslan) told him by his nurse* were true. On the other hand, he does not want to be king,* a fact of ambiguous significance in view of the model of kingship presented by his Uncle Miraz. But the intensity of his desire to live in his imagination* predisposes him to the temptation to power at Deathwater Island* and to his attempted abdication of his throne on the Last Sea.* His desire to go to Aslan's country* cannot be allowed to overrule his vocation to be king. Caspian learns that there is no magical recovery of the old days, and there are no short cuts to happiness. Aslan's restoration of freedom in PC ends in the installation of Caspian as a king who must serve his people; and Caspian's road to the ecstatic reunion with Aslan at the end of SC runs by the tragedies mentioned at the beginning of the same book.

When his insensitive uncle sends Caspian's nurse away at the discovery that she has passed on the heritage of a Narnia Miraz has been striving to erase from the minds of the people, Caspian consoles himself by thinking even more about the old stories of Narnia. His tutor, Doctor Cornelius,* educates the boy in all the subjects Miraz thinks the boy should know as well as in the true history* of Narnia, including the uncomfortable knowledge that Caspian's ancestors enslaved the country. His desire to live in Old Narnia is put to the test by the events that propel him out of his life at Miraz's castle and into the world, at once hostile and hospitable, of the "people that lived in hiding." As he flees from his known world into his believed-in world he experiences the gamut of feelings* from elation to terror.

Caspian is an "it" to the dwarfs* and badger who discover him unconscious. When he comes to, he suffers a shock as he realizes that he is being nursed and spoken to by Trufflehunter.* He suffers a second shock at the realization that his profession of faith in the Old Narnia doesn't mean much to the likes of Nikabrik.* Lewis comments that Caspian matures a little with the knowledge that the horrible people of the old stories are as real as the good people. Caspian is impressed by his first sight of the magnificent Centaur* Glenstorm,* but he is sobered by the Centaur's talk of unavoidable, full-scale war. He has both delightful and thought-provoking experiences as he meets more Old Narnians and as he first faces the prospect and then the actualities and disappointments of war. A test of wills about and visions for how the war should be fought (by foul means or fair) ends in the deaths of Caspian's opponents, and he himself is wounded. Caspian is quite tongue-tied at conversing with Peter, a great personage from out of the past. His sense of nobility moves him to desire to engage in a monomachy* with Miraz to avenge his father, but his wound will not permit such a plan.

After the final victory in the War of Deliverance, Aslan asks Caspian if he feels adequate to the task of ruling Narnia. Knowing what he now knows about the cost of making good dreams a reality, Caspian replies with a humility that Aslan praises. It is the Lion who informs the king about the most important part of the story of his lineage: that he is the offspring of human pirates. This knowledge depresses Caspian, a response that Aslan does not allow to continue, for he reassures him that being a Son of Adam* and Eve is both the most ennobling and the most humbling of heritages. Caspian bows in thoughtful silence* at this lesson.

After three years of setting Narnia in order and learning all he can about navigation, Caspian embarks on a voyage to fulfill the vow he made on his coronation day to find the Seven Noble Lords.* By this time he is a golden-haired sixteen year old, with the eagerness for adventure* and the need for experience that are characteristic of this age. He begins the process of whipping Eustace into shape, a relationship that will culminate in a deep friendship. He frees the Lone Islands* from the tyrannous government* of Gumpas* and would stay to visit with Lord Bern* but for his promise to Reepicheep to journey as far east as they are able. It is one of the tests of his wisdom to balance the weakness of Eustace with the rashness of Reepicheep. Greed* and the lust for power overcome him at Deathwater Island,* until Aslan intervenes to erase even the memory* of the place from his mind. In the Land of the Duffers,* Caspian strategizes and tries to circumvent any confrontation with the invisible beings, but Reepicheep shames him into meeting the challenge head-on. The cowardice* of this people offends him, but their talk of a magician* alarms him. He is anxious for Lucy the whole day she is upstairs with Coriakin.*

At the Dark Island* Caspian halts the advance of the *Dawn Treader* into the darkness, hesitating to make the decision to proceed further. He is impatient with what he considers the mouse's exaggerated sense of honor. In order to avoid making the dishonorable decision by himself, he defers to Lucy, hoping to transfer some of his responsibility. When she indicates that they should continue, he orders all preparations to be made for battle and invokes the name of Aslan.* When they rescue Lord Rhoop,* Caspian's experience of fear makes him very willing to stifle any curiosity* he might have to know what happened to the nobleman on this terrifying island.

He is very cautious as he and his friends explore Ramandu's Island.* And though Reepicheep is the first to rise at the approach of the star's* Daughter,* Caspian is the first to speak: he tells her they have not eaten of the food of Aslan's Table* because they suspect that it might have enchanted the Three Sleepers.* Her beauty moves him to suggest the possibility of kissing her in order to remove the spell over the sleepers (he knows the story of Sleeping Beauty because his friends from earth have told it to him); but she says that he must break the spell before he may kiss her. Ramandu* tells him that only if someone is left at the World's End* will the sleepers' enchantment end. It is at this point that the suggestion that he might be the one to accomplish this enters Caspian's mind, even though he knows that this is also Reepicheep's heart's desire. Caspian sees that his immediate problems are the weariness of his crew and Lord Rhoop's need for healing. Caspian wisely turns the question of who in the crew would want to continue into the question of who would want to remain and thus lose out on the honor* of having partaken in the greatest Narnian adventure.* Before they set sail in the morning (with all the crew save Pittencream*), Caspian tells the star's Daughter of his hope to see her upon his return.

Caspian is the first to taste of the sweet waters of the Last Sea,* and he is the first to attempt to describe this experience of glory. Caspian becomes excited during the discussion of round and flat worlds because he has grown up on the Narnian fairy tales about round worlds.[1] It is one of his great desires to visit a round world. Only after Caspian smells* the fragrance coming from

Aslan's country* does Eustace notice the strange look that comes into his eyes. He addresses the ship's company and gives everyone instructions as though he intends to abdicate his throne.[2] What Drinian and everyone else call abdication and desertion, Caspian calls "going with Reepicheep to see the World's End.*" As Caspian speaks, the look of his uncle Miraz is in his eye; and he will not be told he can't do something he wants to do. Reepicheep, Edmund, and Lucy try to make him see his error. Reepicheep finally provokes a blast from Caspian reminiscent of Henry II's frustration over Thomas à Becket: "Will no one silence that Mouse?" Reepicheep is not daunted, and reminds him of his oath* to be "the good Lord to the Talking Beasts of Narnia." It takes another vision of a stern Aslan to change the king's mind. Caspian has a very deflated feeling, but his hopelessness is ameliorated by Lucy's mention that he should be mindful of the one who is waiting for him back on Ramandu's Island.

A very different Caspian is seen by the reader in the third chapter of SC: a frail old man in his mid-sixties setting sail on a sad journey to try to meet Aslan (rumored to be on Terebinthia*) in the Eastern Islands and to ask him what he should do about his lost son, Rilian.* The Narnians are afraid that the king might pursue his lifelong desire to visit Aslan's country* beyond the World's End. Eustace and Jill hear from Glimfeather* the story of Caspian's grievous loss of his wife and of his son, of how he was so distressed that he almost killed his friend Drinian in a fit of despair. In Chapter 16, the reader learns through the faun* Orruns* that the king had an experience of Aslan (whether a vision or an actual meeting is not known) in which the Lion instructed the king to return to Cair Paravel to meet his son. Caspian arrives back at his capitol long enough to receive his son's embrace and to say a final word to him. The reader next sees the dead king lying on the golden gravel of the stream bed in Aslan's country, the water flowing over him. When a drop of Aslan's blood washes over him, Caspian is transformed into a happy and radiantly youthful man again. He and the Lion embrace and both turn to explain to Eustace and Jill the meaning of what they have just witnessed. Caspian then asks if his desire to visit England* is a wrong and impossible desire. Aslan tells him that he is now incapable of desiring anything wrong, and accompanies him and the two children to visit retribution on the Gang* at Experiment House.* Then Caspian goes back with Aslan to the Lion's country, to be seen for the last time at the Great Reunion* in LB.

---

[1] Lewis means to stretch the imaginations* of his readers to consider that if other worlds exist, there must be other ways of experiencing reality.

[2] Lewis may be giving vent to his frustration over the abdication of Edward VIII in 1939 so that he could marry Wallis Simpson.

CASTLE OF THE WHITE WITCH   Located on the unnamed north-to-south-flowing tributary of the Great River.* The house of the White Witch is a high-walled stone castle with one arched entrance through a pair of huge iron gates and a pincushion of needle-pointed round towers. Complete with courtyard, keep, trapdoors, and dungeons, it is a terrifying, lifeless prison for

all the Narnians whom the Witch has turned to stone. In a scene suggestive of the harrowing of hell,[1] Aslan leaps over the castle wall with Susan and Lucy on his back and proceeds to revive every stone creature with his breath. The girls and the freed Narnians race throughout the castle to discover the other petrified beings and to open every door and window to admit the light and the fresh spring air. At Aslan's request the giant Rumblebuffin* breaks down the gates along with their towers, and all march through the breach to what later is known as the First Battle of Beruna.*

(LWW 88–89, *85–86;* 163, *150;* 167–169, *155–157.*)
[*Credal elements; Holy Spirit.*]

---

[1] The harrowing of hell is a medieval tradition of Christ's descent to the borders of the underworld to free the souls of the Old Testament saints. It is based on the apocryphal Gospel of Nicodemus.

CENTAUR   In Greek and Roman mythology,* a semi-divine being with the head and chest of a man and the body of a horse.* For Lewis the Centaur represents the harmony of nature and spirit.[1] In the *Chronicles,* the Centaur is one of the Nine Classes of Narnian Creatures.* Four great Centaurs are described in LWW: their horse parts are "like huge English farm horses," the human parts are "like stern but beautiful giants.*" In PC we are told that a Centaur's diet consists of oaten cakes, apples,* herbs, wine,* and cheese. They use both swords and hooves in battle, and are good strategists in warfare. They are to be respected: according to Trufflehunter,* no one ever laughs at a Centaur; and in PC the children* ride Centaurs bareback, because "no one who valued his life would suggest putting a saddle" on one. They are informed about the properties of herbs and roots and astrology. In HHB, a Centaur has predicted that Cor will save Archenland* from its greatest danger. The three named Centaurs in the *Chronicles* are Glenstorm,* Cloudbirth,* and Roonwit* —names that have to do with weather, wildness, and wisdom. Other Centaurs in the *Chronicles* include two stone Centaurs in the courtyard of the Castle of the White Witch.* Centaurs are in the war party that marches against Rabadash* in HHB and in the crowd at Cair Paravel in SC.

(LWW 92, *89;* 122, *115;* 134, *125;* 140, *130;* 143, *132;* 165, *152;* 171, *158;* 174, *161;* 179, *165.* PC 47, *50;* 75, *72;* 174, *152.* SC 29, *36;* 204–207, *196–198.* HHB 170, *149;* 198, *173.*

---

[1] C. S. Lewis, *Miracles* (New York: Macmillan Publishing Co., 1978; London: Collins Fontana, 1960) pp. 126 and 161, *130 and 164.*

CHANCE   See *Providence.*

CHARN   The dead city (and likely the country[1]) of which Jadis is empress. Even its sun is dying, and a dull reddish light hangs over the blackish blue sky. It is a cold, silent world where nothing lives. The very name of the city has a sinister sound, and suggests burning. Lewis may have appropriated the name

Charn from *charnel,* meaning "a burial place."[2] Jadis destroyed all living things in Charn with the Deplorable Word* in an attempt to usurp her sister's power. The frozen figures of Charn's royalty (said to have "giantish blood"[3]) that Digory and Polly encounter in the great hall show the degeneration of the kings* and queens from dynasty to dynasty, culminating in Jadis herself. This is almost a tableau of both the history* of Charn and Lewis's own sense of history, based on Chesterton's *Everlasting Man.*[4] The last years of Charn were ones of great cruelty—slavery, human sacrifice, and endless warfare. The pool of Charn in the Wood between the Worlds* has dried up; according to Aslan, "That world is ended, as if it had never begun." He adds that Sons of Adam* and Daughters of Eve should take that as a warning, and it is clearly intended as a warning to the reader that our world, too, may be destroyed through unchecked despotism and the use of ultimate weapons.

(MN 41 ff., *41 ff.;* 177–178, *164.*)
[*Golden bell and hammer; Robes, royal.*]

[1] Jadis refers to Charn as a city in the list she gives, mentioning three other cities of which we are told nothing further: Felinda, Sorlois, and Bramandin. Charn is also called a "world" by Aslan.
[2] Professor T. W. Craik, letter to the author, July 31, 1979.
[3] See *White Witch* for discussion of inconsistencies between Jadis and her alter ego.
[4] G. K. Chesterton, *The Everlasting Man* (New York: Doubleday Image, 1955) pp. 59–60:

> ... the despotism in certain dingy and decayed tribes in the twentieth century does not prove that the first men were ruled despotically. It does not even suggest it; it does not even begin to hint at it. If there is one fact we really can prove, from the history that we really do know, it is that despotism can be a development and very often indeed the end of societies that have been highly democratic."

This devolution is what Digory sees. Two essays that give Lewis's response to evolutionism as one theory of history and to any attempt to understand history are "The Funeral of a Great Myth" and "Historicism," both in *Christian Reflections,* Walter Hooper, ed. (Grand Rapids: Wm. B. Eerdmans Publishing Co., 1967) and the latter in *Fern-seed and Elephants,* Walter Hooper, ed. (London: Collins Fontana, 1975).

CHERVY THE STAG   Chervy is a beautiful animal,* regal and delicate in appearance. Unlike the smaller animals, he is not indecisive when he hears from Shasta of the approach of Rabadash* and his cohort to Archenland* and Narnia. He bounds away and meets Edmund, Susan, and Corin,* newly arrived from their embassy to Tashbaan.* *Chervus* is the Latin word for "deer."

(HHB 165, *145–146;* 170, *149–150.*)
[*Talking Beasts.*]

CHIEF VOICE   Also known as the Chief Duffer and the Chief Monopod, he is the leader of the Duffers,* their spokesman, and, indeed, does all their thinking—such as it is. He leads the Duffers in capturing the exploration party in order to have Lucy's services in breaking the spell of invisibility* that besets him and his followers. A caricature of the pompous leader, he reveals just how dull he is in his first extended speech by referring to Coriakin* over-frequently as though his human listeners are as incapable of sustained attention as his own kind are. His speech is clumsy and filled with hackneyed phrases, such as "to make a long story short," "least said soonest mended," and the like. His lack of any practical sense is evident in the way he expects Lucy to find the proper enchantment in the magician's very large Book.

His master, the magician Coriakin,* tells Lucy that the Chief Duffer is filled with vanity,* as are his companions who believe every word he says. However, Coriakin suggests that though he and they might be better off without the Chief, it is better for the Duffers to admire him than to admire nobody. When the Chief becomes visible, he is wearing a tasseled red cap; and he apologizes to Lucy for his ugly appearance and that of his people. When she contradicts him and praises the Duffers' appearance, his followers typically agree with both of them. And he, incapable of any viewpoint but his own, insists that Lucy must mean that they once looked nice but are ugly now. Finally, when Reepicheep suggests that the Duffers, being monopods, can float upright on the water, the Chief (perhaps feeling his leadership threatened) refuses to try it and warns the others that the water is "powerful wet."

(VDT 112 passim, *115 passim.*)

CHILDREN   Children are the heroes and heroines of the *Chronicles* who are brought to Narnia time and again to clean up the messes made by adults.* Lewis takes them very seriously—more seriously, in fact, than he takes the grown-ups. Upon entering Narnia, children become subtly older and more mature, but they retain their childlike innocence, candor, and innate knowledge* of right and wrong.* As characters, they are far more realistically drawn than any grown-up in or out of Narnia. Lewis has not forgotten what it is like to be a child, and the stories* are told from a child's point of view. Children are often much more intelligent than grown-ups think they are, and can use this to their advantage. Although it is hateful to her, Jill puts on her "most attractively childish smile" and obsequiously addresses the giant* queen at Harfang.* She giggles her way among the giants and giantesses, tricking them into thinking she is harmless while she is actually exploring possible exits. The Gang* at Experiment House* is able to put things over on the Head* because she thinks they are interesting "psychological cases." Lewis takes children's night fears* very seriously, and involves himself and his readers in Shasta's experience of the howling jackals at the tombs. The first chapter of MN is full of things that children like to do: build forts, look for treasure, explore hidden places—especially haunted ones.

Many of the children are left to their own devices at an early age. Shasta is motherless and lives with Arsheesh,* who is not his real father; Prince Corin* has a father, King Lune,* but he has been motherless from an early age; Aravis has a mean stepmother and no affection for her father, who wants to marry her off to the tiresome Ahoshta*; Caspian lives with his Uncle Miraz,* who intends to kill the prince after his own son is born; Digory's father is in India leaving him with his seriously ill mother and his insane Uncle Andrew*; Rilian's mother is the idealized Daughter of Ramandu,* dead from the bite of a serpent; Eustace's parents Alberta* and Harold* are totally lacking in imagination; and the Pevensie children love their parents, but they are left on their own a lot of the time.

Lewis tries to communicate through the *Chronicles* the importance of remaining child*like*—as opposed to child*ish*—in outlook. In Aslan's country,* people are always and forever in the prime of life. Susan, the only "failed child" (she might almost be called a "lapsed child" in the way the Lapsed Bear of Stormness* is a lapsed bear) has fulfilled Lewis's dictum that *in our world, too,* "... it is the stupidest children who are the most childish and the stupidest grownups who are the most grown-up." Hers is a false maturity: "She wasted all her school time wanting to be the age she is now, and she'll waste all the rest of her life trying to stay that age."

CHIPPINGFORD   A small town down-river from Caldron Pool,* where Puzzle* goes to buy food for Shift.* The ape's comment that it's "market day" at Chippingford is a play on words: *chipping* is a common variant of *cheaping,* which means "market" or "market place."

(LB 7, *12.*)
[*Geography, Narnian.*]

CHIVALRY   See *Orders, chivalric.*

CHLAMASH   See *Rabadash.*

CHOLMONDELEY MAJOR   See *Gang, the.*

CHORIAMBUSES   See *Coriakin.*

CHRISTMAS   See *Father Christmas.*

CHRISTOLOGY   See *Credal elements.*

CHRONOSCOPES   See *Coriakin.*

CITY RUINOUS   See *Ruined City of the Ancient Giants.*

CIVILIZATION   See *Technology.*

CIVIL SERVICE, CIVIL SERVANTS   See *Government.*

CLIPSIE   Daughter of the Chief Voice,* she recites the spell of invisibility* in the magician's Book,* which makes the Duffers* disappear. Her father estimates that she is the same age as Lucy.

(VDT 119, *121.*)
[*Magic.*]

CLODSLEY SHOVEL　A mole* to whom Lewis humorously assigns the name of British naval hero Admiral Sir Clodsley Shovel, who died in 1707. He leads a troop of moles to the Great Council*, where he proposes throwing up entrenchments around Dancing Lawn* as the first step in defence. After the War of Deliverance,* he directs his moles to prepare the various earths for the feast of the trees.*

(PC 56, 73; 206, 180.)
[Talking Beasts.]

CLOTHING　See Robes, royal.

CLOUDBIRTH　A Centaur* and famous healer[1] among the Narnians in the later reign of Caspian X. As a Centaur he has knowledge of the healing properties of herbs and plants, and is sent to minister to Puddleglum's burnt foot.

(SC 204, 196.)

---

[1] Orruns* calls him a "leach" in the British edition; "leech" in the American edition.

COL　According to Lewis MS 51,[1] in 180 N.Y. Prince Col leads a group of Narnians to settle the uninhabited country of Archenland.* He is the younger son of King Frank V of Narnia, and becomes the first King of Archenland. In MN, however, Lewis says that the first King of Archenland is the second son of King Frank* and Queen Helen.*

(MN 184, 170.)

---

[1] PWD, p. 41.

COLE　See Darrin.

COLIN　See Darrin.

COLNEY 'ATCH　A voice in the crowd at the lamp-post* calls Jadis* the "Hempress of Colney 'Atch." Colney Hatch was a London insane asylum at the turn of the century. Thus in 1900, "Colney 'Atch for you!" was Cockney slang for "You're crazy!"

(MN 92, 88.)

COMFORT　Comfort and its resulting false sense of security, Lewis seems to say, are the greatest dangers in life.[1] In SC, it is comfort at Harfang* and irritation with lack of comfort on Ettinsmoor* that cause Jill to forget the signs.* It is in HHB, set in the Golden Age, that questions of comfort arise. The smaller woodland animals* are so secure during the Golden Age of Narnia* that "they are getting a little careless." Lasaraleen

Tarkheena* is a slave to creature comforts; and although Aravis is somewhat tempted by luxury, she is glad to escape to the more austere North. Shasta is so comfortable in the Narnian embassy that "none of [his] worries seem so pressing." This gives him a good feeling but a false sense of security. His dinner and conversation with Tumnus* are so enjoyable that they cause him to squelch his worries about Aravis and Bree, and hope that he can stay long enough to be taken to Narnia by ship instead of having to brave the terrors of the Great Desert.*

(SC 36–37, *43–44*; 76–79, *81–83*; 89, *92*; 98, *101–102*; 197, *189–190*; 200, *193.* HHB 60, *58*; 72–73, *69*; 164–165, *145.*)

---

[1] Lewis often reflected on the meaning of comfort and security. One of the most noteworthy instances is found in *The Problem of Pain* (New York: Macmillan Publishing Co., 1962; London: Collins Fountain, 1977) p. 115, *103:*

> The settled happiness and security which we all desire, God withholds from us by the very nature of the world: but joy, pleasure, and merriment He has scattered broadcast. We are never safe, but we have plenty of fun, and some ecstasy. It is not hard to see why. The security we crave would teach us to rest our hearts in this world and oppose an obstacle to our return to God . . . Our Father refreshes us on the journey with some pleasant inns, but will not encourage us to mistake them for home.

CONSCIENCE   See *Right and wrong.*

COR   See *Shasta.*

CORDIAL   Father Christmas's* gift to Lucy in LWW. It is made from the juice of the fire-flowers* that grow in the valleys of the sun,* is kept in a diamond bottle, and is to be used for healing. It is left behind, along with Susan's horn,* when the Kings and Queens* "blunder out" of Narnia. In PC, over half of the cordial is left, and it is said to be able to heal almost every wound and every illness; indeed, it does cure an infected cut in Trumpkin's* shoulder, and it heals Reepicheep's wounds (but it cannot make his tail grow again). Caspian brings the cordial on the voyage of the *Dawn Treader,* and it is now considered one of the royal treasures. One drop cures Eustace's seasickness, and its delicious smell* fills the cabin. Later it helps the dragonized Eusatce reduce the swelling of his arm, and it reduces the pain a little; but it cannot dissolve the gold. In HHB, Lucy does not bring her cordial to the war against Rabadash,* because Peter has "strictly charged [her] to keep it only for great extremities."

(LWW 105, *100*; 176–177, *163.* PC 23–24, *29*; 103, *96*; 201, *176.* VDT 19, *26*; 80, *87.* HHB 172, *151.*)
[*Wine.*]

CORIAKIN[1]   [1]A magician* and master of the Land of the Duffers,* he is an old man with a waist-length beard, barefoot, dressed in a red robe and crowned with a chaplet of oak leaves.[2] His staff is strangely carved. According to Ramandu,* Coriakin was once a star,* and his governing of the Duffers is a kind of punishment for having failed in some way. When he allowed the Duffers* to become invisible, he too became invisible, knowing that Lucy would come along to remove the spell. His invisibility* makes him sleepy, however, and so he misses her arrival. Not surprisingly, the Duffers' leader, the Chief Voice,* describes Coriakin as arbitrary, wrathful, and very direct. He is, however, kind and courteous, and he longs for the day when he can rule the Duffers by wisdom rather than by rough ways. When Aslan presents Lucy to him, the magician shows his courtesy* toward his lord by bowing low and calling his house the least of Aslan's houses. Like Lucy, he is disappointed at Aslan's brief appearance, but he remarks that this is always the way with Aslan: one can't hold on to him as if he were tame.*

Coriakin's magic is evident in many ways. After introducing himself to Lucy, he leads her into a room bright with sunshine and flowers; and aware of the kind of food she would enjoy in England,* he conjures up a proper English tea. Besides Aslan, he is the only one in Narnia who knows of the existence of earth. Later he hosts all the Narnians to a dinner upstairs at which each one eats his or her favorite food, though he himself eats only bread and drinks only wine.* Also indicative of his scientific interests is a room full of polished instruments: astrolabes (instruments to determine altitudes and for solving other problems of practical astronomy); orreries (mechanisms devised to represent the motions of the planets about the sun* by means of clockwork); chronoscopes (instruments for observing and measuring time); poesimeters (imaginary instruments for measuring the meter of poems); choriambuses (imaginary devices for measuring choriambs—a metrical foot consisting of four syllables: long, short, short, long); and theodolinds (portable surveying instruments used in measuring horizontal angles—theodolites). Coriakin's magic is able to create two maps based on Drinian's* observations of the *Dawn Treader's* progress so far. The magician keeps one and gives the other to Caspian. Though his magic does not enable him to tell the adventurers what lies to the East, he does tell them of four Narnian Lords who visited the island: Revilian,* Argoz,* Mavramorn,* and Rhoop.* Finally, he magically repairs the *Dawn Treader's* stern and loads her with useful gifts.

(VDT 117–119, *120–121;* 134, *135;* 137 ff., *138 ff.;* 180, *177.*)
[*Books; House of the Magician; Privacy.*]

---

[1] Spelled Koriakin only in Ramandu's conversation and only in British editions.

[2] Roger Lancelyn Green thinks that crown of oak leaves may be related to those worn by the priests of Zeus at the Oracle of Dodona, but it might also be associated with the Druids (letter to author, May 7, 1979). The image, then, is of some sort of pagan priest to which Lewis adds the Judaeo-Christian association of Melchizedek, the priest-king of Salem, who offered the Most High a sacrifice of bread and wine (Genesis 14:17–20 and Hebrews 7:1–10). Precisely what Lewis intends to signify by Coriakin's priestliness is not clear.

CORIN THUNDER-FIST   Shasta's twin brother, Prince Corin of Archenland.* He is twenty minutes younger than Cor and hence second in line for the throne of his father, King Lune.* He is first mentioned in SC, when Rilian sings an old song about his exploits.[1] Susan has been his best friend since his mother died, and he and Shasta look so alike that Susan mistakes Shasta for Corin. He is a feisty boy, fond of fights, and to defend Susan's honor he knocks down a boy in Tashbaan.* Full of a sense of honor,* he is offended at Shasta's suggestion that he would tell King Edmund and Queen Susan anything but the truth. That he and Shasta become instant friends is indicative of their then-unknown but strong blood bond. He enters the battle of Anvard* against his father's wishes—fighting Thornbut* to do so—and forces Shasta to suit up in the dwarf's* armor and join him in battle. Corin is scolded for his rashness by King Lune, but the King can't disguise his pleasure at his son's bravery.[2] He is the most incensed of the Lords at Rabadash's* insult of the King, and taunts the Calormene,* for which act he is rebuked by Lune. He rejoices that his brother will be king* instead of him, because he knows he will have fun as a prince while Cor must shoulder the responsibility of his vocation. Corin grows up to be the best boxer in Archenland, and earns the surname Thunder-Fist in a thirty-three round fight in which he wins the Lapsed Bear of Stormness* back to the ways of Talking Beasts.*

(SC 171, 166. HHB 58–59, 57; 64, 61; 73 ff., 69 ff.; 169 ff., 149 ff.; Chapter 13 passim; Chapter 15 passim.)
[Courage; Violence.]

---

[1] Another instance of Lewis's inability to edit the Chronicles for inconsistencies. In SC, the name is spelled Thunder-fist; in HHB it is Thunder-Fist.
[2] For discussion of the king's reaction, see Lune.

CORNELIUS, DOCTOR

Caspian's beloved tutor, a half-dwarf* who keeps the facts of his heritage hidden during the fear*-ridden rule of Miraz.* It is easy to keep his identity hidden from the New Narnians, who know nothing of what dwarfs look like. To them he is merely a very small, fat man with a long pointed silver beard. His wrinkly brown face looks at once wise and ugly and kind. It is Doctor Cornelius who enlightens the young prince as to the real history* of Narnia. He longs for the return of Old Narnian values, even though he fears that his dwarf relatives might despise him because of his human blood. Among the subjects Doctor Cornelius teaches are History,* Grammar (for which he uses a book* written by Pulverulentus Siccus) and Astronomy.* Because he teaches the truth about the world, he is obviously the sort of educator Lewis respects, and is certainly so in contrast to the Head* of Experiment House.* His revelation to Caspian that he is a half-dwarf is a numinous* experience for the boy. When Caspian is king, he makes Doctor Cornelius his Lord Chancellor.

(PC 41 passim, 45 passim.)
[Schools.]

CORONET

See Banner, standard, crown, coronet.

CORRADIN

See Rabadash.

COURAGE   True courage is the strength of Aslan, and Reepicheep is its embodiment. Because he has neither hopes nor fears,* his courage in the face of danger is never in question. For human beings, however, courage is a more complex question and their hopes and fears often cause them to waver. As Caspian says to Reepicheep, "There are some things no man can face." In PC, Lucy tries to avoid Aslan's look by hiding her face in his mane; but the magic* in his mane fills her with lion* strength and he calls her a lioness. Miraz* has false courage, which leads him to accept the monomachy* with Peter that ends in his death.* In VDT, Eustace acts bravely "for the first time"* in his life when he attacks the Sea Serpent. And his volunteering to stay overnight on Ramandu's Island* is especially brave because he had never been educated to the fact that courage is a virtue. In HHB, Prince Corin's* courage is not in question but his obedience is.* However, King Lune* and Darrin* seem to speak for Lewis in praise of a rash courage over a planned cowardice.*

(PC 138, *125*. VDT 97, *102;* 157, *156;* 169, *166–167*. HHB 188, *164–165*.)

COURTESY   Narnians show great courtesy to one another. In LWW, Mr. Beaver* defers to Peter (Sons of Adam* before animals*[1]); Peter says to Susan, "Ladies first"[2] (albeit out of fear), and Susan replies that he should go first because he is the eldest. In PC we learn that it is bad manners among squirrels* to watch anyone going to his store or to look as if you wanted to know where it was. Peter defers to Trumpkin* as the eldest in the vote to go upstream or downstream. Nikabrik* shows his true colors when he relegates his oath* of allegiance to Caspian to "court manners," which he feels can be dispensed with considering the tight situation they are in. In VDT, Reepicheep teaches Eustace some manners, respect for knighthood, and respect for mice* and their tails. He also reprimands Rhince* for saying "good riddance" to Eustace, because (1) Eustace is of the same blood as Queen Lucy, and (2) he is a member of their fellowship and thus it is a matter of honor* to find him or avenge him. The entire company stands and uncovers their heads in the presence of Ramandu* and his Daughter* because they are "obviously great people." The life of the sea people includes courtesy along with peace, rest, and council. Out of courtesy, Drinian* offers Caspian a drink of the sweet waters before he takes his own taste. In SC, the reformed Eustace is impressed with the glory and courtesy of the Narnian supper. Glimfeather* courteously offers to catch a bat for Jill as a snack. When Underland* is free, all bow to Rilian, and he in turn is deferential to the eldest dwarf,* whom he calls "Father." Shasta (raised in Calormen* where courtesy is not practiced) was never taught not to listen behind doors. Because Rabadash* has not exercised the courtesy of nations (in which he ought to have declared war on Archenland* by sending defiance), King Lune* declares him unworthy to fight a man of honor. In LB, Tirian* silences Eustace's scolding of the dwarfs: "No warrior scolds. Courteous words or else hard knocks are his only language."

(LWW 123, *117*. PC 70, *68;* 122, *112;* 159, *142;* 180, *157*. VDT 72, *79;* 171–172, *169;* 173, *170;* 176, *173;* 182, *178;* 193, *188;* 198, *193*. SC 39, *46;*

Trufflehunter watches as the Three Bulgy Bears give Caspian the kisses he deserves as a Son of Adam and future King of Narnia. (PC 69, 67.)

44, *51;* 94, 97; 199–201, *191–193.* HHB 4, *14;* 207, *181.* LB 121, *112.*)
[*Hospitality.*]

¹ See *Hierarchy.*
² See *Sexism.*

COWARDICE   A quality despised by all true Narnians, who value courage.* Cowardice is distinguished from fear,* which is a feeling,* and therefore
natural and acceptable. Rather, it is the yielding to the temptation of fear that
leads to cowardice, and thus away from the adventure* that Aslan sends. The
Duffers'* fear of the dark and the invisible magician* has led to a cowardice
so great that they won't ask their own sons or daughters to break the spell.
Pittencream,* who refuses to go with the rest of the Dawn Treaders on their
voyage to the Utter East,* is the embodiment of cowardice. His refusal to meet
the adventure leads to his being cast out from the group and to his degeneration as a teller of lies in Calormen.* In MN, Digory accuses Uncle Andrew*
of cowardice, and Andrew turns the accusation back on his nephew, expressing
the hope that Digory won't show the white feather.¹ Eustace refuses to fight
Reepicheep on the basis of pacifism² rather than cowardice; he says he doesn't
believe in fighting. Here Lewis is giving an image of pacifism that readers must
reject because of Eustace's somewhat ignoble character.

(VDT 27, *34;* 121, *123;* 152, *152;* 169, *166–167.* HHB 187–188, *164–165.*
MN 22–24, *27–28.*)

¹ "To show the white feather" is a phrase from cockfighting. The white feather in a gamecock's
tail is a sign of degenerate stock and thus of cowardice.
² See *Eustace,* note 3.

CREATION OF NARNIA   Aslan creates Narnia with his wild, glorious
song. The stars* are first to appear, simultaneously and in harmony with Aslan,
the First Voice; the Voice rises and with it the sun* rises over Narnia; its light
illuminates the mountains, through which a river runs; and green grass spreads
from Aslan himself to cover all of Narnia with plant life and trees.* As Aslan's
song becomes more tuneful, yet wilder, animals* spring forth from the earth,
which bubbles and boils with their activity; birds shower from the trees, and
bees and butterflies are already busy with the flowers; the Talking Beasts* are
separated from the Dumb Beasts*; and finally, as Aslan commands Narnia to
awake and be divine, the wild people of the wood are called forth.

(MN 96 ff., *91 ff.*)
[*End of Narnia; Music; Mythology; Wood people.*]

CREDAL ELEMENTS   To speak of credal elements in the *Chronicles* is
to try to discern whether there are any lists or formulas that contain the basic
elements of what Narnians believe about Aslan and his ways of working with
them.¹ And though Puddleglum and Mr. Beaver* speak snatches of such
formulas, the clearest example is in Edmund's answer to Eustace's questions
in VDT: Who is Aslan? and Do you know him? Eustace gives a six-fold reply:

"Well, he knows me." This indicates that the important thing is to be known by Aslan and also that a comprehensive knowledge of him and his ways is impossible to achieve.

"He is the great Lion, the son of the Emperor-over-the-Sea." This indicates his basic attributes: his greatness and his relationship to his mysterious Father.

". . . who saved me and saved Narnia." This is the first use of the term "saved" in the *Chronicles,* and the cornerstone of the great supposal that underlies Lewis's intention in writing these books; Aslan fulfilled the demands of the Deep Magic* with respect to Edmund's treachery, and the Lion also delivered Narnia from the Hundred Years of Winter* brought on by the tyrannic magic* of the White Witch.[2]

"We've all seen him." This indicates what Edmund's faith is based on: his actual experience and the experience of his brother and sisters and fellow Narnians.[3]

"Lucy sees him most often." This indicates Lucy's privileged place in the economy, the plan, of Aslan's intervention in Narnian history.*[4]

"And it may be Aslan's country we're sailing to." This not only indicates the goal of their voyage but also the focus of their hearts' desires: to live with Aslan.[5]

Many readers see in the *Chronicles* Lewis's largely successful attempt to remythologize, that is, to give new stories that provide meaning for the Christian Creed. One must remember, however, Lewis's claim that the stories came first.[6] He has not attempted to systematically "storify" the two most ancient Christian formulas or lists,* the Apostles' Creed and the Nicene Creed. But in his story about Aslan he has given new meaning to what Christian theologians call Christology, the systematic study of the nature and activities of Jesus of Nazareth whom Christians believe to be the only begotten Son of God. Lewis therefore has what some traditions call a "high Christology," a clear and prominent picture of Christ, as underlying the supposal[7] of the *Chronicles.*

On the other hand, Lewis has several low-profile doctrines: the Holy Spirit* (or pneumatology); membership in the Church (ecclesiology); and worship and sacraments (liturgiology and sacramentology). With respect to the last, Lewis gives a moving picture of the meaning of baptism in the dragon* Eustace's encounter with Aslan, a scene which might be considered the high point of Lewis's sacramentology in the *Chronicles.* But concerning the other great sacrament esteemed by almost all of the Christian churches, the Lord's Supper, Lewis's picture of Aslan's Table* provides a less focused although very lovely representation.[8]

With these qualifications in mind, consider the following reformulation of the basic Christian Creed in Narnian terms:

I believe in the Emperor-beyond-the-Sea who has put within time the Deep Magic, and, before all time, the Deeper Magic.

I believe in his Son Aslan who sang into being all the worlds and all that they contain: Talking Beasts and humans, dumb animals and shining spirits. And I believe that Aslan was a true beast, the king of beasts, a Lion; that for Edmund, a traitor because of his desire for Turkish Delight, he gave himself into the power of the White Witch, who satisfied the requirements of the Deep Magic by killing him most horribly. At the dawn following that darkest, coldest night, he was restored to full life by the Deeper Magic, cracking the Stone Table and, from that moment, setting death to work backwards. He exulted in his new life and went off to rescue all those who had been turned into stone by the Witch's wand and to deliver the whole land from everlasting winter. He will be behind all the stories of our lives; and, when it is time, he will appear again in our world to wind it up, calling all of his creatures whose hearts' desire it is to live "farther in and farther up" in his country which contains all real countries.

I believe that upon us all falls the breath of Aslan and that ours are the sweet waters of the Last Sea which enable us to look steadily at the sun. I believe that all who have thrilled or will thrill at the sound of Aslan's name are now our fellow voyagers and our fellow kings and queens; that all of us can be for ever free of our dragonish thoughts and actions; and that one day we will pass through the door of death into "Chapter One of the Great Story, which no one on earth has read; which goes on for ever; in which every chapter is better than the one before."

(LB, p. 184, *165*.)

[*Greatness of God.*]

---

[1] Similar lists or fomulas may exist within the Bible itself, around which the later beliefs of Jews and Christians are organized. The basic Old Testament credal formula is found in the Book of Deuteronomy, 26:5–10; and the basic New Testament formula is found in St. Paul's First Letter to the Corinthians, 15:3–8.

[2] At this point Lewis has successfully restrained the moral educator/allegorist in himself, but in LB he abandons this caution in Tirian's* first impassioned speech before the Narnians gathered at the Stable.* Tirian "meant to go on and ask how the terrible god Tash* who fed on the blood of his people could possibly be the same as the good Lion by whose blood all Narnia was saved." Of course only Edmund was saved by the blood of Aslan, and Caspian was rejuvenated by a drop of that blood. But Tirian's statement discloses Lewis's nearly allegorical intention in LB.

[3] This recalls for Christian readers the many New Testament references in which the closest followers of Jesus of Nazareth, the apostles, give witness that they lived with this special man in the most important time of his life. See the Acts of the Apostles 1:21–22, St. Peter's Second Epistle 1:16–18, and St. John's First Epistle, 1:1–4.

[4] This suggests not only the special place St. John, the "beloved disciple," had among the apostles, and the special place that St. Peter and St. James shared with him in Jesus' first circle of friends, but also the position of the four most important women in Jesus' life: the two sisters, Mary and Martha of Bethany, Mary of Magdala, and Mary the Mother of Jesus.

[5] This dimension is a resounding echo of both the Messianic longing* of the Jewish religion and also the eager expectation of Christians for the return of Jesus in glory. The study of this dimension is called eschatology.*

[6] See *Introduction.*

[7] See *Introduction.*

[8] And though there is forgiveness and reconciliation and healing throughout the *Chronicles,* those in the Anglican, Roman, and Orthodox Christian churches perhaps wish that Lewis had been more explicit. But to be explicit was not Lewis's intention with respect to the creative impulse that produced the *Chronicles,* nor with respect to Lewis's entire apologetic effort. He wanted to remain the spokesman for "mere Christianity," as he called it, the heart of the entire Christian tradition. See *Introduction.*

CREEKS   See *Glasswater Creek, Creeks.*

CREW OF THE *DAWN TREADER*   See *Rhince.*

CROWN   See *Banner, standard, crown, coronet.*

CRUELS   Evil* beings, summoned to and present at the slaying of Aslan. Their name reveals their characteristic behavior.

(LWW 132, *123;* 148, *138.*)

CRUELTY TO ANIMALS   See *Vivisection.*

CRYING   In the *Chronicles,* crying is both ignoble and to be avoided, and noble and not to be ashamed of; it is often a sign of despair or self-pity, and it is also a reaction to great beauty or tragedy. While Lewis excuses crying, he also says that it is not the way to get anything accomplished. In SC Lewis comments, "Crying is all right in its way while it lasts. But you have to stop sooner or later and then you still have to decide what to do." In LWW Lucy and Susan cry in despair over Aslan's death,* and in LB Tirian* and Jewel* shed "bitter tears" at the death of their hope in Aslan, and Jill cries over the death of the horses.* There is much more crying in self-pity, however: SC opens with Jill crying behind the gym, and she has a good cry after Eustace plunges over the cliff. She later breaks down and cries from weariness at the castle of Harfang*; and she is so troubled by her dream that she cries into her pillow. It is a sign of her growth that she tries to restrain herself from crying during the killing of the Queen of Underland,* and later her only crying is for the beauty of Aslan and the sadness of Caspian's funeral music. When she notices Eustace crying, she observes that he isn't crying freely like a child or ashamedly like a boy, but like an adult.* Eustace, too, has come a long way from the tears he shed as a dragon* in VDT. In HHB, Shasta feels so sorry for himself on his journey through the fog in Archenland* that he cries. But at the frightening discovery of a large, breathing presence beside him, he stops crying "now that he really [has] something to cry about." At the beginning of MN, Digory is so miserable that he doesn't care who knows he has been "blubbing," and he cries for his mother again in the garden*—but this time Aslan cries with him. In LB, Jill is a much stronger character, and her cry is for joy* at Emeth's* zeal and beauty. Finally, Jill, Lucy, and Tirian cry in mourning the passing of Narnia.

(LWW 148, *136;* 156, *144.* PC 88, *84;* 215, *188.* VDT 74, *80–81;* 82, *89;* 161, *159;* 211, *204.* SC 1, *11;* 15, *24;* 97, *99;* 100, *103;* 161, *158;* 199, *193;* 211, *201.* HHB 155, *137.* MN 2, *9;* 141, *131.* LB 25, *29;* 28, *32;* 121, *112;* 126, *115.*)

CURIOSITY   In Lewis's thinking, curiosity is more than an eagerness and an aptitude for knowledge.* It is also a power of the human mind that is open to abuse. In the medieval tradition,[1] curiosity is a form of intemperance, and studiosity is a form of temperance. The worst distortion of this exaggerated striving for knowledge for Lewis and the medievals is magic.* In VDT, Lucy's desire to know what her friends think of her leads to a disturbing experience with the magician's Book.* Polly's curiosity overcomes her caution and she steps into Uncle Andrew's* study. When Andrew reveals that his godmother's box contained something from another world, Digory becomes "interested in spite of himself." In the great hall of Charn,* his wild curiosity to know what will happen if he rings the golden bell* almost ruins them all. Digory's natural curiosity might have taken him the way of his uncle, the evil* magician, but it did not. Instead he developed his *studiositas* and became Professor Kirke, a man concerned with the correct use of knowledge. The Hermit of the Southern March* has also learned to control his curiosity, and he says of the future, "if we ever need to know it, you may be sure we shall." The calmness and serenity of his enclosure embody the peace that this attitude has brought him.

(VDT 131 ff., *133 ff.* HHB 143, *126.* MN 9, *17;* 20, *25;* 33–36, *36–38;* 43, *44;* 49, *49.*)
[*Positivity; Technology.*]

---

[1] See Josef Pieper's *The Four Cardinal Virtues* (Notre Dame: University of Notre Dame Press, 1966) pp. 198–202 for a succinct treatment of this matter.

CURRENCY   Narnian Lions and Trees, everyday coinage used in Beruna,* are discovered on Deathwater Island.* The Calormene* crescent, chief coin of The Lone Islands,* is worth about "one-third of a pound." Another coin, the minim, is one-fortieth of a crescent.

(VDT 33, *41;* 103, *107.*)

DANCE   Dances and dancing are the chief means of celebration in Narnia.[1] In LWW, all the creatures Aslan revives dance around him, and at the great coronation feast at Cair Paravel there is revelry* and dancing. PC features a number of dances, all of which take place at the Dancing Lawn.* The first dance is that of the fauns* around Caspian at the Great Council*; at the second dance the trees* do a complicated country dance to a familiar tune. The third dance, which takes place just before dawn, is begun around Aslan by the trees and is soon joined by all sorts of revelers, including Bacchus,* Silenus,* and the Maenads.* At the defeat of Miraz's* troops, Aslan leads a singing, dancing group across the countryside. The fourth dance takes place after the victory of Aslan's forces, and this dance of plenty is the wildest of all. In VDT, dancing is said to be the leisure-time activity of the Sea People.* The Great Snow Dance in SC is an annual Narnian event held north of the Great River* on the first moonlit night when snow is on the ground. It is danced by fauns, Dryads,* and dwarfs* to the music* of four fiddles, three flutes, and a drum. Snowballs are thrown with great precision, and if anyone is off-step they get hit.

(LWW 166, *153;* 179, *165.* PC 78, *75;* 112, *103;* 134, *121;* 152, *136;* 195, *171;* 198, *174;* 205, *179.* VDT 193, *188.* SC 191–193, *184–186.*)

---

[1] Though something of a Trufflehunter* at dancing himself (PC 78, *75*), Lewis seems to have been a dancer at heart. He was fond of the Great Dance of the Heavens of the medieval worldview (with its Ptolomeic cosmology full of epicycles and deferents), because it seemed a fitting created reflection of the uncreated Dance within the Trinity* itself, a concept popular with the Christian theologians until the Copernican revolution. For Lewis, the dance is the happiest image for the most important things in life: the place of the human race in the universe, the relationship of humankind with the earth and its creatures, the relationship among human beings (especially between the sexes), the relationship of humankind to God, and the inner life of God himself. The most beautiful description of all of this is in the Song of the Eldila in *Perelandra* (New York: Macmillan Publishing Co., 1962) pp. 214–19; a case could be made that all of Lewis's thinking finds its expression in these six pages. A more systematic explanation of this is found in *Miracles* (New York: Macmillan Publishing Co., 1978; London: Collins Fontana, 1960) p. 124, *128;* and *Mere Christianity* (New York: Macmillan Publishing Co., 1960; London: Collins Fount, 1977) pp. 152–153, *148–150.* For dance imagery and sexual love, see *The Four Loves* (New York: Harcourt Brace Jovanovich, 1960) pp. 145–149; and *That Hideous Strength* (New York: Macmillan Publishing Co., 1965) p. 149.

DANCING LAWN   The traditional site of feasts and councils in Old Narnia, located west of the River Rush* and south of the Great River* and Aslan's How.* Elms border the smooth circle of grass, and there is a well at the margin. It is the site of all dances* in the *Chronicles* except the Great Snow Dance, which takes place north of the Great River* almost directly above Bism.

(PC 70, *68;* 74, *72;* 76, *73;* 135, *122.* SC 191–193, *181–186.*)

DAR   See *Darrin.*

DARK ISLAND   A place of terror where all dreams* come true, including nightmares. For Lewis, the Dark Island seems to be the localization of childrens'* fear* of the dark.[1] It is located fourteen days of gentle wind southeast of the Land of the Duffers.* As first sighted by Edmund, it appears to be a dark mass or mountain; but on closer view, it is seen to be utter blackness, like the interior of a tunnel or the edge of a night without moon or stars.* The waters around the island are greasy and lifeless, and it is impossible to ascertain the speed or direction of the *Dawn Treader* in this murky sea. Piercing cold afflicts all but the toiling oarsmen as the ship moves to rescue the Lord Rhoop.* Exhausted and terror-stricken, Rhoop refuses to talk about the "they" who held him captive on the island; and he asks Caspian to promise that he will not question him further about his experiences. So impressed is Caspian by Rhoop's suffering, that he gladly makes this promise and immediately directs the crew to sail away from the island as fast as possible. At this point, the darkness is so palpable that they expect the ship to be coated with grime, and total silence engulfs them. Yet each one hears a different sound of terror: a gong, a giant scissors cutting, creatures crawling up the side of the ship, "it" landing on the mast. Finally, Rhoop screams in anguish that they will never get out. But after Lucy calls on Aslan for help, a tiny speck of light appears and then a broad beam illumines the ship like a search light. An albatross,* seemingly Aslan or his messenger, appears to lead the ship into the full light of day.

(VDT 150 ff., *150 ff.*)
[*Privacy.*]

---

[1] So important did Lewis consider night-fears that he extensively revised the ending of this twelfth chapter for the American edition of VDT. His aim was to correct any impression that the British edition might have given that night-fears are unreal and ultimately laughable and that they can be obliterated altogether. Thus in the American edition, the Dark Island and its darkness do not vanish but the size diminishes gradually as the *Dawn Treader* sails away. See *Dreams* for a complete delineation of the differences between editions.

DARRIN   A Lord of Archenland,* loyal to King Lune.* He cross-questions Shasta when the boy stumbles onto the King's hunting* party. Later, while remarking on the boy's horsemanship,* he is the first to speculate that Shasta has noble blood. At Anvard,* he fights alongside his brother Dar[1] and kills Ilgamuth. When King Lune reproves Corin for joining in the battle against his express wishes, Darrin reminds the King that he would be more upset if Corin had *lacked* the courage* and inclination to do battle.[2] Darrin is present at the King's luncheon at Anvard after the victory.

(HHB 149, *132–133;* 183–184, *160–161;* 188, *164–165;* 196, *172;* 205–206, *179–181.*)

---

[1] Brothers in Archenland have names that are each part of the other, hence: Cor and Corin,* Dar and Darrin, and Cole and Colin. Tran and Shar are also mentioned, but it is not clear whether or not they are brothers.
[2] This seems to be a literary allusion* to Chaucer's *Troylus and Cresida* (II, 167): "For truly I hold it great deynte, A Kyngis son yn armes wel to do, And been of good conditions per to."

DAUGHTER OF EVE   See *Son of Adam, Daughter of Eve.*

DAUGHTER OF RAMANDU   A tall, beautiful young woman with long golden hair, who greets the travelers when they arrive at Ramandu's Island.* She is dressed in a long blue gown, cut so as to leave her arms bare, and she carries a tall candle in a silver candlestick. Its flame burns with steady intensity as if in a closed room. She is known only by title (Ramandu's Daughter, the Star's Daughter, Caspian's Queen, Rilian's mother) and by no personal name throughout the *Chronicles*—an indication of the awe with which Lewis wished to surround her.[1]

She invites the travelers to dine at Aslan's Table,* tells them all about the Three Sleepers,* and identifies the Stone Knife* enshrined on the Table as being what Lucy senses it is—the instrument used to slay Aslan. When Edmund asks how they can know that she is to be trusted and that the food is safe to eat, she replies that he can only believe she is their friend; he cannot know it. Reepicheep accepts her word and calls for his cup to be filled. This incident reflects Lewis's insights regarding the nature of friendship and the relation of faith to reason.

The Daughter is quick to catch Caspian's meaning in his reference to the Sleeping Beauty story, but she tells him that here it is just the opposite; he cannot kiss the princess until he breaks the enchantment of the Three Sleepers—a task her father will tell him how to accomplish. When her father, a retired star,* appears, she stands with him facing the east; together they extend their arms in welcome to the sunrise and sing their early morning song. When her father places the Lord Rhoop* in an enchanted sleep, she is standing by the Lord's chair. And when Caspian says he hopes to see her again after the enchantment is broken, she smiles, indicating her own attraction for him. In true fairy tale form, she later marries him and sails to Narnia to become "a great queen and the mother and grandmother of great kings."[2]

However, contrary to the "happily ever after" formula, she meets a horrible death when she is bitten by a serpent while resting after going Maying with her son Rilian. She dies quickly, struggling unsuccessfully to give her son a message. Her body is carried back to the city where she is mourned as a gracious and wise lady in whose veins flowed the blood of stars. She is named among the faithful at the Great Reunion.*

(VDT 171 ff., 168 ff.; 216, 210. SC 49–50, 55–56. LB 178, 161.)
[Autobiographical allusions; Literary allusions; Music.]

---

[1] For another view, see Sexism.

[2] Since Lewis completed VDT in February of 1950 and does not seem to have begun working on SC until the fall of that same year, it could be that he did not foresee the tragic death of Ramandu's Daughter. See Introduction.

DAWN TREADER   A Narnian ship built for King Caspian and commanded by the Lord Drinian.* Shaped like a dragon's head, it has green sides and a gilded prow and stern. A square sail of rich purple is rigged to its one mast. Caspian's cabin is small but beautifully decorated in the Chinese style, with birds,* beasts, vines, and crimson dragons* on painted panels. A flat, gold image of Aslan fills the space above the door. There are two long hatches, one fore and one aft of the mast, with benches for rowing. A pit, reaching down to the keel, lines the center of the ship and holds provisions. The crew includes about thirty swordsmen. With the exception of Eustace, who cannot fathom the crew's affection for an unautomated vessel, all on board are fond of the ship.

At Narrowhaven,* the Dawn Treader is stocked with provisions for twenty-eight days, her maximum capacity. After sustaining heavy damage in a storm, she is completely refitted at Dragon Island*—a task that requires three weeks. Later, when her stern is broken in the encounter with the Sea Serpent,* it is magically repaired by Coriakin.* And in the blackness around Dark Island,* lanterns at her stern, prow, and masthead plus two torches amidships give what little light there is. At Ramandu's Island,* the *Dawn Treader* launches a small boat big enough to carry Caspian, Edmund, Lucy, Eustace, Drinian,* Rhince,* Rynelf,* Reepicheep, and four sailors. It is this boat that Caspian wishes to keep when he wants to remain behind to go on to the Utter East.*

When her journey is complete and the adventurers make ready to return from World's End,* the ship flies all her flags and displays all her shields to honor Reepicheep, Edmund, Lucy, and Eustace. She looks "tall and big and homelike" from their low vantage point. And each of them will share her title "Dawn Treader," as will all those who had journeyed to the World's End* with King Caspian. This honor would become their most precious bequest to their heirs.

(VDT 4 ff., *11 ff.; 19* ff., *26 ff.;* 38, *46;* 54 ff., *61 ff.;* 99, *104;* 153, *153;* 185, *181;* 211, *204.*)
[*Splendour Hyaline; Technology.*]

DEATH   Death is called the "long journey" in a conversation between Aslan and Caspian's old nurse.* In SC, Rilian interprets the marvelous transformation of his shield as a sign* that "Aslan will be our good lord, whether he means us to live or die. And all's one, for that." Later in SC, the old King Caspian dies and is reborn as the young Caspian in Aslan's country.* He is truly alive in Aslan's country, although he speculates that he might be a ghost* if he turned up elsewhere. In HHB, Shasta is sure that the Lion is going to kill him, and wonders if anything happens to people after they die. When Frank* comes into Narnia he thinks he has died, and his reaction is remarkable for its piety: he sings a hymn. In MN, Lewis stresses the point that death is not the greatest tragedy. Digory does not want to be immortal; he would rather die and go to heaven. Later Lewis comments that "there might be things more terrible even than losing someone you love by death." The characters in LB spend a lot of time discussing death. Puzzle* says the dead lion* must be given a decent burial; the second mouse says to Tirian* that "It would be better if we'd died before all this began"; Roonwit's* last words are about noble death; Eustace and Jill discuss their possible deaths in the Last Battle*; and Jewel,* in a discussion with Poggin,* Tirian, and Jill, is confident that death is the way into Aslan's country. And, indeed, it is. The Stable* Door* becomes a metaphor for death: on this side of the door death is terrifying, black, unknown; but on the other side lies the glory of Aslan's country.

(LWW 160, *148.* PC 197, *173.* SC 168–169, *164–165;* 209–212, *200–202.* HHB 85, *79.* MN 161, *150;* 175, *163.* LB 6, *11;* 24, *28;* 37, *40;* 91, *85;* 96, *88;* 128, *117.*)
[*Eschatology.*]

DEATHWATER ISLAND   An island about twenty acres in size, the
se___ landing of the _Dawn Treader_. It has two streams—one on the west, the
ot___ on the east—which both flow into the single natural harbor. Dominat-
ing the island is a mountain (perhaps a dormant or extinct volcano) covered
wi___ a little mountain lake that
is ___ ely surrounded by cliffs
(e___ one outlet, the eastern
str___ Lucy discover the rusted
arr___ ___eshore. Then they see a
be___ ___dmund deduces that the
"st___ ___rest gold by the deadly
ma___ ___negative response to the
ma___ ___us wealth. In his greed*
he ___ Island, and attempts to
sw___ ___reat strides he has made
in ___ ___ order to urge, it would
see___ come to blows when a
vis___ ___hing but the awareness
tha___ ___they later decide it has
to ___ the island Deathwater.

(V___
[G___

"D___

DI___ full meaning of which
As___ ___passion. The Deeper
Ma___ ___n of time"). That it is
no___ Deep Magic* is clear
fro___ ___n substituting himself
or ___ ___ the need for sacrifice
in ___ ___ccess finds allies in the
wa___ ___orld's End* in order
for ___ ___ken, and in the spirit
of ___ ___ might be saved.

(LW___

___i___ ___: friend, Arthur Greeves,
writt___ ___WW:

I___ ___nnot do for ourselves and
c___ ___s suffering _for us_ is not a
n___ ___rns the whole world: and
w___ ___, ___ saved others, himself he cannot save," they were
really uttering, little as they know it, the ultimate law of the spiritual world.

From Walter Hooper, ed., _They Stand Together_ (New York: Macmillan Publishing Co., 1979;
London: Collins, 1979) p. 514, _514_. See also the principle of vicariousness in Lewis's _Miracles_
(New York: Macmillan Publishing Co., 1978; London: Collins Fontana, 1960) p. 118, _122_ and
W.H.Lewis,ed.,_Letters of C. S. Lewis_ (New York: Harcourt Brace Jovanovich, 1966) p. 236.

JACKS, A
6195
Monday, September 28, 2020
35143000916953 Companion to Narnia

DEEP MAGIC   A complex term in LWW used by the White Witch and also well-known to Aslan, connoting the demands of justice. Since it has existed "from the dawn of time," it is not eternal justice as we understand it, but the effects of justice in a created world. The words of the Deep Magic are inscribed in the three sacred places: the Stone Table* (a place of ritual sacrifice); on the firestones of the Secret Hill* (another sacrificial context, in the British edition only), or (in the American editions) on the trunk of the World Ash Tree* (with its Odin imagery of inescapable destiny); and on the sceptre* of the Emperor-beyond-the-Sea* (thereby establishing the profoundest basis for the legitimacy of its claims). The Witch understands it only to the extent that she knows that a traitor's blood (i.e., life) belongs to her. Aslan's knowledge of it is far deeper and he will not work against it. Rather, in obedience* to it and to the Deeper Magic,* he offers his own life in Edmund's place.

(LWW 130 ff., *128 ff.;* 152, *140;* 159–60, *148.*)
[*Magic.*]

DEEP REALM   See *Underland.*

DEPLORABLE WORD, THE   A word that has the power to destroy all but its speaker. It is a word that Jadis has learned at great personal cost,[1] and which the great kings of Charn* have long known. Jadis herself used it to defeat her sister, even though the innocent people of Charn were destroyed in so doing.[2] Near the end of MN, Aslan tells the children that the people of their world may soon discover a secret as terrible as the Deplorable Word, a broad hint to humans that there are wicked people with the power to destroy all life on earth, most likely a reference to the newly discovered atom bomb.

(MN Chapter 5 passim; 178, *164.*)
[*Magic; White Witch.*]

---

[1] An echo of Andrew Ketterley's* claim to have learned the secret of Mrs. Lefay's* box at great personal cost, and a warning about the dangers of involvement in magic.*
[2] Another echo of Uncle Andrew, this time about his claim that it is permissible to kill the guinea pigs, if necessary, because he owns them. See *Vivisection.*

DEPRAVITY   In the context of discussing the extent to which the White Witch is human,[1] Mr. Beaver* observes that though "there may be two views about Humans," there is no question about the Witch's evil* nature—because she is not human but only looks like she is, she is "bad all through." Another way of putting this question is to ask whether the Witch is totally depraved, that is, so aligned with evil that she is incapable of being won over to the good. Mr. and Mrs. Beaver* agree that she is entirely evil.

The question remains: how evil are humans? When Mr. Beaver suggests that there are two views on this matter, he is raising one of the major issues of the Reformation. On the one hand, John Calvin, speaking for the Protestant tradition at this point, believed that humankind had no grace in any of its faculties, that is, that its intellect and will were so aligned with evil that in no

It is the worst of nights: the Giant Wimbleweather weeps tears of failure; the bloodied bears, the wounded Centaur, and all the other creatures huddle in gloom under the dripping trees. (PC 87-88, 83-84.)

sense could people attain lasting happiness unless they repented and attached themselves by faith to that perfect man, who is also God: Jesus Christ. Later theologians in the Calvinist tradition understood total depravity to mean not only that humankind was utterly incapable of attaining God on its own, but that humankind was as bad as it could possibly be. This is one view held of humans.

The other view is expressed by the Catholic theological tradition. Agreeing with the Protestants that humankind, apart from the grace of repentant faith, cannot attain lasting joy,* the Catholic tradition distinguished among the various human faculties, saying of the will that though it was entirely incapable of choosing the God of biblical revelation, it was nevertheless able to develop natural (but not *saving*) virtues. And about the intellect, the Catholic tradition maintained that though the mind remained opaque to the truths to be derived from revelation only, nevertheless it was capable of discerning the maker of the universe from the universe he had made. This latter capability is called "natural theology" by theologians in the Catholic tradition. This is a second view held of humans.

In the characters of Andrew Ketterley* and Emeth,* one can discern that Lewis stood on the second or more Catholic side of this particular question. Uncle Andrew is at first capable of hearing Aslan's song, and of recognizing it to be a song. But he chooses to reject this knowledge* because the song stirs up in him unwanted thoughts and feelings.* By the time it is revealed that the Lion is the singer, Andrew has irreversibly convinced himself that the singing is really roaring.[2] On the other hand, Emeth, though he has been consciously seeking Tash* all of his life, has really been serving Aslan.[3] Emeth is the true *anima naturaliter Christiana,*[4] the naturally Christian soul, who has only to be shown the truth of his situation for him to immediately acknowledge his allegiance to Aslan.[5]

---

[1] LWW 77–78, *76–77.*
[2] MN 126, *117.*
[3] LB 164–165, *148–149.*
[4] Tertullian (160–220 A.D.), *Apology,* XVII, 197.
[5] For more about this question, see *Universalism.*

DESIRE   See *Longing.*

DESTRIER   Caspian's horse,* a Dumb Beast,* on whom the prince flees his Uncle Miraz.* It bolts during a thunderstorm and returns to the stables at the castle, thereby unwittingly betraying the fact that Caspian has escaped. *Destrier* is the old French word for "warhorse," and its use by Lewis is another instance of the way in which he creates a medieval atmosphere in the *Chronicles.*

(PC 58, *58.*)

DIGGLE   A dwarf,* spokesman for the group of renegade dwarfs who survive the Last Battle* only to be thrown into the Stable.* He is very cross and disbelieving: he can't see anything in the Stable, and presumes that the Seven Friends of Narnia* can't see either; he takes Tirian's* talk of Aslan as another attempt to lie to the dwarfs. The truth is that Diggle sees only what he wants to see. Although Tirian tells him that the black hole exists only in his imagination,* when he swings Diggle out of the circle of dwarfs Diggle feels like he's been smashed against the wall of the stable.

(LB 144–148, *131–135*.)
[*Plato.*]

DIGORY KIRKE The very wise professor in LWW who welcomes the Pevensie children into his large country home when they are evacuated from London in 1940. He is remarkably understanding of youngsters for a fifty-two-year-old, unmarried man. He is later discovered to be the adventurous, curious Digory of MN, and the handsome Lord Digory, friend of Narnia, in LB.[1] In his anxious concern for his seriously ill mother, he is almost the mirror of Lewis himself, who lost his mother to cancer when he was not quite ten years old.

In the scene where Peter and Susan tell the Professor their concern about their sister, the Professor uses the Socratic method[2] of probing questions to disclose to them that the best evidence they have points to Lucy's essential truthfulness and sanity, and that they should withhold judgment on the existence of other worlds until they have more evidence. Like many adults,* he repeats himself (giving Lewis a chance to express his own question: What *do* they teach children in modern schools*?); but unlike most adults, the Professor is a courteous listener and hears the children out whenever they ask to speak with him.[3] He also helps them to understand that they can't expect to have the same feelings* and adventures* over and over again but that they should hold themselves open to experience new feelings and adventures[4] as they come. When he echoes Aslan's coronation acclamation ("Once a king in Narnia, always a king in Narnia"), he ratifies their experience of a world they can reach only by faith* in good magic.*

In PC the Professor is called the "one very wise grown-up" whom the children had told of their journey to Narnia. In VDT he is Peter's tutor and prepares the boy to take his university examinations. By this time (1942) he is living in a smaller house, a cottage really, with only one spare bedroom, so Lucy and Edmund must spend the summer at the home of Alberta* and Harold Scrubb* while Mr. and Mrs. Pevensie* and Susan are in America.

MN begins with Lewis's announcement that he intends to tell the story* about how the "comings and goings between our own world and the land of Narnia first began." But it isn't until toward the end of the second chapter that the reader learns that the boy Digory will become the Professor Kirke (this is the first time his surname is used) of the other stories. The reader sees the boy through Polly Plummer's eyes: he is a very unhappy person, uprooted from a settled country existence by the illness of his mother and the absence of his father.[5] Polly sensibly distracts his attention by involving him in her world—the attic passageway above their row of houses. His natural curiosity is whetted by her story of the unoccupied house next to his. When they blunder into his Uncle Andrew's* study, Digory is alarmed by his uncle's facial expression.[6] And the boy screams at Polly's sudden disappearance when she touches the ring* the man offers her. Andrew's foul threat to the boy (that one more of his screams might frighten his mother to death) makes Digory ill at the thought that someone could behave so basely; but he will shortly show the same willingness to use violence to get his own way with Polly. Digory's chief concern is to help Polly, but he finds himself almost involuntarily curious about his uncle's explanation of the magic* of the rings. The reader begins to sense a similarity in nephew and uncle: a weakness for hidden knowledge.* But otherwise Digory sees his uncle as a man making highflown excuses for breaking promises,* disobeying rules, and even being cruel to animals.* He sees that he is trapped by Andrew into using his magic to rescue Polly. He shows his mettle in a fine speech in which he confesses that he now knows that magic and fairy tales are true and that his uncle is just another in a long line of evil* magicians. Digory has been properly raised on the right kind of stories, so he concludes that since the stories are true, then their outcome is also true: justice is done to his uncle's kind of magician. As he prepares to go, Digory thinks of his mother and asks what will be said to her if she asks for him. His uncle takes no responsibility, and leaves the boy with no option but to go. However, Digory does not resent this predicament: his standard of decency dictates that he must attempt to help his friend.

In the Wood between the Worlds,* Digory is overtaken by his curiosity. He shows a scientific turn of mind by making the correct hypothesis about the nature of the place, and argues with Polly to carry out a few experiments. In their differing reactions to their situation Lewis shows the dangers of uncontrolled curiosity. Lewis comments that "Digory was the sort of person who wants to know everything." But the desire for knowledge must be tempered with respect for the nature of things, a reverence Digory will have to learn the hard way. Polly has this instinct, but Digory listens to her only occasionally, as when he realizes the grave consequences of not marking the pool that is their route back to earth. Because both have much to learn, they end up quarreling.

Lewis means for the reader to compare Digory's first reactions to Charn* with Polly's. Her response is instinctive and correct; this is not a good place to be. Digory takes a more scientific, even meteorological approach. He senses her fear* but, instead of allowing it to teach him something, he ridicules it and reveals how distorted his perceptions are: "There's not much point in finding a Magic Ring that lets you into other worlds if you're afraid to look at them when you've got there." He forgets that he didn't just "find" the rings. They came to him as the result of his uncle's inordinate curiosity and disregard for promises and for life, animal and human. Digory embarrasses Polly into disowning most of her proper fear.

In the royal hall he is taken with the raw beauty of Jadis[7] and, like his uncle, he will for the rest of his life think her the most beautiful woman he has ever met. His desire to know the story behind the royal statues motivates him to explore the room, where he discovers the golden bell and hammer.* He allows himself to succumb to the spell of the place, an excuse Polly does not want to let him have. They quarrel again, exchanging sexist* and Bulveristic* remarks.[8] He then commits a violent act, the consequences of which can only be compared to Edmund's treachery: Digory reawakens the evil that will come into Narnia and eventually lead to the death* of Aslan. He wrenches Polly into temporary immobility and strikes the bell. And even in the face of the loud noise and earthquake that it causes, he seems unwilling to take responsibility for what he has done.

Digory's reaction to Jadis is the equal and opposite of Polly's. For him, the witch is regal and wonderful and powerful; for Polly, she is simply terrible. Digory is eager to learn Charn's history,* especially who had the power and what the Deplorable Word* is. Digory is not so under her spell that he can overlook the murderous consequences of this woman's reign; but her answer —that her "high and lonely destiny" frees her from common morality, a precise echo of Uncle Andrew's excuse—sounds much grander coming from this magnificent queen.

Digory's infatuation begins to cool when Jadis decides to come to earth and he tries to dissuade her from making this "visit." He can only manage to call Jadis's preposterous explanation for his presence "not exactly" correct. "Absolute bosh" is Polly's accurate judgment of the witch's scenario. In a moment of weakness, Digory pities the queen, who seems immobilized by the atmosphere of the Wood between the Worlds—it is all the hesitation she needs to hitch a ride to Andrew's study by way of Digory's earlobe.

When Digory sees what a mess he's caused, he seeks Polly's help. She first demands an apology, the need for which Digory is so morally obtuse as not to see. When he brushes her request off with another sexist remark, she details his faults. He is surprised at this enumeration, but manages as much of an apology as he is capable of at this point in the narrative. It is really his concern for the effect that Jadis's "visit" will have on his mother that moves Polly to pledge her further help. As he considers how to get rid of the witch, his mind works systematically through various solutions, the hallmark of a future scientist. He overhears a conversation between his Aunt Letitia* and a visitor that rekindles his desperate hope to have his mother well again, "everything right again."[9]

Digory, motivated by the thought that he will explore all the worlds there are until he finds something that will help his mother, takes charge of the situation and escorts the witch and a few passengers first to the Wood and then into a new world. In this new world he is both properly cautious about his uncle or the witch seizing the rings, and properly curious* about the wonders of the place. At the creation of Narnia,* he is entranced by the creation song and by the sight of the Singer-Lion. But he gets nervous as the Lion moves slowly nearer to him: this is not yet awe at the numinous,* but more an instinctive guilt. The scientist in him thrives in this world—Digory is able to explain to his uncle the implications of the growing lamp-post.* Andrew launches into a commercial ecstasy, ending with the observation that this must be the land of youth. Digory's hope for his mother is immediately stirred; and seeing that he will get no help from his uncle, he fixes his hope on the Lion. Out of respect, he doesn't dare to interrupt while the Lion confers the gift of speech* on the animals. But his impatience mounts to the point where he does break into the Lion's council and ask for some magic fruit to heal his mother. He cannot look the Lion in the eyes, and so focuses on his claws throughout all of the dialogue about Digory's responsibility for bringing evil into Narnia. The boy makes a complete confession* of his deeds, with the Lion's help uncovering his deepest motives. Digory goes back and forth between his worries for his mother and the Lion's plans to heal Narnia. He agrees to do whatever the Lion wishes, but inwardly his desperate hope is to bargain with the Lion, something he realizes can't be done. This brings on the worst of his desolate feelings and he looks up into the Lion's eyes for the first time; and there he is shocked to see tears.[10] Aslan commiserates with him and assigns him the task of bringing a seed from the garden* in the West. Digory agrees, not knowing how, but confident of the person who has given him this task. All along, their conversation has moved from solemn confrontation to compassion to light-heartedness. Polly accompanies him on his mission.[11] They discuss the meaning of history* along the way, and they plant the Toffee Tree.* Unlike Jill and Eustace in SC, they repeat the signs* whereby they will find their way to the garden.*

Digory's approach to the garden is in strong contrast to his behavior in the great hall at Charn. His stock responses* alert him to the utter privacy* of the place; he reads the enchanted message on the gates with no effort; and he finds the tree right away. The only mistake he makes, and this is scarcely intentional, is to smell* the apple* before he puts it into his pocket. The temptation to have this pleasure to himself causes him to try to reconstrue the law of the garden (expressed in the verse on the gates) into mere advice. But the roosting bird's open eye serves to remind Digory of the obligations of conscience. This victory over his inclination enables him to immediately intuit the meaning of the witch's eating of an apple: in violating the rules of the garden, she has won her heart's desire, but she has also ultimately undone herself. He flees but she follows and makes an appeal to one of his deepest desires: the thirst for knowledge.[12] Although he claims not to be interested, he actually is. When she appeals to his desire to live forever and to rule as her consort,[13] he rejects her offer with his stated preference to live an ordinary life span and "die and go to heaven." His is a basic faith. His head suddenly clears (as did Puddleglum's in his pain) at the witch's suggestion that he should abandon Polly, who has been so loyal to him, refusing to leave his quest even to get food in England.* Having told the witch off, Digory gets onto Fledge's* back and, with Polly, flies back to Narnia. He is silent on the way back, a silence that Polly and Fledge respect. In truth, he is very sad because his confidence that he has made the right choice is intermittent. But his memory of Aslan's tears serves to reassure him that Aslan really cares about his mother and that the witch does not.

When he returns to Aslan with the apple, Digory goes through the death of human hope* and surrenders the future to the Lion's providence. He finally knows that "there might be things more terrible even than losing someone you love by death."[14] At this moment Digory's basic transformation is complete. He can safely be allowed to take a bit of the apple of youth back to his mother. He and Polly are given a vision of Aslan's glory that will stay with them all their lives. They are transported instantly back to London, and find themselves in front of the Ketterley house. After arranging with Polly to dispose of the rings, Digory rushes in to give his mother the apple. He is gratified by the natural sleep it gives her, but he is torn between hope and despair when he sees no further results. But the next day, when he hears the doctor pronounce her on the road to recovery, Digory's life comes together again and he can continue to grow in the direction of wisdom and knowledge, in the company of his parents, together at last, and his friend Polly.

In the first phase of the Great Reunion* in LB, Peter introduces Tirian to a man with a magnificent golden beard and a very wise face. This is Digory Kirke.[15] He has ceased to be the stiff sixty-one-year-old man he was before the railway accident. In the discussion about the nature of the Stable,* he is the one to observe that its "inside is bigger than its outside," an insight that anticipates the later mention of Plato.* It is especially shocking to him to see Narnia die because he had seen it created. When all are curious about where they are, he quietly says that this Narnia-like place is *more* like the *real* thing —and the reader can sense that Digory is understanding more deeply than anyone else, even than Lucy. It is she whom Digory tells that "all of the old Narnia . . . [has] been drawn into the real Narnia through the door."[16] He tells her that Plato understood all that they are experiencing. And as his story began, so it ends, with the Professor wondering about what kind of education children are getting.

---

[1] When Lewis was writing LWW, he did not yet know that the unnamed Professor and Digory Kirke were the same character. The Professor is modeled both on Lewis's tutor, W. D. Kirkpatrick, a rigorous logician (see *Plato*), and on Lewis himself: he had a great sympathy for children who imagined other worlds, and he opened his own home in Oxford to many children fleeing the London blitz at the beginning of World War II. Lewis found in Digory a way to understand his own disappointed hopes for his mother's return to health. It is not clear from what is now known of Lewis's life if Digory's insatiable curiosity* is something Lewis remembered of himself, or if Digory is only a character through whom Lewis can reveal his beliefs about the limits of knowledge* and other important themes in MN. See *Autobiographical allusions*.

[2] Again, see *Plato*.

[3] Lewis thought that one of the greatest discourtesies a parent can do a child is be dogmatic, interrupting, contradictory, and ridiculing of the things the young take seriously. See *The Four Loves* (New York: Harcourt Brace Jovanovich, 1960) p. 66.

[4] George MacDonald, the Scottish divine and storyteller, was perhaps the greatest single influence on C. S. Lewis. In connection with the Professor's advice, Lewis elaborated on a MacDonald theme: "The door into life generally opens behind us," and "the only wisdom" for one "haunted with the scent of unseen roses, is work. This secret fire goes out when you use the bellows: bank it down with what seems the unlikely fuel of dogma and ethics, turn your back on it and attend to your duties, and then it will blaze." From *The Problem of Pain* (New York: Macmillan Publishing Co., 1962; London: Collins Fountain, 1977) p. 148, *136*.

5 A picture very similar to one of Lewis himself at the same age, his mother dead, his father emotionally so overwrought that the young Lewis distances himself from such display, his boyhood over except for holidays and vacations.

6 Digory's powers of perception are still not too affected by his own potential for the same character defect.

7 Lewis believed of his own male sex the inveterate weakness for extraordinary female beauty.

8 See also *Reductionism.*

9 One does not have to strain to imagine this desire coming from Lewis's own still unhealed heart.

10 Lewis intends to picture how a person moves from fear of God to love of God. "I am sure that God never teaches the fear of anything but Himself," said Lewis to his friend in *Letters to an American Lady,* Clyde S. Kilby, ed. (Grand Rapids: Wm. B. Eerdmans Publishing Co., 1967) p. 58. Other fears are, at their root, temptations to doubt God's providence.* Digory must learn first how just God is, and then how merciful.

11 Digory's expression, "sent on this message," is probably not a misprint for "mission"; "message" in the sense of "errand" is an allowed, if obsolete, meaning.

12 Her appeal to Digory is an echo of one of the most remarkable scenes in Lewis's earliest Christian book, *The Pilgrim's Regress* (Grand Rapids: Wm. B. Eerdmans Publishing Co., 1958) pp. 188–191, the temptation of the pilgrim John by the witch Luxuria (the Latin word for sexual pleasure). Luxuria's five-stage temptation is helpful background to understand what Lewis intends in this scene in MN.

13 This in itself would be a powerful temptation. Recall that Digory found Jadis very beautiful.

14 It may be that in this passage Lewis came to understand one of the deepest hurts he ever received in life: the death of his mother. At this moment Lewis himself was perhaps healed.

15 The American edition accidentally omits the line that identifies Digory as this man. The passage should read:

> He brought him next to a man whose golden beard flowed over his breast and whose face was full of wisdom. "And this," he said, "is the Lord Digory who was with her on that day. And this is my brother, King Edmund: and this my sister, the Queen Lucy."

16 Lewis concludes several of his books with this same theme. See especially *Mere Christianity* (New York: Macmillan Publishing Co., 1960; London: Collins Fount, 1977) p. 190, *188–189;* and *The Four Loves* (New York: Harcourt Brace Jovanovich, 1960) pp. 190–191.

DINOSAURS   See *Dragons, dinosaurs.*

D.L.F.   Abbreviation of "Dear Little Friend," the nickname[1] given Trumpkin* by Edmund. Used by all four children for such a long time that they almost forget what it means. This relating of time span to memory is one instance of Lewis's use of psychological realism in the *Chronicles.*

(PC 105, *97;* 114, *105;* 116, *106;* 122, *111–112;* 142, *128;* 156, *139;* 166, *148.*)

1 The use of acronyms as nicknames is a distinct custom among British schoolboys, thereby giving further credence to the thesis of the renowned Dorothy L. Sayers scholar, Dr. Barbara Reynolds, that the *Chronicles* are the product of an upper-class, Edwardian upbringing.

DOG-FOX   The oldest person present at the party in the woods, which the White Witch breaks up. A dog-fox is a male fox.

(LWW 111, *105–106.*)
[*Talking Beasts.*]

DOGS   Because he considered dogs "honest, humble persons,"[1] Lewis gave them a large part in the *Chronicles.* Their speech reflects doggy sounds:

"How, how? We'll help!" The sheepdog does its job of shepherding by organizing the newly liberated Narnians at the Castle of the White Witch* for their march to battle, and a hound gets the scent. The dogs use their teeth in battle with her forces. At the creation of Narnia,* a Bulldog is among those who tries to decide what form of creature Uncle Andrew* is, and in so doing has an interesting discussion with the She-Elephant about smells* and noses. True to his stubborn nature, he objects strongly on three different occasions. In LB a score of talking dogs are sent to look for Tirian.* Later, dogs are excited about the prospect of seeing Aslan. All fifteen talking dogs rally to Tirian's side in the Last Battle,* and are among those who pass into Aslan's country.* They are very excited about their new life there, and all the new smells. They track down Emeth,* and take exception to his deprecating use of the term "dog" (they call their misbehaving puppies "boys and girls").

(LWW 172, *159;* 174, *161;* 179, *165.* MN 124, *155–166;* 128, *119.* LB 18, 22; 105, *97;* 115–116, *106–107;* 154, *140;* 158–159, *144–145;* 166, *150;* 174, *157.*)

---

[1] C. S. Lewis, *Letters to an American Lady,* Clyde S. Kilby, ed. (Grand Rapids: William B. Eeerdmans Publishing Co., 1967) p. 38.

DOMESTICITY   The *Chronicles* are filled with the delights of domesticity. Elsewhere,[1] Lewis says that *The Wind in the Willows* is not escapism; rather, it makes us more fit to deal with the harshness of life because "the happiness which this kind of story presents to us is in fact full of the simplest and most attainable things—food, sleep,* exercise, friendship, the face of nature, even (in a sense) religion." In LWW Mr. and Mrs. Beaver* enjoy quite a comfy domestic scene, of which the children* are part. In HHB, the scene at the home of the three dwarf* brothers is almost a paean to domesticity. Through Shasta, Lewis contrasts Calormene* meals and homes to Narnian meals and homes, and quite prefers the coziness and homespun, homemade—clearly British—home of the Red Dwarfs.* In MN, after Digory feeds his mother the Apple* of Youth, he looks around him and sees "how ordinary and unmagical" things around him are.[2] In LB, Lewis calls the picture of Tirian,* Eustace, and Jill scrubbing the Calormene pigment off their faces a "homely sight." Jill longs for Narnia to have the "good, ordinary times" that Jewel* recounts in his "history"* of Narnia, which is filled with dances* and feasts. Even Aslan's country* does not exclude these homely delights: in Tirian's reconciliation with his father Erlian,* he remembers the "very smell* of the bread-and-milk he used to have for supper."

(LWW 66 ff., *67 ff.* HHB 166–169, *146–148.* MN 181, *168.* LB 86, *80;* 89, *81;* 177, *160.*)

---

[1] C. S. Lewis, "On Stories," OOW, p. 14.
[2] For Lewis's love of the ordinary, see *Lists,* note 1.

DONKEYS   The first donkey to be created participates in the animals'*
discussion about whether Uncle Andrew* is animal, vegetable, or mineral (he
thinks if Uncle Andrew is a tree,* then he is quite withered). In HHB, Aslan
transforms the unrepentant Rabadash* into a donkey. Puzzle* the donkey is
the unwilling false Aslan of LB. The donkey is a hieroglyph of the stubborn,
foolish, braying person. Puzzle is foolish but he could stand to be more
stubborn in his dealings with Shift.*

(HHB 210–213, *183–185.* MN 132–133, *122–123.* LB passim.)
[*Dumb Beasts; Horses; Talking Beasts.*]

DOORN   The most populated of the three Lone Islands.* Narrowhaven,* the capital of the Islands, is situated here. During the days of Governor Gumpas,* Narnian influence has so declined that courtesy* and cleanli-
ness are almost unknown on the island.

(VDT 29 ff., *35 ff.* [esp. 43, *51.*])
[*Geography, Narnian; Government.*]

DOORS   Doors are a recurrent Narnian motif. In LWW, the Pevensies
enter Narnia through the door of the wardrobe.* In PC, the children* and
the Telmarines* return through a door in the air; and in SC, the door of the
garden wall of Experiment House* leads to Narnia and Aslan's country.* In
VDT, Eustace, Edmund, and Lucy return from Narnia to England through
another door in the air. In LB, the door is an image of death.* The Stable*
Door is viewed darkly by Poggin* and Tirian* and Jill, but with hope by
Jewel,* who perceives that it may be the door to Aslan's country. This Door
is free-standing; it can be walked around and looked at, but when looked
through Old Narnia can be seen. Looked at, the door leads "from nowhere
to nowhere"; looked through, one can see the scene in front of the Stable.[1]
The Door flies open at Aslan's command, and good creatures begin to pour
through into Aslan's country. At the end of Narnia,* when the sea rises, it
never rises high enough to pass through the threshhold of the Door, and when
the giant* Time* snuffs out the sun,* Peter solemnly locks the Door with his
keys.*

(LWW 5, *12;* 7, *13;* 24, *30;* 49, *52;* 185, *170.* PC 208 ff., *183 ff.* SC 8–9, *17–18.*
LB 128, *117–118;* 139–140, *127–128;* 148, *135;* 153, *138;* 156, *142.*)
[*Transitions.*]

---

[1] See *Introduction* for the distinction between looking *at* and looking *along* or through.

DOUBLE STANDARD   See *Right and wrong; Sexism.*

DRAGON ISLAND   A country of mountainous cliffs and crags encir-
cling a bay, like a Norwegian fjord. The island is beautiful to look at but

---

inhospitable. It is here that Eustace finds a dead dragon*—probably the one who devoured Lord Octesian*—and becomes a dragon himself. It is also the scene of Eustace's conversion.* From his dragon's flight perspective, Eustace sees the island to be entirely mountainous and populated only by wild goats and swine.

(VDT 63 ff., 68 ff.)
[Geography, Narnian.]

DRAGONS, DINOSAURS

Dragons, the fire-breathing giant lizards of world mythology,* are certainly related to the giant lizards of prehistoric times. From the Greek word *drakon,* which means "to watch," dragons are usually guardians of some sort.[1] The dying dragon that Eustace encounters is guarding its pile of treasure. Edmund comments later that all dragons collect gold, and indeed it is in appropriating some of the golden treasure for himself that Eustace is transformed into a dragon. Lewis's dragon has a long snout the color of lead, claws made for tearing, a long tail, and bat-like wings. Its favorite food, when it can get it, is fresh dragon. In LWW, a stone dragon is one of the statues in the courtyard of the Castle of the White Witch.* In Underland,* Jill, Eustace, and Puddleglum see dozens of sleeping dragon- and bat-like creatures; at the End of Narnia,* these same beasts awake and go about clearing all life from Narnia. They grow old and die and their skeletons dot the dead countryside.

(LWW 92, 89. VDT 69 ff., 76 ff. SC 125, 126. LB 152, 138.)
[Greed.]

---

[1] In OOW, p. 37, Lewis compares to watchful dragons the kind of religion teacher who insists that his or her pupils have certain required feelings* about Christ and Christian truths. "An obligation to feel can freeze feelings," he says. One of the major reasons he wrote the *Chronicles* was to get past these watchful dragons by allowing children to have their own feelings about matters spiritual. See further comments in the *Introduction.*

DREAMS

Dreams play a large part in the *Chronicles.* Caspian, who misses his nurse* and hates life in Miraz's* castle, dreams of Old Narnia to console himself. In SC, Jill has anxious dreams in which she works out her fears over the possible failure of her quest.* She wants to believe Aslan is a dream so that she won't have to keep going; and her dream (which she does not consciously remember) in which the wooden horse turns into Aslan is perhaps not really a dream at all, but Aslan's way of encouraging her to remember the signs* and to continue. Life sometimes seems like a dream,[1] and the Queen of Underland* tries to make the three travelers think that their previous experience in Narnia was a dream (ironically, after leaving Underland, they think *it* was a dream). In MN, Strawberry compares his vague remembrance of his previous existance as a cabhorse to a dream, and when Helen* first enters Narnia she thinks she is dreaming. Tirian's* vision of the Seven Friends of Narnia* is like a dream in which he cannot make himself heard.

It is in VDT, in the experience of the Dark Island,* that the subject of dreams becomes most vivid, and Lewis considered this so important that he made several substantial changes in the text between the British and American editions of the book.² After the *Dawn Treader* emerges from the darkness, the British edition says: "And all at once everybody realized that there was nothing to be afraid of and never had been. They blinked their eyes and looked about them." In the American edition, Lewis deletes these two sentences entirely, thinking perhaps that he was making too little of the reality of what they were afraid of. He replaces these sentences with one long, beautiful metaphor simile:

"And just as there are moments when simply to lie in bed and see the daylight pouring through your window and to hear the cheerful voice of an early postman or milkman down below and to realize that *it was only a dream: it wasn't real,* is so heavenly that it was very nearly worth having the nightmare in order to have the joy of waking; so they all felt when they came out of the dark."

This is a major change: Lewis here is highlighting the joy* of waking.

The next change comes by way of an omission. Both editions print the expectation the crew has that the ship would be covered with grime and scum. The British edition goes on to say: "And then first one, and then another, began laughing. 'I reckon we've made pretty good fools of ourselves,' said Rynelf." The American edition deletes both sentences, thereby removing another denigration of the seriousness of night fears.

When Caspian asks what boon Lord Rhoop* wishes the King* to grant, the British edition prints:

'Never to bring me back there,' he said. He pointed astern. They all looked. But they saw only bright blue sea and bright blue sky. The Dark Island and the darkness had disappeared forever.
'Why!' cried Lord Rhoop. 'You have destroyed it!'
'I don't think it was us,' said Lucy.

Lewis reconstructs this entirely for the American edition:

"Never to ask me, nor to let any other ask me, what I have seen during my years on the Dark Island."
"An easy boon, my Lord," answered Caspian, and added with a shudder, *"Ask you: I should think not. I would give all my treasure *not* to hear it."

This is perhaps the greatest difference between the editions. The British edition says that our Dark Islands in life can be destroyed; the American edition is much more real in its assessment.

Finally the American edition, having deleted the destruction of the Dark Island, adds a parting note about the experience. Both editions print the sentence: "So all afternoon with great joy they sailed south-east with a fair wind." To this the American edition adds the independent clause: "and the hump of darkness grew smaller and smaller astern."

(PC 41, *44;* 52, *54.* VDT 154 ff., *154 ff.* SC 12, *22;* 66, *71;* 100–101, *103–104;* 154 ff., *151 ff.;* 197, *190.* HHB Chapter 6 passim. MN 122, *113;* 138, *127.* LB 42, *44.*)
[*Sleep.*]

---

[1] See *Plato.*

[2] It could be that between the time Lewis corrected the galleys of the British edition, and the time he corrected those for the American edition, he delivered his address, "On Three Ways of Writing for Children," to the Bournemouth Conference of the British Library Association, April 29 to May 2, 1952. In speaking to the objection that fairy tales are too violent for children, Lewis said: "I suffered too much from night-fears myself in childhood to undervalue this objection. I would not wish to heat the fires of that private hell for any child" (OOW, p. 30). See *Appendix One* and *Violence.*

DRINIAN   A Lord of Narnia and Captain of the *Dawn Treader.* The dark-haired Drinian is a straightforward man and a respected seaman. A stickler for fairness, he discusses with Edmund whether Eustace should be handicapped in some way to compensate for his greater size in his fight with Reepicheep. When he sets sail on a southeast course, he lets everyone not on duty rest. And like Caspian, he wants to board the slave ship and retake the captives. A good sailor, he rigs a jurymast in order to have some sail after the mainmast is brought down in the storm. Coriakin* uses Drinian's knowledge of geography* to make two magic* maps. The Captain's advice is always practical: he advises Caspian not to proceed into the darkness, and asks Reepicheep what practical use it would be to go further. A good leader, he does not hesitate to follow the albatross.* Lord Drinian is the third to tell Caspian that he cannot abdicate the throne, and he supports Rynelf's* comparison of this action with desertion on the part of any common sailor. In SC, Drinian is still in the court of King Caspian. He has become Prince Rilian's chief older friend, and has advised him to give up his quest* for the serpent. He is not taken in by the Queen of Underland,* recognizing her at once as evil.* When Rilian disappears, Drinian is mortified and tells his story to the King. Caspian moves to kill him with an axe and Drinian stands stock still, awaiting his death. But Caspian comes to his senses and lays down the axe, and the two old friends embrace and weep together.

(VDT 14 passim, *22 passim.* SC 50–52, *57–58.*)
[*Slave trade.*]

DRYADS   In Greek and Roman mythology,* wood nymphs* who live and die with the trees* of which they are the spirits. Their creation by Aslan is not specifically noted, but they appear to have come into being in response to Aslan's command for Narnia to awake. They are also part of the wild people of the wood. Dryads like to dance,* and are mentioned as dancing partners of fauns.* Physically they reflect the characteristics of their trees; for example, birch-girls are pale and head-tossing, and the beeches are regal. Perhaps the most poignant passage concerning Dryads is in LB, when a beech Dryad announces that forty of her brothers and sisters have been killed in the name of the false Aslan. As her tree is cut down, miles away, she too dies.[1]

Lewis never makes a clear distinction between Dryads, Hamadryads,* and Tree-people.* In LWW, he states that Tree-women and Dryads are synonymous, although in later use they seem to be separate entities. A case can be made for Tree-women also being Dryads, as Dryads are nymphs and nymphs are always female; but it is difficult to determine what Tree-men are. To add to the confusion, *dryad* is from the Latin *drus,* meaning "oak." Throughout the *Chronicles,* oaks are male. With the birch-girls and willow-women are oak-men and holly-men (who have wives, bright with berries).

(LWW 13, *20;* 92, *89;* 122, *115;* 132, *123;* 164, *152;* 166, *153.* PC 47, *50;* 76, *73;* 112, *103;* 134, *121;* 151–152, *136;* 184, *161.* VDT 16, *24.* SC 36, *43.* HHB 72, *68.* LB 16–17, *20–21.*)
[*Wood people.*]

---

[1] See also Lewis's poem "The Magician and the Dryad" in *Poems,* Walter Hooper, ed. (New York: Harcourt Brace Jovanovich, 1964) pp. 8–9.

DUFFERS   These simple, childish subjects of Coriakin,* also known as Monopods[1] and Dufflepuds, are invisible when first introduced in VDT. The Duffers (once common little dwarfs*) have a single center leg, three feet long, which ends in a large foot that resembles a canoe. They sleep with the foot raised in the air like an umbrella and curl up under it, looking very much like large toadstools. It is a shape Coriakin gave them as punishment when they refused to do what he asked. Thinking this shape ugly, they had the Chief Voice's* young daughter Clipsie* recite a spell to make them invisible. They echo every word of their fatuous leader. But according to Coriakin, it is better that they admire such a leader than admire no one at all. Their foolishness and immaturity show up in many ways: they do not know enough to grow their food, so Coriakin must order them to grow a garden; they water it from a spring rather than from the stream which flows from the spring right by the garden; they wash up the plates before dinner to save time afterwards; and they plant boiled potatoes so that they do not have to cook them afterwards. By the time the *Dawn Treader* lands on the island, they are tired of their invisibility* and threaten to harm Lucy and her companions if she does not read the visibility spell from the magician's Book* (a young girl is the only one who can work the charm). The visible Duffers are a delight to watch: they bounce along on their single feet, cheering for Lucy and agreeing with her opinion that they are not ugly even as they also agree with Chief Voice's opinion that they are. When Reepicheep addresses them as Monopods, they relish the name but cannot get it straight, corrupting it to Moneypuds, Pomonods, Poddymons. Finally, mixing it up with Duffers, they arrive at the name of Dufflepuds, which Lewis says they will probably be called for centuries (even though Narnia has little more than 140 years to go). Discovering, at Reepicheep's suggestion, that their feet made them very buoyant, they take great pleasure

Eustace weeps huge tears when he sees his dragonish reflection. He wishes more than anything to be human again and back with his companions. (VDT 74-75, 81.)

and pride in sailing about the harbor, much to the delight of the adventurers who teach them to race and play games. Only the Chief Voice, perhaps because his authority is threatened, refuses to participate in the fun, warning his fellow Duffers that the water is "powerful wet." As the *Dawn Treader* moves to the north of the harbor, the Duffers accompany it with cheers, and Rynelf* coins a simile for his shipmates, "as silly as those Dufflepuds."

(VDT 112 ff., *114 ff.;* 139 ff., *140 ff.;* 184, *180.*)
[*Land of the Duffers.*]

---

[1] Lewis may have first met the idea of monopods in Pliny's *Natural History* (Book VII, ii, 23), which he studied as a teenager, or in St. Augustine's *City of God* (Book XVI, Chapter 8). Around the time Lewis was writing VDT (second half of 1949), he also wrote a poem which mentions monopods: "The Adam Unparadised," *Poems,* Walter Hooper, ed. (New York: Harcourt Brace Jovanovich, 1964) p. 43.

DUFFLE   The Red Dwarf who rescues Shasta from the indecisive animals* and takes charge. A practical person, he notices Shasta's hunger, mutters a reproach against himself and his neighbors for their inhospitality, and hustles the boy off to a breakfast with Rogin and Bricklethumb, Duffle's brothers. Their home life is the very icon of the loveliness of the ordinary. Any meaning their names might have (*duffle* is a kind of coarse cloth, and *brickle* is an adjective meaning "fragile") is secondary to the quaint, friendly sound the names have.

(HHB 165–169, *145–148.*)
[*Dwarfs; Domesticity.*]

DUFFLEPUDS   See *Duffers.*

DUMB BEASTS   The animals* of Narnia who do not have the gift of speech,* and who are given by Aslan into the care of the Talking Beasts.* Dumb and witless animals are smaller than Talking Beasts—indeed, they are the size of normal animals—and are always grave. Though like all Narnians they are to be respected, it is permitted to kill them for food. Thus Eustace, Jill, and Puddleglum must hunt birds for food, and a hunter has killed the dumb lion* whose skin is worn by Puzzle.* In instructing the Talking Beasts on their responsibilities, Aslan tells them not to go back to their dumb ways.[1] In LB, the reduction of Ginger* to dumbness awakens in all the Talking Beasts their "greatest terror": that any beast who is not good will be struck dumb.[2]

(MN 118, *109;* 119, *110.* SC 71, 76. LB 5–6, *11;* 109, *101.*)
[*Hunting; Reductionism.*]

---

[1] In PC (116–117; *106–107*) the Pevensie children and Trumpkin are stalked by a wild bear, who is killed by the dwarf* just in the nick of time. At this point in Narnian history, so long past the Golden Age,* many Talking Beasts have gone dumb and it is often impossible to tell the two apart. Lucy ponders how awful it would be if human beings could become wild inside but still look the same on the outside. The ever-practical Susan cuts her off, saying they have enough problems as it is. The implication is that this has already happened in our own world, as evidenced

by the tendency to reduce the highest aspirations of humanity to material and technological terms.

[2] Apparently, this edict can also apply to human beings, as in the case of Rabadash.* Although he is repeatedly warned by Aslan, he insists on calling upon Tash* to bring destruction on the Narnians, for which transgression he is turned literally into the figurative ass he has always been. Similarly, the pig-like boys taught by the schoolmistress of the unnamed town* in PC actually become pigs.

DWARFS   One of the Nine Classes of Narnian Creatures* listed by Doctor Cornelius,* this race of subhuman beings comes into existence at Aslan's command for Narnia to awake in MN, figures prominently in PC and LWW (but scarcely in VDT, SC, and HHB), and (after its ranks are thinned by Aslan's judgment) passes into Aslan's country.*

There are three kinds of dwarfs in Narnia: Red Dwarfs, Black Dwarfs,[1] and Duffers.* The Duffers are the smallest and least distinguished of the three; the Red and Black Dwarfs are three to four feet tall, deep-chested, and stocky. All species are bearded, the Red Dwarfs with hair like foxes' and the Black Dwarfs with hard, thick, dark, horse*-like hair. With the exception of the Duffers, Narnian dwarfs are miners, smiths, and metal craftsmen. They excel as tailors and are noted woodsmen. In war, they are fierce axe-wielders and deadly archers, marching and communicating by the sound of drums. In peace, Red Dwarfs are treasure-seekers and love wild dances* and rich feasts and brightly colored clothes (the peacetime activities of the Black Dwarfs are not described, but it is presumed that they are hard workers, though not given to revelry*). No dwarf wives are mentioned but one of the results of the ending of the Hundred Years of Winter* is that young dwarfs will not have to go to school.*

The chief difference between the two main species of dwarfs is seen in their reaction to Aslan in PC: at their first sight of the Lion, the Red Dwarfs are open-mouthed and speechless though they know he has come as a friend, but the Black Dwarfs begin "to edge away." Trumpkin,* Rogin, Bricklethumb, Duffle,* and the Seven Brothers of the Shuddering Wood* are the chief exemplars of the traits of Red Dwarfs. It is to be noted that only groups of Red Dwarfs are called brothers; Black Dwarfs, though they may live together, don't seem to have fraternal feelings. Nikabrik,* Griffle,* Diggle,* and the White Witch's driver are clearly Black Dwarfs. From their feistiness and dry wit, it would appear that the two dwarfs in the Narnian embassy to Tashbaan in HHB are Red. It is not at all clear to what species Poggin* belongs; and since at least one of the renegade dwarfs in the Last Battle* does come into Aslan's country through the Door* of judgment (this one dwarf is not to be confused with the group of dwarfs *thrown* through the door by the Calormene* soldiers), we cannot therefore presume that Poggin or these are Red.

The Talking Beasts* have their own opinions about the dwarfs. Mrs. Beaver* says she knows good dwarfs; but her husband, after admitting that he knows some good ones too, says that their numbers are very few and these are the least like men. Trufflehunter* finds that dwarfs are as forgetful and changeable as humans.* He adds, in defense of Doctor Cornelius,* that dwarfs and half-dwarfs are much less different than are Talking Beasts from Dumb Beasts.*

DWARFS

Concerning half-dwarfs, Doctor Cornelius is the only named example; Caspian's nurse* may also have dwarf blood. During the years of Telmarine* oppression, the dwarfs tried to disguise their race by, in some instances, intermarrying with the conquering humans. The Black Dwarfs consider the half-dwarfs traitors worthy of death.*

Caspian and his son Rilian are especially deferential to dwarfs; the former names Trumpkin his regent and the latter, upon his release from Underland* and his reception of the creatures' obeisance, addresses the oldest of the dwarfs as "father" and seeks his counsel. This mirrors Aslan's own respect when he chooses a dwarf to be a member of the first council (for protecting Narnia against Jadis). Aslan calls upon them to fashion crowns for King Frank* and Queen Helen*; and dwarfs are the King's trainbearers.

The story of the treachery of the renegade dwarfs in LB is one of the saddest in the *Chronicles*. Manifesting the hyper-suspicion their race is prone to and their tendency to follow a leader doggedly (witness the Duffers and their Chief Voice*), the dwarfs echo Griffle's declaration of independence and take up a refrain that is chanted five times in the last half of LB: "The Dwarfs are for the Dwarfs." This harks back to Nikabrik's continuous complaint that his forces are being sacrificed for the protection of Caspian's army in the War of Deliverance.* Because Nikabrik refuses to be "taken in," his ancestors are condemned to repeat their history. Aslan's verdict (that they have rendered themselves incapable of help, chosen cunning instead of faith, locked themselves into the prison of their minds, and are therefore, in the fear* of being taken in, never to be taken out) is strongly reminiscent of the fate of the wise men in Lewis's *Pilgrim's Regress* who have proved conclusively to themselves that the deep desire of the soul has no fulfillment; they are left in limbo, "the twilit porches of the black hole."[2] The renegade dwarfs are last seen "crowded together in their imaginary Stable.*" Nothing further is known of their fate.

(LWW 13, *20;* 27, *33;* 111, *105;* 114, *107–108;* 130, *122;* 149, *138;* 164, *152;* 166, *153;* 174, *161;* 179, *165;* 180, *166.* PC 30, *36;* 33, *39;* 47–49, *50–52;* 63 ff., *63 ff.;* 73, *71;* 83, *80;* 104, *97;* 110, *102;* 199, *175.* VDT 144, *144.* SC 29, *36;* 192 ff., *186 ff.* HHB 68 ff., *51 ff.* MN 117, *109;* 119, *111;* 167, *154;* 171–172, *158–159.* LB 7, *12–13;* 18, *22;* 63, *62;* 67, *65;* 68 ff., *65 ff.;* 104, *96;* 111, *103;* 120, *112;* 126–127, *116–117;* 144 ff., *131 ff.;* 154, *140;* 158, *144.*)
[*Creation of Narnia; End of Narnia; Five Black Dwarfs; Mythology; Salamanders of Bism.*]

---

[1] Red and Black Dwarfs had been metaphors in Lewis's imagination since at least 1934 when in *The Pilgrim's Regress* (Grand Rapids: Wm. B. Eerdmans Publishing Co., 1958) p. 104, the red dwarfs represented the Marxists and the black the Fascists. This particular imagery is not operative in the Narnian dwarfs; but a division according to character is apparent from the Lefay* Fragment (the first draft of MN that Lewis attempted in the Spring of 1942, right after LWW was completed), in which Red Squirrels* (friendly) and Grey (vicious) are distinguished (PWD, pp. 50–52).

[2] *The Pilgrim's Regress,* pp. 178–180.

EARTHMEN   Inhabitants of Underland* and natives of Bism. These pale gnomes[1] come in all shapes and sizes, from less than a foot high to over seven feet tall, and have all sorts of faces—one even has a horn in the middle of its[2] head. They are all profoundly sad and silent. Perenially busy, they move in closely packed groups with padding, shuffling steps. While Jill is gripped with a desire to cheer them up, Puddleglum is delighted to be among such serious people. The Warden of the Marches of Underland* leads a group of one hundred Earthmen armed with three-pronged spears. They do the work of the Queen of Underland,* and have been digging a tunnel to within only a few feet of the Overworld, through which she and Rilian intend to conquer the updwellers. When the Queen has been killed and the enchantments lifted, the Earthmen are freed from her spell to become their true selves—fun-loving, jig-dancing, somersaulting, fire-cracker-firing people who shout in loud voices and dart all over the place. Golg* reveals that they were taken from Bism, deep inside the earth, to become slaves in Underland—what they call the Shallow Lands. Once they remember who they really are, they rejoice that the witch is dead and plan to return home.

(SC Chapter 10 passim; 137, *137;* 148, *148;* Chapter 13 passim; Chapter 14 passim.)

---

[1] According to Paracelsus, gnomes inhabit the element earth. For a more detailed discussion, see *Salamanders of Bism,* note 1.

[2] Although they are named "Earth*men,*" the impersonal pronoun "it" is used by Lewis throughout all appearances or discussions of these gnomes.

EARTHQUAKES   Portents of the coming of the end of Narnia,* especially in LB.[1] When Shift* professes his disbelief the earth shakes, a sign Puzzle* rightly interprets as a sign* that he should not be wearing the lion's* skin. Shift, on the other hand, interprets it to be a confirmation of his plan. Another earthquake is felt at Shift's destruction, and again when Rishda* is thrown into the Stable.* The earth trembles as Aslan approaches the dwarfs* and Aslan growls so mightily at Emeth's* restatement of Shift's lie (that Aslan and Tash* are one) that the earth shakes. In MN, the sound of the golden bell* intensifies until an earthquake destroys the room in which Digory and Polly stand.

(LB 11, 16–17; 115, 106; 131, 120; 146, 134; 165, 149. MN 52, 51–52.)
[Aslan's voice.]

---

[1] Mark 13:8 notes earthquakes as one of the signs of the end of the world.

EASTERN SEA   The ocean that is the eastern border for Narnia, Archenland,* and Calormen.* Aslan's country*[1] is east of this body of water. Where it borders Narnia, the Eastern Sea is saltwater and inhabited by the amphibious Mer-People*; bordering the last wave of the Last Sea* and the plain at the World's End,* its waters are sweet and inhabited by the Sea People.*

(LWW 10, 17; 121, 114; 174, 160. PC 56, 56. VDT passim.)

---

[1] Aslan's country does not connect with any created world.

ECOLOGY   Ecology is the harmony of nature, and the disruption of this harmony in Narnia is always a sign that something is fundamentally wrong. As Edmund is wandering through the forest alone, having already fallen under the spell of the White Witch's Turkish Delight,* he daydreams about what he will do when he is king*:[1] make decent roads, inaugurate railway lines, and make laws against beavers* and dams. In MN, Uncle Andrew* thinks along the same lines: impressed by the fertility of the newly created Narnia, he can hardly wait to begin commercial exploitation of its resources. The Telmarines'* rule is especially marked by disregard for nature: they have felled trees,* defiled the streams, and forced the Dryads* and Naiads*—the very souls and spirits of nature—to retreat into a deep sleep.* The bridge at the fords of Beruna* is also seen as a human imposition on nature, and the River-god* calls it his "chains." At Aslan's command, it is destroyed and reclaimed by nature through the powers of Bacchus.* In LB, the degeneration of society is highlighted by the wholesale felling of talking trees, and the mining of ore by slave labor.

(PC 76, 73; 193, 169.)

---

[1] See Technology, note 1.

EDITH WINTERBLOTT   See Gang, the.

EDMUND PEVENSIE   The second son and third child of Mr. and Mrs. Pevensie,* first a traitor and later King Edmund the Just in the Golden Age of Narnia,* who grows from the sensual, difficult, jealous nine or ten year old in LWW to the handsome and brave twenty-four-year-old king of HHB and the helpful and playful nineteen-year-old youth who is mortally hurt in the railway accident in LB.

Edmund's story begins when he has been separated from his parents by the Second World War. He has been attending a bad school,* which has had a negative effect on him. He is struggling with his older brother Peter, who is always considered better than he, and his older sister Susan, who has appropriated to herself the role of his mother. The only person he ranks above is his younger sister Lucy. Out of this tangle of sibling relationships comes his will to power, his desire to have life his own way. Lewis doesn't try to make the reader feel too sympathetic toward Edmund—he has designed him to be the temporary villain—but Edmund's insecurity, fostered by his war-time dislocation, could make any child a difficult case until he knows he is loved. LWW is the story of both his treachery and his redemption.

Even from the animals* Edmund gets excited about, the reader senses that the boy might be the "bad apple in the barrel."[1] Edmund is seduced by the evil* magic* in the Turkish Delight* the White Witch offers him. And his vanity,* together with the enchantment he is now under, makes him not only try to disguise the fact that he is feeling ill from having eaten too many sweets, but also to commit one of the most despicable acts in the *Chronicles:* he lies about his and Lucy's experience of Narnia, letting her down terribly.[2] His whining question, "How do we know . . . ?" is a refrain throughout the journey to Tumnus's* cave and beyond, to the Beavers'* home.[3]

Because of his enchanted suspicion (rather than faith), Edmund feels only a mysterious horror at the sound of Aslan's name.* His longing,* focused on the power and the pleasure the Witch has promised him, is not open to Mr. and Mrs. Beaver's explanation of the prophecies* and of Aslan. He leaves to accomplish his betrayal of his brother and sisters into the Witch's hands before he hears the explanation of who she is. Lewis is careful to distinguish Edmund's motives at this point: he doesn't want any real harm to come to them but (besides power and pleasure) he does want revenge on Peter, and for the Witch to prefer him to the others. But "deep down inside"[4] he really knows how cruel and evil she is. As he trudges across the frozen landscape to her castle,* he consoles himself with the thoughts of how he can use technology to transform Narnia into what he considers a better place. This planning is a distraction from his earlier desire to give up because of the hardships of his journey and return to make peace with his siblings. He blames Peter for all of his woes.

Arriving at the Witch's castle, he ought to know from the instinctive fear he feels that he should not go ahead with his plan. His guilty conscience is awakened by the sight of the stone lion in her courtyard; but he goes against his conscience by disfiguring the statue and proceeding with his treachery. It is only when the Witch shows her real cruelty on their journey to the Stone Table* that he begins to experience a change of heart: he wants to be a loving and beloved brother again.[5] And he finds no comfort in trying to call all this a bad dream.* It is only when the Witch petrifies the celebrating Narnians that Edmund's conversion really manifests itself in full force: "for the first time"* he feels sorry for someone other than himself. The spring that is bursting forth all around him in Narnia is also happening inside him. Perhaps his winter is equivalent to the time he has spent in school.

After he is freed by Aslan's forces, he and the Lion have a private conversation and then he is reintroduced to his siblings. And though the Witch calls him a traitor, Edmund keeps his eyes fixed on Aslan[6] and instinctively knows that he is expected only to wait and obey. He breaks the Witch's wand* in the first part of the battle, but suffers a wound thereafter. When Lucy heals him with her cordial,* not only does he recover from the injury, but he is rejuvenated as a person. It is possible that Lucy won her argument with Susan and told Edmund what Aslan did for him, for he grows up to be a graver and quieter man than Peter.

When Caspian's winding of Susan's horn* calls the Pevensies back into Narnia at the beginning of PC, Edmund is the second to feel the pull of its magic. He is excited about not having to return to his studies and about having an experience similar to the books* he has been reading about people being shipwrecked and finding fresh water and food in the forests.[7] Compared with his first visit to Narnia, Edmund is delighted to be there; when he is asked to decide whether or not they should follow Lucy, he remembers his betrayal of her in LWW and sides with her. He's not at all happy about losing a night's sleep*; but he follows her nonetheless, and is the second person to be favored with the sight of Aslan. Aslan salutes him with a vigorous "Well done" and breathes on him; an air of greatness henceforth hangs on him, something apparent even to Glozelle* and Sopespian,* Miraz's* treacherous lords. His nobility is also apparent in his genuine sorrow over the fact that Peter and Susan aren't going to be allowed to return to Narnia again.

In HHB King Edmund, on embassy to Tashbaan* with his sister Queen Susan, is the first Narnian adult that Shasta sees and the first adult that Shasta admires. When, in Chapter 12, Shasta is introduced to Edmund, the King assures the boy that he is not a traitor for overhearing their plans—Edmund knows what betrayal is really about. Edmund is furious with Corin* for fighting with his guardian, the dwarf* Thornbut,* against Edmund's order that the boy should not take part in the battle to defend Anvard* against Rabadash.* But he himself has to be restrained by King Lune* from dignifying Rabadash's treacherous attack by accepting the Calormene* prince's challenge. By the time Rabadash's fate is discussed, Edmund is calm enough to remember that traitors may mend if given mercy.

Edmund's reaction to his cousin Eustace is what any regular boy's might be to a boy who is very difficult to get along with. But in the course of VDT he comes to appreciate his cousin as one who has been saved by Aslan from being a really terrible person. He can empathize with Eustace, knowing first-hand what paradoxical pleasure there is in having one's dragon-self pulled away from one like a scab.[8] Edmund is both the scientific observer (he can tell that it would be impossible to lift the solid gold statue from the the bottom of the pool on Deathwater Island* and he is eager to discover what sort of creatures inhabit the Land of the Duffers*) and the natural leader (as Caspian is learning further how to be king* on this voyage). It is a testimony to the extent of Edmund's conversion that he rebukes Caspian for his greed. On Ramandu's Island* he has had enough experience with witches to know that things aren't always what they seem, and so he is tentative about eating at

Aslan's Table*; his question to the Daughter of Ramandu,* "How do we know you are a friend?" is an echo of his questions about Mr. Beaver in LWW. For Edmund, the most exciting moment of the voyage is the sunrise on this island. The scientist in him quarrels with Lucy's description of the smell* of the island as "a dim, purple" fragrance; and he sets her straight when she confuses the Mer-People* and the Sea-People.* And he discusses the difference between a flat world and a round world with Caspian.[9] When Caspian wants to abdicate, Edmund asserts his ancient title for the second time[10] and compares Caspian's proposal to Ulysses's loss of reason under the influence of the song of the Sirens.

Edmund shares with Lucy and Eustace the vision of the Lamb* at World's End.* It is in answer to Edmund's question that Aslan reveals Lewis's intention for writing the *Chronicles.* [11] And in LB Peter introduces Tirian* to Edmund, one of the Seven Friends of Narnia.*[12] Since he is the kind of person who actually understands railway schedules—another hint at his scientific bent—he is the one who explains about the railway accident. Along with the others, he grows in understanding of the meaning of the place they are in. He and Eustace agree on the description of many geographical features and about how unusual it is to swim up a waterfall; but it is Edmund who senses the inner meaning of it all. Tumnus explains to him the mystery of why Professor Kirke's house* is still standing in the England* that they see. Edmund then sees his parents. When Aslan meets the procession that Edmund is part of, the Lion explains not—as they expect—that they will have to return to their world, but that they are never to return there. Edmund recognizes in Aslan the one whom he has gotten to know by his earthly name.

---

[1] It must be presumed that Lewis made the change in the American editions of LWW that replaces the *foxes* that Edmund is excited about on p. 10 of the British edition with *snakes* on p. 3. (The British Susan prefers *rabbits,* while the American Susan enthuses about *foxes,* perhaps a veiled reference to her desire for a high social life, riding to the hounds, and the like.)

[2] This is comparable to Digory's violence to Polly in the royal hall at Charn.*

[3] This skepticism or suspicion comes from Edmund's inability to enjoy Narnia (to look along) in his present condition; he is only seeing or contemplating (looking at) from his enchanted perspective. He hasn't the faith of Lucy or even the beginnings of faith that Peter and Susan have. This same spell is the one the Queen of Underland* tries to cast on the travelers in SC: she would like them to look at the terms they are using to describe their experience (sun,* Narnia, Aslan) rather than to remember the reality of what they had enjoyed in Overworld. See *Introduction.*

[4] See *Right and wrong.*

[5] Recall that it is a similar alienation that moves the dragon* Eustace to seek fellowship with his fellow voyagers.

[6] See *Aslan.*

[7] The *right* books, Lewis might add, ones about adventures. Compare what Eustace is reading at this time.

[8] At this point, Edmund makes the only explicit profession of faith in the *Chronicles.* See *Credal elements.*

[9] See *Astronomy, Narnian* and *Imagination.* Lewis raises this point to reawaken in the reader the wonder of living on a round world, and also to kindle an interest in the medieval worldview.

[10] The other time was on Deathwater Island.*

[11] See *Introduction.*

[12] However, he is *not* the man with the golden beard and wise face. The American edition accidentally omits a line that identifies this handsome man as Lord Digory. Edmund is not described in LB.

EDUCATION   See *Schools.*

EFREETS   Evil* spirits, allied with the White Witch and present at the slaying of Aslan. The word is a variant of *afreet,* which denotes an evil demon or monster of Islamic mythology.* They are often associated with ghouls.*

(LWW 148, *138.*)

ELECTION   See *Aslan,* note 4.

ELEPHANTS   A male and female elephant are created together by Aslan; one of them emerges like a small earthquake* from the biggest of the humps in the ground. The He-Elephant is one of the participants in Aslan's First Council,* and the She-Elephant joins the other beasts in exploring Uncle Andrew.* She speculates that Uncle Andrew might be an animal,* although his nose isn't quite up to the standards set by *her* nose. She and the Bulldog (who has a nose of quite another sort) have a humorous exchange about the meaning of noses and smelling. When Uncle Andrew is planted, on the chance that he may be a tree,* she fills her trunk with water and waters his withered form until he comes to. Just before Fledge* leaves for the garden,* both he and the elephant express their mutual desire that the elephant not ride on the horse's* back. Both elephants, with some dwarfs,* help to dismantle Uncle Andrew's cage.

(MN 114, *106;* 111, *119;* 131–133, *122–124;* 146, *135;* 168–169, *156.*)
[*Andrew Ketterley; Dogs; Smells; Talking Beasts; Vanity; Vivisection.*]

EMETH   The noble Calormene* Tarkaan* who yearns to serve Tash* and ultimately embraces—and is embraced by—Aslan. *Emeth* is the Hebrew word for "faithful, true," and this is a deliberate reference by Lewis, for he was well aware of the meaning.[1] This junior officer is a darkly handsome young man, the son of Harpha* of Tehishbaan,* and has yearned since his youth to serve Tash.* He wants finally to meet him face to face, even if this should mean death*; and convinced that the real* Tash is inside, he enters the Stable* Door.* Once inside, he discovers that his instinctive understanding of Shift's* plot is correct; he slays the Calormene assassin and throws the body outside. Finding himself in a sunlit world, he assumes it is Tash's country and goes in search of his god.* Actually, however, it is Aslan's country,* and he finds Aslan, whom he recognizes as a great Lion. Emeth claims to be unworthy because he has served Tash all his life, but Aslan says that he will account it as service to himself. (This circumstance is not unexpected, and was foreshadowed by Jewel's* earlier comment that the Calormene was "worthy of a better god than Tash.") Emeth's mystical sense is indicated in his sentiment, "It is better to see the Lion and die than to be Tisroc* of the world and not to have seen him."

(LB 110–112, *102–103;* 142–143, *129–130;* 159, *145;* 161 ff., *146 ff.*)
[*Universalism.*]

¹ See C. S. Lewis, *Reflections on the Psalms* (New York: Harcourt Brace Jovanovich, 1958) pp. 60–61.

EMPEROR-BEYOND-THE-SEA¹   Aslan's Father, author of the Deep Magic* and the Deeper Magic* against which Aslan cannot work. In almost every instance where an explanation of Aslan is given, the formula, "the great Lion, the son of the great Emperor-beyond-the-Sea," is used. The Sea here is the Eastern Sea* and "beyond" suggests both Aslan's country* and the transcendence, or greatness, of God.*² The Emperor is never visualized, but his sceptre* is mentioned. In the remarkable scene of Shasta walking in the night fog, his voice is heard as the first "Myself" pronounced by the Large Voice in deep, low, earthshaking tones. The White Witch is the Emperor's hangman, according to Mr. Beaver*; and he is correct in this assessment: death* works by means of God's permissive will. In Aslan's name* and in the name of the Emperor, one of the Seven Kings and Queens,* most likely the High King Peter, dismisses Tash* to go to his "own place" (that is, hell*).

(LWW 75, *75;* 138–139, *128–129.* PC 39, *43;* 91, *86.* VDT 92, *98.* HHB 160, *140.* LB 133, *121.*)
[*Credal elements; Holy Spirit; Trinity.*]

¹ "Emperor-over-Sea" (printed both with and without hyphens) is used interchangeably with "Emperor-beyond-the-Sea" throughout the *Chronicles* in both the British and the American editions.
² There is no mention in the *Chronicles* of where the Emperor might live. Nowhere is he connected with Aslan's country; and we can only guess, on analogy with Christian theology and mythology* on this subject, that he is the ultimate goal of the "farther up and farther in" process. There is, however, one tantalizing clue, found on the last page of VDT, when Aslan tears a door* open in the sky and Edmund, Eustace, and Lucy have a momentary glimpse of a "terrible white light from beyond the sky." In the *Chronicles,* Lewis is trying to restore the medieval worldview; it is always in the background. In this worldview, the spherical earth is the centermost of nine spheres (one for each of the then-known "planets," one for the stars, and one for the "First Movable"). Outside of this system is Heaven itself, full of the light and love of God. (For a fuller explanation of this worldview, see Lewis's *Discarded Image* [London: Cambridge University Press, 1964] pp. 92–121, esp. pp. 96–7.) Because Lewis also has this in mind when he describes Dr. Ransom's experience of an outer space filled with an excess of light, it is quite possible that the three children are seeing into "the very heaven" where the Emperor joyfully reigns. (For Dr. Ransom's experience, see Lewis's *Out of the Silent Planet* [New York: Macmillan Publishing Co., 1965] pp. 29–32.)

ENCORE   See *Right and wrong.*

END OF NARNIA   At Aslan's command, a series of apocalyptic events heralds the end of Narnia. The giant* Time* winds his horn* and the stars* fall from the heavens. The dragons* and dinosaurs round up all living¹ things and send them scurrying toward the stable* door.* When all are safely inside, they eat all the forests until there is nothing left but dead rock. The sea rises, as does the dying red sun.* The moon rises in the wrong position, too close to the sun, which absorbs her. The giant squeezes the sun out, and all is ice-cold, total darkness.

(LB 150 ff., *136 ff.*)
[*Biblical allusions; Creation of Narnia; Father Time.*]

---

[1] There is no general resurrection of the dead or a general judgment at the end of Narnia, though these are both implied.

END OF THE WORLD   See *Eschatology.*

END OF TIME   See *Eschatology.*

ENGLAND   An island nation of western Europe, the birthplace of the Seven Friends of Narnia* and Susan. As seen from the perspective of Narnia, it is less real, and is twice referred to as "that other place." Things Narnian are larger than life when seen against the English sky: Queen Jadis looks more beautiful, fiercer, and wilder in London than she does in Charn*; the Apple* of Youth is filled with a glory that causes earthly things to pale in comparison; and when Jill, Eustace, Caspian, and Aslan come charging out of Narnia and into Experiment House,* the effect is so disconcerting that it causes the Head* to become hysterical. According to Digory, England is only a shadow of something in Aslan's country.* When Peter, Edmund, and Lucy see England and Professor Kirke's house* from the garden,* Tumnus* explains that they are "looking at the . . . inner England [where] no good thing is destroyed."

(LWW 181, *167.* PC 24, *30.* SC 35, *42.* MN 180, *166.* LB 169, *153–154;* 181, *163–164.*)
[*Plato.*]

EPISTEMOLOGY   See *Knowledge.*

ERIMON   One of the great Telmarine* Lords under Caspian IX.* He is executed with Arlian and a dozen other lords under false charges of treason invented by Miraz.*

(PC 56, *56.*)

ERLIAN   Father of Tirian*; second to the last King* of Narnia. Erlian and Tirian are reunited at the Great Reunion* in the real Narnia. In Aslan's country,* Erlian is transformed into a hearty young man, the father Tirian remembers from his youth. The charged emotional quality of Erlian's embrace of his son is unique among the parent-child relationships in the *Chronicles.* Tirian's memories* in conjunction with the reunion are of childhood pleasures so similar to Lewis's own that it is very likely this scene is Lewis's literary reconciliation with his own father.

(LB 177–178, *160.*)
[*Adults; Autobiographical allusions; Jewel.*]

Coriakin the Magician and Lucy can't help laughing at the antics of the Duffers. Visible once more, they are hopping about on their monopods like enormous fleas. (VDT 142-143, 143.)

ESCHATOLOGY   In Christian theology, the study or science of what happens at the end of time.* The "four last things" are: death,* judgment, hell,* and heaven. To live with an eschatological perspective is to live with the expectation that one will die, will be judged, and will enter into either hell or heaven. The first oblique reference to this framework in the *Chronicles* is the expectation that Lord Octesian's* arm-ring will hang on Dragon Island* "till that world ends."[1] The second indirect reference is given by the Daughter of Ramandu,* when she says of the Stone Knife* that it is kept on Aslan's Table* "while the world lasts." In SC, the Warden of the Marches of Underland* repeats the saying that the sleeping beasts and Father Time* "will wake at the end of the world." In the Hermit's* reply to Hwin's question about whether Aravis will survive the Lion's attack, Lewis raises the reader's eyes to the large scope he envisions for the *Chronicles:* "I do not know whether any man or woman or beast in the whole world will be alive when the sun* sets tonight." LB begins appropriately on an apocalyptic note: "In the last days of Narnia . . . " This dying world is marked by the absence of Aslan (and the doubt by many Narnians that he ever existed), and the consequent absence of faith, hope, and longing.* Jewel* says, "This is the end of all things." Jill expresses the hope that, unlike earth, Narnia will go on forever; but Jewel declares to her that "all worlds draw to an end; except Aslan's own country." Roonwit's* dying message is "To remember that all worlds draw to an end and that noble death is a treasure which no one is too poor to buy." Ultimately, Narnia does come to an end, and the creatures of Narnia confront Aslan's judgment before they can pass through the Door.* They must look into Aslan's face; about this they have no choice. Some look at Aslan with hatred, and these disappear into the blackness of his shadow. Others look at Aslan with love, and these are allowed to pass through the Door[2] into Aslan's country.*

(VDT 93, *99;* 173, *170.* SC 126, *126.* HHB 141–142, *125.* LB 1, *7;* 10, *16;* 20, *24;* 24–25, 28–29; 74, *70;* 87, *80;* 89, *81;* 91, *85;* 152, *138;* 158, *144.*) [*End of Narnia.*]

---

[1] The more overt intimations of the world's end do not really begin until HHB. If one accepts the thesis that Lewis originally planned to finish with VDT, then it is apparent that he did not have the eschatological framework of the last three books firmly in mind until HHB.

[2] This is Lewis's evocation of the process of *election,* by which one condemns oneself either to heaven or to hell. Rishda,* for example, condemns himself to "Tash's* own place" by his disbelief in anyone but himself. Emeth* has worshipped Tash all of his life, but he has unknowingly and sincerely worshipped the qualities that rightly belong to Aslan. Indeed, he immediately recognizes Aslan and Aslan's supremacy when he first sets eyes on the Lion; thus he passes into Aslan's country by his own election. See *Aslan,* note 4.

ETTINS   That they are evil* giants* is evidenced by the fact that they are members of the White Witch's party and present at the slaying of Aslan. *Ettin* is another form of the word *eten* (both words mean "giant" and both are obsolete). This is another instance of Lewis's use of old words to evoke the flavor of ancient times in England and Northern Europe.

(LWW 148, *138.*)

ETTINSMOOR The territory north of the River Shribble* and south of Harfang,* near the Ruined City.* It is mentioned first by Glimfeather* as being on Eustace and Jill's path to the North. Puddleglum points out some "hills and bits of cliff" as the beginning of Ettinsmoor, and tells Eustace and Jill that giants* live there. Countless streams cover the moor. The name is derived from *ettin,* an obsolete form of the word *eten,* which means "giant"; and *moor,* [1] an open expanse of fertile land.

(SC 53, 59; 62–63, 68; Chapter 6 passim.)
[*Ettins; Geography, Narnian.*]

---

[1] In the British edition of LB *(153),* Lewis spells the word "Ettinsmuir." *Muir* is another form of *moor,* and it is likely that he forgot how he had spelled it in the earlier books.

EUSTACE CLARENCE SCRUBB[1] The only child and son of Harold* and Alberta* Scrubb, and a cousin of the Pevensie children. He is a victim of his parents' untraditional ways of childraising and of his schooling at Experiment House,* but is reformed in VDT by being transformed into a dragon* (the outer form of his inner disposition), and is transformed again by Aslan himself. Jill's friend and fellow adventurer in SC and one of the Seven Friends of Narnia* in LB, he is one of the most memorable characters created by C. S. Lewis.

A precocious and obnoxious nine year old, Eustace's imagination* and sense of adventure* have been stunted by his upbringing.[2] Since it is possible for him to get seasick by looking at the painting of the *Dawn Treader,* it is not hard to imagine that he is very ill until Lucy's cordial* restores him to his quarrelsome self on board the boat. Lewis wants the reader to see even in Eustace's first diary entry many clues to the boy's character defects: Eustace magnifies the normal sea conditions into a "frightful storm"; he ignores the fact that he has been healed of his seasickness, boasting that he is not ill. He is not grateful; he thinks himself the only one aware of what he supposes to be their alarming condition; he blames the others' not noticing on either their conceit or their cowardice*; he is patronizing, arrogant, jealous, and complaining.

If he were allowed to continue in the direction he is headed in, Eustace would probably either indulge in vivisection* or become a pacifist.[3] Reepicheep "birches" the boy with the flat of his rapier, administering the first corporal punishment he has ever received.

Eustace's experience as a slave on the Lone Islands* seems to reform him not one whit. His later diary entries confirm his complete misperception of himself: "I always try to consider others whether they are nice to me or not," he writes on the very night he attempts to steal water during the shortage. He is the victim of the very wishful thinking he accuses the others of.[4]

His transformation takes place on Dragon Island,* when he wanders away from the group in order to avoid the work of refitting the ship. He tries to make himself comfortable, but he begins to feel lonely "for the first time"* in his entire life. He thinks the others might leave him on the island, a

---

misperception that is as confining to his heart as the narrow valley he stumbles into is to his body. When, in the night, he becomes a dragon, his first thought is one of relief that he will no longer have to be afraid of anyone; but his second and persisting thought is that he is cut off from his companions forever. Becoming a dragon improves Eustace's character because he is concerned about helping his friends. And the pleasure of liking people and being liked is the most powerful antidote to the discouragement he often feels as a dragon. The fact that he is a nuisance as a dragon eats into his mind as painfully as the arm-ring eats into his foreleg. In his providence,* Aslan appears to him in a dream* and cleanses Eustace of his dragonish appearance.[5] When the boy returns to his companions, he tells Edmund his story. Eustace is able to laugh in a way he never could before. He can scarcely believe he has met Aslan, but Edmund assures him that he has.

Eustace begins to be a different, a better person from this point on, though with occasional relapses.[6] He is brave "for the first time" when he fights the Sea Serpent.* Another budding scientist like Edmund, Eustace rejoices to see the water pump in the Land of the Duffers*—the first sign of civilization, to his former way of thought—and is intrigued about the nature of the invisible creatures. Like Lucy, he would rather not enter the darkness at the Dark Island*; but he stands with Edmund, Caspian, and Reepicheep as they proceed. On Ramandu's Island,* he disagrees with Edmund and Lucy about the identity of a bush they are calling heather; they concede the point to him because botany is one of his specialties. When his friend Reepicheep volunteers to stay overnight at Aslan's Table,* Eustace also determines to stay, something Lewis says is especially brave of him because he hasn't even been able to prepare himself by reading about all the things that could happen during the night. He is inquisitive about the nature of the Stone Knife* they see and about how the food keeps. His technological upbringing takes him too far, however, when he equates the composition of stars* ("a huge ball of flaming gas") with their essence; Ramandu* is quick to correct his reductionism.* Eustace grows impatient with the discussion Caspian, Reepicheep, and Drinian* have about falling off the edge of the world, and tries to convince them that their world is spherical; he will discover his mistake at the World's End.* He is the first to notice the odd look in Caspian's eyes, just before the King attempts his abdication. When he and Edmund and Lucy meet the Lamb* at the end of the world, he is silent, even when Aslan refuses to disclose whether he will be allowed to come back to Narnia in the future. Eustace returns to earth with a touch of the Lion's mane and the Lion's kiss. And though his mother finds that his time with the Pevensies has made him boring to her, everyone else finds him a much nicer person.[7]

The reader sees a very different Eustace at the beginning of SC: he is rounding the corner of the gymnasium at Experiment House, hands in pockets, whistling a tune. Even though he is full of empathy for the weeping Jill, he strikes a magisterial pose.[8] Jill is not receptive to any lecture and lets fly with reproaches. Eustace doesn't try to evade responsibility but does want her to see how he's changed—by standing up to Carter,* who was cruel to animals,* and by defending Spivvins.* He wants very badly to share his Narnian experiences, so he risks telling Jill about Aslan. He shows how much he really understands Aslan's ways when he does not permit Jill to try to force her way into Narnia with dark magic.* He knows that the best way in is to ask.[9] He remembers how Ramandu and his Daughter* prayed, and that is how he and Jill call upon Aslan. Surprised by members of the Gang,* they run to the school's perimeter and escape through a door into Aslan's country.* When Jill moves too close to the cliff's edge and appears to be fainting, he grabs for her. She resists him and he loses his balance and falls over. Aslan rushes in and blows him to safety.

When Jill catches up with him, he is put out with her—an unsurprising but regrettable pique, which causes him to miss the first sign.* When Glimfeather* later confirms this, Eustace is not very pleased with himself. Eustace is touchy until the Narnian banquet cheers him up. At the Parliament of Owls, his first concern is to proclaim his loyalty to Caspian and to gauge the loyalty of this secret meeting—an act that is strong testimony to Eustace's maturing sense of honor.* In his zeal, he overreaches himself and tries to expropriate the quest* from Jill, something she does not let him get away with. He almost succeeds in not blaming her for their delay in speaking to Caspian—he only mutters that it was not his fault. Though Jill is slower to respond because this is her first Narnian adventure, the atmosphere of the country has already restored Eustace to the strength he had at the end of VDT. He is not too happy about Puddleglum's talk of difficulties, declaring his faith that Aslan knew what he was doing when he gave them the quest. Jill and Eustace quarrel again, this time over his sexist* assumption that he and the Marsh-Wiggle* should bear the two swords. But later, when Jill suggests that the architects of the bridge might be the architects of the Ruined City of the Ancient Giants* that they are searching for, Eustace praises her. He has no discernment, however, when he is enchanted by the mysterious green lady's promise of beds and meals at Harfang*; Eustace does not distinguish between the Marsh-Wiggle's inveterate gloom and the genuine insight Puddleglum has into her character. He is accurate that Puddleglum's always expecting the worst, but he is wide of the mark when he says that the Marsh-Wiggle is always wrong. The harshness of the winter journey and the promise of comfort* ahead make the two humans careless of Aslan's signs and hostile to one another. But Eustace's sense of the signs painfully returns when he sees the ruined city from Jill's comfortable room at Harfang. His insightfulness resumes as he assesses the reason why they forgot the signs. He also sees that Jill would like to evade responsibility, and that they both must simply confess their fault.[10]

On the journey through Underland,* Jill experiences a claustrophobic panic; Eustace recalls to her how afraid he was at the cliff's edge. There is a hint of reproach in his voice, but he is immediately helpful by suggesting that they link up, hands to heels, in order to crawl through the dark cracks. During this journey, they huddle close to Puddleglum. When at last they meet Prince

Rilian,* Eustace and Jill are far too receptive, perhaps due to the psychological stresses of the past days, to his suggestion that their whole mission has been a foolish response to an archeological accident. Eustace can tell that Rilian is both as heartless as the Queen and a weak, dependent person. But when the prince's fit comes upon him, Eustace nobly offers to stay with him. Eustace exclaims "Oh!" as though he were physically hurt, when the prince adjures them to free him in Aslan's name.* He is not ready to make Puddleglum's affirmation; he is only willing to say that Rilian has said the words of the fourth sign. Eustace wants assurances that it will all turn out right if they release the prince. The Marsh-Wiggle can only assure them about the clear command of Aslan.

When the Queen of Underland* tries to reenchant Rilian and his three rescuers, Eustace is able to argue clearheadedly against the witch's reductionisms. But it is only Puddleglum's brave deed that sets them free. After they pay homage to the miraculous image of Aslan on Rilian's shield, Eustace apologizes to Jill and wishes her well. From this time forward they call each other by their Christian names.

Eustace is far more a product of Narnian adventures than an alumnus of Experiment House when he wants to accept Golg's* invitation to explore Bism.[11] His scientific sense of observation and memory enables him to assure Jill that the rising sea will not flood the caves of Father Time* and the sleeping dragons. They return to the surface and to Cair Paravel in time for Caspian's death,* an event that saddens him to tears. Aslan takes Jill and him back to his country, where they see the rejuvenation of Caspian. Eustace would like to stay there forever; but he willingly goes back to England to administer justice, in the form of corporal punishment, to the Gang.*

The friendship of Jill and Eustace that began in SC continues into LB. They come to help Tirian,* although by a way more abrupt than that of the magic rings,* which had been retrieved for the purpose of conveying them to Narnia. He explains to Tirian who they are, and he speaks up for Jill, who is over-modest about their abilities. He doesn't have the outdoor skills that she does; but he is a good swordsman, as Tirian finds out. When Jill disappears and later returns with Puzzle,* whom she has freed, Eustace is furious with her for giving him such a scare by her absence; but he thinks that she deserves to be knighted for her deed. He is white with fear as he kills the Calormene* guard of the dwarfs.* He is silent during the negotiations with the dwarfs, speaking only once, and then only to reproach them for ingratitude. He and Poggin* spend the next day discussing Narnian fauna and flora. He doesn't get worked up at Tirian's suggestion that they return home; he simply observes that they wouldn't know how to get back. But his cool bravery dissolves into sickening terror as they walk to Stable* Hill. His only consolations are the plans that Jill and he make, and the thought that they might have already died in a railway accident. The Last Battle* finds him hoping that he will be brave, and performing well in the face of his fears.* He is captured and thrown through the Stable Door.* Like the other friends of Narnia, he is miraculously refreshed. He expresses some resentment at Susan for her patronizing attitude toward their enthusiasm for Narnia. He is the first to reach for the fruit of the splendid trees* when Peter says it is permitted. After satisfying this desire, he is also eager to learn how the others came to be inside the Stable. He even interrupts Queen Lucy as she is speaking.[12] When Edmund relates the story of Tash's* eating of Shift,* Eustace expresses his hope that the ape will give the god* indigestion. This is remarkably similar to Rhince's* wish for the dragon whom he believes has swallowed the nuisance Eustace on Dragon Island. Eustace also hopes that Tash has eaten the dwarfs. He gives vent to his rage over their treachery, but Lucy silences him. He is last mentioned as hesitating at the Great Waterfall.* He thinks it crazy to swim up the falls. But he tries Lucy's experiment—to feel afraid—and he can't. So up he swims—a far cry from the insufferable brat of VDT.

---

[1] It is conceivable that Lewis is poking fun at his own name, Clive Staples Lewis, and at how insufferable he thought himself to be when he was a boy only a little older than Eustace. Lewis was known to his friends and family as Jack, a name he chose for himself when he was four. Professor Thomas W. Craik writes that in the 1940s and 1950s there was a cartoon character in a British newspaper, perhaps the *Daily Mirror,* named "Useless Eustace" (Letter to author, September 10, 1979). Although Lewis wasn't a person for reading the newspaper, he may have heard of this fat, middle-aged, comic character.

[2] The British edition rather inaccurately says that he is "far too stupid to make up anything himself." Lewis perhaps felt that this should be toned down for his American audience, because the American edition reads that he is "quite incapable of making up anything himself." A slight difference perhaps, but it may show that Lewis began to like Eustace better as he wrote about him.

[3] Lewis believed that conscientious objection was a legitimate stance one could take toward war; but he felt that pacifism was often a mask for cowardice. See also *The Screwtape Letters* (New York: Macmillan Publishing Co., 1961) pp. 34–35 and 45.

[4] This is the very point that Screwtape tries to make with Wormwood, that it is the plan of hell to keep a person's virtues and that person's imagination and one's vices, unknown, in the will. See *Imagination* and *The Screwtape Letters,* p. 31.

[5] See *Aslan.*

[6] This is Lewis's picture of how repentance is a process, beginning at a definite moment of conversion, yes, but extending through the rest of a person's life. See Lewis's essay, "Man or Rabbit?" in *God in the Dock,* Walter Hooper, ed. (Grand Rapids: Wm. B. Eerdmans Publishing Co., 1970) pp. 108–113; and (London: Collins Fount, 1979) pp. 67–73.

[7] Indeed, it may be that Lewis himself grew so curious about how he was changed that what happened to Eustace is the bridge between the first impulse of composition, which ends at VDT, and the second, which begins with SC. See *Introduction.*

[8] In SC, Lewis comes close to apologizing for Eustace's name, a very different attitude than in VDT, and deliberately intended to highlight the transformation of the boy.

[9] Yet another of Lewis's hints at the obedience* and simplicity required of authentic prayer.

[10] For Eustace's reaction to the discovery that he has eaten Talking Stag, see *Aslan,* especially note 43, and *Talking Beasts.*

[11] He uses his friend Reepicheep's phrase, "a great impeachment to our honour," to try to persuade Rilian to visit Bism.

[12] Lewis calls this a bad habit of Eustace's. This incident, and the further ungenerous remarks about Tash, Shift, and the renegade dwarfs, are included more out of Lewis's intended dramatic effect than out of any difference he might have with the fairly unanimous view among Christian theologians that it is impossible to sin in heaven.

EVE   See *Son of Adam, Daughter of Eve.*

EVIL   Evil stands watching the creation of Narnia* in the person of Jadis, and Narnia is never completely free from its presence. Jadis, driven out of

Narnia in MN, comes back as the White Witch to bring the Hundred Years of Winter* in LWW. And though she is presumed killed by Aslan, in PC the hag* informs Doctor Cornelius* that the Witch is still alive—one can't really kill a witch. This is Lewis's comment that vigilance against evil is always necessary, and it is foolish to slacken for even a moment. During the Golden Age of Narnia,* the smaller animals* have become so comfortable and secure that they fail to recognize the first signs of danger. In MN, Aslan calls the First Council* to discuss what to do about the evil that has entered Narnia. The animals, still innocent, mishear the words "an evil" as "a Neevil," and think it is some sort of creature, perhaps Uncle Andrew.* In this they are not far from wrong, for his dealings in dark magic* have brought the foolish man into direct contact with evil; he is, in fact, in love with the personification of evil, Jadis, whom he calls "a dem fine woman." The children* are called into Narnia each time to help contain evil that has gotten out of hand. In LB, evil has taken over most of Narnia, and its presence is evidenced by the depression and gloom that hangs over that world like a poisonous cloud. Now it is too much even for the Seven Friends of Narnia* to contain, and in the end Narnia is destroyed by Aslan, its creator. The creatures who, at the Door,* look on Aslan with hatred are banished eternally—evil is consigned to "its own place" —thus there is no evil in Aslan's country.*

EXPERIMENT HOUSE   The school* at which Jill and Eustace are students. Lewis's view of modern educational methods[1] is made quite clear in his description of Experiment House. It is coeducational or "mixed" (according to Lewis, "not nearly so mixed as the minds of the people who ran it") and run by a female Head* who is more interested in the bullies than the better behaved children. In fact, Jill and Eustace are very uncomfortable at this school, and are taunted by the Gang.* Students at Experiment House do not receive either a classical or religious education. Thus Jill and Eustace learn more about eluding would-be captors than about French, Math, or Latin; Jill has not learned to curtsey; and the children are unable to identify themselves as Son of Adam* and Daughter of Eve, because they have never heard of Adam and Eve. What's more, they have never heard of the custom of swearing on a Bible to show good faith, and have not been taught to use Christian names. Jill observes in Eustace's desire to explore Bism with Rilian that he is more a product of Narnian adventures* than an alumnus of Experiment House.

(SC 4, *13;* 5, *14;* 8, *16;* 35, *42;* 94, *97;* 168, *164;* 181, *177;* 214–217, *204– 206.*)
[*Books; Courtesy; Stories.*]

---

[1] For a book-length discussion of modern education and its tendency to be value-free and therefore value-less, see Lewis's *The Abolition of Man* (New York: Macmillan Publishing Co., 1965).

FAIRY   A human-like being with magical powers. Although fairies are popularly portrayed in literature as tiny winged creatures, before the sixteenth century they were thought to be the same size as human beings and thus much more ominous. This is what Lewis had in mind when he writes that Andrew Ketterley's* godmother, Mrs. Lefay,* was one of the last mortals in England to have fairy blood in her. Of the two others, one was a duchess and the other a charwoman. Digory's only thought is that Mrs. Lefay was probably a bad fairy.

(MN 19, *24.*)

FAITH   See *Knowledge.*

FARSIGHT   The eagle who brings Tirian* the news of Cair Paravel's capture and Roonwit's* death.* His name reflects both the keen eyes of the bird of prey, and his canny insight into character. Eagles are formidable opponents and Farsight is no exception: Rishda* retreats from engaging Tirian and Poggin,* because Jewel* and Farsight must also be reckoned with; and —together with Jill's shooting—he is the biggest factor for victory in the second sortie of the Last Battle.* He is the first to detect Rishda's surprise and terror at Shift's* destruction, and observes that Rishda "has[1] called on gods* he does not believe in." He goes on to speculate about what will happen if the gods appear.[2] He is among those who enter into Narnia at the judgment, and flies above the Seven Friends of Narnia* announcing that they are in the real Narnia.

(LB 90–91, *83–85;* 95, *87;* 99, *91;* 114, *105;* 115, *106;* 117, *108.*)
[*Animals; Birds; Talking Beasts.*]

---

[1] The word "had" in the American edition is a typographical error.
[2] This may remind the alert reader of Lewis's *Miracles* (New York: Macmillan Publishing Co., 1978; London: Collins Fontana, 1960) pp. 93–94, 97–98, in which he describes the shock of discovering that there is a personal God.

FATE   See *Providence.*

FATHER CHRISTMAS   A huge, bearded man in a bright red robe whose appearance signals the end of the Hundred Years of Winter,* during which time "it was always winter but Christmas never came." He is "big and glad and real," not just funny and jolly like the Father Christmas or Santa Claus we know in the modern world. He brings gifts to the children* and to Mr. and Mrs. Beaver*: for Mrs. Beaver, a new and better sewing machine; for Mr. Beaver* a finished dam with a new sluice gate; for Peter a shield, sword (Rhindon*), sheath, and sword belt—tools, not toys; for Susan a bow and quiver of arrows and a little ivory horn*; to Lucy a healing cordial* in a diamond bottle, and a dagger; and tea for all. In an interesting parallel to the White Witch, Father Christmas too arrives in a sleigh pulled by reindeer, but he is there to tell them that Aslan is on the move, the spring will come again, just as Christmas is the commemoration of the birth of Christ. Father Christmas is a hieroglyph of the joy* that Aslan brings.

(LWW 102 ff., *98 ff.*)

FATHER TIME   An enormous man with a waist-length white beard and a noble face is first encountered asleep in a cave in Underland.* The Warden of Underland* tells Puddleglum that the old man, now Father Time, was once a king* in the Upperworld and will wake only at the end of the world. He is indeed wakened at that time by Aslan's roar, and stands up in Ettinsmoor.* Aslan explains that Time* was his name while he was dreaming, but now that he is awake he will have a new name[1] (he is later called the great Time-giant). He winds a huge horn* that causes the stars* to fall from the skies, signaling the end of Narnia.* Nothing more is said of him.

(SC 126–127, *128.* LB 148, *135;* 156, *142.*)
[*Aslan's voice; Sleep.*]

---

[1] We can only guess that his new name is Eternity. But see *Time*.

FAUNS   In Greek and Roman mythology,* small half-human woodland spirits, followers of Bacchus* and Pan. Linked with satyrs,* they are one of the Nine Classes of Narnian Creatures.* They play wild, dreamy music* on reed pipes, and are described as having curly hair, little horns, and the legs and feet of goats. They are about the same size as dwarfs,* but more slender and graceful. Their faces are described as mournful and merry at the same time, which is suggestive of the innate gravity of the gods.* Like the other mythological creatures (dwarfs, nymphs,* and the like), fauns are not special creations of Aslan but come into existence at the Lion's command for Narnia to awake. The fauns sent by Pattertwig* to dance* around Caspian are named Mentius, Obentinus, Dumnus, Voluns, Voltinus, Girbius, Nimienus, Nausus, and Oscuns. Their vaguely Latin names evoke qualities both of fauns and pagan Roman culture.

Dumnus is probably the diminutive of the Latin *dumus,* meaning "thicket, thornbush, bramble," in which fauns might be expected to live. Mentius is from *mentior, mentitus,* meaning "deceiver, liar, cheater." Fauns are certainly clever seducers. Nausus is perhaps from *nasus,* meaning "nose," or from *nausea,* meaning "seasickness, indigestion." Fauns would be both inquisitive (nosy) and inclined to post-prandial queasiness. Nimienus, a diminutive form of *nimietas,* meaning "superfluity," is a reflection of fauns' tendency to overindulge. Oscuns is perhaps from *osculare,* meaning "to kiss," or *oscitare,* meaning "to be half-asleep, to yawn." Fauns would sneak kisses and might also doze off after a feast. Voltinus, perhaps the diminutive form of *volitare,* meaning "to fly about, flutter," suggests that fauns are unstable pleasure seekers. Voluns is possibly from *volens,* meaning "willing, consenting," which suggests that fauns were predisposed to give in to whatever their love of pleasure brought them. There is no known meaning for the names Girbius and Obentinus (the latter is a diminutive form). Three other fauns are named in the *Chronicles:* Urnus, Trumpkin's* ear-trumpet-holding attendant, and Jill's attendant, Orruns.* The derivation of these names is not known. The best-known faun in the *Chronicles* is, of course, Mr. Tumnus.*

(PC 16, *23;* 47, *50;* 77, 75. SC 34–36, *41–43;* 204–205, *195–197.*)

FEAR   In the *Chronicles,* Lewis teaches children* about the nature and the different kinds of fear. Nikabrik* says to Caspian, Doctor Cornelius,* and Trufflehunter,* "Don't take fright at a name as if you were children." The name, however, is that of the White Witch; Lewis implies that healthy fear is good, and that we can trust a child's reaction to such a name as an instinctive knowledge of right and wrong.* But according to Aslan, Susan has listened to her fears and therefore her faith cannot come to the fore. Fear can also be determined by our preconceptions. The child at the Old Woman's cottage in PC is not afraid of Aslan because he had never even seen a picture of an ordinary lion*; but the Telmarines* are thoroughly terrified at the sight of Aslan because although they knew about lions, "they had not believed in [them] and this made their fear greater." Lewis teaches children about how to get a job done despite fear when he describes Lucy's walk through the House of the Magician.* She has to walk by every room to get to the right room, and in every room an invisible or dead magician* may be hidden. "But," Lewis advises, "it wouldn't do to think about that." Later, at the evening meal, Lucy notices how the fact that she is no longer afraid changes the look of everything upstairs that had frightened her earlier: "The mysterious signs* on the door were still mysterious but now looked as if they had kind and cheerful meanings." Similarly, Shasta finds the tombs frightening and sinister during the night, but relatively harmless in the light of day.

Such night fears are common to all people, and the crew of the *Dawn Treader* instinctively does not want to venture in the Dark Island.* It is only courage* and the spirit of adventure* that allow them to survive the ordeal of nightmare that awaits them.[1] For Reepicheep, yielding to fear is the greatest danger; and Lord Rhoop's* condition shows what harm the extremes of fear

---

127   **FEAR**

can do: his is a voice "of one in such an extremity of terror that he had almost lost his humanity."

In SC, Jill and Eustace experience at least two phobias: Eustace's fear of heights (his worst fear is seemingly fulfilled when he plunges from the cliff, but he has actually fallen safely into Narnia); and Jill's fear of "twisty passages and dark places underground," which intensifies in Underland.* Indeed, much of SC deals with facing fears; and part of Jill's problem in continually forgetting the signs is an indulgence of her fear of taking responsibility. After the slaying of the Queen of Underland* and the fulfillment of Jill's original quest* to rescue Rilian, the prince calls on his companions to bid farewell to hopes as well as fears. Healthy fear, says Lewis, and especially fear of the Lord, can help push us beyond what we think of as our limits. It is fear of a lion—actually, the Lion—that propels Bree and Hwin to gallop flat out.

In Aslan's country,* there is no fear. He says to the newly created Talking Beasts,* "Laugh and fear not." Aslan tells Lucy not to fear the river of death,* which lies across the way to his country, because he is "the Great Bridge Builder." And in LB, in Aslan's country at last, Lucy observes that it is impossible to feel afraid, even if one tries to. Jill, free from fear at last, goes up the Great Waterfall* so high that if she *could* be afraid of heights she would be terrified, but here she can't be, and so the experience is thrilling.

(LWW 127, *120.* PC 148, *153;* 197, *173;* 199, *175.* VDT 124–125, *126;* 148, *148;* 215, *209.* SC 11, *21;* 15–16, *24–26;* 21, *30;* 43–44, *50;* 63–64, *69;* 69, 73–74; 86, *89;* 124–127, *125–128;* 169–170, *165;* 187, *182.* HHB 79 ff., *73 ff.;* 136–137, *121.* MN 118, *110;* 173, *156.*)
[*Autobiographical allusions; Feelings; Imagination; Numinous.*]

---

[1]For further discussion of the Dark Island, see *Adventure,* note 1, and *Dreams.*

FEAR OF THE LORD   See *Numinous.*

FEELINGS   In a letter, C. S. Lewis admits: "My *mind* doesn't waver on that point: my feelings sometimes do."[1] In the *Chronicles,* Lewis teaches children* that nonrational feelings and emotions are natural, acceptable, indeed, unavoidable (kissing and crying* are not frowned upon in Narnia), but that they must not let feelings get them off their path. In LWW, Peter does not feel very brave—in fact, he feels nauseous. But that makes no difference to what he has to do. The theme of expression and acknowledgement of feelings runs through all the books. In PC, the children wish they could go on *feeling* as not-hungry as they did when they were still thirsty; and there is expression of feelings and emotions in their leave-taking of Narnia. In VDT, when Caspian shifts onto Lucy the responsibility of sailing into the darkness, she feels deeply that she would rather not, but says otherwise. In HHB, Hwin shyly suggests that even though she and Bree feel that they can't go on, she knows that

humans can spur horses on in spite of their feelings. And in LB, it is only when Jill and Eustace allow thoughts of the now-chaotic Narnia to come back into their minds that they feel desolate.

A full range of emotions is expressed by the characters in the *Chronicles*. Sadness is often expressed as "term-time"* feelings; Caspian misses his nurse intensely and cries a great deal; as the four children and Trumpkin* grow more and more tired from rowing, their spirits fall; on Dragon Island* Eustace feels sad and lonely; the parting of the children from the *Dawn Treader* is grievous; Jill feels sorrow at the eating of the Talking Stag and notices profound sadness on the faces of the Earthmen*; Digory is miserable at the thought that his mother might die. The entire mood of LB is one of gloom, and at the news that Tash* and Aslan are one the animals* feel depressed. But feelings of sadness are more than balanced by feelings of happiness, joy,* and ecstasy. In PC, feelings of terror and delight simultaneously burst into Caspian's mind;[2] and after their meal, the children feel quite hopeful about the outcome of Caspian's campaign. In VDT, the undragonized Eustace is glad about the process of removal of his dragon* skin—he loves his own body, puny though it may be. After drinking the sweet water of the Last Sea,* the drinkers feel "almost too well and too strong to bear it." In SC, Jill cries out of sheer ecstacy at Aslan's beauty. In HHB, as Shasta rides toward Anvard* in King Lune's* party, he feels happy for the first time since the day he entered Tashbaan.* The paradoxical joy of loneliness is mentioned several times in the *Chronicles:* Lucy regrets the *Dawn Treader* will not land at Felimath,* because she likes to walk there. "It was so lonely—a nice kind of loneliness." At the Silver Sea,* "even . . . the loneliness itself [was] too exciting." In SC, Jill enjoys the loneliness of the moors. And in HHB, the Hermit's* enclosure is "a very peaceful place, lonely and quiet." There is also a place in Narnia for solemnity. Lucy has a solemn feeling as she takes her gift from Father Christmas*; the Dawn Treaders experience the solemn feeling that they have sailed beyond the world. To Shasta, the horns at the opening of Tashbaan are "strong and solemn"; similarly, the preparations for battle with Rabadash* are "very solemn and very dreadful." Anger and other strong feelings are also expressed. Caspian dislikes his aunt, Prunaprismia*; Drinian's* shortness with the King* is explained by the previous day's anxieties; the rainy weather makes Eustace disagreeable; Drinian's rage at Reepicheep is compared to that of a mother who is angry at her child for running out into traffic; at Experiment House* Jill, interrupted in the middle of a good cry, flies into a temper; Digory expresses righteous anger at his Uncle Andrew's* complete lack of principle and honor*; and Polly is angry at the way Digory manhandles her in the great hall at Charn.* Lewis feels that anger can be taken too far, and his comment that talking horses,* when angry, become more horsey in accent implies that anger dehumanizes us. In LB, Tirian* unconciously goes for his sword at Roonwit's* talk of lies; and at the whipping of the talking horse he is overcome by his feelings of grief and anger and rashly commits murder. Lewis comments that he and Jewel* are "too angry to think clearly."

(LWW 127, *120;* 128, *121.* PC 8, *16;* 22, *28;* 24, *29;* 48, *51;* 53, *54;* 109, *101;* 128, *117;* 215, *188.* VDT 30, *38;* 67, *71;* 78, *85;* 96, *101;* 153, *153;* 189, *185;* 197, *193.* SC 3, *12;* 68, *72–73;* 111, *113;* 123, *124;* 211, *201.* HHB 48–49, *49–50;* 81, *75;* 131, *116–117;* 144, *127;* 174–178, *153–156.* LB 15, *20;* 17, *21;* 20, *24;* 32, *35;* 97, *89.*)
[*Crying; Fear.*]

---

¹ *They Stand Together,* Walter Hooper, ed. (London: Collins, 1979) p. 514.
² See *Numinous.*

FELIMATH   One of the Lone Islands.* Uninhabited except for sheep and shepherds, it looks like a low green hill in the sea. It is the scene of the kidnapping of Caspian, Reepicheep, Edmund, Lucy, and Eustace by Pug* and the slave traders.

(VDT 31, *38.*)
[*Geography, Narnian; Slave trade.*]

FELINDA   See *Charn.*

FENRIS ULF   A huge grey wolf, captain of the White Witch's secret police. His name is taken from the great wolf of Scandinavian mythology* who was spawned by Loki—god* of strife and spirit of evil—and who was slain by the fearless Vidar, son of Odin. In the British edition of the *Chronicles,* the wolf is given the name Maugrim, meaning perhaps "savage jaws," or alluding to *maugre,* "ill will."¹

Fenris is not always what he seems. When Edmund encounters the wolf at the Witch's castle, he takes it to be a stone statue, until it challenges him and then takes his message to the Queen. Peter first thinks Fenris to be a bear, but is finally able to kill him when the wolf, unable to control his anger, rises up to howl, enabling Peter to stab him in the heart.

(LWW 55, *57;* 92–93, *90–91;* 127–129, *119–121.*)
[*World Ash Tree.*]

---

¹ No evidence has yet come to light to indicate whether or when Lewis made this change for his American readers. Since he had a predilection for Norse images, he may have thought the name change to be an improvement. Professor Thomas W. Craik disagrees: "The virtue of Maugrim . . . is that [it is] suggestive and not precise. Maugrim . . . has an unpleasant sound; 'grim' carries its sinister adjectival sense; 'mau' *might* be associated with 'maw,' but I think it more likely to connect with all Spenser's evil names beginning with Mal" (Letter to author dated July 31, 1979.) See also *World Ash Tree,* note 1.

FIRE-BERRY   A berry with the appearance of a little fruit or a live coal; it is too bright to look at directly. Every day a Bird of Morning* carries one to Ramandu* and lays it in his mouth to rejuvenate him. The berries are said to grow in the valleys of the sun,* and it is conceivable that they grow from the same bush that produces the fire-flowers* from which Lucy's cordial* is made (although these are said to grow in the mountains of the sun).

Jill and Eustace talk to Puddleglum as the Marsh-Wiggle explains—as Marsh-Wiggles will—that he is fishing for eels, though he doesn't expect to catch any. (SC 59, 65.)

(VDT 178–180, *174–177.*)
[*Birds.*]

FIRE-FLOWERS   The source of the juice used to make Lucy's healing cordial.* They grow in the mountains of the sun,* and may be from the same plant that produces the fire-berries* that the Birds of Morning* bring to Ramandu* to renew his youth (although these are said to grow in the valleys of the sun).

(LWW 105, *100.*)

FIRST COUNCIL   Called by Aslan, when Narnia is barely five hours old, to discuss the advent of evil* into the newly created country. The seven beings invited to the council are the Chief Dwarf, the River-god,* the Oak, the He-Owl, both Ravens, and the Bull-Elephant.

(MN 119, *111.*)
[*Animals; Birds; Dwarfs; Elephants; Owls; Trees.*]

FIVE BLACK DWARFS   Suspicious, rather aggressive dwarfs* who live in a cave near the Seven Brothers of the Shuddering Wood.* Unlike these Red Dwarfs, however, the Black Dwarfs do not seem to be brothers. They define their allegiance to Caspian negatively—they will support him if he is against Miraz,* not because he is for Old Narnia. That they are likely more sinister than the Red Dwarfs is evidenced by their wish to call for the help of ogres* and hags.* Three Black Dwarfs attend the Great Council,* and are sent to investigate the mysterious man (who turns out to be Doctor Cornelius*) with their bows and arrows. One of the dwarfs is ready to kill him if he has to.

(PC 72, *70;* 80–82, *76–78.*)

FLAMING MOUNTAIN OF LAGOUR   An awesome Calormene* volcano. Emeth* uses its force and fury as a simile to describe Aslan's terrifying quality.

(LB 164, *148.*)
[*Numinous.*]

FLEDGE   The winged horse*[1] who carries Digory and Polly to the garden* in the west; originally a cab-horse named Strawberry.[2] As Strawberry he is tired,[3] and when first encountered he is being flogged and maddened by Jadis. But his father was a cavalry horse, and in Narnia his noble heritage is apparent. In the Wood between the Worlds* he already looks and feels better, and it is his desire for a drink that leads the entire London group to Narnia. At Aslan's creation song, he looks and feels stronger, younger, and renewed. Strawberry speaks for all the Talking Beasts* when he declares, "We don't know very much yet"[4] in his "nosey . . . snortey" voice. In fact, he has already forgotten much of his former life, most of it bad—the work, the hard streets, the cart. The best thing he remembers are sugar cubes that riders used to give him. At Aslan's command, he becomes a winged horse named Fledge, the father of all flying horses. His wings sprout chestnut and coppery from his back. Though transformed, he is still Strawberry somewhere inside, for he is puzzled at first that the children* cannot eat grass, and—perhaps because of some primal memory* of his past life—he shivers involuntarily at the passing of Jadis. He is reunited with Digory and Polly at the Great Reunion* in Aslan's country.*

(MN Chapter 7 passim. LB 178, *160–161.*)
[*Creation of Narnia; White Witch.*]

---

[1] See *Horses* for a discussion of the possible meaning of Strawberry's transformation.

[2] In our world, horses named Strawberry are usually strawberry roan in color, a mixture of light brown and white hairs that gives the horse a pinkish tone.

[3] "Cab-horse tired" was an expression Lewis used to describe his dead-tired feeling. See C. S. Lewis, *Letters to an American Lady,* Clyde S. Kilby, ed. (Grand Rapids: Wm. B. Eerdmans Publishing Co., 1967) p. 22.

[4] Lewis may be speculating here about the content of animal knowledge.* When Frank tries to reestablish his relationship with Strawberry, the horse says (1) he doesn't have exact or enough knowledge; (2) he does have an idea that he has met this experience before; and (3) he feels like he has been somewhere else (in another existence) before.

FOOD   See *Lists; Domesticity.*

"FOR THE FIRST TIME"   These words signal that an enormous change is taking place in a character. In LWW, Edmund feels sorry for the feasting animals* turned into stone, and "for the first time in this story felt sorry for someone besides himself." In VDT Eustace, upon leaving the group and wandering around Dragon Island* alone, "began, almost for the first time in his life, to feel lonely." He later acts bravely "for the first time in his life" when he attacks the Sea Serpent. On Ramandu's Island,* when the crew first looks at the Daughter of Ramandu,* they think that they have never before known what beauty means. In SC, Eustace and Jill use one another's Christian names "for the first time" in their departure from the witch's castle. In HHB Aravis, tired of Lasaraleen's* silliness, "for the first time . . . began to think that traveling with Shasta* was rather more fun than . . . life in Tashbaan.*" When Shasta slides off Bree to help Aravis, "he had never done anything like this in his life before. . . ."

(LWW 113, *107.* VDT 65, *71;* 97, *102;* 171, *168.* SC 168, *164.* HHB 99, *90;* 138, *122.*)

FRANK I   The first King* of Narnia; he is a former London cabdriver and the husband of Helen.* The humble, good-hearted Frank is a good neighbor and his coronation is the fulfillment of the prophesy that "the last shall be first."[1] He is kind to his horse* (kindness to animals* is the sure sign of a good person in the *Chronicles*), and kind even to Jadis, whom he takes to be a demented young woman. He is brave, and tries to get close to Strawberry in spite of the threat of the Witch's iron bar. The depth of his simple piety is demonstrated by his thankfulness that no bones were broken in the "fall," and by his calm confrontation of the possibility that they have died, when he suggests that they sing a hymn.[2] He is first encountered in the crowd surrounding the destroyed hansom cab near the lamp-post,* and he is in fact the cab driver hired by Andrew Ketterley* to take him and Jadis shopping. He wears a bowler hat, perhaps a foreshadowing of his future crown. In Narnia, the beauty of Aslan's creation song touches Frank deeply, and he innocently exclaims he would have been a better man if he'd known there were such things. When Aslan announces that Adam's race will help heal the harm that has entered into Narnia, Frank doffs his hat and looks, to Polly, more handsome. Aslan calls him "son," and Frank reveals that he feels he and the Lion have met before. Frank states that he would like to stay in Narnia, but only if his wife could be there. At Aslan's command, Helen is brought to Narnia and the two are named the first sovereigns. Although he feels he doesn't have the right education to be king, he successfully answers Aslan's five questions about the vocation of kingship. King Frank is last seen in LB, sitting with his wife on their thrones in the garden* of the west. Lewis's comment that Tirian* feels, in their presence, as we would feel if we were in the presence of Adam and Eve,[3] is a strong suggestion that this is their role in Narnia.

(MN 86 ff., *82 ff.;* Chapter 8 passim. LB 179, *162.*)
[*Creation of Narnia; Son of Adam, Daughter of Eve; White Witch.*]

---

[1] Mark 10:31.
[2] "Come Ye Thankful People Come," *English Hymnal,* No. 289, of which Lewis cites the third line of the fourth stanza.
[3] Cf. Ransom before Tor and Tinidril in Lewis's *Perelandra* (New York: Macmillan Publishing Co., 1944) pp. 204 ff.

FRIENDSHIP   See *Sea People.*

GALE   Ninth King* of Narnia, a direct descendant of King Frank* and Queen Helen.* He kills the dragon* that has long terrorized the inhabitants of the Lone Islands.* In their gratitude they hail him as their emperor, a title he passes on to all subsequent kings of Narnia.

(LB 88–89, *82.*)

GALMA, ISLE OF   Located a day's voyage north of Cair Paravel. A place that Lucy remembers from past voyages, it is ruled by a duke who holds a week-long tournament for Caspian X, hoping to interest him in wedding his daughter, who has freckles and a squint. Galmians are noted for their nautical expertise. Since Miraz* had forbidden his people the study of navigation, Galma provides a ship and crew for the Seven Noble Lords* sent by the usurper to explore the ocean east of Narnia. Pug* also forces Galmians to man his slave ships. There is mention of an old sailor, "Galmian by birth," concurring with Drinian's* memory of the winds in the Eastern Sea.* Lewis's attention to these details suggests his lifelong love of the sea and his respect for the skills of the sailor.

(PC 107, 99. VDT 17, 24; 36, 44; 183, 179.)
[*Geography, Narnian; Slave trade.*]

GANG, THE   The ten or fifteen bullies of Experiment House* who terrorize Jill, Eustace, and other well-behaved children.* A partial list includes Adela Pennyfather, Cholmondely[1] Major, Edith Winterblott,[2] "Spotty"[3] Sorner, Bannister, the Garrett twins, Carter,* and Spivvins.* These despicable children are special friends of the Head,* who sees them as interesting psychological cases and never punishes them. They intimidate the others with threats of torture (intimated by Carter's cruelty to the rabbit) and are frequently "after" one or another of the children. At the end of SC, they get their come-uppance in a sequence that must be the dream of every child who has ever been picked on by a bully. Accompanied by Aslan, Jill and Eustace and Caspian break through from Narnia in their Narnian robes.* Jill whips the girls with her riding crop, and Caspian and Eustace paddle the boys with the flats of their swords.[4] Lewis does not say whether or not the Gang is thus reformed, but they certainly will not pick on Jill and Eustace again.

(SC 3–4, 12–13; 8, 17; 215, 105.)
[*Vivisection.*]

---

[1] For American readers who may not know, this is pronounced "Chumley."

[2] Note the delightfully suggestive quality of her name. School* and term-time,* already blots on the year, are made even more horrible by people like Edith Winterblott.

[3] He may have been called "spotty" because he had freckles; it is also likely that he had acne, because in England pimples are called "spots."

[4] It should not be inferred that Lewis approved of beating children; in fact, his own school experience was marked by beatings (see *Autobiographical allusions*). For this group of really awful children—spoiled by the Head, and used to a school that does not believe in corporal punishment—however, it is unlikely that anything short of a beating would have made much of an impact.

GARDEN   The spiritual heart of Aslan's country*; it may be reached by going to the Utter East,* or by flying over the Western Wilds.* The fact that it can be reached from either direction is Lewis's comment that even those aspirations that seem to lead away from a spiritual goal may in fact lead to that goal. The garden is located at the top of a steep, green hill, and it has a wonderful smell. Inside a high wall of green turf, which surrounds it, grow trees* with green, bluish, and silvery leaves. Its high gates of gold face the rising sun.* It is here that Digory is sent to pick the silver apple* from which will grow the Tree of Protection.* The good magic* of this place is in strong contrast with the bad magic of the golden bell and hammer.* The garden has an absolute feeling of privacy* and is filled with a sacred silence,* except for the water gently splashing in a fountain near its center. It is far larger inside than it seems outside, a quality which is also found to be true of Aslan's country in LB.[1]

(MN 143, *133;* 156 ff., *145 ff.* LB 176 ff., *158 ff.*)
[*Geography, Narnian.*]

---

[1] Because LB was finished before MN, the garden in MN exactly corresponds to the garden in LB.

GARRETT TWINS   See *Gang, the.*

GENTLE GIANTS   See *Giants; Harfang.*

GEOGRAPHY, NARNIAN   Narnia is the overall name for a flat world that is comprised of three countries: Archenland* and Narnia to the North of the Great Desert,* and Calormen* to the South. All are bordered on the East by the Eastern Sea* and on the West by the Western Wilds,* beyond which is the garden.* Geographically, Narnia is reminiscent of our own world: Calormen is akin to the Near and Middle East, Narnia itself is much like Great Britain and Scandinavia, and Archenland seems topographically like Switzerland. There are rivers and creeks and waterfalls, forests and deserts and moors.

Beginning with his earliest Christian work, the allegory *The Pilgrim's Regress,* [1] Lewis devised a moral geography in which the center of his world was the "countryof Man's Soul." The forces of evil* were operative on two different fronts: in the far North, the region of hyper-rationalism and fanaticism, and in the far South, the region of hyper-sensuality and hedonism. To the East *and* to the West lie the objects of human longing: the land of sunrise, the Landlord's country; and the land of sunset, the Island in the West. Lewis was a man who loved his native Ireland and his adopted England (as an Ulsterman, these two were identical), especially for its temperate climate. Given his attraction for things Northern, his Narnia is situated in the temperate zone above the desert and the middle Europe of his fictional world, Archenland.

Symbolically, however, the geography of Narnia is more complex. It is tempting to ascribe good and bad connotations to its geographical directions, but this soon turns out to be somewhat complex. For example, one might say that the South is bad because Calormen is there, and that the North is good because in that direction lie Archenland and Narnia. But the North is also the home of the very worst and most savage giants,* and it is the direction in which the White Witch goes to learn more of the black art—in fact, the North is the home of all the witches. It is also apparent from VDT that, in traveling East, one gets closer and closer to Aslan's country*; indeed, the East is a very mystical landscape. The breakers are long and slow, a retired star* and his daughter live on an enchanted island, the sea is filled with lilies, the water is sweet, and the rising sun is large and close. And, because Narnia is flat, those who continue to the Utter East* disappear over the edge, presumably into Aslan's country. To the West,[2] however, is another entrance into Aslan's country; it is here that the garden houses the Tree of Protection.* This seeming contradiction is resolved at the end of LB, when, standing in Aslan's country, Lucy, Peter, and Edmund can see that Narnia is ringed by a range of mountains, called the mountains of the Utter East on one side and the Western Wilds on the other side. And the garden in which they stand is really in the middle of the ring: it is the spiritual heart of Aslan's country.[3]

---

[1] (Grand Rapids: Wm. B. Eerdmans Publishing Co., 1958) pp. 11–14.

[2] Probably because the sun sets in the west, "going west" is a euphemism for dying; thus "he has gone west" means "he died." See John Ciardi, *A Browser's Dictionary* (New York: Harper and Row Publishers, 1980) p. 410.

[3] See *Aslan's country*, note 4, for a discussion of this "coincidence of opposites."

GHOSTS   The spirits of dead persons, which remain to haunt the living. In PC, Trumpkin* tells the children* that they don't feel like ghosts, but later adds that the ruined Cair Paravel smells* like ghosts. The Telmarines* think that the Black Woods* are full of ghosts. In SC, Eustace thinks at first that the rejuvenated Caspian is a ghost. Caspian explains that if he were to appear in Narnia, he would be a ghost because he doesn't belong there any more; but "one can't be a ghost in one's own country." He can only speculate about whether he would be a ghost if he were to get into our world. In HHB, Shasta (who is already afraid of ghouls*) is afraid that the breathing presence beside him in the fog is a ghost, but is relieved when it breathes warmly on his face and hand.

(PC 30–31, *34; 36–37, 40*. SC 213, *203*. HHB 157–159, *138–140*.)
[*Aslan's country; Breath of Aslan; Plato.*]

GHOULS   Evil spirits, often associated with graves and corpses, invited by the White Witch to attend the slaying of Aslan. The word ghoul is Arabic in origin, a fact very appropriate in light of the relatively frequent mention of the fear of ghouls that Shasta, Aravis, and Lasaraleen's* groom experience in the shadows of the Ancient Tombs. This is another indication that Lewis's fictional Calormen* is drawn largely from Britain's experience of its Middle Eastern colonies.

(LWW 132, *123*. HHB 82–86, *76–79; 121, 108*.)

GIANTS   A race of tall beings that appears in virtually all world mythologies.*[1] Giants are one of the Nine Classes of Narnian Creatures* as related by Doctor Cornelius.* In Narnia, there are roughly two types of giants: good and bad. Both types use clubs as weapons, and wear knee-high spiked boots.

The bad giants live generally in the North, and are hostile and even murderous toward humans, dwarfs,* and Talking Beasts.* They include the so-called "gentle giants" of Harfang*; the fierce giants of Northern Narnia that are driven back by the Kings and Queens* in LWW; the Northern giants who were defeated by Caspian X in the summer of 2304 N.Y.; and the Ettins* who are part of the White Witch's forces against Aslan. Good giants include Rumblebuffin* (and the entire Buffin* clan), Wimbleweather,* and Stonefoot.* Good or bad, giants are not very intelligent (Tumnus* never knew a clever giant), and ugly (the giants Jill mistakes for rock formations have "great, stupid, puff-cheeked" faces). Giants were apparently once capable of greater achievements, as indicated by the Ruined City of the Ancient Giants,* with its well-engineered bridge and the frieze work that decorates the balustrade. The Queen of Underland* (whose opinions are not to be trusted) distinguishes between the gentle giants of Harfang ("wild, civil, prudent, and courteous") and the Ettinsmoor* giants ("foolish, fierce, savage, and given to all beastliness"). What she neglects to tell the three travelers, of course, is that the "gentle" giants enjoy eating human beings as well as Marsh-Wiggles,* and would be delighted to enjoy Jill, Eustace, and Puddleglum at their Autumn Feast.*

No matter how well meaning the giants may be, human beings have trouble accepting giants as friendly. Jill doesn't even like to read about giants, and Shasta has been taught to fear them since childhood. Other mentions of giants include the two-headed giant Pire, who was turned into stone by King Olvin* of Archenland.* The White Witch has giant blood in her, as does the royal house of Charn.* Shasta mistakes the breathing presence of Aslan beside him in the fog for a giant, which gives some indication of the Lion's perceived size. All giants (both good and bad) are summoned to judgment by Aslan at the Stable* Door.* The stars* are called down from the heavens at the end of Narnia* by the horn* of great giant Time.*

(LWW 77, 76; 92, 89; 132, 123; 166–167, 153–155; 171, 158; 181, 166. PC 16, 23; 47, 50; 56, 56; 80, 76; 95, 89; 173, 152; 181, 159. VDT 15, 22; 165, 162. SC 20, 29; 29, 37; 63, 69; 68 ff., 73 ff.; 89 ff., 92 ff.; Chapter 8 passim; 126, 128. HHB 156–157, 137–138; 170, 149; 177, 155; 213, 186. MN 69, 67; 152, 138. LB 177, 160.)

---

[1] And is also mentioned in Genesis 6:4.

GIFT OF SPEECH   Narnia is set apart from our world if for no other reason than the fact that some of its animals* talk. For Lewis, as for Aristotle, speech is the sign of rational thought in a creature.[1] But in Aristotle's world and in the medieval cosmology, humans are the only talking animals. Not so in Narnia. When Aslan changes some of the animals into Talking Beasts,* he gives them not only speech but themselves, the land of Narnia, and charge over the Dumb Beasts* from which they were taken. With the gift of rational self-possession comes possession of the world, freedom, and moral responsibility. Though all of this would seem to put the Talking Beasts on an equal footing with the humans, they acknowledge the Sons of Adam* and Daughters and Eve as their superiors;[2] further, in many instances the rationality of the Talking Beasts is limited and not quite so well-rounded as that of the children.* The Three Bulgy Bears,* though "talking" and therefore rational beasts, are primarily creatures of appetite. At the council of war the bears, showing little forethought, are "very anxious to have the feast first and leave the council till afterwards: perhaps till tomorrow." Reepicheep and the other mice* are admirably strong on courage* and daring but weak on prudence. They are all for "storming Miraz* in his own castle that very night" with no regard for odds or comparative strength.

(PC 69, 67; 80, 77. MN 117–119, 109–110.)

[1] Aristotle, *Politics,* I, 2, 1253a 9–14.
[2] See *Hierarchy.*

GIFTS   See *Father Christmas.*

GINGER   An orange-colored tom-cat, the atheist struck dumb by Aslan. Poggin* calls Ginger a cunning fellow, although he looks prim and proper.[1] Independent and haughty, Ginger deduces from the fiasco at the Stable* that there is no such person as Tash* or Aslan, and resolves to search out like-minded people and form them into an alliance before the true believers see through Shift's* plot. At the Stable Hill evening assembly he appears to have supplanted the heavily drinking ape and become second in command to Rishda.* He volunteers to enter the Stable (Lewis is at pains to emphasize the cat's haughtiness to highlight his subsequent reduction to dumbness), but soon runs out, completely disheveled and shrieking in terror. He has seen the real Tash, and—for his heresy—has been struck dumb by Aslan. He grows less and less like an intelligent Talking Beast,* and more and more like a wild, Dumb Beast,* and is never seen again.

(LB 32–33, 35–36; 77–79, 73–75; 100 ff., 91 ff.)
[*End of Narnia; Eschatology.*]

[1] Lewis loved cats and owned a number of them, and his letters are full of references to his cats. See PWD, p. 16. See also C. S. Lewis, *Letters to an American Lady,* Clyde S. Kilby, ed. (Grand Rapids: Wm. B. Eerdmans Publishing Co., 1967) pp. 38 and 94.

GLASSWATER CREEK, CREEKS   A small inlet or bay south of Cair Paravel, the head of which is just behind the Hill of the Stone Table.* The D.L.F.* and the Pevensie children row up it to reach Caspian. Shasta and Arsheesh* also live on a "creek"[1] of the sea, and Bree and Shasta and the unknown horse and rider are forced out into a creek, where they begin to talk.

(PC 105 ff., 98 ff. HHB 1, 11; 27, 32.)
[*Geography, Narnian.*]

GLENSTORM   A Centaur.* The father of three sons, he is a noble creature with glossy chestnut flanks and a full golden beard. Being a prophet and stargazer, he knows in advance the mission of Caspian, Trufflehunter,* Trumpkin,* and Nikabrik.* He accompanies Edmund and Wimbleweather* when they deliver Peter's challenge to Miraz* and is appointed one of the Marshalls of the Lists. Glenstorm's life role is "to watch," just as Truffle-hunter's (and all Badgers') is "to remember." He is among the Narnians in Aslan's country* after the Last Battle.* His name suggests that he is a force to reckon with, whose sheer weight makes its presence felt on the pastures.

(PC 73 ff., *71 ff.* LB 178–179, *161.*)
[*Mythology.*]

GLIMFEATHER   A huge white owl,* he is about as tall as a good-sized dwarf* (about four feet tall). His name is derived from the Middle High German word *glim,* which means "to shine or gleam." Thus he is a bird* whose white feathers glow, especially in the moonlight under which he so often flies. He is shortsighted, and (like all owls) his speech is filled with words that rhyme with his "Tu-Whoo" call: to, too, two, who, to-do, you, true. He is a very courteous owl, as evidenced by his offer to catch Jill a bat to eat. He knows immediately that there is some magic* connected with Jill and Eustace, because he alone saw them fly into Narnia. When he hears that they are looking for the lost Prince Rilian, he takes them to talk to Trumpkin.* This proves difficult because the old Lord Regent is so deaf, and Glimfeather—in a scene reminiscent of an English music-hall review—finds himself repeating what the children say until Trumpkin understands.

A short time later, Glimfeather arrives at Jill's window¹ to carry her to the Parliament of Owls,² which takes place in a partially ruined ivy-covered tower in the dead of night (a perfectly reasonable hour for nocturnal birds to meet). The meeting has been called to facilitate the search for Prince Rilian, an effort Trumpkin would have prevented. Another humorous scene ensues when one of the owls imitates the grumpy Trumpkin perfectly. An old owl relates the story of the death* of the Queen and the disappearance of the prince. When he is done, Eustace says that he and Jill must get to the Ruined City of the Ancient Giants,* and the owls are thrown into a state of alarm. They apologize for not offering to accompany the children across the dangerous Ettinsmoor,* saying that the children would want to travel by day while they must fly at night. Glimfeather suggests a Marsh-Wiggle* as the perfect guide, and he and another owl carry Eustace and Jill to the Marsh-Wiggles' camp.

Glimfeather is not heard from again until the end of SC, when Jill (who is trying to wake the others) awakens the owl in late morning. He has been in the dwarf's cheery cave since two, having brought a message to the prince. The sleepy owl goes back to sleep, his head buried in his feathers. He is present for the Great Reunion* in LB.

(SC 31 ff., *38 ff.;* Chapter 4 passim; 203, *194–195.* LB 178, *161.*)
[*Daughter of Ramandu; Humor; Literary allusions; Talking Beasts.*]

---

[1] When he says that Glimfeather landed on the window with a "whirring noise," Lewis shows his lack of knowledge about an important aspect of the behavior of owls, namely the silent flight that allows them to surprise their prey.
[2] This is a humorous allusion to Chaucer's poem, "Parliament of Fowls."

GLOZELLE   A scheming Telmarine* Lord, counselor to Miraz* and his Marshall of the Lists. With characteristic Telmarine treachery, he stabs Miraz to death because of a personal insult. It is presumed that Glozelle is killed by Peter's forces later in the battle.

(PC 174 ff., *152 ff.;* 183, *161;* 189–190, *166–167.*)
[*Sopespian.*]

GNOSTICISM   See *Knowledge; Right and wrong.*

GODS   Specified by Doctor Cornelius* as one of the Nine Classes of Narnian Creatures,* gods are present throughout the *Chronicles.* In fact, the daughters of King Frank* and Queen Helen* marry wood gods and river gods. Narnian gods, goddesses, and semi-deities include Bacchus,* fauns,* Dryads,* Hamadryads,* Maenads,* Naiads,* Nymphs,* Pomona,* the River-god,* satyrs,* Silenus,* Sylvans,* Tree-People,* and wood people.* Calormene* gods and goddesses include Tash,* Azaroth,* and Zardeenah.* The question arises, of course, as to what pagan gods and goddesses are doing in a Christian universe. Lewis replies that it is only in God's name that the spirits of nature can rule their domains with "beauty and security." Without God, they would disappear or "become demons."[1]

(PC 47, 50; 150, *135;* 192, *169.* MN 184, *170.*)
[*Mythology; Revelry.*]

---

[1] C. S. Lewis, *The Four Loves* (New York: Harcourt Brace Jovanovich, 1960) p. 166.

GOLD   See *Greed.*

GOLDEN AGE OF NARNIA   The name given to the time of the reign of the Kings and Queens,* from 1000–1015 N.Y.,[1] in which the adventures* of Shasta and Aravis take place. It is ended when Edmund, Lucy, Susan, and Peter vanish[2] from Narnia during the hunt for the White Stag.* During the Golden Age, all that is best of Narnian life is in full bloom: there are many more Talking Beasts* than ever afterward; Narnia is a great sea power; the smaller woodland people and animals* of Narnia feel so safe and secure that

---

they get a bit careless, even ignoring the Calormene* threat; the fierce giants* are driven away and Narnia forms peaceful, friendly alliances with countries "across the sea."

(LWW 180, *166*. PC 50, *52;* 58, *58;* 67, *66.* VDT 22, *29;* 265–266, *263;* 195, *189.* SC 40, *46.* HHB 1, *11;* 164, *145.* LB 41, *43.*)

---

[1] See Lewis's outline of Narnian history in PWD, pp. 42–43.

[2] Dr. Cornelius* speaks legendarily of Queen Susan vanishing from Narnia *"at the end of* the Golden Age" (my emphasis), whereas Susan herself feels that she had blundered out. See *History* for the meaning of these two perspectives.

GOLDEN BELL AND HAMMER   A golden bell and a little hammer enchanted by Jadis stand on a four-foot high square pillar in the middle of the royal hall at Charn.* The enchantment in the hall enables Digory and Polly to understand the meaning of the writing on the pillar,[1] which beckons them to lift the hammer and ring the bell. Polly is firmly against it but Digory, who has in him the seeds of his Uncle Andrew's* corruption, taps it with the hammer. A sweet[2] note rings louder and louder until it culminates in an earthquake* that destroys the room.

(MN 49 ff., *49 ff.*)
[*Andrew Ketterley; Magic; White Witch.*]

---

[1] The verse on the pillar represents the seduction of evil* by dissipation, whereas the verse on the garden* of the west, which Digory later faces, represents the attraction to good through obedience.*

[2] In the *Chronicles* intense sweetness usually indicates evil*; for example, the Turkish Delight* with which the White Witch enchants Edmund. See *Right and wrong.*

GOLDEN TREE   A tree* made of real gold that grows from two half-sovereigns that fall out of Uncle Andrew's* pockets into the rich Narnian soil. Along with the Silver Tree,* it grows inside the cage in which Andrew is kept.

(MN 132, *122;* 168, *155;* 171, *158.*)
[*Greed; Toffee Tree; Tree of Protection.*]

GOLDWATER ISLAND   See *Deathwater Island.*

GOLG   An Earthman captured by Puddleglum after the death* of the Queen of Underland.* He is three feet tall, has little pink eyes, a hard ridge on his head, and the look of a pigmy hippopotamus. He is primarily a vehicle for conveying the characteristics of Earthmen* and their reaction to the death of the Queen.

When Golg first encounters Rilian, Eustace, Jill, and Puddleglum, he thinks they are out to do him violence in the name of the Queen. Learning that they have killed her, he tells them about his people and their way of life. Trapped in Underland,* they have been planning to fight to go back to their underground kingdom, Bism, because they fear being sent by the Queen to

---

EASTERN OCEAN

SILVER SEA

SEA PEOPLE

DARK ISLAND

RAMANDU'S ISLAND

LAND OF THE DUFFERS

DEATHWATER

BURNT ISLAND

DRAGON ISLAND

LONE ISLANDS

AVRA

BERNSTEAD

NARROWHAVEN

DOORN

FELIMATH

REDHAVEN

BRENN

SEVEN ISLES

MUIL

TEREBINTHIA

GALMA

CAIR PARAVEL

THE *VOYAGE OF THE DAWN TREADER*

N E S W

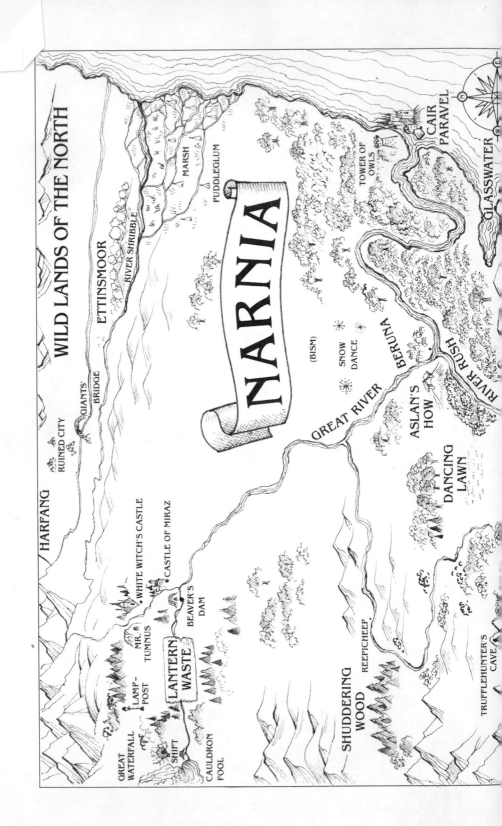

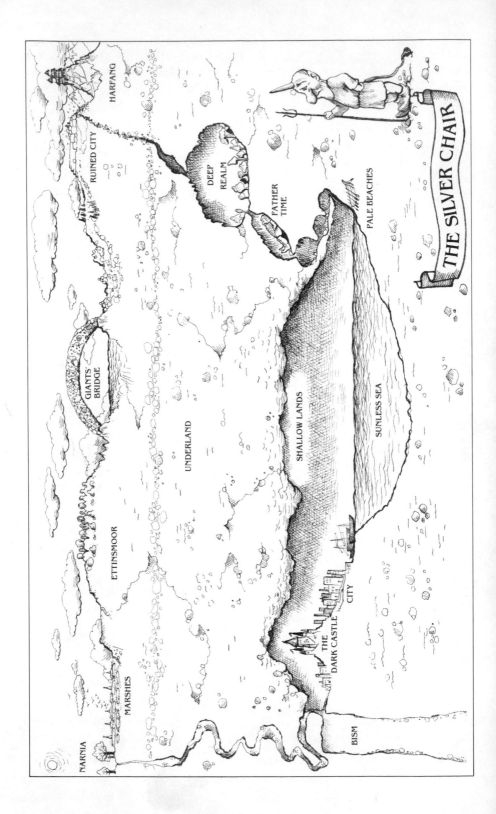

wage war in Overland (which they perceive as a terrible place without a roof and only "a great emptiness called sky"). The four adventurers reassure Golg, and he joyfully tells his people that the Queen is dead and that these travelers can be trusted. He invites the four to visit the land of Bism, where he promises to show them the fiery salamanders.* Golg then shows them the way to the surface, wishing them well.

(SC 173 ff., *169 ff.*)

GOVERNMENT   Narnia is meant to be governed by a Son of Adam* or Daughter of Eve who is guided by the precepts Aslan gave to King Frank* and Queen Helen* in MN. When a king* or queen of Narnia does not rule with humility, honesty, and fairness, the country falls into unhappiness and chaos. In *A Preface to Paradise Lost,* [1] Lewis discusses the medieval concept of hierarchy,* and states that "order can be destroyed in two ways: (1) By . . . Tyranny or [its opposite] Servility. (2) By . . . Rebellion or [its opposite] Remissness." Each of these is in evidence in the history of Narnian governments.

Good Government   The first good government of Narnia is headed by King Frank and Queen Helen. The Golden Age* is so because of the rule of the Kings and Queens.* They "made good laws . . . kept the peace . . . saved good trees* from being unnecessarily cut down . . . and generally stopped busybodies and interferers and encouraged ordinary people who wanted to live and let live." The rule of Caspian X is good because he rules like the High King Peter. (In his desire to go to Aslan's country,* Caspian is momentarily tempted to abdicate; but he is reminded of his solemn oath* by Reepicheep.) Lewis says that Rilian "ruled Narnia well and the land was happy in his days," although this does not happen within the time-frame of SC. King Lune* combines the informality of old clothes with the courtesy* of an emperor, a combination Lewis seems to applaud. Cor and Aravis, Lewis tells us, "made a good King and Queen of Archenland.*" By the time of LB, the world is falling apart; and although Tirian* is a good and well-meaning king, even he is affected by the general disorder of the times. Over all the human kings, of course, is the sovereignty of Aslan and his council, called infrequently and only in times of great danger.

Tyranny   Tyranny in Narnia is marked by unfair laws, random killing or killing for revenge, and a lack of the spirit of revelry.* The first tyrannical rule mentioned in the *Chronicles* is that of the White Witch, who imposed the Hundred Years of Winter* on Narnia and is determined to kill the children* before they can assume the thrones in Cair Paravel. In PC, Narnia is once again under tyranny, this time the Telmarine* rule of the usurper Miraz.* He has intrigued to remove the good lords from his court by murder and false imprisonment, and intends to kill his own nephew, Caspian, to prevent him from ascending to his rightful throne. Under Miraz and others, the Telmarines have imposed high taxes and stern laws, have lost the navigational art that made the Narnians famous, and have destroyed the balance of nature. In SC, the Queen of Underland* rules the Earthmen* by enchantment. Her subjects are her slaves, and they shuffle about in the darkness performing their joyless tasks. In HHB the Calormene* ruler, the Tisroc,* is a consummate tyrant. He kicks his Grand Vizier,[2] threatens his son with death, and will not rest until Narnia is under his power. Because of the rigid class structure of Calormen, its wealthy citizens live in perfumed luxury while its peasants live in servility and squalor. In MN, tyrannical rule is taken to its natural outcome by Jadis, who wanted so badly to rule Charn* that she destroyed the country and all its inhabitants in order to do so. As ruler of a dead land, she is eager to come to earth and add it to her colonies. Andrew Ketterley,* her pale shadow, is obsessed with the commercial possibilities of the newly created and fertile Narnia; his aspirations, however, are soon crushed by the Talking Beasts.* Aslan predicts that our world will shortly be "ruled by tyrants who care no more for joy* and justice and mercy than the Empress Jadis." The final evil government of Narnia is that of Shift* and the encroaching Calormenes. It is marked by slavery, lies, confusion, and overwhelming sadness.

Rebellion   The epitome of a civil servant, Gumpas,* has been allowed to assume rule of the Lone Islands* because they have been excluded from direct Narnian influence for so long. Taking the title "His Sufficiency" (not efficient or excellent, but just independent), Gumpas has created a chaos of bureaucracy. Although he seems to be always "muddling and messing about with accounts and regulations," everything in the islands is a mess. The streets are dirty, the gate's bars and bolts are rusty, and the guards' armor is "disgraceful." Whereas it is the class system that is responsible for disorder in the streets of Calormene, here it is because of their rebellion against the rightful authority of Narnia that the islanders have become so remiss. The slave trade,* which Gumpas defends as an economic necessity, flourishes under his rule. In our world, his counterpart is seen in the Head,* who is so good at interfering with other people's work that she is eventually kicked upstairs to Parliament, where she can happily interfere with all of England.* The one clear example of remissness is Caspian's attempted abdication; an oblique example may be perceived in Susan's refusal to remain a queen in Narnia.

(LWW 180–181, *166*. PC 50, *52; 53, 54; 65, 64; 66, 65*. VDT 42, *51;* 193, *188;* 209, *203*. SC 32, *39;* 216, *206*. HHB 203, *178*. MN 119, *111;* 167, *155;* 178, *164;* 179, *165*. LB 9, *14*.)
[*Ecology; Technology.*]

---

[1] C. S. Lewis, *A Preface to Paradise Lost* (London: Oxford University Press, 1969) p. 76.

[2] According to Professor T. W. Craik, Lewis may have gotten the idea of kicking from William Beckford's *Vathek* (also an Eastern tale), in which it plays a fairly conspicuous part. Cf. Keats's letters in which, after visiting Burns's birthplace and finding the guide wearisome, he says, "I should like to employ Caliph Vathek to kick him" (Letter of July 11–13, 1818). See also *Literary allusions.*

GREAT COUNCIL   Prince Caspian's council of war against Miraz,* held on the Dancing Lawn* under the almost full moon. In attendance are animals,* satyrs,* birds,* Centaurs,* one giant,* and Red and Black Dwarfs.*

Everyone has a different agenda, but Caspian together with the dwarfs and Centaurs prevail in having the council then and there. As Caspian is about to speak, Camillo the Hare* thinks he smells a man, who turns out to be Doctor Cornelius* (half man, half dwarf). Caspian's old tutor brings the news that Miraz knows of the impending rebellion and is on the march, and discussion turns to choosing a defensible position.

(PC 79 ff., 76 ff.)
[*Aslan's How; Trufflehunter; Violence.*]

GREAT DANCE   See *Dance,* note 1.

GREAT DESERT   The hot, arid barrier between Archenland* on the North and the empire of Calormen* on the south. Its northern boundary is the river Winding Arrow.* The desert stretches for untold miles, cold and dead gray at night, burning hot with blinding bright sand by day. Although at night it is silent except for the occasional howls of packs of jackals, birds can be heard singing in the morning. Its central oasis can provide only enough water for small groups. Although it is longer, the western route across the desert is better because it leads to a hidden valley through which a small river runs. Shasta, Bree, Hwin, and Aravis must cross the Great Desert to reach freedom in Archenland and Narnia. Lewis's excellent description of the grueling journey helps us to appreciate the travelers' relief at finding a refreshing pool of clear, cool water to bathe in and to drink.[1]

The southern edge of the desert begins outside Tashbaan,* and the tombs are its gateway.[2] Twelve stone, beehive-shaped tombs are scattered randomly, each with a low doorway that opens into blackness. In the moonlight the tombs seem huge and frightening to Shasta, but in the light of day they seem ordinary. Here Lewis tries to allay children's fear* of the dark.[3]

(HHB 65–66, 62–66; Chapter 6 passim.)

---

[1] The comfort* found at such a place of respite, as well as the trials of a desert crossing, are both traditional Christian images of the ambiguity of the pleasures this world affords and of the struggle (and often the great discomfort) of following Christ. Further, the desert is a symbol of the spiritual combat, the scene where Jesus confronts Satan, the region where the devil seems to hold sway. Because of their desire to imitate Christ in all the mysteries of his life, monks and nuns have lived for centuries in deserts and, more recently, discovered the desert within the city. Finally, the desert is the symbol for the profoundest purifying that God works in a person's life: the dark night of the senses, in which God detaches us from our desire always to have good feelings when we pray; and the dark night of the soul, in which God tests our faith by removing all evidence of his activity in order to reveal to us both the depth of his love for us and the true depth of our love for him. Lewis was well aware of these meanings as can be gauged from his numerous references to Gethsemane, when Jesus was abandoned by his Father; see, for example, *The Screwtape Letters* (New York: Macmillan Publishing Co., 1961) p. 39 letter viii, the last sentence of the penultimate paragraph: "Our cause [the cause of Satan] is never more in danger than when a human, no longer desiring, but still intending, to do our Enemy's will [that is, God's will], looks round upon a universe from which every trace of Him seems to have vanished, and asks why he has been forsaken, and still obeys."

[2] The Calormen culture, which is based on Middle Eastern cultures, has a fear of the dead, ghosts,* and ghouls,* and would of course relegate its cemeteries to the wastes beyond the living city.

[3] See *Dark Island* for a further discussion of this subject.

GREATNESS OF GOD, THE   As children grow older, they discover that the house they grew up in and the familiar sights and people of their childhood have all grown smaller. In a remarkable reversal of this expectation, Lucy, when she meets with Aslan for the first time in PC, comments to him that he seems to have grown bigger. The Lion tells her that he has not grown larger but that, because she has grown, she finds him bigger. He seems to state a principle that as persons continue to grow, they will continue to find him bigger. This revelation makes Lucy so happy that she is silent.* The allegorical intention of this scene is twofold: a person's growth in Christian maturity will always be matched by God's growth in meaning for that person; and yet we will never have a comprehensive knowledge* of God.

Lewis comes at this same insight another way in the discussion between Shasta and the Large Voice in the night fog. Shasta asks the Voice if he is a giant.* It responds that in a certain sense it is a giant but not like the creatures Shasta has in his fearful imagination.* If giants are partly a hieroglyph of power, then God is gigantic, Lewis is trying to say. But this part of the picture needs the complement of the other experiences of God that Shasta has that night: God the provident one, intimately involved in a person's history,* gloriously strong and beautiful and wise.

Theologians use the term transcendence to describe the otherness, the "largeness," and the "overness" of God with respect to all creation. This term is often used as a complement to or in contrast to immanence, the "hereness" and "withinness" of God. This pair of terms must be kept in balance. If God's transcendence is stressed (as in some Eastern religions and in some Christian denominations), then a way is open for a divorce to be decreed between God and what he has made, and creation to be denigrated. If God's immanence is stressed (as in pantheism; or as in naturalism, where Nature is said to have, within her, her own explanation of her existence), then God is in danger of being relegated to the history of ideas. The latter Lewis considered to be the distortion of the last two centuries and he devoted considerable thought to its correction.[1]

(PC 136, *124*. VDT 107, *111*. HHB 157, *138*.)

---

[1] See, for example, *Miracles* (New York: Macmillan Publishing Co., 1978; London: Collins Fontana, 1960), the first eleven chapters; "Religion without Dogma?" in *God in the Dock,* Walter Hooper, ed. (Grand Rapids: Wm. B. Eerdmans Publishing Co., 1970) pp. 129–146; "De Futilitate," *Christian Reflections,* Walter Hooper, ed. (Grand Rapids: Wm. B. Eerdmans Publishing Co., 1967) pp. 57–71; and "De Descriptione Temporum," *Selected Literary Essays,* Walter Hooper, ed. (London: Cambridge University Press, 1969) pp. 1–14.

GREAT REUNION   The reunion of all the good characters in the *Chronicles* takes place in four stages in LB: Tirian is reunited with the Seven Friends of Narnia,* who include his helpers Jill and Eustace;[1] these eight are joined by their comrades-at-arms from the Last Battle*;[2] these meet the heroes from the War of Deliverance* and from the Golden Age of Narnia*;[3] and all of these go on to meet Aslan and Mr. and Mrs. Pevensie.*[4]

(LB 133 ff.; *122 ff.*)

¹ LB 133, *122.*
² LB 154, *140.*
³ LB 176–179, *159–162.*
⁴ LB 182, *164.*

GREAT RIVER   The major river of Narnia, which flows out of Caldron Pool* and runs from west to east across the valley. Created by Aslan on the first day, it is ruled by the River-god* and inhabited by his daughters, the Naiads,* in response to the command "be divine waters." A long stone bridge erected over it by the citizens of Beruna* is destroyed by Bacchus* and his followers at the behest of the River-god, and the command of Aslan.

(PC 45, *48;* 150, *135;* 192–193, *169–170.* MN 101, *95;* 117, *109.* LB 2, *8.*) [*Creation of Narnia; Geography, Narnian.*]

GREAT SNOW DANCE   See *Dance; Dancing Lawn.*

GREAT WATERFALL¹   The farthest western limit of Narnia and the source of the Great River.* It falls from enormously high cliffs and pours into Caldron Pool.* Farsight* leads the company to the waterfall in LB, and Jewel* is the first to go up the Great Waterfall to Aslan's country.* He is followed by Tirian,* Eustace, the dogs,* and Jill.

(MN 143, *132;* 147, *136.* LB 2, *8;* 172–173, *156–157.*) [*Geography, Narnian.*]

---

¹ Waterfalls are a recurrent image in Lewis's writing. In *Miracles* (New York: Macmillan Publishing Co., 1978; London: Collins Fountain, 1960) p. 151, *155,* man is likened to the curve in a waterfall. In *The Abolition of Man* (New York: Macmillan Publishing Co., 1965) p. 14–15, the example Lewis uses is Coleridge's story of the two tourists viewing a waterfall. One called it sublime, and his view both Coleridge and Lewis endorse. In *The Great Divorce* (New York: Macmillan Publishing Co., 1965) pp. 42–46, the lovingly described waterfall is also "a bright angel who stood, like one crucified, against the rocks and poured himself perpetually down towards the forest with loud joy."

GREAT WOODS   The Old Narnian name for the forest that ranges from the Eastern Sea* inland as far as the Hill of the Stone Table,* and from above Cair Paravel on the north to the southern mountains that are the border between Narnia and Archenland.* During the reign of the Telmarine* conquerors, this forest is renamed the Black Woods* when the invaders begin to fear* the trees.* The awakened trees are the deciding factor in the final battle of the War of Deliverance,* when they take advantage of the dendrophobia of the Telmarines and chase the army into the Great River.* As a result of this victory, the forest reclaims its original name.

(PC 50, *53;* 85, *81;* 190, *167.*) [*Geography, Narnian.*]

GREED   The impulse toward greed is almost always the downfall of the overtly wicked characters; but it is also a temptation faced (and overcome) by the good characters of the *Chronicles*. Uncle Andrew* becomes involved in dark magic* because of his greed for power, and in Narnia he is unable to see its glory and is greedy for what the fertile soil can bring him commercially. All of the witches—the White Witch, Jadis, and the Queen of Underland*— are greedy for power over other worlds, be they Narnia or our world. The Calormenes* are perenially greedy for power over Narnia. Edmund's greed for more Turkish Delight* causes him to betray his brother and sisters; Eustace's greed for the dragon's gold causes him actually to become a dragon.* The flush of greed comes over Caspian's face on Deathwater Island* as he dreams about the power this magic* water might bring him.[1] Growing more greedy every moment, he claims the island for Narnia for all time and swears all to secrecy on pain of death. The argument grows greater until Aslan erases their memories; they only remember that something terrible is connected with the place, and they shun it.

---

[1] Alert readers might see here an allusion to King Midas's golden touch.

GREENROOF   One of the Narnian summer months. The name suggests the lush foliage of the season.

(PC 173, *152*.)
[*Calendar, Narnian.*]

GRIFFLE   A cynical black dwarf who is the spokesman for the majority of dwarfs* released by Tirian.* He does not believe in Aslan, and declares that the dwarfs won't be taken in twice by imitations. He is altogether rude: when Jill protests that she has seen the real Aslan, Griffle retorts that she's learned her catechism very well, and when Tirian rebukes him for his discourtesy to Jill, the dwarf replies that he has as little use for more kings* as he has for more Aslans. He declares the dwarfs to be independent of any allegiance. Griffle is present for the final assembly at Stable* Hill. In the struggle between the dwarfs and the Calormenes, Tirian hears Griffle using "dreadful language." Because Diggle* is the spokesman for the dwarfs who survive the Last Battle* to be thrown into the Stable,* it is presumed that Griffle was killed in the battle.

(LB 71–73, *68–70;* 104, *96;* 127, *117*.)

GUMPAS   Governor of the Lone Islands,* called His Sufficiency. Gumpas is the epitome of the petty civil servant, immersed in detail and unmindful of the larger issues. He is completely immersed in accounts, forms, rules, and regulations. He is described as bilious, with mostly gray hair in which there is still a touch of red, and is ill-tempered, angry, peevish, and choleric. Although Lord Bern* has petitioned him a hundred times to put a stop to the flourishing slave trade,* he tolerates the slavers who live in and sail out of

Narrowhaven.* When asked to defend his stand, he cites graphs and statistics to prove the necessity of the slave trade to the island's developing economy. He is removed from office by Caspian, and replaced with Lord Bern, who is made Duke, thus putting an end to corrupt civil government.* The etymological derivation of his name is uncertain. Lewis was aware of the Latin word *gumphus,* meaning "nail,"[1] and probably liked its sound—it certainly suggests grumpiness and pomposity, two of his most striking characteristics. The word *gumpus,* meaning "a foolish person," is found in a letter written by Sir Walter Scott in 1825, in which he says, "Put that [portmanteau] in your mouth, you gumpus."[2]

(VDT 33, *40;* 42, *51.*)

---

[1] *The Discarded Image* (London: Cambridge University Press, 1964) p. 60.
[2] Walter Scott, *Familiar Letters, 1832,* John G. Lockhart, ed., 1894.

GWENDOLEN   A Berunan schoolgirl who disrupts her class by calling attention to the Lion outside. Aslan invites her to join in the party, calling her "sweetheart" (a possible allusion to Lewis's belief that God first loves us, even before we recognize him). She is overjoyed at Aslan's invitation and immediately joins the dancing Maenads.* They help her take off her unnecessary and uncomfortable clothes, an action suggestive of Lewis's admitted abhorrence of school* clothes as the ultimate restraints. Lewis may have taken her name from Gwendolyn Fairfax, the heroine of Oscar Wilde's *The Importance of Being Earnest,* a play Lewis knew quite well.[1] The allusion, however, is to the name only and not to the character.

(PC 194–195, *170–171.*)
[*Autobiographical allusions; Beruna; Literary allusions; Prizzle, Miss.*]

---

[1] See C. S. Lewis, *Selected Literary Essays,* Walter Hooper, ed. (London: Cambridge University Press, 1969) p. 270, and Walter Hooper, ed., *They Stand Together* (New York: Macmillan Publishing Co.; London: Collins, 1979) pp. 182, 248; *182, 248.*

HAGS   Ugly old witches summoned by the White Witch to the slaying of Aslan at the Stone Table.* Four hags bind the Lion, and stand one at each corner of the table, holding torches. Even after the crowning of the four Kings

---

and Queens,* rumors of hags are heard. In PC, the Five Black Dwarfs* are in favor of asking the aid of a hag up in the crags, and Nikabrik's* friend at the council of war is an obsequious hag who claims only minor magical* skills, which she will gladly use against Miraz.* She whines that the White Lady (her name for the White Witch) is not dead—nobody's ever heard of a witch that died. She is beheaded by Trumpkin* as she attacks Doctor Cornelius,* and is presumed dead, although her earlier statement would seem to deny this possibility.

(LWW 132, *123;* 148, *138;* 151, *140;* 180, *166.* PC 72, *70;* 159, *142;* 165–166, *146–147.*)
[*Evil.*]

HAMADRYADS   In Greek and Roman mythology,* a wood nymph* who lives and dies with the tree of which it is the spirit. They are mentioned in conjunction with Dryads* in PC by Lucy and Trufflehunter.* Their creation by Aslan is not specified; they appear to have come into being in response to Aslan's command for Narnia to awake, and for the trees* to be waking trees. They are therefore part of the wild people of the wood. No specific individual Hamadryad or its activity is mentioned in the *Chronicles.*

(PC 112, *103;* 184, *161.* MN 117, *109.*)
[*Tree-People; Wood people.*]

HAMMER   See *Leopard.*

HARDBITERS   The family name of three badgers summoned to and present at Caspian's Great Council,* which plans the War of Deliverance.* When a "man" approaches (it is actually Doctor Cornelius*), Caspian sends two of them to investigate. The name "Hardbiter" evokes the fierce tenacity that is an important ingredient in the hieroglyph "badger."

(PC 76, *73;* 81–82, *77–78.*)
[*Animals; Talking Beasts; Trufflehunter.*]

HARFANG   The name of a mountain and of a castle inhabited by bad giants.* The Lady of the Green Kirtle,* however, says these giants are gentle, prudent, and courteous. If she is to be believed, their life, even in their harsh surroundings, is one of great pleasure and ease. When Eustace, Jill, and Puddleglum first see Harfang it stands high on a crag, looking more like a house than a castle, with low windows outside the wall and little doors in odd places; in fact, its aspect is more friendly than threatening. The children* greet the porter, a short giant—only the height of an apple tree.* After remarking on the blue color of the children's faces (a dislocation of the imagination* for readers), he sends a staring child giant to the main house to announce their arrival and offers Puddleglum a drink from a silver salt-cellar stolen from his masters.

When the King and Queen hear Eustace's speech offering themselves for the Autumn Feast,* they leer at each other. Jill does not like their smiles, and her crying prompts the Queen to order dolls, lollipops, physics (in Lewis's time prescribed for every childhood ailment), possets (hot milk curdled with spices and liquor, also a childhood remedy), caraway candy, lullabies, and toys, which in the children's eyes are crudely made and colored. Lewis appears to make the Queen's response an ironic summary of the many instant and often inappropriate remedies that adults* foist upon children.

(SC 76 ff., *80 ff.*)

HAROLD SCRUBB   The father of Eustace and a resident of Cambridge. Eustace addresses him as Harold, a custom contrary to the attitude of respect that Lewis felt children should have for their parents. When Eustace writes in his diary that Harold maintained that one of the cowardly attitudes of ordinary people is to refuse to look at the facts (in an attempt to explain why the adventurers ignore the fact that the *Dawn Treader* is about to be swamped), Harold's generally arrogant attitude is implied.

(VDT 1, *9;* 24, *31.*)
[*Adults; Alberta Scrubb.*]

HARPHA   A Tarkaan,* the father of Emeth.* Harpha is misspelled "Harpa" in the American edition of the *Chronicles.*

(LB 161, *146.*)

HASTILUDE   A medieval form of spear-play; a kind of tournament which was almost as dangerous as war itself. Rabadash* excels at this form of entertainment.

(HHB 62, *60.*)

HEAD   The unnamed[1] woman who runs Experiment House.* She favors the bullies in the Gang,* finds them interesting psychological cases, and makes them her special friends. Lewis makes a cutting comment on modern education as represented by Experiment House, and modern educators as personified by the Head.[2] After her hysterical reaction to the extraordinary return of Eustace and Jill, her friends see that she can be no further use as a Head, so she is made an inspector to interfere with other Heads. A failure at that duty, she is kicked upstairs to Parliament, where she happily interferes with government* for the rest of her life.

(SC 2, *11;* 215–216, *205–206.*)
[*Schools; Sexism.*]

---

[1] In the first draft of MN, she is named Gertrude, and she is an orphaned Digory's aunt (PWD, p. 48).

[2] Lewis impugns the imaginations of professional educators in his 1952 address to the British Library Association, "On Three Ways of Writing for Children": "I will not say that a good story for children could never be written by someone in the Ministry of Education, for all things are possible. But I should lay very long odds against it" (OOW, p. 34).

HEAVEN   See *Aslan's country.*

HEDGEHOGS   An unnamed hedgehog greets Shasta in a thick and rather wheezy voice coming from "a small prickly person with a dark face." Hogglestock is a large hedgehog who represents his kind at the Great Council.*

(HHB 163–165, *143–145.* PC 76, *73.*)
[*Talking Beasts.*]

HELEN   First Queen of Narnia, wife of King Frank I*; before coming to Narnia she was a London housewife named Nellie. She is transported into Narnia by Aslan, at Frank's wish that his wife be there too. She looks lovely, and her instinctive curtsy in the presence of royalty (Aslan) is one of her stock responses.* She and Polly become friends, and she intercedes with Aslan to ask that Polly be allowed to go on the quest* for the apple* with Digory. At her coronation she wears her hair loose and falling to her shoulders, and her train is attended by the Naiads.* She gives birth to many children (at least two boys and two girls) and her second son becomes the first King of Archenland.*[1] She is last seen on her throne with King Frank in the garden* of the west at the Great Reunion.*[2]

(MN 137, *127;* 145, *135;* 167, *154–155.* LB 179, *162.*)
[*Kings, queens.*]

---

[1] For a different story, see *Col.*
[2] See *Frank I,* note 3.

HELL   Although hell is not specifically mentioned in the *Chronicles,* it can be inferred in at least two instances. In LB, Tash* is dismissed to "his own place," which is implicitly a place of permanent punishment. Since heaven, a place of infinite joy,* corresponds to Aslan's country,* it may be assumed that Tash's place corresponds to hell. Diggle* the dwarf* speaks for his fellows when he calls the inside of the Stable* a "pitch-black, pokey, smelly little hole." This is at least a hell of his own making, and calls to mind the theme of Lewis's *The Pilgrim's Regress,* [1] in which Lewis discusses hell and its fixed pains as God's last "mercy" to those who will let him do no other.

(LB 133, *121;* 144, *131.*)

---

[1] C. S. Lewis, *The Pilgrim's Regress* (Grand Rapids: Wm. B. Eerdmans Publishing Co., 1958) pp. 178–182.

HERMIT OF THE SOUTHERN MARCH   A 109-year-old man who lives on the southern border of Archenland,* north of the Great Desert.* The barefoot hermit is tall and bearded, dressed in an ankle-length robe,* and he leans on a straight staff. His enclosure is perfectly circular (the very picture of the divine wholeness of the place) and his pool—in which he can see events happening elsewhere—is perfectly still (symbolic of the quality and depth of his prayer). A huge, beautiful tree* stands at one end, and the finest grass covers the ground. He lives in an old stone, thatch-roofed house, and keeps goats. In appearance, he is very like two other old men, Ramandu* and Coriakin.* Curiously, although these two are retired stars,* the Hermit is not; but his presence must be equally as commanding as theirs, for Shasta mistakes him for the King* of Archenland.* He is a magician* of sorts, and by his art can read the present but not the future.[1] He loves animals,* calling the goats his cousins and giving Bree and Hwin rubdowns worthy of a king's groom. During a conversation with Aravis about her strangely superficial wounds (which she attributes to luck), the Hermit says that he has never met the thing called luck.[2] He admits he doesn't understand the meaning of it all, but he exercises *studiositas*[3] and hope: "If ever we need to know the meaning, you may be sure that we shall."

(HHB Chapter 10 passim; 149, *132;* 155, *137;* 179 ff., *157 ff.;* 189, *166;* 194, *170.*)

---

[1] He contradicts this by saying that he knows by *art* that Shasta will find the king.
[2] See *Providence.*
[3] See *Curiosity.*

HIERARCHY   According to the principle of hierarchy, which has roots in both biblical and Greek philosophical thought,[1] there is an ascending order of nobility among creatures depending upon their mode of existence. The preeminence of the children* as Sons of Adam* and Daughters of Eve and as humans; the distinction between the Talking Beasts* and the Dumb Beasts*; the importance of rightful authority and its acknowledgement in honor,* obedience,* and courtesy*—all of these elements within the *Chronicles* afford us a glimpse of a cosmos that is shot through with the principle of hierarchy. In LWW, the question of their human heritage is put to the children three times: first, in the meeting between Tumnus* and Lucy; second, when Edmund encounters the White Witch; and finally, when Mr. Beaver* establishes contact with the four children. When they are introduced to Mrs. Beaver,* her awed response raises our expectations of these children precisely as humans, as descendents of Adam and Eve.[2] We then learn, as Mr. Beaver quotes the old prophecies, that Aslan's advent to "put all to rights" will be accompanied by the appearance of four human children and their enthronement at Cair Paravel.[3]

In PC, Caspian is acknowledged as the rightful ruler of Narnia by the Talking Beasts not only because of his immediate lineage, but also because he is a human and a Son of Adam. "Narnia was never right except when a Son of Adam was King," Trufflehunter* says in response to Nikabrik's* hatred and suspicion of humans. This acknowledgement is seconded by the Three Bulgy Bears* and then by the great Centaur* Glenstorm,* who announces that "a Son of Adam has once more arisen to rule and name creatures." In MN we learn about King Frank* and Queen Helen*—the cabby and his wife who are chosen to be the first rulers of Narnia by Aslan. "You shall rule and name all these creatures, and do justice among them, and protect them from their enemies when enemies arise."

In all these instances it is the humans who are clearly born to rule and to make history; how they choose to respond in the face of Aslan's initiatives is decisive for the history* of Narnia, though Aslan always has the last word. It is, for example, a human choice that brings evil* into Narnia at its creation, setting the stage for both Edmund's betrayal and Aslan's suffering in LWW. In the final chapter of MN, Aslan warns the children of the destructive possibilities of human freedom. A whole world—Charn*—has been blotted out through the evil choices of Empress Jadis: "Let the race of Adam and Eve take warning."[4]

But humanity is not arbitrarily placed in such an awesome position of responsibility over material creation, including Narnia: it is naturally suited to this role. And here the traditional philosophical estimate of humanity's place in the cosmic hierarchy dovetails with the biblical one. Humans are the ruling animals because they are the rational animals. The meaning of humanness as rational and free existence is as important a theme in the *Chronicles* as is the historical lineage of the children as Sons and Daughters of Adam and Eve. It might be argued that the Talking Beasts, to whom Aslan gave the gift of speech* and dominion over the Dumb Beasts, are on an equal footing with the humans.[5] The same might be said of the dwarfs,* who are certainly human-like; in fact Caspian does make Trumpkin* his Lord Regent. Why, then, is there not greater equality between these creatures and human beings? The explanation is that Lewis's innovation, far from collapsing the hierarchy into a democracy, introduces a new rung on the ladder of being. Just as the logic of the medieval hierarchy allowed for a fuller, more perfect rational life above the human level (the angels), Lewis provides for a less perfect one below. To this metaphysical explanation a theological consideration must also be added: God surely equips each creature for its task within the overall hierarchy of being and presumably could equip a Talking Beast to rule Narnia. Even when the cabby and his wife are made the first rulers of Narnia, and when the children become kings* and queens of Narnia, they have to grow into these positions. Why, then, must a Son of Adam always rule in Narnia? Because, says Lewis,[6] with the incarnation of Christ as man on the earth, the universe has turned a corner.[7]

(LWW 9, *16;* 29, *35;* 63, *64;* 68, *68;* 74 ff., *74 ff.;* 104, *99–100.* PC 65, *65;* 69, *67;* 74, *72.* MN 136–138, *126–128;* 178, *164.*)

---

[1] For Aristotle, the more a being approaches a conscious, personal mode of existence (that is, the more spirituality or immateriality is a factor in its makeup) the greater and more perfect its activity of being and the higher it is on the hierarchy (*On The Soul,* I, 1, 403ᵃ 3–10; Aquinas follows Aristotle in *Summa Contra Gentiles,* IV, 11). Lewis illustrates this hierarchical interpretation of reality in "Imagination and Thought in the Middle Ages" in *Studies in Medieval and Renaissance Literature,* Walter Hooper, ed. (London: Cambridge University Press, 1966) p. 50: ". . . stones, for example, have only being; vegetables, being and life; animals, being, life and sense; man,

When Scrubb, Jill, and Puddleglum discover the giants' recipes for cooking Men and Marsh-Wiggles, they realize they must flee Harfang before the giant cook wakes up and turns them into dinner. (SC 114-115, 115.)

being, life, sense and reason." Although each of the creatures mentioned occurs in the same cosmos, each one exists in a deeper, more profound way than what precedes it on the scale. Without entering into metaphysical explanation, Genesis assumes and implies a hierarchy when it places humanity at the summit of material creation as its steward. Again, the New Testament implies a hierarchy in the significance it assigns to human decisions with regard to the fate of the whole cosmos. Medieval thinkers combined these metaphysical and biblical insights into a finely detailed cosmology, which Lewis recounts in *The Discarded Image* and adapts for use in his Space Trilogy.

2 There even seems to be a faint echo of Simeon's *nunc dimittis* from the gospel of Luke (2:29–32). "At last! To think that ever I should live to see this day!"says Mrs. Beaver.

3 The titles Son of Adam and Daughter of Eve are again invoked when Father Christmas* fits Peter, Lucy, and Susan out with gifts* appropriate to their respective tasks in the struggle against the evil* Witch.

4 The crucial role assigned to human choice parallels the biblical estimate of humanity's place in the cosmos. Its free, personal decision in the face of God's initiative decides the fate of the entire created cosmos, first in the catastrophic disobedience of the old Adam; and second in the eucatastrophic, redemptive obedience of Jesus, the new Adam who is not only true God but true man.

5 See *Gift of speech* for an explanation of this argument.

6 See *Perelandra* (Macmillan Publishing Co., 1962) pp. 62, 82 and 215.

7 In the medieval vision reality is headed by God, the source of all being. From that unreachable apex one crosses over into creation and the scale works itself down from the highest angel to the lowest inanimate material being. Christ has a special place in the whole system since he is on both sides of the great divide between Creator and creature. In Narnia, the hierarchy is topped by the transcendent Emperor-beyond-the-Sea.* Aslan—as Son of the Emperor-beyond-the-Sea, and Lord of the Wood, and King of Beasts—has one foot in Narnia and one foot in the realm across the sea. Ultimately, he is the bridge between the two realms; this becomes clear at the end of LB. But the analogy to Christ must not be pushed too far here. Aslan comes on the scene always and already a lion*: he didn't become incarnate as a lion in order to save Narnia. Aslan is followed in nobility by the humans, who are in turn followed by the various other personal and rational species to be found in Narnia.

HISTORY   Lewis names *historicism* "the belief that men can, by the use of their natural powers, discover an inner meaning in the historical process."[1] He argues with the historicists who say that we can explain reality by looking at history, commonly defined as wars and dates. In contrast, he says that what is really important is the peace between wars, and the lives of ordinary people. When Digory wishes to know the names of the places in the newly created Narnia that he and Polly are seeing from the air, Polly reminds him that they won't have names until there are people in those places. Digory is excited at that because then there will be histories, which Polly (speaking for Lewis) equates with the very dull learning of battles and dates. In LB, Jewel* comments that history is made up of big events, but that the times of peace flow on with no chronology. He explains to Jill (an incipient historicist) that there's *not* "always so much happening in Narnia," and that in between the visits of the English children* there were "hundreds and thousands of years . . . in which there was really nothing to put into the history books."

Tirian,* the last king of Narnia, has been a good student of history, and is inspired to recall all the interventions of the children into Narnian distresses. In Aslan's country,* he remembers that Susan should be among the Seven Friends of Narnia,* and asks where she is. The schoolmistress of the unnamed town* near Beruna is in the midst of teaching a history class when Aslan comes by, and Lewis comments that history as taught under Miraz's* rule was "duller than the truest hisory you have ever read, and less true than the most exciting adventure* story."

[*Books; School; Stories.*]

---

[1] "Historicism" in *Christian Reflections,* Walter Hooper, ed. (Grand Rapids: Wm. B. Eerdmans Publishing Co., 1967) pp. 100–113, and *Fern-seed and Elephants and Other Essays on Christianity,* Walter Hooper, ed. (London: Collins Fontana, 1975), pp. 44–64. Lewis first published this essay in October of 1950. It is crucial to understanding a major theme in the background of the *Chronicles.* See *Appendix One.*

HOGGLESTOCK.   See *Hedgehogs.*

HOLIDAYS   See *Term-time.*

HOLMES, SHERLOCK   The famous fictional sleuth created by Sir Arthur Conan Doyle. He is mentioned by Lewis in the first few paragraphs of MN to set the times. Since Narnia is a work of fiction, it really exists in the world of fiction in which Holmes is also real.

(MN 1, 9.)
[*Bastables.*]

HOLY SPIRIT   In the Judaeo-Christian tradition, the Spirit of God is the creative, strengthening, renewing power of God, symbolized by the breath of life, the wind, fragrant oil, water, and fire. In the Christian doctrine of the Trinity,* the Holy Spirit is the third Person, the principle of sanctification; in the tradition of Western Christianity, he comes forth from the Father and the Son, as in the gospel scene where Jesus, after his resurrection, breathes on his apostles and says, "Receive the Holy Spirit."[1] In the *Chronicles* Lewis reflects his profound assimilation of this Judaeo-Christian tradition in the rich symbolism with which he surrounds Aslan.

The most explicit Narnian reference to the Holy Spirit is in the marvelous scene where the Large Voice speaks a three-fold "Myself" in answer to Shasta's question, "Who *are* you?" The third "Myself" is a nearly inaudible whisper that seems to come from everywhere, as if the leaves rustled with it.[2] Lewis here intends to give a sound-picture of the subtle, yet all-pervasive, activity of the Spirit of God.

Another allusion to the activity of the Spirit is found in Father Christmas's* outfitting of Peter, Susan, and Lucy with their gifts* from Aslan. They are given instruments of combat, surely an allusion to Ephesians 6: 11–18, in which the virtues of truth, righteousness, peace, faith, salvation, and the word of God are the belt, breastplate, shoes, shield, helmet, and sword of the soldier.

Beyond these two allusions, Aslan's breath (with its sometimes emphasized fragrance) is the chief symbol of the Spirit's activity in the *Chronicles.* After his resurrection Aslan breathes on Susan to reassure her that he is not a ghost*;

---

he breathes on the creatures turned to stone in the White Witch's castle* and they return to life. In PC he breathes on Susan to quiet her fears* and twice on Lucy—once in a sheer outpouring of love, and a second time to give her strength to face her companions; Edmund looks formidable to the Lords Glozelle* and Sopespian* because, when Aslan and Edmund had met, the Lion had breathed on him "and a kind of greatness hung on him"; and when Aslan's breath comes over the brave Telmarine* soldier, the man wears a happy but startled look, "as if he were trying to remember something"—he now has the courage* to walk through the door.* In VDT Lucy is heartened by Aslan's voice,* speaking through the albatross,* and by the "delicious smell*" of his breath. In SC Eustace and Jill are blown into Narnia from Aslan's country* and from Narnia back into his country by Aslan's gentle but powerful breath. In HHB the Large Voice breathes on Shasta to assure the boy that it is not a ghost. In LB, in his last gesture before he leaves to make his final appearance at the giants'* stairway, Aslan breathes on Emeth,* taking away the Calormene soldier's fear.

In MN the allusions to the creative and spiritualizing activity of the Holy Spirit are very strong. After the creation of the stars,* "a light wind, very fresh, begins to stir." This will remind the adult reader in the Judaeo-Christian tradition of the first verses of the Book of Genesis, the first book of the Bible. That Lewis intends this allusion is clear from the next reference to the wind, in which he uses the definite article: "the light wind could now be ruffling the grass." When Aslan confers the gift of speech* on the chosen animals,* his "long, warm breath . . . seemed to sway all the beasts as the wind sways a line of trees. . . . Then came a flash of fire (but it burnt nobody) either from the sky or from the Lion itself, and every drop of blood tingled in the children's bodies. . . ." This passage is remarkable for the intense breath image and the addition of the fire image (from the first conferral of the Holy Spirit in the New Testament on Pentecost; see the Acts of the Apostles 2:3–4).[3]

One of the most striking symbols for the Spirit's activity in Narnia is the sweet waters of the Last Sea.* These fortify all who drink them with the power to look directly at the sun* and they diminish the need for food and sleep.* In Christian theology, the Spirit prepares the person to see the glory of God by transforming the person gradually into God's likeness.[4]

Lewis talks relatively little about the Holy Spirit in his writings, and could therefore be said to have a low pneumatology (theology of the Holy Spirit). But his sense of the all-pervasive activity of the Spirit in a person's moral and devotional life, especially as seen in the *Chronicles,* should eliminate anyone's doubt about the completeness of Lewis's Christian experience and theologizing.

(LWW 159, *147;* 164, *152.* PC 136, *124;* 138, *125;* 148, *133;* 174, *153;* 213, *186.* VDT 160, *159.* SC 13, *23;* 22, *31;* 210–211, *201.* HHB 157 ff., *138 ff.* MN 100, *94;* 104, *97;* 116, *108.* LB 165, *149.*)
[*Biblical allusions; Credal elements; Memory.*]

---

[1] Gospel of St. John 20:22.
[2] Alert readers of Lewis will recall a similar, powerful image in his sermon "The Weight of

Glory" in *The Weight of Glory* (Grand Rapids: Wm. B. Eerdmans Publishing Co., 1965) p. 13, and *Screwtape Proposes a Toast* (London: Collins Fontana, 1965) p. 107.

[3] For the allusion in the tingling feeling in the children's blood, see *Gift of speech.*

[4] II Corinthians 3:18.

HONOR   To seek honor unselfishly and to behave honorably may be said to be one definition of a true Narnian. In PC, Caspian is ashamed that he comes of such a dishonorable (Telmarine*) lineage. Aslan replies, "You come of the Lord Adam and Lady Eve. And that is both honor enough to erect the head of the poorest beggar and shame enough to bow the heads and shoulders of the greatest emperor in[1] earth. Be content."

Reepicheep characterizes the voyage of the *Dawn Treader* as a search for honor and adventure,* and honor is often the companion of adventure in the *Chronicles.* Thus Rilian wonders if in passing up the chance to explore Bism, a "marvelous adventure" in itself, he might not fulfill the "honor" expected of him. In HHB, it is in defense of Queen Susan's honor that Prince Corin* knocks down the boy in the streets of Tashbaan.* Uncle Andrew,* who has no sense of honor, is able still to use honor and chivalry as weapons against Digory—who does understand such things—to get him to go to Polly's rescue. In LB, Tirian* is profoundly ashamed of having murdered the two unarmed Calormene* drivers of the talking horse* without first having challenged them; he considers himself a dishonored knight.*

The correlative of honor is to avenge honor, and in slaying the Queen of Underland* Rilian is able to avenge his mother's honor. Vengeance,[2] however, is quite a different thing. It is vengeance that makes Corin want to see Rabadash* dead, but Lune* points out to him that Rabadash is not worthy— not *honorable* enough—of such a death.

(PC 211–212, *185*. VDT 152, *152; 155, 154; 157, 156; 169, 166–167*. SC 46, *52; 161, 158–159; 182–183, 177–178*. HHB 75, *71*. MN 27, *30*. LB 24, *28; 259, 145*.

---

[1] This is a typographical error of "on," which is correct in the British edition.

[2] Prudence, Justice, Temperance, and Fortitude are the four cardinal virtues of both medieval thought and Christian philosophy. Vengeance is considered a form of intemperate anger, an excessive response to a disordered situation, which—no matter how innocent in intent—can only lead to more disorder. See Josef Pieper, *The Four Cardinal Virtues* (Notre Dame: University of Notre Dame Press, 1966) pp. 193–197.

HOPE   See *Longing.*

HORN   Susan's gift* from Father Christmas,* which if blown in great need will always bring help. Its sound,* richer in tone than a bugle, is first heard when the horn is used to call for help against Fenris Ulf.* It was left behind when the children* returned to England* at the end of LWW. This loss, which seems tragic, was really a providence*: by the time of Prince Caspian it is the greatest and most sacred treasure of Narnia, and it is given to the young prince by Doctor Cornelius.* Deciding that this is indeed a time of great need, Caspian blows the horn and succeeds in calling the Pevensies back to Narnia. Its sound this time is described more fully: "strong enough to shake the woods," as "loud as thunder" and longer in duration, cool, sweet notes that fill the air. At the end of PC, Caspian offers Susan the horn but she says he may keep it. Two other horns are mentioned in the *Chronicles:* Father Time's* horn is used to signal the end of Narnia.* Its sound is "high and terrible . . . of a strange, deadly beauty." The horn is thrown into the sea.[1] King Frank's* horn is heard summoning all to process to their meeting with Aslan in the real Narnia.

(LWW 104, *100;* 126, *119.* PC 24, *29–30;* 58, *58;* 89, *85;* 94, *89;* 215, *189.* LB 150–157, *136–143;* 182, *164.*)

---

[1] This is a biblical allusion* to the Book of Revelation, Chapter 8 passim, 9:1, 13, 10:7, and 11:15.

HORRORS   Evil* beings, present at the slaying of Aslan. No precise definition of "horrors" exists for the way Lewis uses the term, but their name reveals something of their characteristic behavior.

(LWW 148, *138.*)

HORSES, HORSEMANSHIP

Horses play a large part in Narnian life and are found throughout the *Chronicles.* The horse, for Lewis, is a complex symbol, the personification of all that is best in our natural desires. Thus good horsemanship, the harmonic interaction of horse and rider, is symbolic of the ultimate reconciliation of our spiritual and physical natures; more specifically, our physical natures give movement to our spirits, which in turn gently guide them.[1] Shasta's increasing skills in horsemanship are probably a symbol of the gradual reunification of spirit and nature Lewis speaks of in *Miracles,*[2] whereas Aravis's Calormene* style of riding—rider as total master of the horse—is typical of the Calormene disregard for nature. In Bree and Hwin, the two most fully developed animal* characters in the seven books, the characteristics of horses that every rider knows are brought to their most noble. That "no one can teach riding so well as a horse" is given its highest meaning when Bree actually tells Shasta how to ride. The acute sense of hearing in horses is acknowledged by Bree's ability to tell by the sound of a horse in the distance that it is a thoroughbred mare being ridden by a fine horseman. Lewis also instructs the reader in proper treatment of horses when he notes that galloping day and night is only for stories,* and that real horses must alternate brisk trots and short walks to stay in the best condition. He also notes the importance of grooming and rubdowns, and the pleasures of water, grass, and hot mash. Of Narnian talking horses in particular we learn that, contrary to Bree's fears, they do love to roll in the grass like other horses, and that although they are not usually mounted they don't mind being ridden on "proper occasions," such as to war.

Strawberry, the cab-horse whose transformation into Fledge* is the very image of risen nature in its glory, is another striking horse character whose treatment at the hands of human beings partially determines their fate. Frank,* the cab-driver, is always considerate of his horse and eventually is crowned the first King of Narnia. Jadis, the villainous witch who flogs Strawberry unmercifully and maddens him with her whispered words, is eventually killed. (She is also a good rider, which seems at variance with Lewis's thought; however, she is undoubtedly of the "horse and master" school of riding.) The winged Fledge carries Digory and Polly to the garden,* and is the vehicle of their ultimate salvation, illustrating Lewis's feeling that humanity and nature must be in harmony in order to enter Aslan's country.* Even the noble Jewel* the Unicorn* is in awe of Fledge's beauty.

Other horses mentioned by name in the *Chronicles* include Destrier*; Pomely*; the Queen of Underland's* horse, Snowflake; and Rilian's horse, Coalblack. A stone horse is mentioned as being in the courtyard of the Castle of the White Witch.* The plight of the talking horse who is harnessed and whipped in LB causes Tirian* and Jewel to commit murder; and over twenty horses are released by the mice* but are slain by the dwarfs* while on their way to help Tirian. Of course, horses are among those who come into Aslan's country after the judgment.

(LWW 92, *89*. SC 167, *163*. HHB passim. MN 86–87, *82;* 144 ff., *133 ff.* LB 178, *160–161;* 120, *111–112;* 154, *140;* 178, *160.*)
[*Animals; Centaurs; Dumb Beasts; Talking Beasts; Violence.*]

---

[1] C. S. Lewis, *The Great Divorce* (New York: Macmillan Publishing Co., 1949) pp. 103–107.
[2] C. S. Lewis, *Miracles* (New York: Macmillan Publishing Co., 1978; London: Collins Fontana, 1960) pp. 126, 161–163, *130, 164–167.*

HOSPITALITY
Freely given hospitality is a fundamental aspect of Narnian life. Mr. and Mrs. Beaver* open their home to the the Pevensie children in LWW; Trumpkin* cares for Caspian in his home, and differs from Nikabrik* about killing the prince because "it would be like murdering a guest." Pattertwig* offers nuts, and the Centaurs* share their food. In VDT, Coriakin* provides a magic* meal for Lucy, and the crew and the Duffers* enjoy a feast. By contrast, Calormenes* demand hospitality. In HHB Arsheesh,* fearful of reprisal, dares not refuse the Tarkaan.* Escaping this Calormene brand of hospitality, Shasta flees to the north and has his first Narnian meal in the home of the dwarf* brothers Duffle,* Rogin, and Bricklethumb. The giants'* hospitality at Harfang* is even worse: they are only kind to Jill, Eustace, and Puddleglum because they intend to eat them at the Autumn Feast.*

[*Courtesy.*]

HOUSE OF PROFESSOR DIGORY KIRKE
A large, complicated country house in the south of England* located ten miles from the nearest railway station. It is full of all sorts of rooms and places to hide—an armor room, a harp room, a billiard room, rooms and rooms full of books,*[1] and one room with only a wardrobe* in it. Old and famous, it is mentioned in guidebooks and histories of the area. In his younger days, Digory lived in the house with his mother Mabel,* his father, and Uncle Andrew.*

---

[1] Lewis's own book-filled boyhood home is lovingly described in his autobiography, *Surprised by Joy* (New York: Harcourt Brace Jovanovich, 1955) p. 10.

HOUSE OF THE MAGICIAN   The home of Coriakin* is located in the Land of the Duffers.* A long, grey, two-story stone house, grown over with ivy, it sits at the end of a tree-lined avenue. The nicely cut lawns that surround the house remind Lucy of England.* A gateway leads to a paved courtyard, in the middle of which is a pump. The house has many windows and at least one fireplace, as smoke can be seen rising from the chimney. There is a long dining hall. The sunlit passage on the second floor that runs the whole length of the house is carpeted, and its walls are carved and panelled. Masks also hang on the wall, and the doors are painted with strange undecipherable lettering. A bearded glass hangs just past the sixth door. The last door on the left leads into the room of the magician's* Book,* and the room itself is lined with books. The room where Coriakin and Lucy eat is sunny and filled with flowers, and another room has several mysterious instruments in it—astrolabes, orreries, chronoscopes, poesimeters, choriambuses, and theodolinds.

(VDT 111 ff., *114 ff.*)

HUMAN RESPECT   See *Vanity.*

HUMILITY   See *Obedience.*

HUMOR   The *Chronicles of Narnia* are filled with humor from beginning to end. In fact, the creation of Narnia* is no sooner accomplished than the First Joke is made by the Jackdaw,* and ". . . all the other animals* began making various queer noises which are their way of laughing and which, of course, no one has ever heard in our world."[1] Then, with Aslan's permission, they all abandon themselves to merry laughter. The Jackdaw not only *makes* the first joke, he becomes the first joke.[2] Many scenes in the *Chronicles* are reminiscent of music hall routines, the British vaudeville with which Lewis was familiar. Some striking examples include Glimfeather's* impossible conversation with the deaf Trumpkin*; the newly created Talking Beasts'* discussion of whether Uncle Andrew* is animal, vegetable, or mineral, and their chase of poor Andrew in a reverse fox hunt; the old owl's* imitation of Trumpkin at the Parliament of Owls; and the interplay between the arrogant Tisroc,* the obsequious Ahoshta Tarkaan,* and the firebrand Rabadash,* which moves from burlesque to wry wit.

In the opening epigraph of *The Screwtape Letters,* Lewis quotes Luther as saying, "The best way to drive out the devil, if he will not yield to texts of scripture, is to jeer and flout him, for he cannot bear scorn."[3] In the *Chronicles,* Lewis employs humor to drive out the devil in as many ways as he possibly can.

He succeeds in making evil figures ridiculous—and thus defuses their power—by poking fun at them. When Aslan transforms Rabadash into an ass, it is impossible for the Calormenes* to take him seriously as a tyrant. Andrew's descent into ridicule happens almost immediately. He doesn't need Aslan to make a fool of him; he's perfectly capable of doing it himself. His potential for evil,* which is great in the beginning of MN, is almost nil by the end, especially after he has been chased and caged by the animals in a neat reversal of his own cruelty to animals. The *Chronicles* have become quite grim by LB, and there is little laughter left in Narnia. But there is always laughter in Aslan's country,* and at the Great Reunion,* one of the best features is the retelling of old jokes. Lewis makes his own joke when he adds, "You've no idea how good an old joke sounds when you take it out again after a rest of five or six hundred years."

---

[1] Lewis says "of course" because animals are grave and solemn in our world and they are thus because they are dumb and witless. Risibility (a term coined by Boethius in the sixth century) is for many philosophers one way of defining the human being: a person is a being with a sense of humor (Aquinas, *Summa Theologica* III, 16, 5). Lewis prized Boethius, calling his *De Consolatione Philosophiae* "one of the most influential books ever written in Latin. . . . To acquire a taste for it is almost to become naturalized in the middle ages." (*The Discarded Image* [London: Cambridge University Press, 1964] p. 75.)

[2] For a discussion of Lewis's authorial lapse at this point, see *Jackdaw*.

[3] *The Screwtape Letters* (New York: Macmillan Publishing Co., 1978; London: William Collins Publishers, 1979).

HUNDRED YEARS OF WINTER
The period of time (900–1000 N.Y.)[1] in which Jadis ruled Narnia, when it was always winter but never Christmas. Tirian remembers this time from Narnian history. Lewis uses winter as a metaphor for the enthrallment of evil* or sin.[2]

(LWW 11 passim; *17 passim.* LB 41, *43.*)
[*Enchantment; Father Christmas; White Witch.*]

---

[1] Lewis's outline of Narnian history (PWD, p. 42) calls it the "Long Winter."

[2] For the meaning of summer in Lewis's personal iconography, see *Aslan,* note 1.

HUNTING
Hunting animals* for meat is an accepted practice in Narnia, with one important stipulation: only Dumb Beasts* may be killed and eaten; to kill and eat a Talking Beast* is both murder and cannibalism.[1] Truffle-hunter* discusses the meaning of hunting in PC, and on their trip across Ettinsmoor* Jill and Eustace and Puddleglum live off moor-fowl, which Jill observes are messy to prepare. The giants* of Harfang* hunt on foot (there are no giant horses*), and in LB a hunter has killed the dumb lion* whose skin is worn by the miserable Puzzle.* When first met, King Tirian* is at his hunting lodge.

(PC 67, *66.* SC 71–72, *76;* 107, *109.* LB 6, *11;* 12, *17.*)
[*Vivisection.*]

---

[1] See *Talking Beasts* for discussion of this subject.

HWIN
The mare ridden by Aravis in HHB. Like Bree, she is a Narnian talking horse who was captured in her early youth and enslaved in Calormen.*

Her name is evocative of the "whinny" sound horses* make. Although she was necessarily silent in Calormen, she is forced to speak in order to stop her mistress's attempted suicide. She will not be silenced by Aravis either: "This is my escape just as much as it is yours," she tells the Tarkheena. She is a highly bred mare, "a very nervous and gentle person who was easily put down," but sensible and brave nonetheless. She is crushingly patronized by Bree, who thinks he has more experience and superior knowledge of the capability of horses. But although both horses are exhausted, and she perhaps more so than Bree, it is Hwin who sets the pace. Nearing Narnia, she is all for moving on and does not understand Bree's reluctance until she discerns that his vanity* has been injured by the shabby condition of his tail; she laughingly compares him with Lasaraleen Tarkheena.* Her stay in the Hermit's* enclosure seems to enhance her courage* and enthusiasm, and though she is shaking all over when she sees Aslan leap over the Hermit's wall, she waits only a short time before giving "a strange little neigh, and trots across to the Lion." She tells Aslan that he may eat her if he likes: "I'd sooner be eaten by you than fed by anyone else." Aslan, of course, does not eat her, but kisses her and tells her that she shall have joy.* This is a moment of high mysticism.[1] Hwin experiences the terror and the beauty of Aslan and draws near, almost eager to be devoured. She meditates on this experience for two hours. Hwin strolls along toward Anvard* "in a happy dream," in strong contrast to Bree, whose apprehension only increases. She does not care what anyone thinks: she will roll in the dust when and as she pleases. Hwin lives happily ever after in Narnia, marrying and living to a ripe old age, and visiting her friends in Archenland* often.

(HHB Chapter 2 passim.)
[*Animals; Talking Beasts; Sexism.*]

---

[1] Lewis returns to this theme in *Till We Have Faces* (Grand Rapids: Wm. B. Eerdmans Publishing Co., 1956), in which the full significance of loving and devouring being at root the same thing becomes apparent. There he explains that philosophy ("Greek wisdom") does not understand what religion ("sacred language") knows; see pp. 49–50, 69 ff.

ILGAMUTH   See *Darrin.*

ILKEEN   Site of a lake and the palaces of wealthy Tarkaans.*

(HHB 97, *88.*)
[*Ahoshta Tarkaan.*]

ILSOMBREH TISROC   Paternal great-great-grandfather of Aravis.

(HHB 33, *37.*)
[*Ardeeb Tisroc; Tarkaan; Tisroc.*]

IMAGINATION   Lewis felt very strongly that children's* imaginations should be nourished and encouraged to grow.[1] When asked about the practical use of fantasy for a child, he "agreed that practical things were first class, but that although fantasy might not help a boy to build a boat, it would help him immensely if he should ever find himself on a sinking ship."[2] Indeed, because Edmund's imagination is stimulated by reading *Robinson Crusoe,* he knows the elements of survival that help keep the children going when they are "shipwrecked" in the ruins of Cair Paravel.[3] Of course, imaginations can go bad or interfere with reality. Uncle Andrew's* vain imagination causes him to play down Jadis's fearsomeness, and to exaggerate her beauty and his handsomeness. But when she bursts in on him and Letitia,* her real presence dissipates all of his daydreaming. In LB, Tirian* tells Diggle* that the black hole is all in his imagination. But when Tirian swings the dwarf* by his belt and hood out from the circle of dwarfs, Diggle claims he has been smashed against the Stable* wall and even appears injured. Thus for Diggle the imaginary has become real.[4]

In order to encourage children's imaginations, Lewis often employs an inversion of ordinary reality[5] to jog them into awareness of the ordinary. There are a number of these dislocations of the imagination in the *Chronicles.* Among them: the books* on Tumnus's* bookshelf, including *Is Man a Myth?;* Caspian's sudden realization in Trufflehunter's* cave that Old Narnia really exists; the porter at the giants'* castle at Harfang* who speaks to Jill and Eustace as if they were beetles, saying he supposes they look "quite nice" to one another; Caspian's dreams of living on a round world, which he has read about but never believed was real; Golg's* horror at the thought of living in Overland, with "no roof at all . . . only a horrible great emptiness called sky"; Shasta's first experience of talking horses*; Bree's reference to Shasta in horse terms, as a "foal"; and Tirian's realization that he is in a "very queer adventure*" when he notices fruit trees* *inside* the Stable.

(LWW 12, *19.* PC 5, *14;* 62, *62;* 191 ff., *188 ff;* 201, *196.* SC 91, *94;* 179, *174;* 182, *177.* HHB 8–11, *17–19;* 22, *27;* 30, *34.* MN 75–76, *73–74;* 79, *76.* LB 135, *124;* 146, *134–135.*)

---

[1] Lewis conceived of the human soul as having three concentric circles: the imagination outermost, the intellect next, and the will innermost; see *The Screwtape Letters* (New York: Macmillan Publishing Co., 1978) p. 31. His own return to Christianity was occasioned by what he himself called the "baptism" of his imagination by his reading *Phantastes,* a novel by George

MacDonald, when he was sixteen; see *Surprised by Joy* (New York: Harcourt Brace Jovanovich, 1955; London: Collins Fontana, 1959) pp. 178–181, *144–146*.

² See Gilbert Meilaender, *The Taste for the Other: The Social and Ethical Thought of C. S. Lewis* (Grand Rapids: Wm. B. Eerdmans Publishing Co., 1978) p. 48.

³ Lewis no doubt felt that he was helping children with all the practical notes* he included in the *Chronicles*. Lewis almost surely was alluding here to G. K. Chesterton's comment on Robinson Crusoe in *Orthodoxy* (New York: Doubleday Image, 1959): "Crusoe is a man on a small rock with a few comforts just snatched from the sea: the best thing in the book is simply the list of things saved from the wreck." See *Lists*.

⁴ See *Plato*.

⁵ Chesterton might have called this "topsy-turveydom"; see *Orthodoxy*, pp. 46–65.

IMMANENCE   See *Greatness of God.*

IMMORALITY   See *Right and wrong.*

INCUBUSES   Evil* spirits of the night, present at the slaying of Aslan. According to medieval thought, an incubus is the personification of the nightmare, a demon who descends on people, especially women, while they sleep.

(LWW 148, *138.*)

INSECTS   Narnia is filled with humans, dwarfs,* animals,* gods,* and trees,* but the only insects specifically created by Aslan are butterflies (perhaps for their beauty) and bees (undoubtedly for pollination of the plant life). Eustace and Edmund discuss grasshoppers in the Land of the Duffers,* but decide not to mention them to Lucy, who doesn't like insects—especially large ones.¹

(VDT 124, *125.* MN 114, *106.*)

---

¹ Lewis did not like insects either, and that is probably why Narnia is so lacking in them. See OOW, p. 30.

INVISIBILITY   The experience of invisibility in the Land of the Duffers* is complex, and operates on several different and quite distinct levels for the various characters affected. For the Duffers,* invisibility is a self-imposed enchantment that enables them to escape their real shame at their supposed ugliness. For the voyagers from the *Dawn Treader,* fighting an invisible enemy is demoralizing: there is no way to tell what sort of creatures they are; it is no good trying to hide from people you cannot see; and it is no good trying to fight invisible enemies, because no onlooker would take it seriously enough to know that help is needed.¹ For the magician* Coriakin,* subject to the enchantments of his own Book,* invisibility is merely a tiring experience. For Aslan, the fact that *he* is also subject to the enchantment (at least as far as the Land of the Duffers is concerned) is a secondary point Lewis is trying to make. Enchantment in Narnia is almost equivalent to natural moral law in our world. As in nature God keeps the law even in making miracles,² so in Narnia Aslan obeys the good enchantments. Finally, all things are not invisible in the same way. That is, spears become visible when they leave the hands of the Duffers, but the food at the banquet is visible before it is set in front of the Narnians.

(VDT Chapters 9 through 11.)
[*Honor.*]

¹ Lewis was well aware that Christians "are not contending against flesh and blood, but against . . . the spiritual hosts of wickedness in the heavenly places." (Ephesians 6:12.) But the tone of this passage is so natural that it is not possible to discern whether Lewis intended this meaning.

² A discussion of the relationship between God and nature occupies a major portion of Lewis's *Miracles* (New York: Macmillan Publishing Co., 1978; London: Collins Fontana, 1974), especially chapters 8, 12, and 14. An earlier essay (1943) that deals with the allied question of the relationship of God to the moral law is "The Poison of Subjectivity" in *Christian Reflections* (Grand Rapids: Wm. B. Eerdmans Publishing Co., 1967), especially p. 80.

ISLAND OF THE THREE SLEEPERS   See *Ramandu's Island.*

ISLAND OF THE VOICES   See *Land of the Duffers.*

IVY   One of three servants to Professor Digory Kirke. The other two are Betty* and Margaret.*

(LWW 1, 9.)

JACKDAW   A small bird* of the crow family that can be taught to talk. The Jackdaw's gaffe soon after the creation of the Talking Beasts* (continuing to talk when the others had fallen silent) is the occasion for the first laughter in Narnia. He truly enjoys the joke at his own expense, and asks if everyone will always be told how he made the First Joke.¹ The Jackdaw labels the bear's pratfall as the third joke.

(MN 118–119, *110–111;* 131, *121.*)
[*Humor.*]

¹ This instance of the Jackdaw's awareness of history is probably a lapse on Lewis's part, for it seems to come out of the author's consciousness of the significance of the incident rather than that of the newly created bird. Later, when the Jackdaw falls from his perch between Strawberry's ears and only just remembers his wings, Lewis comments that the animals were still new to it all and implies that the bird could not have been aware of the "first-ness" of the incident as much as Lewis was. See *History.*

JADIS   See *White Witch.*

JEWEL   A creamy-white Unicorn,* noble and delicate, with one blue horn in the middle of his forehead and a gold chain around his neck. He is King Tirian's* best friend. Soft-spoken and gentle, he is fierce in battle and uses his horn as a weapon. Throughout LB, he steadfastly refuses to believe in the false Aslan, reminding Tirian that Aslan is not a *tame* lion. For many readers, Jewel is almost too noble to be true. A heraldic figure, Jewel seems to have stepped right off of a banner*[1] and never comes across as three-dimensionally as do other horse* figures—notably Bree, Hwin, Glenstorm,* and Roonwit.*[2] Even the bewildered Puzzle is more "human." Jewel is given to noble speeches (his reply to the King's farewell and request for forgiveness is quite moving), even paraphrasing Scott's "Lay of the Last Minstrel" (VI, i, "This is my own, my native land") when he discovers that Aslan's country* is the fulfillment of his heart's longing.*

When Jill mentions that things always seem to be happening in Narnia, Jewel corrects this mistaken assumption by telling her that, in the history* of Narnia, Sons of Adam* and Daughters of Eve are only called in times of crisis; the rest of the time Narnia is peaceful and uneventful. In a foreshadowing of the culmination of LB, Jewel tells Jill that, with the exception of Aslan's country, all worlds come to an end. In Aslan's country at last, he swims up the Great Waterfall.* He shows his respect and lack of jealousy by giving Tirian time alone with his father, Erlian.* Finally, he issues the call to go "farther up and farther in!"

(LB Chapter 2 passim.)
[*Eschatology.*]

---

[1] The antipathy between Scotland and England in the seventeenth century has traditionally been symbolized as a battle between the Lion and the Unicorn, because the Unicorn upheld the Royal Arms of Scotland on its seals and banners, while the Lion (along with the Dragon) graced England's flag. A famous battle between the Lion and the Unicorn takes place in Lewis Carroll's *Through the Looking Glass,* and undoubtedly Lewis knew of this when he wrote LB. In Jewel's role as a true believer, Lewis may have been making a point about the ultimate reconciliation of enemies at the judgment.

[2] The Narnia of LB is notable for the absence of Aslan. In some ways, Jewel takes over one of Aslan's roles in the other books: keeping the travelers on the right path. In Christian mythology,* the Unicorn is often a symbol of the Word of God, or even of Jesus himself. While Jewel is in no way to be taken for Aslan himself (his overwhelming rage at the mistreatment of the talking horse, and his subsequent murder of the Calormenes,* militate against this), he may mirror Aslan in much the same way as, in Christian angelology, Michael is "one like God."

JEWELS   See *Robes, royal.*

JILL POLE   She and her schoolmate Eustace Scrubb are the first products of the modern coeducational school* system to have Narnian adventures.* It is to escape the harrassment of the Gang* at Experiment House* that she finds a way into Narnia; and it is partly to be strengthened for returning to this situation that she has been called into Narnia. Her chief failure in Narnia—

The Queen of Underland transforms herself into a hideous, seething serpent and coils herself around Rilian. Scrubb and Puddleglum come to his rescue with swords at the ready while Jill looks on in horror and tries not to faint. (SC 160-161, 157-158.)

forgetting the signs* Aslan gives her, by which she and Eustace are to find the lost prince Rilian—is connected to the fact that she is a fearful person and doesn't like physical discomfort. She likes the thought of having adventures but not the actual ardures. Her time in Narnia in SC (during which her emotions are the extremes of delight and depression) prepares her for her role in LB (in which she has matured into a steady, reliable guide).[1]

She and Eustace have a lot to learn about cooperation when they first meet, and they quarrel a good bit in SC. Not yet aware that one can't force good magic* to happen[2] but must ask to enter Narnia, she first proposes to use a darker magic. She and Eustace have scarcely begun their prayer to Aslan (a name that does not excite her as it did the Pevensie children in LWW) when they find themselves chased by members of the Gang into Aslan's country.* Her desire to show off the fact she isn't afraid of heights leads to Eustace's falling into Narnia. She tries to avoid her responsibility in this by calling her experience a dream*; but her memory of his scream, her tears, and the sight of the Lion force her to confront herself.[3] She can hardly believe that she is being called to a task; she thought she had been calling Aslan.[4] In light of the insight the Lion gives her, she accepts her task and is blown into Narnia to take up her quest.* She will be looking for the lost prince, but she will also be discovering herself. As the Lion predicted, the sights and sounds of this new world crowd out the signs she has committed to memory; and when she does remember, Eustace is still angry with her. This ongoing rivalry between them is responsible for much loss of time with respect to accomplishing their task. She is not allowed to get too comfortable in Cair Paravel before Glimfeather* takes her away and helps her commence the Lion's assignment. At the Parliament of Owls she is not about to let Eustace arrogate the search for the prince to himself. And her insightfulness is shown by her immediate identification of the serpent as the woman. However much she might want to be known as the person to whom the Lion assigned the task and to be known as an adventurer, the actual experience is not nearly as romantic as she thought it would be. This is a motif that runs through all of SC.

Jill doesn't like the thought of meeting giants,* a fact that only heightens her surprise when she muses that the rocks along the gorge in Ettinsmoor* could be imagined to be giants and they actually *are* giants.[5] But these prove to be foolish children, unlike the savage "gentle giants" Jill and Eustace and Puddleglum will meet at Harfang.* Her desire for comfort* grows with every chilly hour out on the inhospitable moor. She is entranced by the sight of the Lady of the Green Kirtle[6] and readily thinks the Black Knight shares the same enchantment—the re-reader of SC would certainly appreciate the irony here. Though Puddleglum tries to remind Jill of the signs, her obsession with getting away from the harsh weather takes her over and she leaves off repeating the signs as the Lion has told her.

As they stumble through the trenches on the plain in front of the Hill of Harfang, Lewis reveals that Jill has a fear* of twisting passages; she will meet far worse below the earth in a few days. That she considers Puddleglum's reminder about the signs inconvenient (rather than the providence* that they are) shows how bewitched she is by the thought of creature comforts at the giants' castle. She repeats the signs out of order (another thing she would not have done if she had worked on her memory* every day) and another opportunity is missed for taking up the quest by a more direct route. Her conscience is bothering her (this is the meaning of the phrase "deep down inside") but her fatigue is the greater motive, greater even than the instinctive fear she feels in the face of the giant gate-keeper and the giant king* and queen.[7]

After her dream about the Lion, she awakes quite refreshed, only to face the unpleasant vision of the Ruined City* outside her window. She partially takes the blame for muffing the signs, but she also tries to evade her guilt by considering the possibility of Aslan's putting the letters of the sign into the city *after* they had passed through. Eustace sees through this evasion, however, and shares her guilt with her.

The most terrible moment she has ever faced in life is when she feels all alone at the bottom of the cave they have fallen into. Her fear increases to the point that she can't go any further. But Eustace comes to her aid with the reminder that he knows how she feels because of his fear of heights. The touch of her companions helps her though the tight spots. Puddleglum's assurance that they must be doing right because they are finally following the Lion's directions is the only thing that keeps her from despair. When she meets the enchanted prince, she sees immediately that something is wrong with him. It is only when he returns to his senses in his daily imprisonment in the silver chair* that she thinks him a nicer looking man. His request of them in the Lion's name stuns her, and she would rather not confront this decision. But when Puddleglum correctly distinguishes between consequences and commands, she leads the way in releasing the prince. In the final encounter with the Queen of Underland, the magic almost overtakes Jill; but she is able at the last moment to mention the Lion's name, and thus begin the process by which all are freed from the witch's snare.

After the witch's death, all pay homage to the miraculously refurbished image of the Lion on Rilian's shield. Jill and Eustace apologize to each other, wish each other well, and use one another's Christian name for the first time. The natural smell of the stable (such a contrast to the witch's spell) refreshes Jill who, as a budding equestrienne, has no fear of stepping between the frightened horses.[8] She, in her empathy, is thrilled to learn that the Earthmen* were sad only because of the witch's enchantment,* that they are really happy people. She is adamant about their returning to Narnia, and their way to the surface is full of frightening moments for her. She nearly faints with delight at coming up in the middle of the Great Snow Dance; its music pierces her with its beauty and good magic. It takes her only a little while to forget the smothering quality of Underland. And after one relapse of fear (when she awakens in the dwarf's* cave, she thinks she is still in Underland), she bids Puddleglum an affectionate farewell; she has seen through his manner and declared him to be as happy and as brave as a lion.

The reader experiences the pathos of Caspian's funeral through Jill. It is she who notices that Eustace is crying* over the dead king as an adult* would cry—though it is hard for her to place his age on Aslan's mountain. She is overwhelmed by tears at Aslan's beauty and by the mournfulness of the funeral music.* She and Eustace are sent back to Experiment House as administrators of the Lion's justice upon the Gang (she keeps her Narnian finery and wears it to a holiday dance*). A lifelong friendship with Eustace has begun.

When they return to help Tirian* in LB, she is sixteen years old and very businesslike in rescuing the King; she becomes excited only at the King's suggestion that they disguise themselves. She is overly modest about her abilities as an archer, so Eustace speaks up for her. She is an excellent guide for the group, very wood-wise, and has in fact become a leader. She takes matters into her own hands and rescues Puzzle, pleading for his life with Tirian. Her stock responses* are evident: she is outraged at the dwarfs' lack of allegiance to Tirian, awed by Eustace's bravery, and enchanted by Jewel's* beauty. Her very limited experience of Narnia has persuaded her that "there's always so much happening"—she is an incipient historicist. But when Jewel enlightens her on Narnia's relative dearth of what is normally considered history,* she is persuaded of this viewpoint and hopes this good ordinariness goes on forever.[9]

She will not obey Tirian's command for her and Eustace to return home.[10] But her courageous feelings fail her on the way back to the Stable.*[11] She and Eustace discuss their possible deaths,* and she determines that she'd rather die fighting for Narnia than decline into decrepitude in England.*

The reader sizes up the situation at the Stable through Jill's eyes, wonders at Shift's* possible insanity, and then figures out the fiendish cleverness of his scheme. Jill is moved to tears by the handsome Emeth's* youthful zeal for his god* Tash.* She slays three enemies and wins Tirian's praise; he assigns her to cover for the rest of their company as they make a preemptive strike. And though she feels "terribly alone," she does her duty. She throws herself into the Last Battle,* is captured and thrown through the Stable Door.*

When Tirian walks through the same door, he sees a transformed Jill, ageless and beautiful and fresh; she laughs at his amazement. It is she who introduces him to the High King Peter. Like the other friends of Narnia, she is negative in her assessment of Susan. And although her contact with Narnia has been relatively short, she mourns the destruction of that world, a response Lewis thinks quite in order.[12] She is the one who asks Emeth to tell his story; and she recognizes Puzzle and runs to embrace him. Since she is the last to ascend the Great Waterfall,* the reader sees the rest ascend through her eyes. She is part of the great procession to meet Aslan for the final scene of the *Chronicles.* From a frightened nine-year-old, she has grown to be a loving, fearless queen in the Narnia that lives forever.

---

[1] She is also the last female character Lewis creates in the *Chronicles,* and her character reveals a Lewis trying very hard to overcome his sexist* outlook. The next women he writes about will be Orual and her sister Psyche in the book he considered his masterpiece, *Till We Have Faces* (New York: Harcourt Brace Jovanovich, 1980).

[2] See Professor Digory Kirke's advice to the Pevensie children at the end of LWW.

[3] For the meaning of Jill's three experiences of the Lion, see *Aslan.*

[4] Part of a profound experience of prayer is the awareness that this dialogue with God and reality is first, last, and always a gift, a grace: Lewis, in a long line of Christian thinkers, believes that before a person addresses God, God—especially the Holy Spirit*—has been addressing that person.

[5] John the Pilgrim has the same experience in Lewis's *The Pilgrim's Regress* (Grand Rapids: Wm. B. Eerdmans Publishing Co., 1958) when he meets the giant, the Spirit of the Age (p. 60).

[6] See *Queen of Underland.*

[7] She is uncomfortably aware, however, of the smiles the two giants exchange with each other. Recall Jane Studdock's similar sensitivity to Feverstone's smile and laughter in *That Hideous Strength.* Jill also notices the unreal quality of the enchanted prince's laughter.

[8] In this scene Lewis may only be saying that people have different fears*: Jill may have claustrophobia, but she is not afraid of horses. He may also be suggesting that Jill's fearlessness may be her response to Rilian's speech about bidding farewell to hopes and fears, or it may be the result of their liberation from the Witch's enchantment.

[9] See *Domesticity* and *History.*

[10] A testimony to the kind of freedom Lewis is willing to let women have by the time of LB. She has the right to differ with what she considers to be an irrational order, and to claim her part in the Last Battle of Narnia. The fact that her facial coloring changes from white to red to white again indicates her violent emotional changes: from fear to anger to firm resolve.

[11] The British expression "to get the wind up" means "to be thoroughly frightened."

[12] See *Lucy,* note 21.

JOY   Lewis uses this word to describe the "want" of something that is better than the "having" of any particular thing. Joy is not an uncontrolled ecstasy, but a feeling of innate dignity. The garden* is "a happy place, but very serious."[1] Emeth describes his joy as a "happiness so great that it even weakens me like a wound." The older friends of Narnia laugh at Digory's refrain that "it's all in Plato,*" but they become grave again "for, as you know, there is a kind of happiness and wonder that makes you serious."

(MN 158, *146.* LB 165, *150;* 170, *154.*)
[*Longing.*]

[1] "Joy is the serious business of Heaven," said Lewis in his fictional *Letters to Malcolm: Chiefly on Prayer* (New York: Harcourt Brace Jovanovich, 1964) p. 93.

JUDGMENT   See *Eschatology.*

KEYS   Tirian* carries a "nice bunch of keys" made of gold, which Lewis carefully describes to remind the reader of the contrast between royal life in untroubled times and the present Narnian crisis. At Aslan's command, the High King Peter closes and locks the Stable* Door* with a golden key.

(LB 52, *52;* 157, *143.*)
[*Biblical allusions.*]

KIDRASH TARKAAN   The name borne by both the paternal great grandfather and the father of Aravis. The latter is married a second time to a woman who is jealous of Aravis. The stepmother persuades him to give his daughter to Ahoshta Tarkaan,* a wealthy and powerful man whom Aravis despises. When Kidrash realizes that his daughter has fled in order to escape this marriage, he goes to Tashbaan* in search of her.

(HHB 33 ff., *37 ff.;* 92–95, *84–86.*)
[*Autobiographical allusions.*]

KINGS AND QUEENS   The two Kings* and two Queens who rule Narnia in its Golden Age*: the High King Peter, King Edmund, Queen Lucy, and Queen Susan. Their thrones have been waiting for them in Cair Paravel,* and their coronation is the fulfillment of an ancient prophecy that Sons of Adam* and Daughters of Eve will again sit on the thrones at Cair Paravel. Even though they are children* in England, when they return to Narnia, they are still Kings and Queens in that country.

KINGS, QUEENS   All true kings and queens of Narnia are human beings[1] who rule by the wiill of Aslan. In MN, Aslan outlines to King Frank I* and Queen Helen* the five necessary qualities of their vocation:[2] (1) to work with their hands to raise their own food; (2) to rule the people[3] as free subjects and fellow human beings; (3) to educate their offspring to rule in the same way; (4) to prefer none among their offspring or their subjects and to tolerate no abuse of one by another; and (5) in the event of war, to be first in battle and last in retreat. Most important, they must rule with humility. In Narnian countries, bad rulers are so precisely because they lack humility and hold themselves to be above the law. These tyrants and despots include the White Witch (and her alter ego, Jadis), Miraz,* the Tisroc,* and the Queen of Underland.* The named kings and queens of Narnia and Archenland* are: Frank I, Helen, Frank V, Col* (of Archenland), Gale,* Olvin,* Peter, Edmund, Susan, Lucy, Lune* (of Archenland), Cor (of Archenland), Aravis (of Archenland), Ram* (of Archenland), Swanwhite,* Caspian I,* Caspian VIII,* Caspian IX,* Nain* (of Archenland), Caspian X,* the Daughter of Ramandu,* Rilian, Erlian,* and Tirian.*

(PC 21, *26;* 27, *33.* VDT 117, *119;* 195, *189.* SC 199, *191–192;* 213, *203.* HHB 56, *57;* 160, *140;* 214–215, *186–187.* MN 139, *129;* 172, *158.*)
[*Government.*]

---

[1] One of the reasons that English children* are kings and queens in Narnia is Lewis's firm belief in the Christian tradition of royal symbolism (C. S. Lewis, "The Weight of Glory" in *The Weight of Glory and Other Addresses* [Grand Rapids: Wm. B. Eerdmans Publishing Co., 1965] pp.

7–12 and *Screwtape Proposes a Toast and Other Pieces* [London: Collins Fountain, 1977] pp. 100–106). Because "the dullest, most uninteresting person you talk to may one day be a creature which, if you saw it now, you would be strongly tempted to worship"—because we live in a "society of possible gods* and goddesses"—Lewis believed we should take one another seriously and love one another "with a profound and costly love" (*The Weight of Glory and Other Addresses*, p. 15; *Screwtape Proposes a Toast and Other Pieces*, p. 109). Lewis means his readers to take his analogy seriously: just as the Pevensies are children in England and *at the same time* kings and queens* in Narnia, so he means us all to live our lives as though we are kings and queens in Narnia. See *Hierarchy*.

² In Narnia, one has a vocation not by personal choice but by the will of Aslan, and it must be taken seriously. Cor does not want the responsibility of being King of Archenland; like his brother Corin,* he realizes it would be much more fun to be a prince. But, as King Lune* explains, he has no choice. He is the older by twenty minutes and thus he is born to be king. It is the law, not a question of what he wants. Lewis is educating children that with vocation and adulthood comes responsibility. In VDT, Caspian's wish to abdicate the kingship in order to venture to the Utter East* is a wish to avoid his vocation (in this Lewis may have been influenced by the real abdication of King Edward VIII from the throne of England).

³ The word "people" as used in this sense includes Talking Beasts,* dwarfs,* and other nonhuman residents of Narnia.

KNIGHTS, LADIES, SQUIRES

Mentioned only in passing, it is presumed that they are part of the chivalric order* in Narnia. Many knights are among the champions who searched for Rilian and never returned. Rilian himself is said to be a very young knight. Squires and ladies went Maying with the Queen and Rilian the day of her death.

(SC 48–49, 55.)
[*Hierarchy.*]

KNOWLEDGE

The venerable philosophical question "How do we know?" is one of the keynotes of the *Chronicles*. How are the children to know whether or not Lucy's story of the magic* wardrobe* is true? How do they know, the Professor unexpectedly asks, that it is not true? Once all the children* have gotten into Narnia they find themselves following a robin into the forest. Under the influence of Turkish Delight,* Edmund stridently questions Peter. How do they know which side the robin is on? that the fauns* are good and the Witch bad? that the faun Tumnus* really saved Lucy?

Behind these recurring questions lies a quest* and a struggle for reality that is waged all through the *Chronicles* and is finally won only in the closing pages of LB. The fact of the quest and the struggle already suggests the beginnings of an answer: truth is not an issue for a being who has no access to it. People who are completely deaf from birth do not find themselves trying to sort out whether or not they heard what they thought they heard. The children would not find themselves on their quest if they did not have some real capacity and desire for the deepest reality. Against any sort of ultimate skepticism or irrationality Lewis holds that humanity can, by virtue of its rationality, know much of reality, make true judgments, and recognize objective values.¹

Rationality is an inborn capacity for reality, an openness to things as they are that makes objectivity and communication possible. Insofar as a person is reasonable, that person surmounts the immediate tumult of fears, desires, and needs in order to consider and appreciate things for what they really are.² Rationality, as a receptive appreciation surpassing fear and desire, also means that one has surmounted merely private, subjective, immediate experiences to gain an objective vantage point where shared meanings and thus communication become possible. Much more than just thinking is included here: freedom, moral responsibility, valuation, love, and humor all follow on this fundamental openness to reality.

In MN, the reader witnesses the dawning of rational life. Aslan creates Narnia and confers the gift of speech* on some of the animals.* Their response is, "Hail Aslan. We hear and obey. We are awake. We love. We think. We speak. We know." He then gives the newly created Talking Beasts* responsibility over themselves, Narnia, and the Dumb Beasts.* With rational self-possession and moral responsibility comes humor* too. Shortly after the conferral of speech the first joke and the first laughter occur. ". . . Jokes as well as justice come in with speech," Aslan says.

While rationality means that humanity has access to reality and can know a great deal about it, this capacity must not be taken for granted. Like the gears of a car, this inborn capacity works tolerably well if we take its inner workings seriously and handle it carefully and correctly. It is possible, however, to "strip the gears" through carelessness and neglect, to seriously impair the ability to take in reality.[3] Aslan warns the Talking Beasts not to slip into their old animal ways "lest you cease to be Talking Beasts. For out of them you were taken and into them you can return."

In PC, when the dwarf Trumpkin* kills an attacking bear, Susan hesitates letting go an arrow because she is concerned that it might be a talking bear. Trumpkin assures her that it wasn't, but confesses that it is sometimes difficult to tell, especially "when most of the beasts have gone enemy and gone dumb. . . ." Lucy then has a chilling thought: What if the same thing happened in our world, if people continued to look human on the outside but went wild and beastly within? In a book written after Auschwitz this can be no idle speculation. Against any facile and optimistic rationalism, Lewis knows that our rationality is not only fragile and finite but fallen. Knowing would not be a quest or a struggle at all if it were not exacting and perilous, if mistakes were not possible, or if a fall into unreality were not a constant threat.

Edmund's state of mind and heart in LWW illustrates how desire may affect one's openness to truth. Under the influence of Turkish Delight and the promise that he will be made King of Narnia, he gives his allegiance to the White Witch, who after all is a counterfeit. "She calls herself the Queen of Narnia though she has no right to be queen at all," Lucy tells him. Edmund's unbelief and skepticism about the realities that contradict his desires do not stem at all from any kind of hard-headed rationality. Quite the opposite: his will and desire override his reason. The pursuit of what he desires entails an intellectual dishonesty which he willingly embraces.

As Edmund is drawn deeper into a web of lies (for example, he denies that he has actually been in Lucy's Narnia), his perception of things becomes increasingly distanced from that of the other children. They naturally trust the robin and Mr. Beaver.* Their hearts are in the right place with regard to ultimate reality. Among all who have remained faithful to Aslan there is a natural kinship. But Edmund hangs back and projects his own wrong-heartedness onto the others. At the name of Aslan* he feels "a sensation of mysterious horror," while the others have only positive reactions.

Another striking example is that of Uncle Andrew* in MN. He sees only "dangerous wild animals walking vaguely about," when in reality Aslan is carefully selecting pairs of beasts. He initially recognizes that the sound* at the creation scene is singing; but since this song makes him think and feel things he does not want to think and feel, he writes it off. Lewis comments, "Now the trouble about trying to make yourself stupider than you really are is that you very often succeed. Uncle Andrew did." Andrew completely misinterprets the intentions of the Talking Beasts toward him, his awareness of the situation clouded by a fear and hatred of animals that stems from years of vivisection.* The Talking Beasts, from their side, are unable to make out what Uncle Andrew is, not just because of the clothes he is wearing but because although he can mouth words, he is no longer "open" to any reality beyond himself, and is therefore incapable of communication.[4]

The distortion of human awareness and knowledge through egoism and immorality is a recurrent theme in the *Chronicles.* Various characters lose touch with their real situation or become doubtful and skeptical to the extent that they become morally lazy and cowardly, preferring comfort* and security to duty. Moral weakness, self-absorption, and blindness all increase in direct proportion to one another. In PC Lucy is able to see and communicate with Aslan while to Peter, Edmund, and Susan he is not only invisible but silent as well. Susan later admits that she could have seen Aslan all along if she had "let herself," but her desire to leave the wood got the better of her. The usurper Miraz* and the false political order he represents is an exercise in willed self-deception on a grand scale. The truth about Old Narnia has been methodically suppressed and replaced with lies. This is not a rational procedure, but one motivated by a mixture of fear and desire.[5]

The loss of humanity that accompanies the shrinking of the heart and mind is cleverly illustrated in the adventures of Eustace in VDT. Having fallen asleep on a dragon's* hoard with "dragonish thoughts in his heart," he actually turns into a dragon. His first thought upon discovering what has happened to him is that now, as a dragon, he can terrorize everyone. But almost immediately a deeper, more human Eustace breaks through: a lonely little boy who wants "to get back among humans and talk and laugh and share things."

Once he realizes that he is "a monster cut off from the whole human race," he works through a sort of examination of conscience. But the process of conversion is only just starting. When the others discover what has happened they can't help but notice that, if anything, becoming a dragon has improved Eustace's character. Only Aslan can make the enchanted boy fully human again, and that only at the cost of a deep tear into the beastly hide and heart Eustace has developed.

A third crucial, if somewhat paradoxical, point about human knowledge as it is portrayed in the *Chronicles* must now be added. It has become clear that for Lewis thought never occurs in a vacuum but is always shaped by moods, attitudes, and character. Emphasis so far has fallen on those instances in which the capacity to know has been impaired by negative moods and egotistical attitudes. But Lucy's character and profound grasp of reality in the tales should warn us against drawing any hasty conclusions. One such conclusion would be that knowledge of reality requires complete neutrality and the noninterference of emotions. Lewis would have it otherwise. Reason always needs more than itself in order to remain reasonable. Openness is a positive posture, not a neutral one. In the character of Lucy we see that the fullness of reality is disclosed only to the one who waits upon it, hopes in it, heeds it, and welcomes it. Of all the children in the *Chronicles,* Lucy is the one with the deepest love for Aslan.

Despite the temptation to give in and deny the wonderful reality that has been disclosed to her, Lucy holds firm at the outset of LWW to her story of the magic wardrobe. In PC, amid the skepticism and even spitefulness of her brothers and sister, she persists in her certainty that she has seen Aslan. In each of these cases belief gives stability to knowledge already gained in previous experience.

In SC, it is Puddleglum's obstinate fidelity to what he has known that saves the day against the narcotic enchantment of the Queen of Underland.* "... You can play that fiddle till your fingers drop off, and still you won't make me forget Narnia; and the whole Overworld too." When all the logic the Queen can muster has nearly destroyed whatever defenses the children have, it is Puddleglum who again comes to the rescue. His confession of faith in Aslan is a refusal to budge, no matter what. Earlier, Puddleglum didn't want them to go to the city of the giants because it didn't figure in with Aslan's signs*—the signs that were to guide their quest. His attentiveness is contrasted with the forgetfulness of Jill and Eustace. "They never talked about Aslan, or even about the lost Prince, now. And Jill gave up her habit of repeating the Signs over to herself every night and morning."

All of this points to the fact that knowledge needs more than itself in order to fulfill itself. Faith, as Lewis sees it, helps to keep reason alive and fighting when feelings,* circumstances, and imagination* tempt one to abandon what one knows to be true. It is "the art of holding onto things your reason has once accepted, in spite of your changing moods."[6] Faith is not knowledge, but gives psychological stability to knowledge.

---

[1] "In thinking, we are not reading rationality into an irrational universe but responding to a rationality with which the universe has always been saturated." ("De Futilitate," *Christian Reflections,* Walter Hooper, ed. [Grand Rapids: Wm. B. Eerdmans Publishing Co., 1967] p. 65; see also in the same volume "On Ethics" and "The Poison of Subjectivism.")

[2] In Lewis's science fiction work *Out of the Silent Planet* (New York: Macmillan Publishing Co., 1965), the ruling angel of Mars confronts Ransom and Devine and questions them to determine "if there is anything in your mind besides fear and death and desire." Since Ransom acts on principles, however distorted, he is only *bent.* But the Oyarsa pronounces Devine *broken,* for in his mind there is nothing but greed. Reasoning, however corrupted, is still operative in Ransom's calculations, whereas Devine's mentality has become that of sheer egoism (pp. 134–139).

[3] See Gilbert Meilaender's excellent analysis of this question in "The Primeval Moral Platitudes," in *The Taste for the Other* (Grand Rapids: Wm. B. Eerdmans Publishing Co., 1978) pp. 179–234.

[4] Lewis knew well the medieval philosopher Boethius, who said: *"Omne quod recipitur in aliquo*

---

recipitur in eo per modum recipientis." ("The way anything is received depends on how the receiver is fitted to receive it.") (*De Consolatione Philosophiae* [*On the Consolation of Philosophy*] V, 4.) Edmund is very little disposed to the truth about what he is doing, and misinterprets reality accordingly. In MN, Lewis gives Uncle Andrew's point of view on the creation of Narnia.* In an editorial paragraph, Lewis restates the adage of Boethius: "For what you see and hear depends a good deal on where you are standing: it also depends on what sort of person you are" (p. 125, *116*). Lewis dramatizes this principle most notably in his short story "The Shoddy Lands," in which the main character, Lewis himself, is somehow made able to view the world from the stifling perspective of a young woman named Peggy. (OOW, pp. 99–106; *The Dark Tower and Other Stories,* Walter Hooper, ed. [New York: Harcourt Brace Jovanovich, 1977] pp. 104–111.)

⁵ Miraz wishes, as Eric Voegelin says in his description of modern ideologies, to prohibit his subjects from asking questions concerning the sectors of reality he has excluded from his personal horizon. ("Remembrance of Things Past," *Anamnesis* [Notre Dame: University of Notre Dame Press, 1978] p. 3.) If we wish to cultivate understanding, Lewis seems to be saying, we must also cultivate the heart and the will. Chesterton says that if one doesn't learn how to go soft in the heart (think of Edmund and Eustace), he will soon go soft in the head. Lewis speaks at length and brilliantly to this topic in *The Abolition of Man* (New York: Macmillan Publishing Co., 1965).

⁶ C. S. Lewis, *Mere Christianity* (New York: Macmillan Publishing Co., 1960; Collins Fount, 1977), pp. 123, *121–122*.

KORIAKIN   See *Coriakin.*

KRAKEN   A large, dark, mythical sea monster, said to dwell in Norwegian waters. Described as one of the most remarkable of all animals, it belongs, along with the Sea Serpent* and the squid, to the group of three dangerous beasts of the deep feared by the Sea People.*

(VDT 193, *188.*)
[*Mythology.*]

LADIES   See *Knights, Ladies, Squires.*

LADY, THE   See *Daughter of Ramandu.*

LADY LILN   See *Olvin.*

LADY OF THE GREEN KIRTLE   See *Queen of Underland.*

LAMB   In Christian art, both a symbol of innocence and of Christ the Redeemer. Both of these usages appear in the *Chronicles.* At World's End* Edmund, Eustace, and Lucy encounter a Lamb who is transformed into Aslan.

In LB, the Lamb who observes that Narnia is Aslan's and Calormen* is Tash's,* and that there should be no friendship between them, is a hieroglyph[1] of innocence.

(VDT 214–215, *208–209;* 31, *34.*)
[*Talking Beasts.*]

---

[1] See *Introduction* for a discussion of Lewis's use of hieroglyphs.

LAMP-POST   Marks the westernmost boundary of Narnia. It grows from a cross-bar of the lamp-post outside the Ketterleys' London residence, which is damaged in the crush. Brandished by Jadis as a weapon, it fells two policemen and is transported with her to Narnia. She throws it at Aslan, but it drops to the ground, where it grows into a complete—already lit—Lamp-post that shines day and night and gives the name Lantern Waste* to the region. Encountered first by Lucy, it is rediscovered and marveled at by the Royal Party while on the hunt* for the White Stag* that brings the Golden Age of Narnia* to a close.

(LWW 7, *14;* 26, *25;* 174, *160;* 182–183, *168–169.* MN 87, *82;* 92 ff., *88 ff.;* 105, *98;* 108 ff., *99 ff.,* 184, *170.*)
[*White Witch.*]

LAND OF THE DUFFERS   Also known as the Island of the Voices, this island, the estate of the magician Coriakin,* is located within a fortnight's voyage east of Deathwater Island.* Its park-like grounds are dominated by a low Georgian-style manor house, built of warm stone with many windows.

(VDT 111 ff., *113–116.*)
[*Duffers; Geography, Narnian; House of the Magician.*]

LANTERN WASTE   The area surrounding the Lamp-post,* which marks the westernmost boundary of Narnia, takes its name from the eternally lit lamp. It is an uncultivated tract of wilderness, of which Edmund is Duke. An ancient forest of talking trees*—including the Golden Tree,* the Silver Tree,* and the Tree of Protection*—has grown up here. Many of the trees are felled in LB. Lantern Waste is mentioned in passing in HHB as within the western limits of the Hermit's* vision in his pool. Tirian's* grandfather had built three protective towers in Lantern Waste[1] to maintain law and order against the robbers who then plagued the area. These towers were simple, functional structures, dark and damp but well-stocked with provisions. It is here that Tirian, Jill, and Eustace return after their failed negotiations with the dwarfs.*

(PC 91, *86;* 173, *152.* HHB 180, *158.* MN 184, *170.* LB 1, *7;* 12, *17;* 17, *21;* 21, *25;* 48, *48;* 51 ff., *51 ff.*)
[*Geography, Narnian.*]

---

[1] In 2534 N.Y., according to Lewis's outline of Narnian history (PWD, p. 44).

As the four overlanders—Puddleglum, Jill, Eustace, and Rilian—look on, the gnomes rejoice at the news of the wicked Queen of Underland's death. (SC 179-180, 175.)

LAPSED BEAR OF STORMNESS   A talking bear who has gone back to the marauding habits of a wild bear, sallying forth from his den on the Narnian side of Stormness Head* and attacking travelers. He is reformed by Prince Corin, who earns the title "Thunder-Fist" when, in the dead of winter, he finds and boxes with the bear for thirty-three rounds.

(HHB 216, *188.*)
[*Corin Thunder-Fist; Talking Beasts.*]

LASARALEEN TARKHEENA   A childhood friend of Aravis. Clothes, parties, and gossip are the top priorities of this paragon of vanity.* A habitual giggler, she loves to attract attention and travels in a litter "all a-flutter with silken curtains and all a-jingle with silver bells," from which emanate the rich scents of perfumes and flowers. She is married to a great Calormene* and has a summer home in Mezreel.*

Her lack of depth is readily apparent in her encounter with Aravis. Though she asserts her eagerness to hear Aravis's story,* she hardly listens at all. And when she does, she is horrified at Aravis's harsh words for her intended husband, Ahoshta,* whom Lasaraleen thinks a great match because of his palace, pearls, and position and because he is favored by the Tisroc.* A bearer of tales and upholder of rank, she points out the horrors of Narnia to Aravis and chides her for the impropriety of traveling with a "peasant" boy. Typically, Lasaraleen becomes hysterical with fright at the prospect of helping Aravis escape, but finally cooperates when Aravis threatens to expose them both. The picture Lewis paints of her is really a caricature of the kind of dissipation the leisured class is prone to. Her name, in fact, is derived from *lasar,* an obscure Scottish form of "leisure";[1] the suffix *een* is the Gaelic feminine diminutive.

(HHB 41, *43;* Chapter 7 passim; 114, *102;* 117 ff., *105 ff.*)
[*Tarkaan.*]

---

[1] Martha C. Sammons, *A Guide Through Narnia* (Wheaton: Harold Shaw, 1979) p. 150.

LAST BATTLE   The final struggle of the forces of good (Tirian's* "army") with the forces of evil* (Rishda's* Calormene* cohort) in Narnia. It is in four phases, the final one of which is the "Last Battle." Tirian has Jewel,* Puzzle,* Poggin,* Jill, Eustace, Farsight,* fifteen dogs,* mice,* moles,* squirrels,* a boar, a bear, and twenty horses* (in reserve) on his side. Rishda* has fifteen Calormene veterans, a bull, a wolf, Slinkey,* and Wraggle* on his side. Aloof from the battle are the renegade dwarfs.*

In the first phase,[1] the Calormenes attack but are beaten off with the loss of two soldiers, the bull, the fox, and the satyr. Three dogs are killed and one is wounded. The bear is also killed. The horses, freed by the mice, are killed by the dwarfs before they can come to Tirian's aid.

In the second phase,[2] Tirian's forces sortie but fall back to a white rock when the Calormene troops are reinforced. The Calormene side loses several men and the wolf but Tirian loses Eustace.

In the third phase,[3] Rishda divides his force, one group to guard the Narnians at the rock, and the other to attack the dwarfs who had been shooting at the Calormene soldiers. When those dwarfs who have been taken alive are sacrificed to Tash* in the Stable,* Rishda turns his attention to the remaining Narnians.

Thus the final phase,[4] "the last battle of the last King of Narnia," begins. The boar is the first to go down. Jill is captured and thrown into the Stable Door.* The Last Battle ends for Tirian when he pulls Rishda into the Door.

The stark courage* and the hopeless quality of the Narnian fighters evoke in anyone who has read Norse mythology* the clear allusion to *Ragnarok,* translated variously as the last battle of the gods,* the twilight of the gods, or the "destruction of the powers," in which the monsters slay the gods and destroy earth and heaven.[5]

(LB 113 ff., *105 ff.*)
[*End of Narnia; Eschatology; Violence.*]

---

[1] LB 118–119, *109–112.*
[2] LB 122–125, *113–115.*
[3] LB 126–128, *116–117.*
[4] LB 129–131, *118–120.*
[5] H.R. Ellis Davidson, *Gods and Myths of Northern Europe* (Harmondsworth: Penguin, 1964) p. 236.

LAST SEA   The body of water between Ramandu's Island* and World's End,* it lies beyond the known Narnian world. The crew of the *Dawn Treader* finds, in at least three specific ways, that all is different there: (1) everyone needs less sleep, less food, and less conversation; (2) there is too much light; the sun* at dawning looks two or three times its normal size; and (3) the song of the Birds of Morning,* flying overhead every day, gives a special atmosphere to the place.

Its waters are so clear that Lucy can see the shadow of the *Dawn Treader* on the sea floor. She also begins to see countryside and farms and forests below, and notices the depths of deep green water and the "sunny places" of ultramarine blue, then the city of the Sea People* and their park in the shallows.

The waters of the Last Sea are sweet, not salt, a fulfillment of the prophecy* of the Dryad* at Reepicheep's birth. After a sip of it, Caspian drinks deeply and everything about him becomes brighter. He compares the water to light; and Reepicheep calls it "drinkable light." The taste is dazzling, "stronger than wine and somehow wetter, more liquid, than ordinary water." They can now bear the ever-increasing light and look straight at the growing sun without blinking; everything and everyone is transfigured. The rising sun is now five or six times its normal size, and they do not need to eat or sleep at all. Some of the older sailors are growing younger. The stillness of the sea overtakes them all. When they notice whiteness up and down the horizon, the ship turns south along it and they discover that the current is only forty feet wide.

Outside the current, the sea is as quiet as a lake. The region here and at World's End is named the Silver Sea.*

(VDT 189 ff., *185 ff.*)
[*Geography, Narnian; Holy Spirit; Imagination.*]

LAUGHTER   See *Humor.*

LEFAY, MRS.   Andrew Ketterley's* godmother, and according to him "one of the last mortals in this country who had fairy* blood." Although she is known to Mabel Kirke,* Digory's mother refuses to discuss her. Uncle Andrew tells Digory that Mrs. Lefay was "queer," and that she did unwise things for which she was put in prison. (To Andrew, "unwise" implies that her deeds were not wrong or unlawful, but that she should have been more careful.) But Mrs. Lefay was always kind to him, and he was one of the few people she called to see her in her final days. Like Andrew, she didn't associate with "ordinary, ignorant people."[1] Although Uncle Andrew promised her that he would destroy a secret box, he does not.

(MN 16 ff., *21 ff.*)
[*Magic; Rings.*]

---

[1] The adjectives "ordinary" and "ignorant" here are equated in the minds of amoral magicians as well as amoral technologists. See *Technology.*

LEOPARD   A Narnian constellation, seen in the summer sky along with the Ship and the Hammer. The Leopard is Lucy's favorite, and it shines on her the night she attempts to awaken the trees.* The sight of this trio of "friendly" constellations would have cheered her greatly during her first anxious night on Ramandu's Island.* Lewis's attention to such detail comes from his desire to restore a greater sensitivity to the beauty of nature.

(PC 111, *102.* VDT 170, *167.*)
[*Astronomy, Narnian.*]

LETITIA KETTERLEY   Digory's great-aunt Letty; she is an old maid who lives in London. Lewis calls her "touchy," but her character is really quite embracing—she has taken in her strange and difficult brother Andrew* (who calls her a hot-tempered old woman) and her seriously ill niece Mabel Kirke,* Digory's mother. She doesn't seem to like Andrew: she forbids Digory from entering Andrew's study and she won't allow Andrew to speak to the boy. She is a good housekeeper who puts out fresh vases of flowers and mends her mattress. She has a firm, quiet voice. Her brother has succeeded in spending much of the money she inherited, and she refuses to lend him any more to waste on brandy and cigars. Her house, according to Lewis, is of the sort that "gets very quiet and dull in the afternoon and always [seems] to smell of mutton." She certainly does not like Jadis, and does not hesitate to confront the Queen of Charn.* When Jadis seems to be slurring her English (she is actually trying to cast a spell), Aunt Letty operates out of her culture's stock response* to what appears to be a loose woman and decides she is drunk.

Digory later overhears Letty's comment that it will take fruit from the land of youth to cure his mother, and decides he must get that fruit from Narnia. As Digory's mother recovers, Aunt Letty brightens up the house and is finally relieved of the burden of her brother, who goes to live with the Kirkes in their country house.

(MN Chapter 1 passim.)
[*Adults; House of Professor Kirke.*]

LILITH   A female demon of both Babylonian mythology* and the Hebrew tradition, who murders newborn babies, harms women in childbirth, and haunts wildernesses on the lookout for children. In the *Chronicles,* she is said to be the wife of a Jinn and mother of the White Witch (who, true to her heritage, spends most of LWW trying to do away with the Pevensie children).

(LWW 77, 76.)

LILYGLOVES   The funny old chief mole,* whom Peter remembers from the old days. Leaning on his spade, he says that some day King Peter will be glad of the newly planted orchard.

(PC 18, 24.)
[*Apples, apple trees; Talking Beasts.*]

LILY LAKE   See *Silver Sea.*

LIMITS OF KNOWLEDGE   See *Knowledge.*

LION   The king of beasts. Any lion ought to be feared, and Edmund is afraid of the stone lion at the Castle of the White Witch* for quite a while until he realizes it is stone; when he scribbles a moustache and spectacles on it, it still looks so terrible and sad and noble. Aslan, a lion himself, favors the species. Thus in the Witch's courtyard he breathes* first on a stone lion. Aslan and the now-revived lion lead the others into battle, to the lion's delight. This lion is among those who receive honors at the the coronation of the Kings and Queens.* In LB, Puzzle* shows proper respect for his lion's skin disguise, and recognizes that the dignity of Aslan's lionhood is present even in a dumb lion.

(LWW 90, 89; 164, 152; 171–172, 158; 179, 165. LB 6, 11–12.)
[*Animals; Dumb beasts; Talking Beasts.*]

LISTS   Lewis's love of the ordinary[1] shows up in many ways in the *Chronicles:* his attention to the details of smells,* tactile images,* sounds,* domesticity,* and especially lists. In LWW, he lists the items to be found in the Beavers'* house, the menu for the Beavers' meal, the list of happy animal-person sounds as the statues in the courtyard of the Castle of the White Witch* come alive. In PC, he lists the treasures of Cair Paravel, and the foods eaten at the feast after the war with Miraz.* In VDT, Lewis outlines the provisions in the *Dawn Treader;* the number of things on Gumpas's* table that come down in a cascade; the list of things worth having (including beer, wine,* timber, cabbages, and books*); the menu for the Duffers'* hearty supper; the menu of Lucy's magic* luncheon with Coriakin*; the list of real and imaginary instruments in the House of the Magician*; and the menu of the continuous banquet on Ramandu's Island.* In SC, the menu for supper at Cair Paravel is given. In HHB, the description of Tashbaan* from a distance and its crowded streets is accomplished by lists, as is the menu for Shasta's Calormene* and Narnian meals.

(LWW 69, *70;* 70–71, *70–71;* 166, *153.* PC 22, *28;* 205, *180.* VDT 19, *26;* 45, *53;* 47, *55;* 124, *126;* 139, *139;* 141, *141;* 166, *163.* SC 39–40, *46.* HHB Ch 4 passim; 71, *67–68;* 167–168, *147.*)

---

[1] See *Imagination,* note 3.

LITERARY ALLUSIONS[1]   Lewis was known as one of the best- and most widely-read persons of his times, and he shares his great fund of knowledge with the readers of Narnia. Soon after his death, Lewis was accused by friends and critics alike of borrowing perhaps too much from other writers at the expense of his own originality. In *C. S. Lewis,* Roger Lancelyn Green comes to Lewis's defense:

> This background of thought is apparent throughout the Narnia stories, and for this reason it is of little importance to look for 'sources' and 'originals'. Such research might tell us what books Lewis had read, and where some of his ideas came from: but pure invention is almost impossible, and all authors receive their inspiration with the aid of suggestions or trains of thought induced by the odd word, line, sentence or even idea in another man's books—or in the general background of myth from which as often as not the previous writer himself had drawn. What matters is the use made of these hints, ideas and inspirations . . . the old universal pieces, now arranged in a new pattern.[2]

In PC, Lewis calls Reepicheep "the Master Mouse," a term suitable enough to Reepicheep's station in life but actually drawn from Henryson's version of Aesop's lion-and-mouse story in the *Morall Fabillis.* No doubt Lewis was tickled by the expression and amused by the new currency he was giving it. He may even have looked ahead with pleasure to the possibility that a few of his child readers, going on to study literature, would meet Henryson's original Master Mouse. Children might sooner recognize Puddleglum's testing of the bottle by degrees as an allusion to Pooh's testing of the honey-jar in the Heffalump Trap. Lewis may also be trying to educate modern children, as Professor Kirke often echoes Lewis's own feelings: "What do they teach them in school nowadays?" Thus in VDT, Edmund infuriates Caspian by comparing Reepicheep's plan to tie him up with the crew's binding of Ulysses to the mast so that he could do nothing beyond hearing the sirens' song. Lewis perhaps hoped that children might be curious enough to find out for themselves what this Ulysses story was all about. Other literary allusions are noted in the entries to which they apply.

LONE ISLANDS   Felimath,* Doorn,* and Avra,* a cluster of three islands east of Cair Paravel. Until the time of the further explorations of Caspian X, they are considered the last known outpost of civilization. They have had many rulers since the time of King Gale,* who kills the dragon* that terrorized the islanders (302 N.Y.).[1] These grateful people name Gale their emperor, a title that thereafter becomes hereditary with the kings* of Narnia (during the Hundred Years of Winter* in 900–1000 N.Y., Queen Jadis appropriates this title to herself). When Aslan kills her, the title falls to Peter, now the High King. Queen Lucy's fond memories of the Islands come from this Golden Age.* At the time of the *Dawn Treader*'s voyage (2306–2307 N.Y.), Gumpas* is the legitimate governor of the Islands; but he takes advantage of three hundred years of lack of supervision on the part of the Telmarine* kings of Narnia by allowing the slave trade* to flourish. Thus when the *Dawn Treader* makes its stop at the Lone Islands (they are the fourth stop on the voyage), Caspian unseats Gumpas and makes Lord Bern* the duke. When the *Dawn Treader* docks at Narrowhaven* on its return voyage, Pittencream* deserts his companions and flees to Calormen* where he lives out his days.

(LWW 55, 57. PC 107, *99; 172, 151*. VDT 18, *25; 30 ff., 36 ff.; 187, 183*. SC 38, *45*. LB 88–89, *82*.)
[*Geography, Narnian.*]

[1] When Lewis was writing VDT, he hadn't invented the history of how the Lone Islands came to be Narnian. He promises (on p.30, *36*) that if he learns this history, he might include it in another book. He makes good this promise in LB 88–89, *82*. The way in which he phrases his explanation ("I have never heard how . . . if I ever do. . . .") may be an indication of his creative process; that is, he might hear stories in the same way he sees images.

LONGING   A nameless longing to which Lewis believed he could put the name of God.[1] It is the term Lewis uses to express the sort of experience within life that opens us up beyond appearances to the transcendent; the craving suggested but not fulfilled by pleasure. In LWW, the girls have longed ever since they first saw him to bury their hands in Aslan's mane. In PC, the young Prince Caspian longs for Old Narnia, and Doctor Cornelius* has been looking for traces of it all his life. At the sight of the Narnian sunset, Jill is filled with a longing for adventure.* In HHB, both Bree and Shasta long to go to Narnia; Bree because he remembers how free he was as a colt, and Shasta because he has had a somewhat mysterious desire to go there all his life.

The feeling of being pleasantly reminded of something just out of reach is also an image of longing. Thus the Telmarine* soldier in PC has a startled, happy look, "as if he were trying to remember something"; and Frank,* Polly, and Digory, entranced by the joy* of Aslan's song of creation, look "like they are being reminded of something." In LB, Aslan is referred to as Tirian's* "heart's desire"; Emeth's* desire since boyhood has been to serve and know Tash* and to look upon his face; and Jewel* says of Aslan's country,* "This is the land I have been looking for all my life, though I never knew it till now."

(LWW 147, *136*. PC 38, *42;* 49, *52;* 52, *54;* 64, *63;* 112, *103;* 132, *120;* 196, *172;* 213, *186*. VDT 16, *24*. SC 9, *19;* 36, *43;* 214, *204*. HHB 12, *20*. MN 100, *94*. LB 146, *134;* 162, *147;* 171, *154*.)

[*Joy.*]

---

[1] Longing is often manifested as hope. In the Ruined City of the Ancient Giants,* "the one voice in the whole world which each [of the three travelers] had been secretly hoping to hear." See Lewis, *The Pilgrim's Regress* (Grand Rapids: Wm. B. Eerdmans Co., 1958) p. 10. This is one of the most important themes in Lewis's life and thought. For a book-length treatment, see Corbin S. Carnell, *Bright Shadow of Reality: C. S. Lewis and the Feeling Intellect* (Grand Rapids: Wm. B. Eerdmans Publishing Co., 1974).

LOYALTY   See *Honor.*

LUCK   See *Providence.*

LUCY PEVENSIE   The youngest child and second daughter of Mr. and Mrs. Pevensie*; she is known as Queen Lucy the Valiant in the Golden Age of Narnia,* is one of Aslan's closest friends, and is perhaps the best developed character in the *Chronicles.* She is the person through whom the reader sees and experiences most of Narnia in LWW, PC, and VDT; she is absent from only SC and MN, is in the background of HHB, and figures in the last quarter of LB. She is a fair-haired, happy, and compassionate person, deeply sensitive and intuitive, but somewhat fearful and vain. Her story is one of growth from fear* to courage* so that she becomes what her cognomen signifies, a valiant person. It is through her character that Lewis expresses his own religious and personal sensibilities. Through her, as well, the reader sees the connection between the first hearing of Aslan's name (at the sound of which she has a beginning-of-vacation, waking-up-in-the-morning feeling) and the last words of Aslan ("The term is over: the holidays have begun. The dream is ended: this is the morning."). From beginning to end, she is concerned about other people: her first question of Aslan is to ask him to do something about her brother Edmund; she pleads for mercy for Rabadash*; almost her last question is to ask the Lion to try to help the renegade dwarfs.* She is the one who notices how terrible Aslan's paws are and the one to experience their playfulness and caresses. He shares with her his laughter and happiness as well as his sadness. It is part of Edmund's "credal statement" that Lucy sees Aslan most often. To her is given the gift of healing in the cordial* made from the juice of the sun's* fire-berries.*[1] Her capacity for instant friendship endears her to Tumnus,* Aravis, Reepicheep, her brothers, and even the mysterious Sea-maiden.

In LWW she is between eight and nine years old, subject to both the fatigues and the enthusiasms of the very young. All the charms of the new world of Narnia come to the reader through her lively senses. Through her, the two-sided effect of Aslan's submission to the Deep Magic* is experienced as a presentiment both of evil* falling upon the Lion and of the Lion's doing something dreadful.[2] She is swept up in Aslan's explanation of the meaning of his resurrection, so much so that she does not know why she is laughing as she scrambles over the top of the broken Stone Table* to reach him.[3] The one fault she commits in LWW is her desire to see the results of her cordial upon the wounded Edmund.[4] She is cross with Aslan, but responds immediately to his growl both with words of contrition and with actions on behalf of the other wounded. And it is she who notices the depth of Edmund's transformation. Lewis never says whether Lucy wins her argument with Susan over telling Edmund that Aslan died in the boy's stead; but, since Edmund and Lucy talk a great deal about Narnia back in England and since Edmund seems to operate from this knowledge in his profession of faith,* the reader can assume that Lucy told him. A vignette of her activities in the Golden Age is given in HHB when she rides to Archenland's* aid.

Lucy is the first in PC to feel the tug from Narnia. Her question of Peter ("Do you think we can possibly have got back to Narnia?") anticipates an almost identical scene when the Seven Friends of Narnia* arrive in Aslan's country* in LB. Chapter 9, "What Lucy Saw," emphasizes her gifts of insight. Her special kind of wakefulness is an ineffable signal to go out to meet the trees* and attempt to awaken them. She, unlike her "practical" sister Susan, is able to understand the implications for humankind of the attack by the bear.[5] She has a momentary vision of Aslan that her companions ought to trust but don't; though she is angry at their contrariness, she very generously does not criticize them. Aslan favors her with an ecstatic, nighttime rendezvous; but he does not let her complain about her companions—he means only for her to strike out on her own if they do not listen to her. This is a hard lesson for her to learn and she would rather escape it in the intimacy of their relationship; but this intimacy itself strengthens her. It is very difficult for her to hear the grumbling of her companions, but she forgets her harsh responses by keeping her attention focused on the Lion who walks ahead of her.[6] She is compensated for this hardship by the many dances* that take place in Narnia as Aslan liberates the country and its people. Her sorrow that Peter and Susan will not be able to return to Narnia is genuine; she is a very selfless person.

Lucy's love of sailing and the sea is everywhere apparent in VDT.[7] Her respect for Reepicheep's dignity prevents her from embracing him until the very last moment they are together.[8] She cares for Eustace even before he has come to the point of being able to think of anyone besides himself: she uses her cordial to heal his seasickness, and shares her water with him during the rationing. Even before she knows he is the dragon,* she eases its pain with her cordial and kisses it. Lucy's horror at the realization that the statue on Deathwater Island* was a man is heightened by the fact that she first perceived the statue as the most beautiful work of art she had ever seen. She does not hesitate to intervene in the fight between Caspian and her brother, calling them both "swaggering, bullying idiots." She has only to hear of the need of the invisible people before she volunteers to seek out the magic* spell for them. Her apprehension is great as she anticipates going upstairs (she takes fright at the sight of the bearded glass, something she will laugh at only after her fears are relieved).[9] In the scene at the magician's Book,* Lucy's faults become most evident. She is insecure: she thinks herself inferior to her sister, especially in physical beauty; and she worries about how devoted her friends are—she wants very much to be liked.[10] So strong is her desire to be accepted that when she is prevented from reciting the spell that would make her irresistibly beautiful, she rushes to recite the very next spell that would have a bearing on this desire—the spell to know what her friends think about her. But hearing her own voice raised in anger at her friend Marjorie Preston's* betrayal reminds her that she is talking only to a picture and not really to her friend.[11] She then recites the spell for the refreshment of spirit, which is such a lovely story* that she wants to read it over again but finds that she cannot have an encore: the pages only turn forward. She can remember only a few main images from the story.[12] Lucy finally finds and reads the spell to make hidden things visible. Aware that she has made *all* things visible, she turns to face the open doors of the library (their being opened had made her somewhat uncomfortable when she had first come into the room). She is transfigured by what she sees—"Her face lit up till, for a moment (but of course she did not know it), she looked almost as beautiful as that other Lucy."[13] What she sees is Aslan.[14] He explains to her the meaning of her experiences with the various spells in the Magician's Book and then leads her to Coriakin.* Her first sight of the Duffers* makes her convulse with laughter, but she regains her composure to sincerely suggest to them that they aren't the ugly creatures they believe themselves to be.

Though she feels otherwise, she tells Caspian she is willing to sail into the Dark. The reader senses the complete horror of the Dark Island* from her vantage point in the fighting top. It is she who notices the total darkness, the cold, and the mounting hysteria in the voices of the crew. Along with the rest, she recalls the worst of her nightmares; but she hangs on tight and whispers a prayer* (the first explicit prayer in the *Chronicles*) for Aslan's help. The darkness does not diminish but she feels almost imperceptibly better; she consoles herself with the thought that at least the situation hasn't worsened. Because of her faith in the face of this great trial, she is rewarded with the words of the albatross* (whose voice and breath are the Lion's, she is sure). As soon as they are out of the dark, she goes down to the deck to extend whatever help she can to Lord Rhoop.*

At the thought that hers might be the first eyes that see the new constellations in the southeastern night sky, she has a numinous* experience. As precious as this is to her, she finds the new stars* "strange" and "burning." Her homesickness for Narnia causes her to long to see her "old friends," the familiar constellations of Narnia. On Ramandu's Island,* she forgets her desire to return because of the excitement of the magical place and because she wants to wake the Three Sleepers.* She is among the volunteers who stay on the island overnight and she is the first to see (and the only one who would recognize) the Stone Knife* on Aslan's Table,* in the light of the candle held by the Daughter of Ramandu.* The reader sees Ramandu through Lucy's eyes and the fire-berry* that the Bird of Morning* brings. Her sympathy is evident in her delight that the retired star can offer Rhoop oblivion. She prods Reepicheep to speak out during the attempted mutiny of the crew (and later cools the hottest part of the dispute with Caspian over his attempted abdication with the reminder to him that he has pledged to return to the Star's Daughter).

The wonders of the Last Sea* are, for the reader, largely Lucy's experience. She becomes absorbed in trying to understand the life and culture of the Sea-People whose country she sees beneath the clear waves. When Lucy tastes the sweet waters, she gasps that this is the loveliest thing she has ever tasted, but so very strong and nourishing that she will need to eat no further. The waters so strengthen her that (though she feels some pangs at leaving the *Dawn Treader* behind at World's End*) she is too excited by the light, the silence,* the smell,* and even the special kind of loneliness of the place to mourn too long over the parting. Lucy is the only person who has ever tried[15] to describe the fragrance and music* of Aslan's country. In dialogue with Lewis, who intrudes himself into the narrative at this point, she explains that they would break your heart, not with sadness, but with the special kind of joy* that is experienced in this life only as longing.*

She and Edmund and Eustace no longer feel as grown-up as they do in Narnia, but very childlike.[16] Lucy asks the Lamb* they see if this is the way to Aslan's country. As he tells her no, he is transfigured into the Lion. As he moves to show them the door to their own country, Lucy begs him to let them return soon. Hearing his "never again," she cries out his name in despair. She sobs her most beautiful lines in all of the *Chronicles:* "It isn't Narnia, you know. It's you. We shan't meet you there. And how can we live, never meeting you?" Hearing that she *will* meet him in "our world," but under another name, and that the reason they were brought to Narnia was to know him better there, she plays a "St. Peter" and asks about Eustace, a "St. John." Will he ever get to come back? Aslan calls her "child" and explains to her that she doesn't need to know that. He sends her and the two boys back with a caress and a kiss into Lucy's back bedroom at the Scrubb residence in Cambridge.

In LB, Lucy accompanies Polly, Digory, Jill, and Eustace on the train that will meet Peter and Edmund. Unknown to her, her parents are also on the train. She finds herself arrayed as a queen and standing with her friends in the middle of a discussion about the meaning of a Stable* whose Door* alone she can see. She does not speak until the end of this conversation; when she does, she speaks with a thrill of joy in her voice that communicates itself immediately to Tirian* ("She was drinking everything in more deeply than the others. She had been too happy to speak."). Her first observation links the meaning of Narnia's Stable with the stable at Bethlehem, which also sheltered something —some*one*—larger than the whole earth.[17] Now the reader not only sees with her eyes but understands the meaning of everything through her understanding. She explains why the Calormene* assassin who cannot[18] see anything in Aslan's country can yet see Tash.* Lucy instinctively likes Emeth.[19] In her delicacy, she cannot bring herself to relate Tash's eating of Shift.* She has tried to befriend the renegade dwarfs,* but to no avail. She won't tolerate any of Eustace's anger at the dwarfs (nor did King Lune* of his son Corin* at Rabadash) and bids Tirian to do something for the dwarfs. She pleads with them again, calling them "poor,[20] stupid dwarfs." In the middle of his attempt, Aslan appears; and she tearfully pleads with him. He calls her "dearest" as he promises to do what he can for them. Later, when Narnia is ended, Lucy weeps at its demise and defends her right to mourn.[21] She runs to meet Puzzle,* along with Jill. She assures him that when he meets Aslan, things will go well. She tries to understand the meaning of where they are by asking Peter. As he and the others point out the striking similarity of their surroundings to old Narnia, Lucy sees more of the dissimilarities; it is only after Digory's explanation that they all understand. At the Great Waterfall,* she observes that one can't feel afraid even if one tries: fear is conquered in this country. After flying up the falls and across the west to the garden,* they all meet Reepicheep, then Tumnus, and all their friends. Lucy sits with Tumnus (her first Narnian friend) on the wall of the garden overlooking Narnia and again tries to comprehend what has happened to them. Her graced vision enables her to take in all of Narnia and then to notice how its east and west are part of a chain of mountains that ring that world and connect it with the mountains they are near. Then she sees, to her great excitement, England jutting off as another peninsula from the same mountain range. The Pevensies see their parents and wonder how to get to them. Tumnus tells them; but then King Frank's* horn calls them to meet Aslan. Through Lucy's eyes, the reader sees Aslan bounding toward them. Hers are the final words addressed to him in the *Chronicles;* she speaks their fear that they will be sent back into their world. He removes this fear forever and announces the real, everlasting adventures farther up and in his country.

---

[1] A Christian reader might see in her activity and sensitivity the apostle John (Lucy leans on Aslan's breast in PC); the apostle Peter (she asks about Eustace at the end of VDT); Mary Magdalene (she is with Aslan in his agony in LWW and she is the first to see him in PC); and even Mary, Jesus' mother.

[2] This is how Lewis views the death of Christ, as both tragic and necessary, as catastrophic and eucatastrophic (to use Tolkien's term); as the awful and awesome consequence of that other paradoxical event, the fall of Adam of Eve, which Christian tradition views as the *felix culpa*— the happy fault that necessitated the advent of the Son of God into human history.

[3] This is the first manifestation of Lucy's true mysticism: she finds her religious experience ineffable.

[4] See *Aslan,* note 11.

[5] Lewis sets up a deliberate contrast here between the two sisters to persuade the reader that Lucy's seemingly theoretical observation has great practical value. See *Dumb Beasts,* note 1.

[6] See *Worship.*

[7] Lewis loved the sea too.

[8] Since Lewis did not detail Lucy's reunion with Reepicheep in LB, it is only speculation to say more.

[9] Compare Shasta's experience of the horns at Tashbaan.* When he is excited, they sound wonderful; later in the day, when he is abandoned and alone, they sound terrifying. Lewis is commenting on the experience of fear.

[10] See *Vanity.*

[11] This same realization helps free the hero, John, from the enchantment of the Spirit of the Age in Lewis's allegory, *The Pilgrim's Regress* (Grand Rapids: Wm. B. Eerdmans Publishing Co., 1958) p. 70. The glances of the Spirit of the Age produce as false a picture of the insides of things as the magic spell produces of the insides of people's conversations and motivations.

---

[12] Yet another indication that Lewis intended to end the *Chronicles* with VDT is the parenthetical remark he makes at this point in the story: "... ever since that day what Lucy means by a good story is a story which reminds her of the forgotten story in the Magician's Book." The verb in the present tense ("means") implies that Lucy is continuing to make this judgment now, as though she were alive. She was ten at the time of VDT and had, as we can see in LB, only seven more years to live.

[13] Lewis believed that a person's beauty *belonged* to the beholder: one ought not want others to find one desirable and desired but enjoyable and enjoyed. For the distinction between contemplation and enjoyment, see *Introduction* and *Vanity*. See also Jane Studdock's experience in *That Hideous Strength* (New York: Macmillan Publishing Co., 1965) p. 63.

[14] For the significance of their conversation, see *Aslan*.

[15] Except for C. S. Lewis, who tried to describe his experience of joy and longing all his life. In an epigram, Lewis comes to a very similar point to the one he has just attempted to depict in his "dialogue" with Lucy:

Have you not seen that in our days
Of any whose story, song, or art
Delights us, our sincerest praise
Means, when all's said, 'You break my heart'?

(Epigram 2, *Poems*, Walter Hooper, ed. (New York: Harcourt Brace Jovanovich, 1964) p. 133.

[16] Lewis is suggesting the humility requisite for the vision of Aslan they are about to have. Recall the thesis that Lewis may have intended to end the *Chronicles* with this book.

[17] An allusion of G. K. Chesterton in *The Everlasting Man;* see *Stable.*

[18] This is an oblique reference to Lewis's theology of grace. The Calormene has no connaturality with Aslan or anything pertaining to Aslan; he is able to see only Tash because the assassin shares the same treacherous outlook as his god.

[19] Lewis mentions this twice. Her attraction and his attractiveness must have been remarkable.

[20] The British edition accidentally deletes "poor," thereby giving the impression of impatience on Lucy's part.

[21] That it is proper to mourn the passing of old Nature is a point Lewis makes in *Miracles* (New York: Macmillan Publishing Co., 1978; London: Collins Fontana, 1960) pp. 66–67, 70–71.

LUNE   King of Archenland,* father of Cor and Corin.* From Lewis's description, he looks very much like a Santa Claus; but his deep voice and the "hungry" expression with which he first greets Shasta give him a more serious aspect. His company at the Battle of Anvard,* where he kills Azrooh* in hand-to-hand combat, includes the brothers[1] Cor and Corin, Dar and Darrin,* Col and Colin, and Tran and Shar. That he is a good and fair ruler is shown over and over: he prevents Edmund from killing Rabadash* by declaring the Calormene unfit for a gentleman's death because he has breached the code of war-courtesy; he reproves his son Corin for joining the battle, but only thinly disguises his pleasure over his son's bravery[2]; he was merciful to Lord Bar,* his chancellor, when he discovered that Bar was an embezzler (however, when he found out that Bar was also a Calormene spy and had kidnapped the King's son, he pursued and killed him); he explains to Cor that he must be king, for this is his inescapable duty and vocation.* An unpretentious man, he greets Aravis not in his royal robes* but in his oldest clothes.

(HHB 72, *68;* 184, *160–161;* 196 ff., *172 ff.;* Chapter 15 passim.)
[*Government; Kings and Queens.*]

---

[1] See *Darrin* for more on brothers' names.

[2] Lewis seems to be saying that rash courage is better than planned cowardice.* He treads very close here to a false sense of courage,* and probably does so in exaggerated reaction to pacifism, which he could not abide.

MABEL KIRKE   Mother of Digory Kirke, niece of Andrew Ketterley* amd Letitia Ketterley.* For most of MN she is seriously ill. Her character is not particularly well drawn, and it is primarily her illness that is important— Uncle Andrew uses it as a condition of extortion over Digory; and its cure by the Apple of Youth is seen as a miracle. She seems to be a kind woman who sings and plays the piano and enjoys playing games with Digory and Polly. She is very strict about keeping promises, and has taught Digory not to steal—a virtue that serves him well when he is tempted in the garden.* She awakens at the smell of the Apple of Youth and is given the strength to eat the whole thing. Eventually, she recovers completely. Her husband, who has been away in India, inherits his great uncle's estate and decides to retire and come home forever. Mr. and Mrs. Kirke and Digory go to live in a house in the country and take the irascible Uncle Andrew with them.

(MN 2–3, *9–10;* 15–16, *21–22;* 26, *30;* 74, *72;* 82, *78;* 85–86, *81–82;* 112, *104;* 120, *111;* 134, *125;* 136, *126;* 141–142, *130–131;* 161–163, *150–151;* 175, *163;* 180 ff., *166 ff.*)
[*Adults; Apples, apple trees; House of Professor Kirke.*]

MACREADY, MRS.   Housekeeper to Professor Digory Kirke. She is not fond of children and dislikes being interrupted when she is telling visitors all she knows about the house. A stereotype of the British housekeeper, she is bossy and full of instructions. When the children return from Narnia, she is still talking with the visitors outside the spare room—an indication of the wide discrepancy between English time* and Narnian time. Mrs. Macready's name is probably based on Mrs. McCreedy, a woman who kept house for Lewis's parents when he was two years old,[1] although it may also be a play on the words "make ready."

(LWW 48, *51;* 185, *170.*)
[*Autobiographical allusions.*]

---

[1] Kathryn Lindskoog, *Voyage to Narnia* (Elgin: David C. Cook, 1978), p.13 of the Response Book.

After their trek across the Great Desert, Aravis, Bree, Hwin, and Shasta plunge into a broad pool to cool off. (**HHB** 128, 114-115.)

MAENADS   In Greek and Roman mythology,* the female members of Bacchus's* company. They leap, rush, turn somersaults, and dance the dance* of plenty.¹

(PC 192, *168*.)
[*Gods.*]

---

¹ For the meaning of their cry, *Euan, Euan, euoi-oi-oi-oi,* see *Bacchus,* note 1.

MAGIC, MAGICIAN   Magic at first calls to mind various evil* enchanters, enchantments, and instruments we encounter in Narnia: the petrifying wand* of the White Witch in LWW; Turkish Delight*; the spell of the Hundred Years of Winter* that lies over Narnia; Nikabrik's* willingness in PC to tap dark magical forces, if necessary, to overthrow Miraz*; the spell of forgetfulness cast over Prince Rilian* by the Queen of Underland* in SC; the Deplorable Word* of Empress Jadis of Charn*; and Uncle Andrew's* magic rings.* But the wardrobe* that lets the children into Narnia is also magic; there is a hint from Lewis that good magic may have chased them into Narnia, and Narnia knows good magicians like Coriakin* and Doctor Cornelius.* The Deep Magic,* which the Witch counts on to insure her triumph over Aslan, is not quite what she takes it to be—its real dimensions include a yet Deeper Magic* that undoes all her evil. In short, the *Chronicles* do not present a battle between the ordinary, natural scene and dark, unnatural magical powers. The ordinary, natural scene is rather the battlefield¹ on which the good magic confronts the bad, just as ultimately the human heart is the stage on which the mystery of grace wrestles with the mystery of evil.

The *Chronicles of Narnia* are themselves a kind of magic, a seven-volume magician's book devised by Lewis to break bad enchantments of technology* and vanity* and curiosity* and bring about re-enchantments by means of honor,* courage,* and obedience by reawakening a longing* for Aslan and Aslan's country.* Lewis spoke in *"The Weight of Glory"*: "Do you think I am trying to weave a spell? Perhaps I am; but remember your fairy tales. Spells are used for breaking enchantments as well as for inducing them. And you and I have need of the strongest spell that can be found to wake us from the evil enchantment of worldliness which has been laid upon us for nearly a hundred years."²

---

¹ See *Aslan,* note 2.
² *The Weight of Glory and Other Addresses* (Grand Rapids: Wm. B. Eerdmans Publishing Co., 1965) p. 5, and *Screwtape Proposes a Toast and Other Pieces* (London: Collins Fountain, 1977) p. 98. For a discussion of magic as curiosity,* or an immoderate striving for knowledge,* see Josef Pieper, *The Four Cardinal Virtues* (Notre Dame: University of Notre Dame Press, 1966) p. 199.

MAN-HEADED BULL   A mythological creature, enthusiastically on Aslan's side in the war against the White Witch. He is not to be confused with any of the Minotaurs,* bull-headed men who are invariably on the Witch's side.

(LWW 122, *115;* 139, *129.*)
[*Mythology.*]

MARGARET   One of three servants to Professor Digory Kirke. The other two are Ivy* and Betty.*

(LWW 1, *9.*)

MARJORIE PRESTON   An intimate, older school chum of Lucy Pevensie. Lucy "overhears" Marjorie betray her during the eavesdropping enchantment. In order to gain Anne Featherstone's* respect, Marjorie asserts that she doesn't care for Lucy as much as she appears to. Lucy, surprised and hurt, asserts that Marjorie, who is apparently the kind of girl who has few friends, should be grateful for all that Lucy has done for her.

(VDT 131 ff., *133 ff.*)
[*Privacy.*]

MARSH-WIGGLES[1]   Human-like beings that live in marshes and subsist on a diet of eels and a strong, alcoholic beverage. The derivation of the name is apparent; "marsh" from their habitat and "wiggle" from their rather rubbery physiques and affinity for eels. They refer to themselves as "wiggles." Their feet are webbed and cold-blooded, "like a duck's."[2] They value their privacy,* and live in wig-wams[3] spaced far apart. They smoke* a heavy tobacco, perhaps mixed with mud. Internally, they are quite different from human beings—although in what way is not specified. However, Puddleglum's hand, chewed by Golg* the earthman,* would have been a bloody pulp if he were not a Marsh-Wiggle. Marsh-Wiggles do the Narnian work that is concerned with water and fish, and Jill and Eustace are ferried across the fords of Beruna* by a ferry-wiggle. Marsh-Wiggles are at duty at Cair Paravel and fasten the hawsers when ships dock there. The general disposition of Marsh-Wiggles is dour and pragmatic, and they generally expect the worst of any situation. Glimfeather* suggests them as the best guides to take Jill and Eustace across Ettinsmoor.*

(SC 53, *59;* 56 ff., *62 ff.,* 158, *155;* 174, *170;* 208, *199.* LB 178, *161.*)

---

[1] The word Marsh-Wiggle is hyphenated in both the American and British editions of SC, but it is unhyphenated in both editions of LB. It is likely that by the time he wrote LB, Lewis simply forgot the word was originally two words.

[2] A mistake. As everyone knows, ducks are warm-blooded.

[3] Perhaps an abbreviation, in this case, for "wiggle-wams."

MASTER BOWMAN   The unnamed leader of the bowmen aboard the *Dawn Treader,* he speaks for his archers and many of the crew when he expresses the fear that, with the seas becalmed, they might never return to Narnia. The Lord Drinian* derides this suggestion as "landsman's talk."

(VDT 182, *179.*)

MAUGRIM   See *Fenris Ulf.*

MAVRAMORN   One of the Seven Noble Lords* and one of the four Telmarine* visitors to the Island of the voices* in the years 2299–2300 N.Y. He is one of the Three Sleepers* at Aslan's Table.*

(VDT 16, *23;* 149, *149;* 168, *165.*)
[*Sleep.*]

MAZERS   Hardwood drinking bowls used at the feast celebrating the victory of Old Narnia over Miraz* and the Telmarines.* Mazers are cups or goblets without feet, which were originally made out of mazer wood (wood derived from gnarled tree burls) and often richly carved or ornamented with silver and gold or other metals. The "great wooden bowl, curiously carved" mentioned in LB could be a mazer.

(PC 205, *180.* LB 14, *18–19.*)
[*Revelry; Wine.*]

MEMORY   Lewis felt that one's memory of an experience actually improves that experience, and might, indeed, be *better* than the original. This idea was a part of Lewis's mental furniture from at least his twenty-second year, when he wrote in a letter to his father of the "images and ideas which we have put down to mature in the cellerage of our brains, thence to come up with a continually improving bouquet."[1] Elsewhere, he says, "A pleasure is full grown only when it is remembered."[2] Thus when he speaks of memory[3] in the *Chronicles,* it is with deliberate meaning. In PC, Lucy has a thrill of memory as she recognizes three of Narnia's summer constellations. When Lucy tries to remember the story* that is the spell for refreshment of the spirit in VDT, it fades on her: she cannot have it again because the pages turn only forward, not back. However, she experiences *reminders* of it for the rest of her life in other stories that she reads, and she judges a story as good to the extent that it "reminds her of the forgotten story in the magician's* Book.*" Rilian is concerned that he will remember to his dishonor how he passed up the "marvelous adventure* of exploring Bism." Perhaps the most vivid memory in the *Chronicles* is Tirian's* memory of his childhood, which comes flooding back with his father's embrace.

Lewis also stresses the importance of remembering as a spiritual discipline. Jill thinks she should say something courteous to Aslan when he finishes giving her the four signs,* so she says "Thank you very much. I see." Aslan, who really *does* see, gently says that she may not really see as well as she thinks she does, and tells her that the first step toward seeing is remembering—and the first step toward remembering is repeating. He commands her four times to remember the signs, adding the fourth time that she should also believe them. He adds that, in the thicker air of Narnia, it may be hard to remember her quest,* and that unless she learns the signs by heart it will be easy to forget them.

(PC 110, *102;* 213, *186.* VDT 133, *135;* 169, *167;* 177, *173;* 190, *186.* SC 8, *17;* 20, *29;* 181, *176.* MN 28 ff., *31 ff.;* 76, *73;* 99, *93;* 110, *102;* 164, *152;* 178, *165.* LB 43, *40–41;* 175, *158;* 177–178, *160.*)

¹ *Letters of C. S. Lewis,* W. H. Lewis, ed. (New York: Harcourt Brace Jovanovich, 1966) pp. 71–72 (August 31, 1921).
² C. S. Lewis, *Out of the Silent Planet* (New York: Macmillan Publishing Co., 1965) p. 73.
³ For a discussion of the meaning of memory of events which have not really happened, see *Longing.*

MER-PEOPLE   Inhabitants of the Eastern Sea* on its border with Narnia. These mermen and mermaids sing at the coronation of Peter, Edmund, Susan, and Lucy. Their unforgettable music* differs from ordinary music in its strangeness, sweetness, and profoundly piercing character. Lucy confuses them with the Sea People* of the Last Sea* (as do many readers), but Edmund reminds her that the mer-people are able to live in air and in water, whereas the Sea People live only in water.¹

(LWW 179, *165.* PC 16, *23.* VDT 196, *191.*)

¹ When writing LWW, Lewis probably did not know he would create in VDT a separate species, called by the proper name, the Sea People. Hence he uses the phrase generally in LWW.

MEZREEL   A summer resort of the wealthy in Calormen.* Its attractions include a lake, famous gardens, and the Valley of the Thousand Perfumes— an area of especially fragrant flowers and blossoming trees and shrubs. To Lasaraleen Tarkheena,* whose summer home is here, Mezreel is the epitome of sensual delights.

(HHB 41, *43.*)

MICE   Mice figure prominently in the *Chronicles.*¹ They were not created as Talking Beasts,* but because they were kind enough to gnaw through the ropes to free the dead Aslan, they were given the gift of speech.* Ever helpful, mice rally to Tirian's* side and are sent to free the horses* in LB. They are over two feet tall, and stand on their hind legs. Perhaps the most famous mouse is the courageous Reepicheep.

(LWW 156, *144.* PC 203, *178.* SC 29, *37.* LB 116–117, *107–108.*)
[*Animals; Peepiceek.*]

¹ Lewis's love of mice is evident in many of his works, and a lovely passage can be read in *That Hideous Strength* (New York: Macmillan Publishing Co., 1965) p. 149.

MINOTAURS   Enormous, earthshaking men with bulls' heads, totally devoted to the cause of the White Witch. They are present at the slaying of Aslan and take an active role in the battle with Aslan's armies. They are not to be confused with the man-headed bull* who fights on Aslan's side. In Greek mythology* the Minotaur was the Cretan monster who, housed in the labyrinth, devoured his annual tribute of seven Athenian youths and seven Athenian maidens until he was slain by Theseus.

(LWW 132, *123;* 148, *138;* 154, *143.*)

MIRAZ   The Telmarine* king of Narnia, Prince Caspian's uncle, and the husband of Prunaprismia.* Affectionate to Caspian only out of necessity, he is hoping for an heir of his own. He spends as little time as possible with the young prince, and educates him only on the off chance that the boy may someday be king.* He is almost a stereotypical adult* who does not believe in fairy tales, the possiblity of talking animals,* or anything that he sees as impractical (such as the idea of two kings and two queens ruling at the same time). Miraz himself is a usurper. Calling himself the Lord Protector, he weeded out the great lords through hunting* "accidents," dangerous assignments, and false charges of treason and madness. When his own son is born he decides to murder Caspian, and spends the rest of PC tracking him down. Challenged to a monomachy* by King Peter, he shows himself to be brave but irascible and vain. Although Miraz's army has the advantage and he could easily win in that way, Lords Glozelle* and Sopespian* flatter him into accepting the duel. He fights well but trips over a tussock and is stabbed to death by Glozelle.

(PC 37 passim, *42 passim;* 53 ff., *54 ff.;* 83, *80;* 170 ff., *150 ff.*)
[*Ecology; Government; Technology.*]

MOLES   These burrowing animals* do much of the digging in the *Chronicles,* and at that they are as good as dwarfs.* Led by Lilygloves,* they dig the apple* orchard at Cair Paravel.* In SC, moles are chiefly responsible for digging Jill, Eustace, Puddleglum, and Rilian out of Underland.*

(PC 18, *24.* SC 194–195; *187–188.*)
[*Talking Beasts.*]

MONOMACHY   The term is used by Peter in his challenge to Miraz. It means single combat, an ancient form of battle often used in order to decide the outcome of a war without resorting to general bloodshed. Lewis seems to favor monomachy as an act of extraordinary bravery, exemplified by Ransom's fight with the Unman in *Perelandra*[1] and Orual's fight with Argan of Phars in *Till We Have Faces.*[2] Reepicheep, that heiroglyph of courage, takes an interest in the conversation of the pre-dragoned, pre-converted Eustace only because the boy demands of Caspian that he be allowed to "lodge a disposition" with the nearest British consul; the mouse thinks lodging a disposition might be a new form of single combat. Later, Reepicheep desires to challenge the dragon* Eustace to a monomachy. The image of single combat has been used frequently throughout the Christian era to describe one aspect of the theology of the atonement.* Thus Christ's temptation in the desert was viewed as a monomachy with Satan; and Christ's death on the cross was a monomachy with Death. The biblical foundation for this image is found in Romans 5:12–21.

(PC 173, *152.* VDT 21, *28;* 78, *84–85.*)

[1] C. S. Lewis, *Perelandra* (New York: Macmillan Publishing Co., 1943) Chapter 12 ff.
[2] C. S. Lewis, *Till We Have Faces* (New York: Harcourt Brace Jovanovich, 1980) Part 1, Chapter 19.

MONOPODS   See *Duffers.*

MOONWOOD   A Narnian talking hare with hearing so acute that he is able to hear what is whispered in Cair Paravel from his position below the Great Waterfall.* According to Lewis's outline of Narnian history,[1] Moonwood lived around 570 N.Y.

(LB 88, *82.*)
[*Talking Beasts.*]

[1] PWD, p. 42.

MORALITY   See *Right and wrong.*

MUIL   The westernmost of the Seven Isles.*

(VDT 18, *25.*)
[*Geography, Narnian.*]

MULLUGUTHERUM   The only named gnome-in-waiting to the Queen of Underland.* Eager to keep with her wishes, he is all for imprisoning Jill, Eustace, and Puddleglum, but the Prince intervenes and has the three brought to him. The gnome tries to remind the Prince of the Queen's orders, but is overruled. It is probable that Mullugutherum is the "prying chamberlain" who helps to strap Rilian into the silver chair and who is told, when he inquires about the guests, that they have gone to bed. He may also be one of the two gnomes who bow to the Queen as she enters the Prince's apartments. The sound of his name is suggestive of the obsequious nature of his personality.

(SC 131, *132;* 142, *141;* 149, *148.*)
[*Earthmen.*]

MUSIC   Along with dance,* music is part of the revelry* and celebration of Narnian life; indeed, the creation of Narnia* is accomplished by Aslan's song, which calls forth animals* from the earth and causes birds* to shower from the trees.* One of Frank's* first actions in Narnia is to sing the thanksgiving hymn, "Come Ye Thankful People Come." In LWW, songs are sung at the crowning of the Kings and Queens.* The Dawn Treaders hear Ramandu* and his Daughter* sing their long, strange song of welcome to the rising sun.* In SC, the Queen of Underland* attempts to enchant the three travelers and Rilian with her "sweet" song and monotonous thrumming. In contrast, the good music of the fiddles, flutes, and drum that accompany the Great Snow Dance is "wild . . . intensely sweet and . . . just the least bit eerie," and Jill feels she could almost "faint with delight" at hearing it. The funeral music for King Caspian is "a tune to break your heart," and the fact that it continues to play in Aslan's country* is a comment on its spiritual quality. Songs are apparently used to transmit Narnian oral history,* and Rilian sings snatches of an old song about Corin Thunder-Fist.* In LB, Tirian's mood so lightens that he hums "an old Narnian marching song."[1]

---

[1] The full text of this song is the second part of the *Narnian Suite* and has the title "March for Drum, Trumpet, and Twenty-One Giants." It was first published in *Punch,* November 4, 1953, and was later reprinted in revised form in *Poems,* Walter Hooper, ed. (New York: Harcourt Brace Jovanovich, 1965) pp. 6–7.

MYTHOLOGY The proliferation of mythological themes and figures in the *Chronicles* reflects C. S. Lewis's lifelong immersion in the wonders of mythology. In fact, he recovered his Christian faith through his love of mythology.[1] He felt that Christianity was founded on the great myth of the dying and rising god who has somehow communicated a new life to humanity,[2] with the distinction that this myth had become fact in this historical figure of Jesus of Nazareth.[3] And although modern biblical scholars have done much to uncover the mythical elements in the Bible, Lewis was distressed both at their aversion to myth (they wished to strip the Scriptures of all myth and leave only the facts), and also at the consequent mythopathy of many Christians who wanted to rescue the Scriptures from the efforts of such scholars. Lewis believed that faith was based both on the facts and also on the mythic elements which gave meaning to those facts.[4] Just as Ramandu* explains to Eustace that a star* is not what it is made of but what it *is,* Lewis felt that myths were a "real though unfocused gleam of divine truth falling upon human imagination,"[5] the distilled essence of a story which communicates entire truths to a reader that could otherwise not be expressed by mere abstractions.[6]

Mythological gods* and spirits abound in Narnia: Bacchus,* Centaurs,* dragons,* Dryads,* dwarfs,* fauns,* Fenris Ulf,* giants,* Hamadryads,* the Kraken,* Maenads,* the man-headed bull,* Minotaurs,* Naiads,* nymphs,* the Phoenix,* Pomona,* the River-god,* satyrs,* Silenus,* silvans,* and Unicorns.* These creatures are not expressly created by Aslan, but spring forth naturally as a response to his command to Narnia to awake and become divine. Thus all of nature lives: the rivers are inhabited by a god and his daughters, the trees* speak, and the forests contain a multitude of wild people. In the foreground of the Narnian tapestry are the grave and playful characters from classical Greek and Roman mythology, the fauns and satyrs and Dryads who bring a spirit of revelry* to Narnia. Lewis has woven the background in the darker colors and less distinguishable patterns of the stark and terrifying characters from the North, the witches and giants* and black dwarfs* of Celtic, Norse, and Teutonic mythology.

Lewis reveals his feeling for myth in his reiteration of the truth contained in stories.* Prince Caspian consoles himself in Miraz's* castle by dreaming of the tales his nurse* has told him of Old Narnia, which the Telmarines* consider to be fairy tales. It is his belief in these stories and the wisdom they impart, that saves him from the same fate as his ancestors and allow him to become a true king* of Narnia in the tradition of the High King Peter. His realization in Trufflehunter's* house that the stories are true is a numinous* experience that Lewis wants his readers to share.

[1] See his autobiography, *Surprised by Joy* (New York: Harcourt Brace Jovanovich, 1955; London: Collins Fontana, 1959) pp. 234–236, *187–189,* and his letters to his oldest friend, Arthur Greeves, October 18 and November 8, 1931, printed in *They Stand Together: The Letters of C. S. Lewis to Arthur Greeves (1914–1963),* Walter Hooper, ed. (New York: Macmillan Publishing Co., 1979; London: Collins, 1979) pp. 426–431, *426–431.*

[2] *Mere Christianity* (New York: Macmillan Publishing Co., 1960; London: Collins Fount, 1977) p. 54, *51.*

[3] "Myth Become Fact," *God in the Dock,* Walter Hooper, ed. (Grand Rapids: Wm. B. Eerdmans Publishing Co., 1970) pp. 63–67, and (London: Collins Fount, 1979) pp. 39–45.

[4] "Modern Theology and Biblical Criticism," *Christian Reflections,* Walter Hooper, ed. (Grand Rapids: Wm. B. Eerdmans Publishing Co., 1967) pp. 152–166 and as the title essay in *Fern-seed and Elephants and Other Essays on Christianity,* Walter Hooper, ed. (London: Collins Fontana, 1975) pp. 104–125.

[5] *Miracles* (New York: Macmillan Publishing Co., 1978; London: Collins Fontana, 1960) pp. 133–134, *137–138.*

[6] *An Experiment in Criticism* (New York: Cambridge University Press, 1961) pp. 40–41. See also PWD, pp. 16–19.

NAIADS   In Greek and Roman mythology,* water-nymphs. In the *Chronicles,* Naiads are one of the Nine Classes of Narnian Creatures*; and one of Narnia's epithets is the country of "Visible Naiads." These four daughters of the River-god* emerge with him from the Great River* at Aslan's command to the waters of Narnia to be divine; they are Queen Helen's* train-bearers at her coronation. The young Prince Caspian calls them "nice people" who used to live in the streams of Narnia; since the coming of the Telmarines* and their pollution of the rivers, however, the Naiads have fallen into a deep sleep. In LWW Lewis mentions Well-Women who play stringed instruments and are frightened by the wolf attack, and it is probable that they are Naiads.

(LWW 122, *115;* 126, *119.* PC 38, *43;* 47, *50;* 76, *73.* MN 117, *109;* 167, *154.*)
[*Ecology; Gods.*]

NAIN   King* of Archenland* in the reign of Miraz* the usurper. He is named as a possible refuge for the fleeing Prince Caspian by Doctor Cornelius.*

(PC 57, 58.)

NARNIA   The enchanted world of Lewis's *Chronicles;* also the name of the country that is the northern neighbor of Archenland.* Lewis probably chose the name Narnia for his imaginary world because he liked the sound of the word. There is no indication that he was alluding to the ancient Umbrian city Nequinium, renamed Narnia (after the river Nar, a tributary of the Tiber) by the conquering Romans in 299 B.C. Since Lewis's first successes at Oxford were in the classics and ancient history, it is quite possible that he came across at least seven references to Narnia in Latin literature.[1] The creation of Narnia* is accomplished through Aslan's song; and the end of Narnia* is also at his bidding. The history* of Narnia lasts 2555 Narnian years (N.Y.), which corresponds to forty-nine earthly years (1900–1949 A.D.).[2] Its geography* is as varied as our own; the world of Narnia has deserts and moors, oceans and rivers, mountains and valleys. Politically, it is composed of three kingdoms: Narnia and Archenland to the north of the Great Desert, and Calormen* to the south. The history of Narnia is largely uneventful, consisting of long stretches of peace punctuated by wars and invasions. Aslan's country* exists outside of Narnia; indeed, it is not physically connected to any country.

Old Narnia   The physical world created by Aslan in MN; characterized by the presence of all manner of fauna and flora who, at Aslan's command, become divine and alive. Old Narnia is meant to be ruled by humans, who do so with humility. It is a country where courtesy,* honor,* and the spirit of adventure* are the respected virtues, and in which hospitality* is graciously offered.[3] Old Narnia exists before, during, and after the rule of the New Narnians. This world is destroyed by the dragons* and dinosaurs at Aslan's command.

Old Narnians   Specifically, the nonhuman residents of Narnia: Dumb Beasts* and Talking Beasts,* dwarfs* and giants,* gods* and goddesses, creatures of mythology,* and wild people of the wood. During the rule of the New Narnians they are silenced and forced into hiding, and many of the wood and water spirits go to sleep to await the War of Deliverance.*

New Narnians   The Telmarines*; specifically, the dynasties of Caspian I* through Miraz.* "New Narnians" is a term distinct from "New Narnia." The rule of Caspian X restores Old Narnian rule.

New Narnia, Real Narnia   The heart of Narnia, which has always existed in Aslan's country,* on the other side of the Door.* From the garden,* the children behold Narnia, which they have just seen destroyed. But what was destroyed was the Old Narnia, the Shadow Lands;[4] the renewed Narnia—the real Narnia—exists externally in Aslan's country.

[*Astronomy, Narnian.*]

[1] Four references are found in Livy's *History* (10:10, 27:9, 27:50, and 29:15) (the history of the Roman conquest of Narnia and the consequences of its refusal to furnish soldiers and money to Rome in the war against Hannibal). The fifth reference is found in Tacitus's *Annals* (3:9). The sixth is in Pliny the Elder's comment in *Natural History* about its unusual weather (it became drier in the rainy season). The seventh is in Pliny the Younger's letter to his mother-in-law, in which he mentions the excellence of the accommodations of her villa at Narnia, especially its beautiful baths. Of all of these references, Lewis mentions only Pliny the Younger, in a letter to Arthur Greeves (*They Stand Together,* Walter Hooper, ed. [New York: Macmillan Publishing Co., 1979; London: Collins, 1979] p. 171, *171*).

[2] PWD, pp. 41–44.

[3] For a comparison of Narnian and Calormene ways, see *Calormen.*

[4] See *Plato.*

NARROWHAVEN

A white seacoast town. Although it is small, it is large enough for several bells to ring from many parts of the town. It is the capital of Doorn,* one of the Lone Islands,* and the seat of government for Governor Gumpas,* whose castle is outside the town. Its slave market is near the harbor, where there are facilities for repairing the *Dawn Treader;* but three pirate ships guard the harbor, lest anyone interfere with the town's lucrative slave trade.*

(VDT 32, *39;* 41, *49.*)
[*Geography, Narnian; Government.*]

NEW NARNIA, NEW NARNIAN   See *Narnia.*

NIGHTMARES   See *Dreams.*

NIKABRIK

A Black Dwarf* in PC, the second voice Caspian hears upon regaining consciousness. From his first appearance he shows the nature "soured by hate" that Caspian later attributes to him. Naturally suspicious, he is for killing Caspian immediately but is prevented by Trumpkin* and Trufflehunter.* He would also do away with the half-dwarf Doctor Cornelius,* whom he sees as a renegade. But his greatest aggravation is Trufflehunter, the faithful badger. Nikabrik is not only negative, he is a downright disbeliever. When asked if he believes in Aslan, he answers that he believes in *anyone,* be it Aslan or the White Witch, who will liberate Narnia. This equating of Aslan's power with that of the Witch intensifies his confrontation with Trufflehunter, who sees the Witch as Narnia's worst enemy. Nikabrik protests that she was good to the dwarfs, and for him this is all that matters: dwarf interests come first. He has no use for the simple pleasures of pipe smoking,* and he does not join in the dance* before the Great Council.*

When it appears that Susan's horn* has failed to bring help to the beleagured group, Nikabrik's anger and doubt surface even more. He calls Aslan that "performing lion,*" asserting that he never *did* come back to life. He sneers at Caspian to whom he had earlier given his oath* of allegiance, referring to him as "this Telmarine* boy" and saying that oaths of allegiance are no more than "court manners." Given a chance by Caspian to state his case, he calls all the stories of the Golden Age of Narnia* into question; but he also says that should they be true, the Witch is to be turned to as one whose power long outlasted that of the Kings and Queens.* Countered and crossed by everyone, Nikabrik finally explodes and attacks Trufflehunter. He is killed by no-one-knows-whom. Caspian recognizes that the dwarf's antagonistic nature is the result of intense, prolonged suffering, and says he might have changed in time of peace. His body is given to the dwarfs to be buried in honor according to their custom.

(PC 61 ff., *61 ff.;* 157 ff., *140 ff.*)

NINE CLASSES OF NARNIAN CREATURES   According to Doctor Cornelius,* they are: Waking Trees,* Visible Naiads,* Fauns,* Satyrs,* Dwarfs,* Giants,* gods,* Centaurs,* and Talking Beasts.* He adds that Old Narnia is not the land of men.[1]

(PC 47, *50.*)

---

[1] Lewis's handling of humans is inconsistent. Later in the *Chronicles* he indicates that humans have been present (indeed, that they have been at the apex of the hierarchy*) in Narnia since the beginning. One indication of this is the place Lewis assigns to King Frank* and Queen Helen* (MN 138–140; *128–130*).

NINE NAMES OF ASLAN   See *Aslan.*

NORTHERN FRONTIER   The region where the Northern giants* live. Much of SC is set here, including the Queen's Maying party, her death,* and Rilian's wanderings for vengeance. Lewis probably intended the region to suggest the environment and beings of Norse mythology.*

(PC 56, *56.* SC 20 passim; *29 passim.*)
[*Daughter of Ramandu; Geography, Narnian.*]

"NOTHING BUT . . ."   See *Reductionism.*

NUMINOUS   The simultaneous awe and delight felt in the presence of something holy is the content of a numinous experience.[1] In the *Chronicles,* most characters experience the numinous in Aslan's presence. Their first sight of Aslan in LWW cures the children* of the mistaken notion (held by all who have not been to Narnia, says Lewis) that a thing cannot be good and terrible at the same time. Caspian has a numinous experience when he realizes that all the stories* about Old Narnia are true: he feels terror at the thought that the dwarf* is "not a man at all," and delight that "there are real Dwarfs still, and I've seen one at last." When Aslan turns to face the children and Trumpkin,* he looks so majestic that "they feel as glad as anyone can who feels afraid, and as afraid as anyone can who feels glad." At Lucy's first sight of the new constellations in VDT, she is filled "with a mixture of joy* and fear.*" At the sound of Aslan's voice, Jill's fear turns to awe and she is "frightened in rather a different way," that is, with a fear of the numinous. The depiction of the experience of the numinous that is most natural—in the sense that it is un-

*The dwarf brothers Rogin, Bricklethumb, and Duffle serve the starving Shasta his first Narnian meal. (*HHB 166, 147.*)*

forced and therefore a good example of Lewis's craft—is Shasta's encounter with the Lion. It begins with the fear of being devoured, or of the preternatural, and ends in the "revelation" of the Trinity* and Shasta's "new and different sort of trembling," which is also a feeling of gladness. In MN, Digory finds Aslan to be "bigger and more beautiful and more brightly golden and more terrible" than he had thought."[2] Emeth experiences the numinous in the extravagant Calormene* fashion, and compares the tenor and beauty of Aslan to the Flaming Mountain of Lagour* and a rose in bloom.

(LWW 122, *115*. PC 48, *51;* 148, *132–133*. VDT 163, *161*. SC 16, *26*. HHB 155 ff., *137 ff.;* 192, *168*. MN 108, *100;* 117, *109;* 134, *124*. LB 164, *148*.)
[*Longing.*]

---

[1] For Lewis's views on the numinous, see *The Problem of Pain* (New York: Macmillan Publishing Co., 1967; London: Collins Fountain, 1977) pp. 16 ff., *4 ff.* See also Rudolf Otto, *The Idea of the Holy* (London: Oxford University Press, 1968) pp. 31 ff.
[2] See *Digory*, note 10.

NURSE   The beloved nurse of Prince Caspian, to whom she tells tales of Old Narnia. Miraz,* displeased with her stories,* banishes her from the castle without even a chance to say goodbye; and Caspian misses her greatly. (She also incurs the wrath of Nikabrik* for having told Caspian about Old Narnia.) Later in Caspian's adventures, near Beaversdam,* a little old woman who looks as if she might be part dwarf* is found near death by Aslan. She makes her final peace, professing her lifelong faith and trust. Then, calling Aslan by name, she asks if he has come to take her away. Instead, he makes her well. Bacchus* offers her well-water that has been transformed into rich red wine.* After drinking it she jumps out of bed, and Aslan invites her to ride on his back as they go off to join the war against Miraz. She appears to be modeled on Lewis's beloved nurse, Lizzie Endicott, who introduced him to the stories of Beatrix Potter and to Irish folktales.[1]

(PC 65, *64;* 197, *173*.)
[*Autobiographical allusions; Biblical allusions.*]

---

[1] Roger Lancelyn Green and Walter Hooper, *C. S. Lewis: A Biography* (New York: Harcourt Brace Jovanovich, 1974 and London: Collins, 1974) pp. 20, *21*. Chesterton calls the nurse "the solemn and star-appointed priestess . . . of democracy and tradition." See *Orthodoxy* (New York: Doubleday Image, 1959) p. 49.

NYMPHS   In Greek and Roman mythology,* beautiful semi-divine maidens who live in a variety of natural habitats—trees,* rivers, mountains, and so on. In LWW they are mentioned as dancing with fauns* at midnight festivals. In PC they rise out of the river at Aslan's roar. In MN, four river-nymphs—the Naiad* daughters of the River-god*—bear Queen Helen's* train. The sons of King Frank* and Queen Helen marry nymphs.

(LWW 13, *20*. PC 150, *135*. MN 167, *154;* 184, *170*.)
[*Dance; Dryads; Hamadryads.*]

OATHS Narnian oaths and promises are to be taken seriously, and several oaths are specifically mentioned in the *Chronicles*. All kings* and queens of Narnia must swear a coronation oath (Reepicheep reminds Caspian of his solemn oath to serve Narnia in order to dissuade him from his planned abdication). Caspian also makes an oath to seek out the Seven Noble Lords.* Eustace swears an oath to Jill that he is telling the truth, and Puddleglum makes the condition of his visiting Harfang* an absolute promise from the children* not to tell the giants* their Narnian origin or their destination. Later in SC Lewis reinforces this cardinal moral tenet for children when he says that the children couldn't tell without Puddleglum's consent, because they had promised. In HHB, Shasta's promise to meet his companions at the tombs keeps him there in spite of his fears,* and Aravis's similar promise keeps her from the temptation that Lasaraleen* offers. Bree swears by "the Lion's mane," as do all Narnians. Breaking promises can lead to great evil.* Promises mean nothing to Andrew* (who broke his promise to Mrs. Lefay* not to open her box); both Jadis and her sister had promised not to use magic* but they each did, and then Jadis used the Deplorable Word*; and part of the Witch's temptation of Digory is to get him to neglect his promise to Aslan.

OBEDIENCE The word *obedience* is from the Latin *oboedire,* which means "to listen"; and it is in this very specific sense that Lewis uses the word in the *Chronicles.* For Lewis, the primal stance of human beings before God is to be obedient: not to be slavishly devoted, but to be freely attentive. The first response of the newly created Talking Beasts* is to pledge their obedience to Aslan with the words "We hear and obey." This concept survives in its submissive form in Calormen,* where his subjects answer the Tisroc* with "To hear is to obey." It is characteristic of the despotic rulers of the *Chronicles* that they desire to be unswervingly obeyed. Obedience to Aslan, however, is not something that must be enforced; the Narnian knows the proper response innately: for example, Peter doesn't feel brave when he anticipates fighting Fenris Ulf,* "but that made no difference to what he had to do."

A correlative of obedience is humility: accepting and living in the truth of obedience. When Aslan asks Caspian if he feels sufficient to rule Narnia, Caspian demurs, citing his youth and inexperience. Aslan approves of his humility, saying, "If you had felt yourself sufficient, it would have been proof that you were not." Rabadash,* on the other hand, is infuriated to the point of tears by King Lune's* treatment of him as a traitor. Lewis comments, ". . . he couldn't bear being made ridiculous. In Tashbaan* every one had always taken him seriously." In Aslan's presence, the good Narnian must have humility; Digory forgets his fame among the Narnians because he is looking at Aslan.[1]

(LWW 127, *120*. PC 200, *175*. HHB 206 ff., *180 ff*. MN 166, *154*.)

---

[1] See *Biblical allusions*.

OCTESIAN One of the Seven Noble Lords.* His device, a hammer and a star,[1] marks the arm-ring found on the dragon Eustace. It is not certain whether he became a dragon* or was devoured by one, but he did meet his end on Dragon Island.*

(VDT 16, *23;* 81–82, *88;* 92–93, *98–99*.)

---

[1] Lewis may have patterned Octesian's device on Durin's Emblem, the hammer and anvil crowned with seven stars, from J. R. R. Tolkien's *The Lord of the Rings* (Boston: Houghton Mifflin Co., 1965), Second Edition, Vol. I *(The Fellowship of the Ring)*, p. 318.

OGRES Man-eating monsters, the size of giants,* summoned by the White Witch to the slaying of Aslan. They are eagerly present for the murder, and one of them shears off Aslan's mane with its "monstrous teeth." At least three are present at the following day's battle, for Edmund kills that many. Ogres seem to remain in Narnia, for the Five Black Dwarfs* are in favor of enlisting an ogre or two to overthrow Miraz.* *Ogre* is a French word related, through a complex history, to *Orcus,* the Latin name for the god of the infernal regions; readers of Tolkien will note the significance of this.

(LWW 132, *123;* 148–150, *138–139;* 176, *160*. PC 72, *70*.)

OLD MAN See *Ramandu*.

OLD NARNIA, OLD NARNIAN See *Narnia*.

OLVIN The fair-haired king of Archenland who in 407 N.Y.[1] defeats Pire, the two-headed southern giant, and turns him into stone (thus *Mount Pire*, the two-forked mountain). As the result of this exploit the Lady Liln becomes his wife and queen. Their story becomes the subject of many a minstrel's song.

(HHB 213, *186*.)
[*Music; Stories*.]

---

[1] PWD, p. 42.

ONE'S OWN STORY See *Privacy*.

ORDERS, CHIVALRIC   The code of chivalry is an especially important feature of Narnian life, and the lack of chivalry on the part of the Calormenes* and Telmarines* is one of their most fatal flaws. Two orders are
mentioned in the *Chronicles:* The Most Noble Order of the Lion (MNOL),
named, of course, after Aslan; and the Noble Order of the Table, after the
Stone Table* of Aslan's sacrifice. Peter confers the MNOL on Caspian,
and Caspian confers the order on Trufflehunter,* Trumpkin,* and Reepicheep.

(PC 172–173, *151–152;* 204, *178.*)
[*Knights, Ladies, Squires.*]

ORKNIES   Monsters, present at the slaying of Aslan on the Stone Table.*
Beowulf (line 112) mentions "orcheas" among other monsters, and Lewis is
content to allude to them in order to add to an atmosphere of horror surrounding Aslan's death.* The allusion to Tolkien's *orcs* is inescapable.

(LWW 148, *138.*)
[*Literary allusions; Ogres.*]

ORRERIES   See *Coriakin.*

OVERWORLD   See *Underland.*

OWLS   Nocturnal birds* of prey. A He-Owl, the embodiment of the idea
of wisdom, is present at Aslan's First Council.* In SC, Glimfeather* and the
Parliament of Owls aid Jill and Eustace in their search for Prince Rilian.

(MN 119, *111.*)
[*Talking Beasts.*]

PACIFISM   See *Eustace Clarence Scrubb,* note 3.

PAIN, ANIMAL   See *Vivisection.*

PARLIAMENT OF OWLS   See *Glimfeather.*

PASSARIDS   A family of great Telmarine* lords in the reign of Caspian IX.* They are sent by Miraz* to fight giants* on the northern frontier, where they fall one by one.

(PC 56, *56*.)

PATTERTWIG   A magnificent red squirrel,[1] nearly the size of a terrier and very hospitable. He is a chatterer, and when he attends the Great Council* he runs around frenetically, calling for silence. Though Nikabrik* thinks squirrels to be generally flighty, he considers Pattertwig trustworthy enough to go to Lantern Waste* to await the help summoned by Susan's horn.*

(PC 69–70, *67–68;* 80, *77;* 92, *88.*)
[*Lefay, Mrs.; Talking Beasts.*]

---

  [1] In the "Lefay Fragment," an early draft of MN, Pattertwig is met by Digory. The red squirrel offers Digory a nut and some advice, especially about Grey Squirrels, who are almost always evil (PWD, pp. 50–52). The Red-Grey contrast is suggestive of the Red-Black difference among Dwarf species. It is also possible that Lewis modeled Pattertwig on Ratatosk, the squirrel and message bearer of Yggdrasill, the World Ash Tree* of Norse mythology.*

PAVENDERS   The delectable and beautiful rainbow-colored saltwater fish served at the royal banquets at Cair Paravel.[1]

(PC 33, *39.* SC 39, *46.*)
[*Literary allusions.*]

---

  [1] There was a humorous verse popular with scholars in the 1920s and 1930s in which the writer, after alluding to the "Chavender (or Chub)," goes on to mention the "Pavender (or Pub [i.e., public house]), Gravender (or Grub [i.e., food])," and then "Clavender (or Club)." The entire allusion is to Isaac Walton's *Compleat Angler* (1653). The Fifth Edition (by Sir John Hawkins in 1791) refers to the chub or chavender at the end of Chapter II, and this fish is the subject matter of the entire Chapter III. Professor Thomas W. Craik provided the lead and the humorous verse here.

PEEPICEEK   One of the mice* in Reepicheep's company. He is devoted to his leader and vouches that all the mice are prepared to cut off their tails if Reepicheep must go without his. Reepicheep designates Peepiceek as his successor as part of his declaration to Lucy that he will go as far towards Aslan's country* as he can, even if he drowns in the attempt.

(PC 203, *178.* VDT 184, *180.*)
[*Talking Beasts.*]

PEOPLE OF THE TOADSTOOLS   Evil* spirits, probably responsible for the poisonousness of toadstools. They are summoned by the White Witch to the Stone Table.*

(LWW 132, *123.*)

PERIDAN   A Narnian courtier in the embassy of King Edmund and Queen Susan to Tashbaan* in 1014 N.Y. He escorts Shasta to the royal quarters, and closes the door to keep the escape plans secret. He leads the Narnian war party, riding a bay horse* and carrying the great banner* of Narnia. When King Lune* asks what should be done about Rabadash,* Peridan reminds Lune that he has the right to behead the Calormene* ruler.

(HHB 56, 55; 62, 60; 69, 65; 169, 149; 205, 179–180.)

PETER PEVENSIE   The oldest child and son of Mr. and Mrs. Pevensie*; Sir Peter Fenris-Bane[1] and High King Peter the Magnificent; victor over the Northern Giants* in the Golden Age of Narnia*; Aslan's helper in renewing Narnia in PC; a student preparing for university entrance examinations with his tutor, Professor Kirke, in VDT; and the one who consigns Tash* to his "own place" in the name of Aslan and his Father in LB. He is the figure of the fine older brother to his brother and sisters, and the paradigmatic king in Narnia.[2] With very few setbacks, he grows from a thirteen-year-old boy in LWW to a splendid, twenty-seven-year-old king in HHB and a twenty-one-year-old university student with his heart still in Narnia when he meets his death in the railway accident that sends the Seven Friends of Narnia* and the Pevensie parents into Aslan's country* forever in LB.

From the fact that he is interested in eagles, stags, and hawks in the first pages of LWW, the reader can discern that Peter is predisposed to love and rule Narnia. After Lucy claims to have visited Narnia, he wonders if his sister is well; but the professor challenges him to find her a liar, or crazy, or telling the truth—the only alternatives.[3] Peter provisionally decides on the latter, but reserves judgment until he has more data. Once in Narnia himself, he thinks that Lucy ought to be the leader. He feels obligated to try to rescue Tumnus,* and defends their guide, the robin, by citing the fact that in the stories* he has read they are always good birds.* By this enumeration Lewis means to suggest that Peter is a natural leader, discerning and well-read and imbued with the right stock responses.*

When he first hears Aslan's name, Peter's response is to feel brave and adventurous, two qualities he will need in the years ahead. Mr. Beaver* ratifies Peter's paradoxical reaction to the thought of meeting Aslan: "I long to see him, though I am thoroughly frightened"—a classic numinous* experience. From Father Christmas* he receives Aslan's gifts of a shield, a sword—Rhindon*—and sheath and sword belt with the silence* and solemnity called for at such an occasion. After some prodding from Susan, he leads his group forward to meet the Lion. A proper sense of responsibility makes Peter acknowledge his fault in Edmund's treachery—he had stayed angry with his brother instead of seeking to be reconciled with him immediately.[4] Peter is also properly silent after Aslan shows him the country he is to rule; but he goes into immediate action at the sound of Susan's horn. Ignoring his feelings of fear,* which make him nauseous, he assails the wolf and kills him. Afterwards, he feels more tired than brave; he kisses and cries with Susan, two emotional displays that are noble in Narnia. That he should always clean his sword is the first of many practical notes* Lewis makes throughout the *Chronicles.* Peter welcomes the traitor Edmund back. When it appears that he might have to lead the fight against the Witch's forces without Aslan's help, he worries through the night. After the battle, Lucy sees that his face has become pale and stern and that he seems much more mature. Peter shows his selflessness by giving Edmund the credit for the success of the first attack. LWW ends with the tall, deep-chested king urging his royal companions on in their hunt for the White Stag.*

In PC, Peter is the third person to feel the pull into Narnia.[5] He resumes his role as leader in the explorations of the island they find themselves on. And when Susan finds the ancient chesspiece, he constructs a hypothesis that their discovery of the treasure room bears out. When Susan doesn't want to investigate, Peter tries to encourage her by reminding her that in Narnia she's not a child anymore, but a queen. And after the contests he devises to convince Trumpkin* of their authenticity, he organizes the return to Aslan's How.* After rowing all day, he is pardonably irritated at Susan's "I told you so" attitude; he takes the blame for coming what he thinks is the wrong way; and he nearly loses his temper at Trumpkin's correct observations about their route until the dwarf* explains himself. Peter, in his fatigue, is perhaps overreacting because of his own uncertainties.

Peter would like to make peace between Lucy, who has seen Aslan, and the others who doubt her vision, but his solution—a vote[6]—is really more of an abdication of his responsibility to make the decision for them. If he had acted on his instinct, he would have chosen to follow Lucy; but he decides on the more logical path. When it becomes obvious that he has made the wrong decision, he admits it without too much grumbling, and sets about undoing his error. He is the third person in the group to see Aslan; and when he approaches the Lion, he readily expresses both his joy at seeing the Lion and his sorrow at having misled his companions. Meeting Caspian for the first time, he sets the prince at ease; he has come not to replace him but to set him in his place. And he is warmly affectionate to Trufflehunter* and all the animals. In his challenge to Miraz* to meet him in a monomachy,* Peter lists his titles, the first of which is "by the gift of Aslan," a sign that Peter has a faith perspective on his leadership. With wisdom he negotiates among the various animals clamoring for their rights; with courage* and courtesy* he fights Miraz; and with equanimity he accepts the fact that he and Susan won't be returning to Narnia again.[7]

In Tirian's* vision in LB, Peter is the mirror of bravery to the last Narnian king. Peter and Edmund disguise themselves as workmen in order to retrieve the magic* rings* from the old Ketterley place in London. But death,* not the rings, brings him to Narnia on the other side of the Stable* Door.* His is the voice, "strong and calm as a summer sea," that dismisses Tash to the Narnian equivalent of hell.* After Jill introduces Tirian to Peter, Peter introduces him to Lord Digory[8] and Lady Polly. Asked about Susan, Peter answers briefly (as if he were in pain) and solemnly declares that she has ceased to be a friend of Narnia. He changes the subject to the matter of the lovely fruit all see growing on the trees in Aslan's country. He is able to intuit why all are reluctant to eat it and proclaims that their desire is allowed, because everything they can desire in this place is right,* not wrong. At Aslan's bidding, he locks the door on the end of Narnia.* His remark about Emeth* reflects a high standard of honor*: "Whether he meets us in peace or war, he shall be welcome." The sights of the new country confuse him: it all seems a bigger Narnia; and yet he remembers that he is not to reenter Narnia. More puzzling still is his sighting of England* and Professor Kirke's house.* But everything becomes plain to him when Aslan reveals that they have died and have come into the real Narnia, which is connected with the heart of every real land.

---

[1] In the British editions, "Wolf-Bane." This change was made by Lewis at the same time the name "Maugrim" was changed to "Fenris Ulf" in the American edition. See *Fenris Ulf* for an explanation of the difference in the editions at this point.

[2] Doctor Cornelius* tells Caspian that if he can be a king* like Peter, he will have lived up to the vocation of being king.

[3] Lewis uses the very same argument numerous times in discussions about the claims of Jesus Christ to be the Son of God. See, for example, *Mere Christianity* (New York: Macmillan, 1960; London: Collins Fount, 1977) pp. 54–56, 51–52. It is an argument that might have been suggested to him by G. K. Chesterton's *Orthodoxy* (New York: Doubleday, 1959) pp. 24–25.

[4] Recall the Gospel of Matthew 5:21–24. And notice how in other scenes of judgment before Aslan, other children* have to be brought to confess their misdeeds (e.g., Jill and Digory); Peter is exceptional in his immediate candor.

[5] That he precedes Susan is indicative of their relative childlike receptivity to the call into Narnia. This becomes apparent in the scene where Aslan becomes progressively visible to the Pevensies and Trumpkin. See *Aslan,* note 16.

[6] Democracy is theoretically only the second-best form of government,* says Lewis. Practically, it is the best. But Lewis expressed his preference in his address, "Membership," in *Weight of Glory and Other Addresses* (Grand Rapids: Wm. B. Eerdmans Publishing Co., 1965) p. 37, and *Fern-seed and Elephants and Other Essays on Christianity,* Walter Hooper, ed. (London: Collins Fontana, 1975) p. 19: "I believe that if we had not fallen . . . patriarchal monarchy would be the sole form of government."

[7] His remark to Lucy shows that he knows the difference between what difficulties human imaginations can anticipate and the actual difficulties as people experience them.

[8] Digory is accidentally omitted in the American edition.

PEVENSIE, MR. AND MRS.   The parents of Peter, Susan, Edmund, and Lucy Pevensie. Although they are hardly mentioned at all, they seem to be good and thoughtful, because in LWW they have sent the children* from their London home to the country house of Professor Kirke* to escape the air raids of World War II. Mr. Pevensie is also a professor, and in the summer of 1942 he and his wife take a sixteen-week trip to America where he has been invited to lecture. The journey is Mrs. Pevensie's first real vacation in ten years, and she takes Susan along. In 1949, the Pevensies are on a train to Bristol—providentially, it is the same train that Lucy, Edmund, Peter, Polly, Digory, Eustace, and Jill are on—when the train is wrecked. From the garden* in Aslan's country* Peter, Edmund, and Lucy see their mother and father waving to them from what seems to be England.* Aslan explains to them that they have all been killed in the railway accident, and that since the real England is connected to Aslan's country, a short walk will take them to their parents.

(LWW 1, 9. VDT 2, 10. LB 138, 125–126; 182–183, 164–165.)
[*Adults; House of Professor Kirke.*]

PHOENIX   A symbol of resurrection, the Phoenix is a mythological bird that periodically burns itself to death on a funeral pyre, and is reborn from the ashes. It sits in the tree above the thrones of King Frank* and Queen Helen,* surveying the Great Reunion.*

(LB 179, *162.*)
[*Mythology.*]

PIRE   See *Olvin.*

PIRE, MOUNT   See *Olvin.*

PITTENCREAM   A cowardly milquetoast (his name suggests someone who is pitiful or a pittance)[1] and the only sailor on the *Dawn Treader* whom Caspian does not allow to go to World's End.* Fearful of such a journey, Pittencream is even more afraid of being left behind on his own. But this is just what happens. He stays on Ramandu's Island,* remorseful at not having gone on with the others, and finds his situation intolerable. It rains too much, conversation with Ramandu and his Daughter* is most unsatisfactory, and dining at Aslan's Table* with four enchanted sleepers is not at all comfortable. He boards the *Dawn Treader* on its return voyage, but feels so left out, not having shared any of the crew's recent adventures, that he deserts ship at the Lone Islands* and goes to live in Calormen.* There he tells tall tales of his voyage to the end of the world until he comes to believe them himself. Lewis's final comment, "So you may say, in a sense, that he lived happily ever after," suggests Pittencream's mediocrity and inability to deal with reality. And the final irony that he could never bear mice* confirms his cowardice,* since the chief mouse Reepicheep is a hieroglyph of courage.*

(VDT 187–188, *183–184.*)
[*Fear.*]

---

[1] Professor Thomas W. Craik observes that the resemblance of the name Pittencream to Pittenweem (a fishing village in Fife) "cannot be accidental. That association suits a sailor, and I should not be surprised if 'cream' came in from Macbeth's cream-fac'd loon (Act V, Scene 3), since Pittencream hangs back from volunteering for the adventure, and since there are enough allusions to Fife in *Macbeth* to have set off this train of thought in Lewis's mind." (Letter to author dated July 31, 1979.)

PLATO   A Greek philosopher (427?–347 B.C.) who believed that earthly things are copies of transcendent ideas. When Digory says, "It's all in Plato, all in Plato," at the end of LB, we are given a broad hint as to a major theme that underlies the *Chronicles.* Lewis, as a scholar and a teacher, was well-acquainted with the Platonic tradition; and his own deepest experiences are recognizably one with the Platonic-Augustinian "ascent of the soul" in which the human heart, incited by the limited goods and beauties of creation, discovers within itself a restless, piercing desire for the unlimited source of all reality and perfection.[1] Thus, in addition to some obvious uses of Platonic thought and imagery at various key points of the tales, there is an almost continuous Platonic undercurrent which is often hardly noticeable.

In LWW the Pevensie children, troubled over Lucy's story of visiting another world, come to the Professor for advice. In admirable Socratic fashion he replies not with answers but with questions that invite the children to step beyond their typical unexamined opinions about what is and what is not possible. The net effect of the conversation is to steer the children into a searching and thoughtful openness, which is precisely the method Socrates employs throughout the dialogues of Plato. When Susan protests that "all this about the wood and the Faun" couldn't be true, the Professor replies as Socrates often does to the unfounded assertions of his conversation partners: "That is more than I know." Peter then comes forward with his own objection to the credibility of Lucy's story, a version of the modern principle of verification (which states that a thing is real only so long as it is publicly observable). When he and the others looked into the wardrobe, *they* did not find Narnia. The Professor challenges their underlying assumption ("if things are real, they're there all the time"). Peter is speechless. Not only is this method of examining one's fundamental assumptions recognizably Socratic, but an important Platonic theme is touched upon here which Lewis develops throughout the remaining books.

True knowledge* of reality is for Plato an art, a struggle, and a discipline, not something easy or obvious or automatic as the principle of verification assumes. Those who would learn must turn not to the average, run-of-the-mill public consciousness of things but to genuinely philosophical and morally upright individuals. Within Christian Platonism, this position is amended so that it is God and especially Christ that one must turn to for guidance, since he is not only the Way and the Life but the Truth. But the basic Platonic insight that knowledge requires a special maturity and state of mind and heart remains unchanged. The truth about Narnia is not a neutral bit of transmittable public information for just anyone at all; it is something that one must experience and be initiated into. Digory is actually preparing the children,* as Socrates prepared the Athenian youth, for an experience of another reality that he himself has known firsthand, although the reader doesn't discover this connection until MN.[2] There is a hint of this personal connection, however, in the fact that LWW ends with Digory telling the children not to mention Narnia to people who have not had similar adventures.

In order to understand how Lewis expands upon this Platonic theme in the subsequent tales, one must realize that Plato saw the Socratic method of questioning as a necessary consciousness-raising antidote to the human tendency to shrink back from the fullness of reality into a superficial existence. In such a reduced state the human spirit will mistake the most immediate appearances for reality itself.[3] Self-deception is a recurring factor in this constriction of consciousness since it is easy enough to hold an opinion but hard work to actually know what one is talking about. The contrast between appearance and reality is, then, a related and central Platonic theme. The quest* for reality and the clash of appearance and reality are taken up in PC. As in LWW, Lucy has an experience that the others will only subsequently share. She is the first to catch sight of Aslan. Her sighting and insistence that Aslan wants them to go "the opposite of the way you want to go" are met with immediate suspicion and skepticism from the others. Susan repeats almost verbatim Peter's objection from LWW: no one except Lucy saw anything. And the idea of going up the gorge instead of down it doesn't appear to be the best course. They would rather trust the appearances than Lucy's testimony. But Lucy's experience is right while the expectations and opinions of the others are dead wrong. A clue to the superiority of Lucy's disposition to reality is given when she next sees Aslan and speaks with him. Aslan is bigger, she says. He responds that it is not he but she who has changed: "every year you grow, you will find me bigger."[4] Lucy's capacity for taking in the most important and sublime realities (especially Aslan himself) is expanding. By contrast Peter, Edmund, and Susan have become narrow and seem to have lost the openness they gained in LWW.

They cannot see Aslan at all when Lucy wakes them from their sleep. Edmund accuses her of seeing things and Susan smugly asserts that Lucy has only been dreaming "because there isn't anything to see." Peter wonders why Aslan should be visible to Lucy but not to the rest of them. Lewis stresses the fact that now the others must follow Lucy's lead because Aslan was not only invisible to them but silent as well. Begrudgingly, the little party follows Lucy on what appears to be a mad course—she seems to go right over the edge of the gorge. But, as Edmund soon discovers, there is a way down the other side. Edmund and Peter now begin to make out first Aslan's shadow and then Aslan himself, but Susan and the dwarf,* who claims to "know nothing of Aslan," are still in the dark. Susan makes an important admission when she is finally able to see Aslan: she could have seen him all along if she had let herself. But instead she had resisted. Her blindness was self-imposed.[5]

Susan's egotistical resistance to Aslan and Lucy all throughout this episode in their adventures is especially disturbing because it is not very far removed from the mindset of the false political order they have come to overthrow. The usurper Miraz* wants to suppress all knowledge of Old Narnia ultimately out of a fear* of and resistance to Aslan himself. Lies have been invented to conceal the truth, and those who are in the know not only propagate these lies but wish to believe them. "They feel safer," Doctor Cornelius* tells Caspian, "if no one in Narnia dares to go down to the coast and look out to sea— towards Aslan's land and the morning and the eastern end of the world." They want, in other words, a closed and manageable horizon. Reality is too threatening.

Lucy, the apparent dreamer among her more sober-minded brothers and sister, is the one who is really wide awake, just as Plato portrays Socrates as the one wide awake man in ancient Athens.[6] In her encounters with Aslan, Lewis tells us that Lucy is "wide awake, wider than anyone usually is." It falls upon her to awaken the others from more than one kind of sleep.* In The Apology, Socrates likens the city to a large thoroughbred horse "which is inclined to be lazy and needs the stimulation of some stinging fly." He continues: "It seems to me that God has attached me to this city to perform the office of such a fly."[7] Though Lucy would never speak of herself in this way, such is surely her office too.

In SC, Lewis's recourse to Platonic doctrine and imagery is much more obvious, especially in Chapter 12, where the Queen of Underland* and her captives argue about the reality of an overworld. The earliest pages of the book, which find Jill and Eustace in the closed, oppressive atmosphere of Experiment House* and describe their escape, foreshadow what is at stake in the whole story: the recovery of reality and of one's true identity. The kind of education to be had at Experiment House is one which cuts the children off from their own past, including their Judaeo-Christian roots. When Trumpkin* addresses them as Son of Adam* and Daughter of Eve, Jill and Eustace don't know what he is talking about because "people at Experiment House haven't heard of Adam and Eve." Ironically, Aslan's task for the two is the liberation of Prince Rilian from the similarly closed, oppressive Underland of the witch. Her underworld prison is the external expression of the false consciousness she has instilled in the Prince. She has filled his head with a "script" which lamely saves all the appearances but keeps him in the dark about his Narnian past and royal identity.

The pattern of Rilian's predicament and his liberation from it has thoroughly Platonic elements. For Plato, the human soul in its depths knows that its present bodily existence is a fall from a sunny overworld of truth into a shadowy underworld of shifting appearances.[8] This fall, however, is simultaneously a fall in consciousness. The soul forgets its immortal identity—in other words, it loses touch with its own true dimensions. Real education, real learning consists in overcoming this forgetfulness and rediscovering the soul's openness to and foothold in a higher, timeless realm. Liberation, which occurs definitively at death with the separation of the soul from the body,[9] is prefigured in each genuine act of knowledge, because in each act of knowing the soul rises from mere sensation of time-bound material appearances to contemplation of immaterial, timeless ideas. The whole movement is one of recovery, recollection, coming home to what one already is and knows in one's depths. Once Rilian is freed from the enchantment, it is clear that he has regained full possession of his own consciousness.

Chapter 12 of SC is a variation on Plato's famous Allegory of the Cave.[11] What appear there to the cave-dwellers on the wall in front of them seem to be real, but they are only the flickering shadows cast by more original objects held up against a fire behind their backs. Plato calls them artificial objects, human images and animal shapes wrought in stone and wood. Liberation comes when one of the prisoners is forced to turn around and see what is behind his back and behind the wall-appearances. He then ascends out of the cave into the open world above and sees that the artificial objects and the fire within the cave were themselves only inferior copies of yet more original realities—real living beings and the sun. In SC, the Witch seeks to halt the similar ascent of Rilian, Puddleglum, and the children out into the Overworld. Her tactic is to argue, much as Susan does in PC, that they can't return to Narnia because there is no Narnia to return to. The Queen is the archetypical reductionist,* trying to convince the cave-dwellers that the shadows of their immediate experience are all there is. Their conversation even taps the "original copy" thesis of Plato. In trying to defend their belief in the Overworld, the children liken the sun* of that realm to the lamp in the Witch's apartment, and Aslan to a huge cat with a mane. The Witch counters that the lamp and the cat are the "realities" and the sun and Aslan are glorified, make-believe "copies." Her position is the antithesis of Platonic metaphysics, and the effect of her discourse, her music,* and her magic* powder is to induce forgetfulness and weakness of thought. Jill has trouble remembering the names of things in the world from which she originally came and begins to fall under the full force of the enchantment. The Witch almost succeeds because "the more enchanted you get, the more certain you feel that you are not enchanted at all." Platonism is absorbed into Christian theology at this point because it is Puddleglum's bravery, obedience, and obstinate faith in Aslan that finally breaks the enchantment—not some sort of philosophical attainment or illumination.

The Platonic theme of the shrunken and self-deceived consciousness returns in MN in the person of Uncle Andrew.* Years of pursuing knowledge that promises power—at the expense of truth and morality (precisely the ailment Socrates diagnosed in his contemporaries)—have blinded Andrew to things and people as they actually are. Things make an impression on him only insofar as they present themselves as usable and exploitable. Digory, Jill, and the guinea-pigs have no significance outside of being material for Andrew's experiments. As he witnesses the founding of Narnia the striking thing is its "commercial possibilities."[12] Openness to and respect for the other, which make genuine perception and communication possible, are almost totally lacking in Andrew. That is why, at the creation of Narnia,* he misinterprets everything and is incapable of communication with the Talking Beasts.* Lewis emphasizes the key role of self-deception in Andrew's condition: he could have recognized the scene and Aslan's song for what they were, but instead he chose against reality. This choice carries so much weight that it hinders even Aslan from helping him. "If I spoke to him, he would hear only growlings and roarings. Oh Adam's sons, how cleverly you defend yourselves against all that might do you good!"

The foregoing is some preparation for the explicit and full-blown Platonic metaphysics that emerge in the closing chapters of LB. Digory's remark—"It's all in Plato"—refers to Plato's original-copy thesis, which we have already touched upon. So that we might see the full extent of Lewis's Platonism at the climax of the *Chronicles,* it will be helpful to elaborate a bit on Plato's theory of the forms and the Good. For Plato, every intelligible appearance that we meet with in the material world is a participation in a higher, more perfect, spiritual reality. Every human being that we encounter, for example, is an instance that approximates the ideal form of humanity. But this idea or form of humanity is never exhausted or perfectly fulfilled by the material instances, taken singly or altogether. Likewise, anything of beauty attempts to capture the quality of beauty itself, but no art object or natural splendor captures the reality of beauty perfectly. So the ideal surpasses its material approximations as an original surpasses the imperfect copies it inspires. There is, then, beyond the world of material things, an overworld of self-subsisting ideas. In turn

Queen Jadis hangs on in rage as the magic rings transport Digory and Polly out of Charn and into the timeless Wood between the Worlds. (MN 65, 63-64.)

these ideas or forms are themselves participations in the one single highest reality that gives being to everything else: what Plato calls "the Good."[13] It was not difficult for medieval thinkers to press this three-tiered interpretation of reality into the service of Christian theology. Plato's "Good"—that supreme reality that grounds everything else—becomes God himself, creator of heaven and earth. Plato's ideas, the intelligible blueprints for material realities, become creative thoughts in the mind of God or what he has in mind when creating. Creatures are thus intelligible instances of designs "thought up" by God.[14] It follows, as Aquinas says, that whatever is of value or excellence in any creature pre-exists in God.[15] Were one able to go "farther up and farther in"—into the very mind and being of God—one would find not an utterly new reality but something strangely familiar, something "like" what one had always known before, only supremely better. This, along with resurrection theology and eschatology,* is the Divine economy, or plan, which the children meet when they enter Aslan's country* after witnessing the passing of Narnia. Digory explains to Peter that the Narnia that has passed away was but the shadow of the real Narnia "which has always been here and always will be here: just as our own world, England* and all, is only a shadow or copy of something in Aslan's real world." And Lucy need not mourn over the Narnia that was but is no more because everything that mattered in the Old Narnia has come home to the new.

Lewis follows this passage with a fascinating but somewhat puzzling suggestion that likens the difference between the eternal sunlit Narnia and mortal Narnia to a landscape viewed in a mirror. The images in the mirror are "like" the real thing outside the window and yet somehow "deeper, more wonderful, more like places in a story." This might at first seem like a reversal of the Platonic thesis, for on the face of it the images or copies in the mirror are said to have more depth and reality than the original objects. But if we think of the looking glass as the mind reflecting on the world of experience and feeling its full weight, things begin to fall into place.[16] For this reason art is able, at times, to capture and represent what is significant in life better than life does. Lewis thought that story* was one of the ways in which the eternal might be glimpsed within the temporal, and in the passage just cited he likens what the mirror does to what a good story can do.

The immanence of the Good to the Platonic forms, and in turn of the forms to material things, is the paradoxical presence of the greater "in" the lesser. So as the company penetrates more and more into the heart of Aslan's country everything becomes greater. The hub of the wheel is larger than its perimeter. "The farther up and the farther in you go," Tumnus* explains to Lucy, "the bigger everything gets. The inside is larger than the outside." The company itself has grown in stature with its ascent; Lucy is now able to take in the whole world and see its relation to the great mountains of Aslan. Lewis again reminds us of Plato's Allegory of the Cave when Aslan tells the children that they are home to stay; he refers to their earthly existence, now left behind, as "the Shadow-Lands."[17] The Platonic quest for reality, the return of the soul to its eternal ground, has come full term. But the Christian perception of things has intervened, for much more that mattered has also been drawn through the Door.*

(LWW 43–46, 46–50; 186, 170. PC 51, 53; 121–123, 110–113; 135–136, 124–125; 140, 127; 142, 129; 144, 130; 147, 132. SC 35, 42; 132 ff., 133 ff.; 148, 147; 149 ff., 150 ff. MN 111, 103; 125–126, 116–117; 130, 120–121; 171, 158. LB 169–170, 153–154; 180–183, 162–164.)

---

[1] C.S. Lewis, *The Weight of Glory* (New York: Macmillan Publishing Co., 1966) pp. 3–6; *The Pilgrim's Regress* (Grand Rapids: Wm. B. Eerdmans Publishing Co., 1968) pp. 5–11.

[2] If we accept the thesis that Lewis intended to end the *Chronicles* with VDT (see *Introduction*), then we may also assume that Lewis was unaware of the Professor's motivations. However, the Professor indisputably accepts the children's Narnian experiences as real.*

[3] See *Dreams*.

[4] For another interpretation of this meeting, see *Aslan*.

[5] The famous Aristotelian dictum that "all men want to know" (in the opening line of his *Metaphysics*) must always be balanced by Plato's dialogues. All people, says Plato, also have a desire *not* to know, a tendency to resist the truth, a tendency toward self-deception. For a discussion of the self-imposed blindness of the renegade dwarfs, see *Imagination* and *Stable*.

[6] See *A Mind Awake: An Anthology of C. S. Lewis*, Clyde S. Kilby, ed. (New York: Harcourt Brace Jovanovich, 1969).

[7] Socrates, *The Apology* (30e–31a), from *The Last Days of Socrates*, Hugh Tredennick, trans. (Harmondsworth, Middlesex: Penguin Classics, 1954).

[8] *Phaedrus*, 246–251.

[9] See Plato, *The Phaedo*.

[10] Plato, *The Meno*, 80e–82, 85e–86b.

[11] Plato, *The Republic*, book seven, 514a–521.

[12] See *Ecology* and *Technology*.

[13] See especially the simile of the sun in *The Republic*, 504d–509d.

[14] Thomas Aquinas, *Summa Theologica*, I, q. 15.

[15] *Summa Theologica*, I, q. 14, article 6.

[16] In Lewis's *Out of the Silent Planet* (New York: Macmillan Publishing Co., 1965) p. 73, the hross Hyoi says to Ransom that reality remembered, recollected, reflected, "caught" again in a mirror of consciousness comes into a focus and grows to a fullness rarely achieved in the immediacy of life. That is where the real meeting with life takes place. See *Memory*.

[17] A term reminiscent of the Earthmen's* name "Shallow Lands" for a world that was for them a pale version of the brilliant world of Bism.

PLEASURE   See *Right and wrong*.

POESIMETERS   See *Coriakin*.

POGGIN   A helpful dwarf* who leaves the renegade dwarfs and joins Tirian's forces at the Last Battle,* putting himself in the King's* and Aslan's service. He perceives the situation at the Stable* clearly, having overheard Ginger* and Rishda* in a plot to neutralize Shift.* He is very helpful: he shoots a rabbit for breakfast and cooks it with Wild Fresney,* and he also makes the soap needed to wash the Calormene* pigment off Tirian, Eustace, and Jill. He makes significant contributions to the discussion of options, and Tirian later discusses strategy with him. Poggin's decision to divorce himself from his dwarf brothers enables him to save himself from their unhappy fate: and ultimately, he comes into Aslan's country* and is greeted by the Seven Friends of Narnia.*

(LB 75, 71; 77, 73; 83, 77; 85, 79; 87, 81; 90, 85; 94, 86; 97, 89; 102, 95; 121–122, 113; 154, 140; 171, 154.)
[*Diggle; Griffle; Hunting.*]

---

[1] His persistent cheerfulness is in direct contrast to their bleak cynicism.

POLLY PLUMMER The first human child[1] to enter the Wood between the Worlds* by means of the magic* rings.* She is a very balanced person, a good judge of character, perceptive, imaginative, and filled with the spirit of adventure and creativity. Her only fault is her womanly vanity,* a weakness that stems perhaps more from Lewis's unconscious sexism* than from a real character defect. When she appears for the last time in LB—forty-nine years after her first appearance—she is unmarried and is addressed as Lady Polly.[2] Much of MN is told from her perspective, because she has the requisite childlike perceptions and freedom from the enchantment of exaggerated curiosity* and bad magic that afflict Digory.

After a rather rough introduction to Digory in which Polly learns the reason for his misery, she distracts his attention from his problems by asking if his Uncle Andrew* is really insane. This is the first hint the reader has of her active imagination, a suggestion confirmed almost immediately by the sight of her smugglers' cave (a refuge she has constructed in the attic of her house), by her cashbox full of personal treasures, and by the copybook that contains a story she is writing—she is an independent Victorian girl.

A brave person, she leads the way into what she and Digory will discover is Uncle Andrew's study; and she becomes frightened only when he locks the door. Lewis seems to say that she is right to feel afraid and ought not to have dropped her guard; but Andrew appeals to his lonely old age and her vanity, enough to persuade her to pick up a yellow ring. She is instantly transported to the Wood between the Worlds. When she is joined by Digory and they both adjust to the atmosphere and figure out where they are, they decide to return to England.* When they can't return, she becomes as frightened as one is able to become in such a peaceful place.[3]

Even here her rationality and leadership prevail: she becomes absorbed in Digory's explanation of the place and gives it its name; she takes charge of the situation because of her instinctive sense that Digory isn't very prudent when his curiosity is roused; she insists that they test a sure way back before they continue their explorations, and that she be the one to signal when they should end their experiment. And when Digory intends to run off exploring, she has the presence of mind to question whether they should mark their conduit-to-earth pool. The fear* that they might otherwise never return grips them both.[4] She ridicules Digory's lack of foresight and prides herself on her good sense; if she had avoided either excess, she might have exercised more control over Digory's precipitous curiosity; as it is, they have the first of many quarrels. She lets her guard down a second time when, at their first attempt to enter another world, they get nowhere. This lapse of vigilance seems unfortunate, Lewis implies, in light of the trouble they get themselves into when their second attempt works.

POLLY PLUMMER   228

Polly's first *and* second reaction to the new world is "I don't like it." Lewis implies that she ought to have listened to her feelings about this place and told Digory of her fear, a proper fear. But her pride intervenes; and then her weakness for splendid attire sweeps her into the royal hall at Charn* ahead of Digory.[5] But unlike Digory, she sees nothing extraordinarily beautiful about the last queen and she wants nothing to do with danger; therefore, she is not at all tempted by the enchanted golden bell and hammer's* invitation to "know what would have happened."[6] Lewis emphasizes that Polly sees clearly that Digory is consenting to the temptation and will try to shift the blame to magic. Her remarks hits home and he retorts with a sexist remark.[7] She ignores this for the moment because she sees a very telling resemblance between Digory's facial expression and his uncle's. And Digory confirms this parallel by duplicating one of his uncle's stock evasions of responsibility. This incenses her and she retorts with another sexist remark of her own. They grapple and Digory violently immobilizes her, twisting her wrist.

Polly's perception is keen, and she sees the Empress Jadis for what she is: "a terrible woman." She calls her a beast for her callous disregard for life. At Jadis's long and totally vain explanation of why Digory was "sent" to Charn, Digory waffles but Polly calls it as she sees it: "absolute bosh from beginning to end." Lewis means for his readers to cheer at this remark, which cuts through the fog, and to wince at the unfortunate outcome: Jadis pulls Polly's hair and so is brought back to the Wood. Here Polly again takes charge, but to no avail: Jadis is carried all the way back to Andrew's study.

Seeing the witch and the magician side by side, she notices their similar facial expression. Polly has every reason to abandon Digory to the consequences of his mistreatment of her, but she hears his plea to help keep Jadis from hurting his mother. She promises to return and goes back to her home by the now very prosaic secret tunnel: the imaginary magic has paled in comparison to the real magic Polly has just experienced.

She rejoins Digory at the tumultuous scene in front of his house; and she is swept back into the Wood and then into a new world. Again her instincts prompt her to side with Frank* and she joins him in his hymn. At the first sound of the Lion's creation song she is transported with joy, another indication of how good she is. And when she sees the Lion, she falls instantly in loving awe of him, the proper stock response.* Through her eyes and ears, the reader experiences the connection between the song and the creation of Narnia. It is so exciting that she does not become frightened as the Lion wends his way closer to them. After the witch attempts to hurt the Lion, and after Andrew's third suggestion that the Lion be shot, she again sees the similarity in the reaction of the two villains. When Aslan confers the gift of speech on the animals,* Polly—in her great ability to rejoice with others[8]—is thrilled that the cabhorse has also received the gift. And though she is alarmed at Digory's decision to present his mother's case to the Lion, she is true to her pledge and walks with him. She is properly awestruck by the Lion when he calls her into his council. He calls her "little Daughter" as he completes her forgiveness of Digory's violence* toward her. Her instant friendship with Queen Helen* and the Queen's intercession with Aslan enable Polly to accompany Digory

POLLY PLUMMER

on his quest* for the silver apple. Unlike Digory, who is excited about the names and the eventual histories of the places over which they are flying, she equates this with the dull learning of dates and battles that passes for history* in her school. But she wisely observes that places will have names only when people inhabit them. And though she can't understand why Aslan needs to be asked before he would provide food for their journey,[9] she is not about to go back on her promise even if she is hungry enough to contemplate using her ring to return to England. She knows instinctively that she is not meant to enter the garden*; and she stays out of the conversation between Digory and the witch because she knows that Mrs. Kirke's life is at stake.

Like Lucy interceding for the renegade dwarfs,* Polly asks Aslan to help Andrew in whatever way he can. This gives Aslan a chance to explain what he can and cannot do for people with hardened hearts. And when she asserts that the witch cannot be afraid of the Tree of Protection* because she has eaten of it, Aslan explains the meaning of pleasure. He gives her and Digory an unforgettable vision of his beauty. Polly and Digory become very good friends; and the next time the reader sees her, she is host of a banquet for the Seven Friends of Narnia.* Lewis emphasizes her "wise, merry, twinkling eyes." She dies in the railway accident, on her way with her friends to obtain the magic rings from Peter and Edmund for Jill and Eustace to use to get back into Narnia. She finds herself restored in health on the other side of a Stable* Door.* She is rather ungenerous in her remark about Susan's disinterest in Narnia because of her preoccupation with a false notion of maturity. Polly, with Digory, seem to be Lewis's picture of what gracious old age should look like. She turns her attention to the wonders of the end of Narnia* and the greater wonders of the New Narnia. Her last words in LB are "Do you remember?" as the sights and smells* awaken in her the hope that she has arrived at the goal of her longing.* This hope is confirmed.

---

[1] And one of the first humans to enter Narnia. If Lewis intended that the Telmarines* were earthly pirates from the nineteenth century or before, then they would have arrived in Narnia before Polly but only by means of a wrinkle in time.* It is clear that Lewis did not harmonize his account of human* presence in Narnia in the first three *Chronicles* (by means of the Telmarine incursion through a magic cave on an island in our earth's south seas) with his account in the last four books (by means of Frank* and Helen,* as well as Digory and Polly). It is conceivable that Lewis liked his later explanation better than his earlier and, had he lived longer, he would have explained the Telmarines differently.

[2] A sign of her status in Narnia rather than an earthly honorific.

[3] Recall Lucy's experience in LB at the Great Waterfall* when she notices that it is impossible to feel afraid in New Narnia. The Wood between the Worlds partakes of something of the same quality.

[4] It is the quality of this fear that Lewis seems to intend his readers to remember, to foster the stock response* to unpremeditated experimentation of any kind.

[5] Whatever might be thought of Lewis's implicit sexism in his belief that women are almost uncontrollably interested in fashion, he is clear in his assumption that (1) she should have been honest about her fear and expressed it, and (2) in a prideful reaction to what she probably considered a weakness (her fear), she leads the way into the hall, a place neither of them should have entered.

[6] For the futility inherent in knowing what would have happened, see *Positivity.* Lewis's craftsmanship as a writer is quite evident here. He surrounds the heart of the exchange between Polly and Digory with an envelope of the twice-said "No fear!" Their reactions are exactly the

opposite: Polly has no fear that she will succumb to the enchantment, and Digory has no fear that he will *not* succumb.

[7] See *Bulverism.*
[8] Recall Romans 12:15: "Rejoice with those who rejoice, weep with those who weep."
[9] See *Eustace Clarence Scrubb,* note 9.

POMELY   Lord Glozelle's* horse.* Glozelle wagers his mount that Edmund's approach to the camp of Miraz* signals a challenge rather than a surrender. "Pomely" is an adaptation of the old French word for "dappled," and alludes to the Reeve's horse in Chaucer's "Prologue" to *The Canterbury Tales.*

(PC 175, *153.*)
[*Literary allusions.*]

POMONA   The Roman goddess of gardens and fruit trees. Peter says she put good spells on the apple* orchard.

(PC 18, *24.*)
[*Gods; Mythology.*]

POSITIVITY   A term that denotes Lewis's feeling that what has actually happened is most important; and that it is futile to speculate about what might have happened had another choice been made. In PC, Aslan tells Lucy that nobody is ever told what would have happened *if* . . . In VDT, the pages of the magician's* Book* cannot be turned back for a rereading of the spell for the refreshment of the spirit. When he has become visible, Aslan reminds Lucy that no one is ever told what would have happened. In MN, the verse on the pillar taunts Digory with the idea that not knowing what would have happened will drive him mad; but Polly, as the voice of reason, states that it doesn't matter what would have happened. In the garden,* Aslan tells Digory what would have happened if someone had stolen a silver apple* for Narnia, and what would have happened if he had taken the apple directly to his mother. But because he did the right* thing, these circumstances did not occur, and healing is possible.[1]

(PC 137, *125.* VDT 133, *134;* 136, *137.* MN 175, *162–163.*)

[1] See *Right and wrong* and *Providence.*

POWER   See *Magic; Technology.*

PRACTICAL NOTES   Lewis's inclusion of practical notes helps to make the fantasy world of Narnia quite real. A great lover of walks and the outdoors, Lewis was not fond of camping. He managed instead to walk from inn to inn where he could sit down to a hot meal and a fresh bed. Thus in PC he notes the discomfort of sleeping outside, and the difficulty of eating roasted apples* and hot fish without forks. From his great experience as a walker, he can comment about how easy it is to find imaginary paths in the woods. Helpful to the modern reader is the fact that swords aren't very useful for cutting ropes, because they can't be held anywhere lower than the hilt. In PC, Trumpkin's* problem in the rowboat (where his feet don't reach the floor) is a problem common to all children* in an adult* world. Lucy knows that the best way of getting to sleep is to stop trying. In VDT, Lewis's great love of boats comes into play, and he notifies readers that in order to read the book* intelligently, they must be able to distinguish *port* from *starboard*. When thrown into deep water, Lucy kicks off her shoes—as anyone should to keep from drowning. In SC, Lewis comments that like other deaf people, Trumpkin is not a "good judge of his own voice." And when Eustace loses his temper at Puddleglum, Lewis remarks parenthetically that people who have been frightened often do. Just as it is difficult to see after gazing into a bright light, the travelers can't see after gazing into the bright depths of Bism. In HHB the reader learns all sorts of practical information about horses,* including the fact that they shouldn't sleep in their saddles. And at the enclosure of the Hermit of the Southern March,* Lewis comments that goat's milk has a rather shocking taste to those not used to it.

(PC 26, *33;* 30, *37;* 100, *93;* 109, *101;* 110, *102;* 115, *106.* VDT 4, *12;* 8, *16;* 31, *38.* SC 15, *24;* 63–64, *69;* 180, *175.*)

PRAYER　　See *Eustace Clarence Scrubb,* note 9.

PRIDE　　See *Vanity.*

PRIVACY　　Respect for the privacy of "one's own story" is important in Narnia. Lewis himself had an intense sense of privacy,[1] and this theme is apparent in the *Chronicles.* In VDT, the reformed Eustace does not pry when Edmund tells him that he himself was a traitor on *his* first time in Narnia. In the Land of the Duffers,* Lucy comes across a spell in the magician's* Book* that enables her to know what her friends think of her. As a result of this invasion of their privacy, she will never be able to forget what they said. Ramandu* quells Caspian's curiosity* by telling him "it is not for . . . a Son of Adam* to know what faults a star* can commit." In HHB when Shasta asks the Lion why he wounded Aravis, Aslan replies, "Child, I am telling you your story, not hers. I tell no one any story but his own." When Aravis asks what harm might come to the slave she drugged, Aslan again replies, "I am telling you your story, not hers." This is Lewis's doctrine of privacy, and it is not to be broken.[2] The garden* in the west is obviously private: "Only a fool would dream of going in unless he had been sent there on a very special business." Finally, arousing the curiosity of many readers, Aslan's words to Puzzle* at the end of LB are for the donkey's* ears alone.

(VDT 92, *97;* 131 ff., *133 ff.;* 180, *177;* 216, *209.* SC 57, *63.* HHB 32, *35;* 159, *139;* 194, *170;* 199, *175;* 204, *178–179.* MN 48–49, *49;* 157, *146.* LB 183, *165.*)

² Cor wants his story told to King Lune,* but when Aravis does go he finds that it's not as enjoyable as he thought it would be—in fact, he tires of Lune's constant retellings. This may be one of the punishments for violating the rule prohibiting personal storytelling.

PRIZZLE, MISS   The schoolmistress at the Beruna* girls' school. She reprimands Gwendolen* for looking out the window at Aslan's holiday party, and accuses her of talking nonsense when she claims to see a Lion. When Miss Prizzle herself sees Aslan, she flees, taking her "dumpy, prim little girls" with her. The name "Prizzle" may be an allusion to Miss Prism, the governess of Cecily Cardew in *The Importance of Being Earnest* by Oscar Wilde.

(PC 194, *170–171.*)
[*Literary allusions; Prunaprismia.*]

PROFESSOR KIRKE   See *Digory Kirke.*

PROGRESS   See *Government; Technology.*

PROMISES   See *Oaths.*

PROPHECIES   There are three prophecies in LWW and one in VDT. Mr. Beaver* tells the children* that old rhymes have kept the knowledge that (1) spring will return to Narnia when Aslan comes; (2) evil* will be gone from Narnia when Adam's flesh and bone sit on the thrones at Cair Paravel; and (3) four thrones are there, two for Sons of Adam* and two for Daughters of Eve. In VDT, Reepicheep relates the Dryad's* prophecy that he will seek the Utter East.* All these prophecies are fulfilled in the *Chronicles,* and Lewis felt that prophecy could be used in a story for giving a sense of how free will and destiny work together.¹

(LWW 74, *75;* 76, *76;* 78, *77.* VDT 16, *24;* 198, *193.*)
[*Providence.*]

¹ See "On Stories" in OOW, p. 15.

PROVIDENCE   When Cor reflects that Aslan "seems to be at the back of all the stories," this is a summary statement of Lewis's theology of providence. How Aslan takes care of all of Narnian history and the lives of each person and animal* is one of the major themes of the *Chronicles.* Lewis did not believe in luck or fate;¹ rather, he believed in providence: that God's care and foresight is behind all activities, on a scale so large it is impossible for the human mind to comprehend. It seems a misfortune, for example, that Susan has lost her horn* somewhere in Lantern Waste* when the children* "blunder" out of Narnia in LWW. But Lewis as subcreator has a providence in mind for events in the *Chronicles* just as Aslan has a providence for the Narnians. The loss of the horn is actually providential, because in PC it turns up as one of the old Narnian treasures and its note brings the Pevensies back into Narnia to aid Caspian against the Telmarines.* In VDT, Reepicheep comforts Eustace with the reflection that his becoming a dragon* is only a most unusual instance of the way fortune has dealt with royal persons, scholars, and ordinary people in the past: their fall from prosperity and their recovery leads to the eventual happiness of many. It is indeed providential that Rilian calls on the three travelers in the name of Aslan to untie him, for this is just the sign* they have been waiting for. In HHB, Aravis says it is "luck" that the lion* did not wound her more seriously; but the Hermit* refers to providence when he says he has "never met any such thing as Luck." And Shasta shows how well he has learned his lesson when he first attributes his arrival through the mountains into Narnia to luck, but corrects himself with, ". . . at least it wasn't luck at all really, it was *Him.*" Finally, it is not tragedy that the Seven Friends of Narnia* and Mr. and Mrs. Pevensie* are killed in a train wreck, for they are all reunited in the glory of Aslan's country.*

---

[1] See *The Four Loves* (New York: Harcourt Brace Jovanovich, 1960) p. 126.

PRUNAPRISMIA[1]   Caspian's aunt, the red-haired wife of Miraz.* Caspian dislikes her because she dislikes him. The thirteen-year-old Caspian's life is put in jeopardy when she gives birth to Miraz's son.

(PC 37, 42; 53–57, 55–57.)

---

[1] Readers of Charles Dickens will recognize that Lewis has modeled her name on the characteristic exclamation of Mrs. General in *Little Dorrit:* "prunes and prisms." The suggestion of "prunes" in her name is significant in that Lewis loathed prunes (OOW, p. 34). See *Literary allusions.*

PUDDLEGLUM   A Marsh-Wiggle* who serves as Jill's and Eustace's guide and companion on the journey across Ettinsmoor* in SC. His name implies his marshy origin and his glum outlook (although, ironically, he is considered "flighty" by the other Wiggles). A typical Marsh-Wiggle, he is all arms and legs, marsh-colored, long and thin, beardless, with greenish-gray hair that is perhaps more weed-like than hair-like. He wears a high pointed hat with a wide flat brim, and earth-colored clothes. He is, in fact, a practical, down-to-earth sort of person and a complete pessimist. His qualities are perfect for the job at hand, however, and he is the voice of reason and the steadying influence for the children* in their trek across the frightening Ettinsmoor, to the Ruined City of the Ancient Giants,* and to the confrontation with the Queen of Underland* and the freeing of Rilian. That his guidance will be so necessary is not at first discernible, however; when the children first meet him he paints such a bleak picture of their prospects that he scares both Jill and Eusatace badly. However, his suspicious nature pays off: he refuses to let Jill tell the Green Lady and the Black Knight any details of their journey; he is skeptical of what the adjective "gentle" might mean when applied to a giant; he is the only one who is able to keep his head during the witch's attempt at enchantment*; and indeed it is he who breaks the spell. Allegorized, he may be said to be the skeptical nature that we all need to keep us on the right path.

Puddleglum is a Marsh-Wiggle of much faith, and he trusts to Aslan's instructions even when things look worst. When Rilian laughs at Jill's exposition of the signs,* Puddleglum jumps to the defense of their mission. His profession of faith consists of the following: (1) "There are no accidents";[1] and (2) "Our guide is Aslan." When he breaks the witch's spell and she shrieks at him, clearing his head, he is able to assert that though Narnia and Aslan may not exist, "the made-up things seem a good deal more important than the real ones."[2] This assertion is so strikingly similar to the conclusion of Lewis's essay "The Obstinacy of Belief,"[3] written at around the same time, that one cannot escape the conclusion that Lewis means Puddleglum to be a figure of the way in which Christians adhere to their faith after it has once been formed.[4]

Puddleglum is also something of a fatalist. Profoundly despondent at Jill's supposed death,* he groans that he was meant to be a misfit and as fated to be responsible for Jill's death as he was to eating the Talking Stag at Harfang.*[5] But he accepts his own fault in both matters.

By the end of the adventure,* Jill and Eustace are quite fond of Puddleglum. Ever the pessimist, he is sure his injured foot will have to be amputated, but of course it heals in three weeks thanks to the ministrations of Cloudbirth* the Centaur.* Jill puts the lie to his pessimism when she says, "You sound as doleful as a funeral and I believe you're perfectly happy. And you talk as if you were afraid of everything, when you're really as brave as—as a lion" (this simile, of course, being the highest compliment in Narnia). After Jill kisses him goodbye, Puddleglum displays a degree of vanity* heretofore unsuspected when he says to himself, "Well, I wouldn't have dreamt of her doing that. Even though I am a good-looking chap." Finally, Puddleglum's skepticism foreshadows future events in Narnia. Lewis comments that even though Rilian's reign was a happy one, Puddleglum "often pointed out [that] you couldn't expect good times to last."

(SC Chapter 5 passim.)

---

[1] See *The Four Loves* (New York: Harcourt Brace Jovanovich, 1960) p. 126. See also *Providence*.
[2] See *Plato*.
[3] In *The World's Last Night* (New York: Harcourt Brace Jovanovich, 1959) especially page 29 ff.
[4] See *Introduction* and *Appendix One*.
[5] See *Dumb Beasts*, note 1.

PUG   An obsequious, oily pirate on the island of Felimath* who is engaged in the slave trade.* He siezes Caspian, Reepicheep, Lucy, Edmund, and Eustace with the intention of selling them along with other captives at auction in Narrowhaven.* But when he is in the midst of this sale, Caspian, now free and recognized as King,* declares Pug's life forfeit and demands that he free all his slaves and give back the money he received for those already sold, including Lucy, Edmund, and Reepicheep. Pug protests that this will leave him a beggar. To this Caspian replies that it is better to be a beggar than a slave, and he accuses Pug of having lived on broken hearts all his life.

(VDT 32 ff., *40 ff.;* 49–51, 56–58.)

PUGRAHAN   The site of the Tisroc's* salt mines in Calormen,* for which the smaller animals* and dwarfs* are destined.

(LB 69, 65.)
[*Slave trade.*]

PUZZLE   A gray donkey,* Shift's* one "friend" and neighbor at Lantern Waste.* He is a decent sort, but has lapsed into the habit* of letting the ape do all his thinking for him. He sometimes questions Shift's motives, but is easily intimidated and persuaded into doing his bidding. He shows his innate goodness in several ways: he is concerned about the dead lion* from whose skin his coat is made,[1] and wants to give it a good burial;[2] he refuses to pretend to be Aslan, as that would be wrong (but the deception is perpetrated nonetheless); and when the earthquake* and thunderclaps come, he correctly discerns them as signs* of divine disapproval. Jill saves him from execution by Tirian,* and Jewel* the Unicorn* speaks to him kindly of horsey matters. He is the first to shiver at the sight of Tash,* and hides in the tower. In Aslan's country* at last he appears as he really is—a lovely gray donkey with an honest face. Aslan, on his final return, seeks the donkey out before all others, and whispers something that first causes Puzzle to be humbled, and then elated.

(LB passim.)
[*Horses.*]

---

[1] Recall Aesop's fable, "The Ass in the Lion's Skin."
[2] He says that all lions, even dumb lions, are somewhat solemn because Aslan himself is a lion; thus he shows his basic faith in Aslan.

QUEEN OF UNDERLAND   The ruler of the underground kingdom that lies directly beneath Narnia; she is also known as Queen of the Deep Realm, and the Lady of the Green Kirtle. The poison-green dress she wears foreshadows her transformation into a shiny, great, poisonous green serpent. She is related to the White Witch; and (according to the oldest owl*) one of the "same crew" of evil* witches. It is later concluded by Rilian and the wise animals* and dwarfs* that, just as the White Witch intended to rule Narnia with the Hundred Years of Winter,* the Queen of Underland intended to rule

*The animals of Narnia spring joyously from the earth, brought forth by Aslan's song of creation. (*MN 113-114, 105-106.*)*

Narnia through Rilian as slave-king in his rightful kingdom. The eldest dwarf comments that "those Northern Witches always mean the same thing, but in every age they have a different plan for getting it."[1] She rides a white[2] horse,* Snowflake, whom Rilian says is worthy of a better mistress. Like her sisters, she is beautiful and specializes in sweet seductions: the spells woven by her "sweet, quiet voice," and her sweet suggestion to the children and Puddleglum that they tell the giants* at Harfang* they have arrived for the Autumn Feast*—which is actually an offer of themselves as the main course. Her realm is an unhappy one populated by enslaved gnomes. She first appears in serpent form, to kill the Daughter of Ramandu,* Rilian's mother and Caspian's wife; and it is as a serpent she dies, at the hands of Eustace and the truly disenchanted Rilian. At her death, all of Underland rejoices.

(SC Chapters 4 through 8.)
[*Earthmen; Reductionism.*]

---

[1] See *White Witch* for a discussion of the recurrence of evil.
[2] See *White Witch,* note 3, for the meaning of "white."

QUEENS   See *Kings and Queens;* Kings, queens.

QUEST   To quest is to seek; in medieval times knights-errant set out in quest of adventure* and knowledge.* The *Chronicles,* in which the medieval worldview is foremost, has its share of quests. It is important to understand the difference between a quest and an adventure: there may be many adventures within the framework of the quest. For example, Caspian's oath to sail east and find the Seven Noble Lords* is a quest, during which he and the crew become involved in such adventures as Ramandu's Island,* the Land of the Duffers,* and the Dark Island.* His quest is ended when the Seven Noble Lords have been located, and his oath is fulfilled.

In LWW, the Kings and Queens* vanish from Narnia while on a hunt— a quest, really—for the Talking Stag,* who when caught grants wishes to his captors.

In HHB, Shasta is on a quest for his true identity; and even though he has only subconscious knowledge—his longing* for the north—that he doesn't belong in the south, this is enough to push him along toward Narnia. Jill's quest for Rilian is the most complete quest of any in the *Chronicles.* She is charged with her task by Aslan, who gives her signs* that she must watch for. Although she is often tempted to give up her quest, and although she often does not (through her own doubt and inexperience with adventure) recognize the signs when she sees them, at the Parliament of Owls she recognizes the quest as hers and hers alone and takes it for herself from Eustace, who would have it for his own. At the end of SC, her quest complete, she has a longing for home. Aslan tells her, "You have done the work for which I sent you into Narnia." Since children* are brought into Narnia only to save it, in some sense they are all on this same quest.

RABADASH   The crown prince of Calormen* during the Golden Age of Narnia,* the eldest of the eighteen sons of the Tisroc,* would-be suitor of Queen Susan and would-be conqueror of Archenland* and Narnia. When first seen in HHB he is a tall, dark, and handsome young man, wearing a "feathered and jeweled turban on his head and an ivory-sheathed scimitar at his side." His face bears an excited expression and his eyes and teeth have a fierce glint. His name suggests his menacingly wild (rabid) and precipitous (dash) personality. His experience with Aslan at Anvard* changes him into what his people call him to his face—Rabadash the Peacemaker—and what they call him behind his back—Rabadash the Ridiculous. Afterward, to be called a second Rabadash in Calormen is to be insulted.

Rabadash meets the freedom of Narnia for the first time on his visit there to follow up on the report of his ambassadors about the beauty of Queen Susan. His suit for her hand in marriage may be only a cover for a planned annexation of the kingdoms of Archenland and Narnia. When, out of courtesy,* Susan and Edmund make a return embassy to Tashbaan,* they discover his sinister intentions and flee on the *Splendour Hyaline.* * Rabadash demands a meeting with his father, the Tisroc, and the Grand Vizier, Ahoshta Tarkaan.* From their conversation the reader gathers much information not only about the plot the crown prince is proposing but also about the total lack of affection between fairly representative Calormene adults. Rabadash soon learns that his naturalistic explanation of the change in Narnia's climate is even more erroneous than is the Grand Vizier's.[1] Rabadash also completely misjudges Peter when he assumes that the Narnian high king will not attempt to rescue Susan —Rabadash's sexism* is apparent in discounting her desires because they are a woman's.

Rabadash leads a troop of two hundred horsemen against King Lune* at Anvard; his force includes Corradin of Castle Tormunt, who is killed by Edmund; Azrooh, who is felled by Lune; Chlamash, who surrenders to Edmund; Ilgamuth of the twisted lip, who is killed by Lord Darrin*; and Anradin,* who seems also to have been captured alive. The crown prince himself is literally held up to ridicule—the very thing he hates most, even than physical torture—by a hook on the castle wall.

He is treated very well by the Archenlanders, but he is so caught up in his fury that he does not eat or sleep.* He hardly lets King Lune announce his mercy before he insults Lune and promises vengeance. His irascibility is so great that only the intervention of Aslan himself has a chance of changing him. But Rabadash, in his assinine stubbornness, refuses to accept even the Lion's mercy. For this he is transformed into an ass.[2] Since Rabadash is incapable of acknowledging the Lion, the Lion decides to reach him through the only divine personage the crown prince has any respect for—Tash.*[3] Aslan gives Rabadash one more chance by assuring him that he will be healed in the temple of his own god* and will remain healed only if he stays within ten miles of the temple.

(HHB 61–62, 59–60; 94, 86; 98, 89; Chapter 8; 153–154, 135–136; 178 ff., 156 ff.; 205 ff., 179 ff.)

---

[1] See *Aslan*, note 60.
[2] See *The Great Divorce* (New York: Macmillan Publishing Co., 1946) p. 70, in which a grumbling lady is turned into a grumble.
[3] See *Universalism*.

RAM   Surnamed "the Great," he is the son of King Cor and Queen Aravis. He becomes the most famous of all the kings of Archenland,* though the reason for his fame is not given.[1]

(HHB 216, 188.)

---

[1] According to Lewis's outline of Narnian history, he succeeds his father and begins his reign in 1050 N.Y. (PWD, p. 43).

RAMANDU   A star* at rest, first referred to as "it." "It was an old man," with silver hair and beard down to the floor. Tall and straight, he is clothed in a robe* that appears to be made of the fleece of silver sheep, and his feet are bare. He is mild and grave of demeanor, seeming to radiate light and commanding silence* and respect. At his first appearance he does not greet the travelers, but joins his daughter; with her he raises his arms toward the East and sings a ritual song of welcome to the sun.* Afterwards a bird* flies by and places a bright fruit in the old man's mouth.[1] This is the fire-berry,* which will renew Ramandu each day until he is able to rejoin the Great Dance. He does tell Caspian that in order to break the enchantment of the Three Sleepers,* it is necessary for someone to sail as far East as possible and to leave there a volunteer who will continue on to the Utter East.* However, he cannot give Caspian navigational information about the journey there, because he has had only a star's perspective of Narnia.

When Ramandu tells the visitors his name and there is no recognition, he is quick to realize that he ceased being a star long before they were born. He corrects Eustace for equating what a star is made of with what it is; and he informs the adventurers that they have already met another star, Coriakin,* who, he indicates, is earthbound because of some personal failure. However, he will not reveal the circumstances of Coriakin's fall on the grounds that humans are not meant to know such things about stars.

Dismissing this line of questioning as useless, he presses Caspian to decide about sailing East. When the King mentions the weariness of his crew, Ramandu says that great enchantments can be broken only by knowledgeable and willing participants. He also assures them that should the adventurers wish to winter on his island, Aslan's Table* would supply them daily with royal fare. Finally, Ramandu lays his hands, radiant with a faint silver glow, on the head of the Lord Rhoop,* so that he may experience the refreshment of rest in the company of the Three Sleepers.

(VDT 174 ff., *171 ff.*)
[*Astronomy, Narnian; Deeper Magic; Knowledge; Privacy; Reductionism.*]

---

[1] Though this image is reminiscent of Isaiah 6:6, the purification of the prophet Isaiah, the dynamic of Ramandu's rejuvenation* is very dissimilar.

RAMANDU'S DAUGHTER   See *Daughter of Ramandu.*

RAMANDU'S ISLAND   Also known as World's End[1] (Island), Island of the Three Sleepers, and Island of the Star. This island, with its gentle hills and attractive smells, is first sighted in the setting sun.* The sound of the long waves breaking on its shore is all-pervasive (the company of five is especially conscious of this during their night of waiting at the magic table). At the head of the island's shallow bay is a level valley with springy turf and a few low bushes resembling heather. It has no roads and shows no evidence of human habitation. This island is the site of Aslan's Table* and the home of Ramandu and his Daughter.* Seated at the head of the Table, in an enchanted sleep, are the Three Sleepers,* lords Argoz,* Revilian,* and Mavramorn.* There is a magic about the island that helps Caspian convince his reluctant voyagers to continue their journey to the Utter East.*

(VDT 163 ff., *161 ff.; 210, 216.*)
[*Geography, Narnian.*]

---

[1] This island is not to be confused with the true World's End.* Daughter of Ramandu says that though some call Ramandu's Island the World's End, it is more properly the beginning of the end (VDT 174, *171*).

RAVEN OF RAVENSCAUR, OLD   Apparently an Old Narnian of some renown. He is in attendance at Caspian's Council of War, but would rather orate than get down to serious planning. "Ravenscaur" may be a community of ravens, because *scaur* is the Scottish word for "cliff."

(PC 80–81, *76–77.*)
[*Birds; Talking Beasts.*]

REDHAVEN   The main city on Brenn,* one of the Seven Isles.* The people are very hospitable and feast the crew of the *Dawn Treader** royally.

(VDT 18, *25.* HHB 180, *158.*)

REDUCTIONISM   The idea that things can be defined by what they are physically, or that a situation can be reduced to the facts about it. Lewis abhorred the sort of person who "sees all the facts but not the meaning";[1] such persons are always given away by their use of the words "nothing but," "merely," or "only." One can almost hear the words "nothing but" in Eustace's declaration to Ramandu* that a star* is only a ball of flaming gas; Ramandu speaks for Lewis when he replies that gas is not what a star is, only what it is made of. In her enchantment of the three travelers, the Queen of Underland* tries to reduce Aslan to "nothing but" a lion,* a large cat; and the sun* into "nothing but" a large lamp. According to Lewis, "as long as this refusal to see things from above . . . continues, it is idle to talk of any victory over materialism."[2] In LB, materialism has consumed virtually all that is noble in Narnia: the talking trees* are reduced to dead lumber; the nobility of humans is perverted by the imposter ape Shift*; and Aslan, whose presence actually *gives* the "meaning from above" to Narnia, is physically absent from the country for the first time in the *Chronicles.*

(VDT 180, *177.*)
[*Plato; Technology; Vivisection.*]

---

[1] C. S. Lewis, *The Weight of Glory and Other Addresses* (New York: Macmillan Publishing Co., 1966) p. 28.
[2] *Ibid.*

REEPICHEEP   A talking mouse who stands between one and two feet tall, and has ears nearly as long as a rabbit's. The very soul of courage,* his head is filled always with battles and strategies, honor* and adventure.* Unlike humans, he has no hopes or fears* to contend with. He wears a rapier at his side and, in PC, leads a fully armed band of twelve valiant mice.* He fights bravely at the battle against Miraz* and the Telmarines,* and is brought back more dead than alive. Healed by Lucy's cordial,* he is horrified to find that his tail has been cut off. He apologizes to Aslan for appearing before him in such unseemly fashion, asserting that "a tail is the honor and glory of a Mouse." Aslan restores his tail because of his love for the courage of mice and their ancient kindness in eating away the cords that bound him to the Stone Table.* Reepicheep, who never shirks danger, volunteers to take eleven mice through the door* back to earth in the Telmarines' stead, but Aslan tells him that if he did, he would only be shown off at fairs.

By the time of VDT, Reepicheep has been designated Chief Mouse, and wears a thin headband of gold with a crimson feather stuck in it. He is one of the heroes of the second battle of Bernua.* He reveals that at his birth a Dryad* spoke a prophecy* over his cradle that told of sweet waters, and that he would find what he sought in the Utter East.* Although he never knew what it meant, it becomes increasingly apparent that in sailing with the *Dawn Treader** to the Utter East, he will fulfill the prophecy. On the voyage it is Reepicheep who keeps the crew on the path of adventure, and spends his days far forward, gazing always to the east. When Eustace insults the mouse by swinging him by the tail, the mouse gives Eustace the first physical punishment of his life, beating him with the flat of his sword. Fair in every way, however, he later upbraids Rhince* for saying "good riddance" to the lost Eustace, and when the dragon-Eustace appears he solicits its promise of friendship. It is his plea with the crew to push on instead of fighting the Sea Serpent* that saves the Dawn Treaders. In the Land of the Duffers,* he is all for fighting the invisible enemy. His greatest courage comes in his urging the crew to forget their fears and venture into the darkness of Dark Island.* In that darkness, he is the only crew member who keeps his head and remains unaffected by the nightmares. And on Ramandu's Island,* when the crew hesitates to move closer to the tower-like shapes there, Reepicheep announces that "the way to find out is to go right in among them."

When Ramandu* praises Caspian for a decision to sail to the east and leave someone there, rather than to sail west, Reepicheep sees clearly that it is part of their quest* to "rescue these three lords from enchantment." As they sail toward the Utter East and the waters grow sweet, he is excited to find out what lies over the edge of the world—"Aslan's country,* perhaps. Or perhaps there isn't any bottom. Perhaps it just goes down for ever and ever." He is the second to say "no" to Caspian's intention to abdicate, because such an act would go against the King's solemn oath.* When the *Dawn Treader* runs aground at the World's End,* Reepicheep lowers the coracle,* throws aside his sword, saying he won't need it any more, and bids goodby to Edmund, Lucy, and Eustace. He tries to be sad for their sakes, but he is really quivering with happiness at what lies ahead. He vanishes over the wave of the Last Sea* and is never seen again, although Lewis comments that he is probably safe in Aslan's country; and in LB he is indeed found to be safe there. Saying "Welcome in the Lion's name," he gives the last summons to "come farther up and farther in," and Edmund, Peter, and Lucy kneel in greeting as he prevails upon them to come into the garden.*

[*Literary allusions.*]

REFRESHMENT OF THE SPIRIT   See *Aslan; Jill Pole.*

REMEMBER   See *Memory.*

RESTIMAR
One of the Seven Noble Lords.* He is judged by the children* and Coriakin* to be the beautiful golden statue lying in the lake at the top of Deathwater Island,* since they are able to account for the whereabouts of his six companions. His armor is lying on the shore and Edmund speculates that Restimar, unaware of the water's Midas touch, decided to go for a swim and was instantly transformed into the statue.

(VDT 16, *23;* 149, *149.*)
[*Greed.*]

REVELRY
The spirit of revelry is a fundamental part of Narnian life, a correspondence to the medieval world in which feast days were plentiful. One of the sure signs of enchantment and the work of dark magic* is an unending

sameness and dreariness, such as can be seen in Underland* and Charn.* In the very beginning of LWW, Tumnus* informs Lucy that, in the days before winter came to Narnia, the world was full of nymphs,* and fauns,* and Dryads,* and wild Red Dwarfs,* and even Bacchus and Silenus* would come, and "the whole forest would give itself up to jollification for weeks on end." PC is filled with celebration, feasts, and dances,* and it is significant that the chief meeting place in Narnia is the Dancing Lawn.* In VDT there is a feast at Lord Bern's* house and another at Narrowhaven.* The Duffers* serve the Dawn Treaders a hearty meal, and the feast at Aslan's Table* on Ramandu's Island* is replenished each day. In SC, banners,* trumpets, and kettledrums announce each course of the supper at Cair Paravel. During the feast celebrating the justice over Rabadash,* Aravis and Cor hear real Narnian poetry and song. The complete lack of revelry and the overwhelming sadness of LB is a sign that the very heart has gone out of Narnia.

[*Autumn Feast; Wine.*]

REVILIAN   One of the Seven Noble Lords.* He is one of the four Narnian visitors to the Island of the Voices* in 2299–2300 N.Y., and one of the three who is found at Aslan's Table* in an enchanted sleep* on Ramandu's Island.*

(VDT 16, *23;* 149, *149;* 168, *165.*)
[*Three Sleepers.*]

RHINCE   The first mate on the *Dawn Treader,* he is an old salt who hopes to be home before his supply of tobacco runs out. He is talking with Lucy when the Lone Islands* are first sighted. Throughout the rest of the voyage, Rhince is often heard to remark what everyone else, including the reader, might be tempted to say. He says "good riddance" when Eustace is missing and presumed dead; and upon seeing the dead dragon,* he mutters that Eustace probably poisoned him: "he'd poison anything." Even Lucy feels the bite of his tongue when he calls her description of the fragrance on Ramandu's Island* "rot."

The *Dawn Treader* is under his command when the other adventurers go ashore at the Land of the Duffers.* He and his men are amused at the way the monopod creatures can sail on their one giant foot, and they have great fun sponsoring races for the Duffers.* At Dark Island,* Rhince and his fellows at first agree with the Captain's advice not to venture further into the darkness. Later they verge on changing their minds, mistakenly thinking Dark Island a land where daydreams come true. Upon learning how treacherous a place it is, they threaten mutiny.

At Ramandu's Island, Rhince's forthrightness returns, and he is all for "falling to" the sumptuous banquet on Aslan's Table.* But he and his men see the wisdom of Caspian's warning that the food might be harmful. Having greeted Ramandu and his daughter with due respect, they are eager to winter on the Island, especially after hearing that Aslan's Table will provide their daily banquet. Ultimately, the crewmen are persuaded to continue the voyage by Caspian's directive to Drinian* and Rhince to select for the journey only "the hardiest in battle, the most skilled seamen, the purest in blood, the most loyal to [the King's] person, and the cleanest of life and manners." Of course, no one (except perhaps Pittencream*) wants to be left out of such august company. Some of the crew even fawn on Drinian and Caspian to make sure they are chosen for this ultimate voyage.

(VDT 20, *28; 29, 36;* 72, *79;* 77, *84;* 109, *112;* 147, *147;* 152 passim, *152 passim.*)
[*Dreams; Daughter of Ramandu; Rynelf.*]

RHINDON   The name of Peter's sword, one of his gifts* from Father Christmas.* It has a hilt of gold, and fits in a sheath and belt. He uses it to slay Fenris Ulf* (Maugrim).

(LWW 104, *100;* 127–129, *120–121.* PC 25, *30.*)

RHOOP   One of the Seven Noble Lords,* first mentioned by Coriakin* as one of the four Telmarine* visitors to the Land of the Duffers* in 2299–2300 N.Y. A prisoner on Dark Island,* he is first identified by his cry "made inhuman by terror." He begs to be taken aboard the *Dawn Treader* even if it means death or worse—if it is only a dream: "In the name of all mercies, do not fade away and leave me in this horrible land." When he is welcomed aboard the ship, his appearance is that of a man who has known harrowing experiences. Pale, gaunt, and wild looking, he wears only a few wet rags and though he is not old his hair is completely white. His wide-open eyes stare "as if in an agony of pure fear." He urges those on board to row for their lives, and he is enraged at the naiveté of the sailors who think it would be ideal to live in a place where all one's dreams* come true. Rhoop tells them that there is a great difference between daydreams and dreams. Ignoring this difference got him imprisoned on Dark Island, a fate that made him wish he had never been born. As the ship tries to leave the island, Rhoop lies in a heap on the deck for several minutes. But when the crew panics, fearing they will never escape the darkness, he lets out a screaming laugh affirming their fears: "What a fool I was to have thought they would let me go as easily as that."

The ship does finally enter daylight, and Rhoop is speechless; tears of joy* line his face as he stares at the sun and the sea and repeatedly feels the bulwarks to make sure what is happening is real. He introduces himself by name; and having learned Caspian's identity, he begs the favor of never being asked anything about his experiences on the Dark Island—a request readily granted.[1] When the voyagers disembark at Ramandu's Island,* Rhoop at first stays on board, wanting no more of islands.

Later Caspian describes Rhoop's condition to Ramandu,* who suggests that he can give the weary Lord what he needs most—a long, uninterrupted sleep without a hint of dreams. When Rhoop finally does leave the ship to join the group, he sits down next to the Lord Argoz* at Aslan's Table.* There

Ramandu gently places his hand on the head of the exhausted Lord; and Rhoop, a momentary smile on his haggard face, slips into a deep and peaceful sleep.* He is not mentioned again in the *Chronicles.*

(VDT 155 ff., *154 ff.;* 181–182, *178;* 186, *182.*)

---

[1] In the British editions, Rhoop's request is a simple plea, "Never to bring me back there," followed by everyone looking in the direction he points and discovering that the Dark Island has disappeared altogether. Because Lewis felt that this might lead children to expect that such fears could be eliminated from life, he rewrote this section for the American editions of VDT, in which Rhoop's request is elaborated, Caspian responds, and the island recedes in the distance. For a complete discussion of these differences, see *Dreams.*

RIGHT AND WRONG   Lewis believed there was a clear distinction between right and wrong; between morality and immorality; and between good acts and bad acts.[1] With the proper education, any person should be able to develop the stock responses* to allow that person to know that good is to be done and evil* is to be avoided.[2] When Digory asks his Uncle Andrew* whether anything was "wrong" about Mrs. Lefay,* he replies with a chuckle, "Well, it depends on what you call *wrong.*" The evil in Andrew's outlook and activities is echoed and amplified to its most terrible consequences in Jadis's use of the Deplorable Word* to destroy Charn.* Like him, she has broken oaths* and paid a terrible price to learn her magic*; like Andrew with his guinea pigs, she does what she wishes with her people because she thinks she owns them; like him, she pleads that her role in society exempts her from ordinary moral considerations; and like him, her greedy look betrays her lack of principle. Digory is capable of following either the right or the wrong path; although he is initially overcome by the witch's beauty, he is eventually repelled by her. Ultimately, he is tested in the garden* of the west, from which he must bring a silver apple* back to Aslan without eating or stealing it. The element of potential pleasure[3] lends an ambiguity to the distinction between right and wrong. When Digory smells the silver apple he has plucked in the garden of the west, he has "a terrible thirst and hunger . . . and longing to taste the fruit." It suddenly seems right that he should do so, even though he knows it to be wrong. Digory has been brought up correctly, however, and knows it is wrong to steal and wrong to break promises. He resists; but Jadis does not. When Digory returns the apple, untouched, to Aslan, the Lion explains that the fragrance of the Tree of Protection* will be a horror to the witch, because "that is what happens to those who pluck and eat fruits at the wrong time and in the wrong way. The fruit is good, but they loathe it ever after."

The problem of right and wrong does not exist in Aslan's country,* because just as there is no evil in that place, it is also impossible to do wrong there.[4]

---

[1] And this distinction is the cornerstone of Lewis's argument for the existence of God in *Mere Christianity* (New York: Macmillan Publishing Co., 1960; London: Collins Fount, 1977).

[2] The instinctive and educated knowledge of what is good and what is evil is called conscience. In the *Chronicles,* it is often expressed as the feeling "deep down inside" that something ought to be done or ought to be avoided.

[3] Lucy experiences intense pleasure in the spell for the refreshment of the spirit that she reads in the magician's Book,* and desires to read it again. But the pages cannot be turned back. Lewis says there is nothing wrong with her experience of pleasure, but there *is* something wrong with the wish to experience pleasure over again, which he calls "the desire for an encore." He even speculates that the root problem with money is that it can purchase for us an unlimited number of encores. Recall Ransom's experience with the fruit in *Perelandra* (New York: Macmillan Publishing Co., 1962) pp. 42–43, 48, 50, 83.

[4] See *Letters to Malcolm: Chiefly on Prayer* (New York: Harcourt Brace Jovanovich, 1964) pp. 114–117, for a discussion about the absence of morality in heaven.

RILIAN   A king of Narnia, the son of King Caspian X and the Daughter of Ramandu.* Throughout most of SC he is held captive by the enchantment of the Queen of Underland,* who killed his mother when the prince was about twenty years old. Seeking to avenge his mother's death, Rilian instead falls under the witch's spell and goes to live with her in her underground kingdom. The story of Rilian's enchantment and subsequent disenchantment is superficially a story of the illusions of romantic love, but beneath that is the grim plot of the Queen of Underland to invade and rule Narnia. Rilian is first met as the mysterious Black Knight who accompanies the equally mysterious Lady of the Green Kirtle across Ettinsmoor.* Because he wears no identifying device on his shield, and "no banneret[1] on his spear," there is no way to know his identity.

When Rilian is at last met in Underland* by Jill, Eustace, and Puddleglum —who have been commanded by Aslan to save Rilian and restore him to the throne—he is about thirty years old. He has been held captive for a decade, and though he is still handsome and kind-looking, the enchantment gives an odd cast to his face. Lewis comments that he looks "a bit like Hamlet," the tragic prince of Denmark; indeed, Prince Rilian speaks in Elizabethan language throughout. His first words to the travelers, "What coil are you keeping down there, Mullugutherum*?" is an allusion to Shakespeare.[2] In his enchanted state he is silly and talkative, and engages his would-be saviors in an exercise in reductionism* concerning the signs.*

Rilian has no memory of who he is except for one hour each night, when he returns to his normal state and must be strapped into a Silver Chair* to be prevented from leaving Underland. This state, however, he perceives during the rest of the time as a fit. All of his reactions are, in fact, upside down. In his enchantment he is convinced that his "all but heavenly Queen" has *saved* him from an evil enchantment, which is how he thinks of his one hour of normality. He asks the three travelers to stay with him during his "fit," so that he will not be alone, but to pay no attention to anything he may say in his altered state. In his sanity, however, he tells them his story and begs them in Aslan's name* to release him. This throws the rescuers into a crisis: the fourth sign has been been spoken, but it is so unlike what they thought it would be that they debate about whether or not to obey.

Once released, Rilian looks his most insane as he leaps to destroy the Silver Chair and end his captivity. When he is finished, the "something wrong" in his face has vanished, he remembers himself once again, and he announces that he is the very Prince Rilian whom they have come to save. He and Eustace finally avenge his mother's death by decapitating the Queen in her serpent form. After their adventures* with the Earthmen* in Bism, they return to Narnia to see King Caspian once more before he dies. Rilian is recognized immediately by the dwarfs* and animals* who are enjoying the Great Snow Dance,* and he proceeds to Cair Paravel on Trumpkin's* instructions. He meets his father on the King's deathbed, and Caspian blesses his son before he dies. After burying his father, Rilian goes on to rule Narnia well and happily.

---

1 Lewis may be confusing *bannerette,* a small banner, with *bannaret,* a rank between baron and knight, abolished in England in 1611, that was usually conferred on the field of valor.

2 *Comedy of Errors* (III, i.48). "What a coile is there, Dormio? Who are those at the gate?" A *coile* or *coil* is a disturbance. See *Literary allusions.*

RINGS   Four paired rings—two yellow, two green—which Andrew Ketterley* has made from the magic* dust in Mrs. Lefay's* box, and which transport Digory and Polly to the Wood between the Worlds.* Shiny and beautiful, they work only when they touch bare skin (although, like electricity, the magic* will run through one person to another if they are touching). Uncle Andrew, a typical magician, has a limited understanding of how the rings work —he thinks that the yellow rings lead out of our world, and the green rings lead back. Actually, they are far less specific. Since the rings are made of material that originated in the Wood between the Worlds, the yellow rings want to get back to the wood, while the green rings want to go out of the wood. In a telling statement about the essential triviality and trickery of any magic in the presence of God, Aslan tells the children* that they "need no rings" when he is with them, and commands them to bury the rings, which they do—at the foot of the apple tree* in Digory's back yard. Although the Seven Friends of Narnia* resolve to use the rings again and recover them, they are never used.

(MN 9 ff., *17 ff.;* 21 ff., *26 ff.;* Chapter 3 passim; 64–65, *65–66;* 177, *164.* LB 50, *50.*)
[*Transitions.*]

RISHDA TARKAAN   The Calormene* captain who joins with Shift* in the plot to subjugate Narnia by means of the lie about the false Aslan. He is obsequious and throughly corrupt; his first actions in LB are to steal Tirian's* crown and then to tell the lie that he has captured Tirian and Jewel* by skill and courage.* He does not really believe in either Tash* or Aslan, and says that Aslan means no more and no less than Tash. He calls the dwarfs* "children of mud" and offers them as a burnt sacrifice to Tash. He is horrified by the sight of the real Tash, whose name he had invoked without faith, and disappears under the arm of the god to Tash's "own place," presumably hell.*

(LB 26, *29;* 30, *33;* 32, *35;* 100 ff., *91 ff.;* 114–115, *105–106;* 132, *121;* 161–162, *146–147.*)
[*Tashlan.*]

RISHTI TARKAAN   Paternal grandfather of Aravis.

(HHB 33, 37.)
[*Tarkaan; Tisroc.*]

RIVER-GOD   He arises from the waters of the Great River* (accompanied by his daughters, the Naiads*) at Aslan's command to the waters of Narnia to be divine. He has a deep voice, a weedy beard, and a larger than human head crowned by rushes. He considers the bridge at Beruna* to be his chains, and at Aslan's command Bacchus* destroys it. The River-god is one of the seven beings invited by Aslan to the First Council.*

(PC 150, *135;* 192 ff., *169 ff.* MN 117, *109;* 119, *111.*)
[*Gods.*]

RIVER RUSH   A tributary of the Great River,* joining it at the Fords of Beruna.* In ancient days it is a small, young river; but by the time of Prince Caspian it has carved a deep gorge.

(PC 144, *105.*)
[*Geography, Narnian.*]

RIVER SHRIBBLE   A major Narnian river, it marks the boundary between the northern marshes and Ettinsmoor.* Contrary to Puddleglum's misgivings, the river is easily crossed by all the travelers.

(SC 62 ff., *68 ff.*)
[*Geography, Narnian.*]

ROBES, ROYAL   Narnian clothes in general look, feel, and smell good (there is no flannel, starch, or elastic in all of Narnia), and royal robes are no exception. At their coronation King Frank* and Queen Helen* are dressed in "strange and beautiful" clothes, and their long trains are attended by dwarfs* and nymphs.* The clothes of the Narnian embassy to Tashbaan* are comfortable and colored in strong earth tones. In comparison to the fabulous Middle Eastern–style clothes of the Calormenes* and the expensive, jewel-encrusted clothes of the enchanted royalty at Charn,* the royal robes of Narnia are simple and direct. In fact, it may be said that in Narnia "the man makes the clothes" rather than the other way around: King Lune* greets Aravis in his oldest clothes; and the young Tarkheena (who is used to the formality of Calormen) is a bit put off. In comparison to English clothes, Narnian robes are brighter and easier to wear. In a foreshadowing of their later elevation to royalty, the four Pevensie children* borrow coats from the wardrobe* to wear into Narnia. Too big for them, the coats hang down to their heels and look like royal robes. Each thinks the other looks much better and more suited to the landscape. At the end of PC, they must remove their royal robes and change back into their school clothes in order to reenter England* from Narnia—none are at all happy about this prospect, and several Telmarines* typically make fun of their drab outfits. Lewis seems to have the same feeling about school clothes as he does about schools*; the little girls at Gwendolen's* school in Beruna* wear tight, itchy uniforms. Tirian* thinks Jill's and Eustace's clothes are dingy, and in SC the children themselves look dingy in comparison to their Narnian surroundings.

(LWW 52, *54.* SC 27, *35;* 28, *34–35;* 36–37, *43–44.* MN 46–47, *47–48;* 167, *155.* PC 215, *188.* HHB 54–55; *54.* LB 45, *46;* 133–134, *123.*)
[*Banner, standard, crown, coronet.*]

ROGIN   See *Duffle.*

ROONWIT   A great, golden-bearded Centaur* whose voice is as deep as a bull's. Like all Centaurs, he can read the stars*; indeed, in Old Norse, *roonwit* means "he who knows how to read the sacred language." He tells Tirian that he has seen bad portents in the stars all year, and there are disastrous conjunctions of planets in the heavens. He drinks to Aslan and truth; and because the stars never lie, he concludes that the rumor that Aslan is in the country is untrue. Roonwit is sent to rally Narnian forces against the Calormenes,* and much depends on him. But the Calormenes take Cair Paravel and Roonwit is killed by a Calormene arrow. Farsight* the eagle shares the Centaur's last hour, and bears his last message to Tirian*: "Remember that all worlds draw to an end[1] and that noble death* is a treasure which no one is too poor to buy." He is among those who pass the judgment into Aslan's country,* and is the first to raise the cry to go "farther in."

(LB 14, *18;* 57, *57;* 84–85, *78–79;* 91, *85;* 154, *140–141.*)
[*Astronomy, Narnian; Eschatology.*]

---

[1] The same sentiment is voiced by Jewel.*

RUINED CITY OF THE ANCIENT GIANTS   The ruins of an enormous city, formerly inhabited by an ancient race of giants.* It lies north across Ettinsmoor,* just outside the castle of Harfang.* Aslan instructs Jill to find it as her second sign.* The Lady of the Green Kirtle calls it the City Ruinous, and claims she doesn't know where it is. It is so huge that the children and Puddleglum wander through it unknowingly, thinking it is a very strange landscape. From the perspective of her high window at Harfang,* however, Jill and Eustace recognize it at last. The cliff-like ruins of one wall are five hundred feet high, and the broken pavement is dotted with broken pillars, which the children had thought to be factory chimneys. Stairs go up one side and down the other, and across the middle of the pavement are written the letters "UNDER ME." They are carved so deeply that, the day before, the travelers had walked through the second "E" thinking it was a deep trench.

(SC 20, *29;* 62, *67–68;* 75–76, *79–81;* Chapter 7 passim; 101 ff., *104 ff.*)
[*Glimfeather; Queen of Underland.*]

Sorely tempted to disobey Aslan and eat a silver apple from the Tree of Protection, Digory wrestles with his conscience. He is watched by the evil witch and a wonderful, mysterious bird. (MN 158-160, 147-149.)

RUMBLEBUFFIN   A good giant,* freed by the breath of Aslan from imprisonment as a statue in the White Witch's courtyard. Aslan enlists him to break down the gate and the towers of the Witch's castle.* Winded and sweaty from this effort, Rumblebuffin asks for a handkerchief to wipe his brow. When Lucy offers hers, he picks her up bodily, thinking she is the handkerchief. In true giant fashion, he clubs and tramples in battle, but always on the side of good. He is rewarded and honored at the feast of the crowning.

(LWW 166 ff., *153 ff.;* 174, *161.*)
[*Buffin.*]

RYNELF   A sailor on the *Dawn Treader,* fashioned by Lewis after the dutiful, articulate, and experienced seaman of many a sea story. At Narrowhaven,* he brings refreshment to the three children* after they are rescued from Pug.* When the *Dawn Treader* approaches Dark Island,* Rynelf stands in the bow prepared to take soundings. His fear surfaces as he tells Eustace that he hears "them" crawling up the sides of the ship.[1] As the adventurers escape from the darkness, he is the first to perceive a speck of light.[2]

On Ramandu's Island,* he seeks to persuade his fellow crewmen to continue the journey by pointing out that they had come on board as volunteers in search of adventure* and that many in Narnia would have given anything to have come in their place. When the ship arrives at the Last Sea,* Rynelf brings the bucket that Caspian uses to draw up some of the sweet water. He is one of those in the small boat who investigate the mysterious whiteness of the Silver Sea.* When Caspian argues his right to remain behind and continue to the Utter East,* Rynelf has the temerity to suggest that this would be desertion. The prince rebukes him for presuming too much on his long service. Nothing further is mentioned of this loyal sailor in the *Chronicles.*

(VDT 9, *17;* 153 ff., *153 ff.; 159;* 183, *179;* 198, *193;* 205 ff., *199 ff.*)

---

[1] This remark is incorrectly attributed to Rhince* in the American editions.
[2] In the British editions Rynelf speaks the line, "I reckon we've made pretty good fools of ourselves." To correct any impression that night-fears are foolish, Lewis deletes this line in the American edition in his complete revision of the ending of chapter twelve, "The Dark Island," in VDT. See *Dreams* for a complete discussion of these changes.

SAFE, SAFETY   See *Comfort.*

SALAMANDERS OF BISM   Small, dragon*-like creatures that live in the rivers of fire[1] in Bism and, like the sun,* are too white-hot to be looked at directly. They are very eloquent. When a hissing voice announces the closing of the rift of Bism, Lewis notes that the four travelers are not sure if it is the voice of Fire itself or of a salamander.

(SC 181, *176*.)
[*Golg; Underland.*]

---

[1] Lewis reflects an ancient belief, to which Pliny refers in his *Natural History* (X, 86 and XXIX, 23). Paracelsus (Theophrastes Bombastus von Hohenheim, 1490–1541) later designated a creature to inhabit each of the elements: Salamanders or Vulcans in fire, Gnomes or Dwarfs* in earth, Sylphs or Silvans* in air, and Undines or Nymphs* in water (Lewis, *The Discarded Image* [London: Cambridge University Press, 1964] p. 135).

SALLOWPAD   The large raven in the Narnian embassy to Calormen* in 1014 N.Y. He has a birdseye view on everything, and is the most informed about the Great Desert* and possible routes across it. His is the voice of wise counsel in the deliberations of Edmund, Susan, and the Narnians who are hostage to Rabadash's* whim. Like many an elder statesman, he is inclined to use proverbs. His name, appropriate for a raven, means "yellow-footed."

(HHB 61 ff., *59 ff.*; 87, *80*.)
[*Birds; Talking Beasts.*]

SARAH   Uncle Andrew's* housemaid. She is the unnamed servent whom Andrew sends to call a hansom cab, and the maid who finds the morning of Queen Jadis's arrival to be "beautifully exciting." Later she stands at the door watching the fun when Digory, Polly, and Uncle Andrew return.

(MN 76, *74*; 81, *77*; 179, *166*.)
[*Betty; Ivy; Margaret.*]

SATYRS   In Greek and Roman mythology,* wood gods* who have goat legs, pointed goat ears, and sprouting horns, and who are considered to be quite lascivious; they look more like goats than do fauns,* who are only half-goats. One of the Nine Classes of Narnian Creatures,* they are among the wild people who emerge from the wood at Aslan's command to Narnia to awaken.[1] Reddish-brown in color, satyrs are seen feasting at the squirrel's* party in LWW, and the Kings and Queens* free young satyrs from the drudgery of attending school.* Jill sees satyrs together with fauns at Cair Paravel. Wraggle,* the only named satyr in the *Chronicles*, fights against Tirian* in the Last Battle.* They are summoned to judgment at the Stable* Door* with all the living creatures at the End of Narnia.*

(LWW 111, *105*; 166, *153*; 180, *166*. PC 47, *50*; 80, *76*. SC 29, *36*. MN 117, *109*. LB 118, *109*; 152, *138*.)

---

[1] Like all mythological creatures in the *Chronicles*, they are not expressly created by Aslan.

SCEPTRE   The royal staff or rod, the symbol of the authority of the Emperor-beyond-the-Sea,* Aslan's Father. The words of the Deep Magic* are engraved on it. Nothing more is said of it; but as a symbol of good power, it is to be contrasted with the Witch's wand.*

(LWW 138, *128.*)

SCHOOLMISTRESS OF UNNAMED TOWN   First encountered unhappily teaching arithmetic to a group of pig-like boys, she responds joyously to Aslan's invitation to join him. Aslan calls her "Dear Heart."

(PC 196, *172.*)
[*Dance.*]

SCHOOLS   Lewis considered schools a necessary evil,*[1] and the schools mentioned in the *Chronicles* reflect this. The trouble with schools in general, Lewis hints, is that instead of teaching values through stories* they teach dry subjects. When Professor Kirke wonders in LWW what they teach children* these days, he is implying that they certainly do not teach them about adventure,* and especially about the adventure of faith. Children in the Narnian adventures simply do not want to go to school. In PC, the Pevensie children consider themselves lucky to have been swept into Narnia just at term-time,* and Shasta (now Cor) laments that Bree will have a much better time because he does not have to get an education. Mythological creatures seem to be metaphors for the free spirits of children in at least two instances: one of the first commands of the new Kings and Queens* is that the young dwarfs* and satyrs* be released from the bondage of school; when Gwendolen* leaves the girls' school at Beruna* to join Aslan, the Maenads* free her from her tight school uniform.

Although Lewis dislikes most schools, he particularly dislikes modern schools like Experiment House.* Here bullies are treated like interesting psychological cases instead of being punished, and ordinary children live in terror. Although Jill has somehow managed to see pictures of mythological creatures, Eustace is a victim of his education, at least at first. He actually enjoys looking at pictures of foreign children doing exercises, and knows nothing of adventure or honor.* In fact, he is well on his way to becoming a model civil servant in the government* of England* when he is transported into Narnia. It is here that his real education begins, and Jill notes that he seems more a product of Narnia than Experiment House.

Headmasters are not well-treated in the *Chronicles;* the fate of the Head* is especially ironic. Trumpkin* is compared to a crusty but lovable old headmaster, and the loud greeting of Puddleglum fades to a dead silence* comparable to the silence that falls over a dormitory when the headmaster unexpectedly arrives. Doctor Cornelius* is the only likable educator in the *Chronicles.* Although he teaches Caspian the usual dry subjects, he also teaches him the truth and awakens him to his destiny.

(LWW 177, *163;* 180, *166;* 186, *171.* PC 15, *22;* 43, *47;* 52–53, *54;* 193, *170.*
VDT 169, *167;* 187, *182.* SC 1 ff., *11 ff.;* 29, *36;* 47, *53–54;* 199, *191.* HHB
201, *176;* 147, *159.*)
[*Adults; Alberta Scrubb; Autobiographical allusions; Books; Gang, the; Knowledge;
Stories.*]

---

[1] Lewis's own experiences in school were not happy. He learned French and Latin from his
mother, and other primary subjects from a governess, all at home. A month after his mother's
death in late August of 1908, the nine-year-old Lewis began almost six years of misery in boarding
schools. So bitter was his experience of his first headmaster, the Rev. Robert Capron (who was
certified insane in 1910 and died in 1911), that Lewis was able to forgive this cruel man only in
the last years of his own life (see Clyde S. Kilby, ed., *Letters to an American Lady* [Grand Rapids:
Wm. B. Eerdmans Publishing Co., 1967] p. 117, letter of July 6, 1963). In the fall of 1914 Lewis
began three of the happiest years of his life living with his tutor, W. T. Kirkpatrick. For details,
see Lewis's autobiography, *Surprised by Joy* (New York: Harcourt Brace Jovanovich, 1955; London: Collins Fontana, 1959); and *C. S. Lewis: A Biography,* by Roger Lancelyn Green and Walter
Hooper (New York: Harcourt Brace Jovanovich, 1974; London: Collins, 1974); and the excellent
"Chronology of the Life of C. S. Lewis," published by the New York C. S. Lewis Society. For
Lewis's criticism of education, see his *Abolition of Man* (New York: Macmillan Publishing Co.,
1965). And for perhaps the best commentary on Lewis's educational thought, see Gilbert Meilaender, *The Taste for the Other* (Grand Rapids: Wm. B. Eerdmans Publishing Co., 1978) especially
pp. 179–234.

SEA PEOPLE   Inhabitants of the Last Sea,* they are a race of aquatic
beings (not to be confused with the Mer-People,* who are amphibious). Their
cities are sea-mounds, their farms and pastures the shallows, their places of
danger (and therefore of adventure*) the sea valleys. This inversion of human
experience in which the valleys are our havens and the mountains our challenges is another instance of Lewis's deliberate dislocation of our imaginations.* Lucy is the first to see Sea People, a hunting party comprised of royalty,
knights* and ladies, all mounted on sea-horses and "hawking" with hunting*
fish instead of falcons. They appear to be a fierce people, immediately challeng-
ing the threat of the *Dawn Treader* sailing overhead. It is in answer to this
challenge that the courageous Reepicheep dives overboard and thereby discovers that the waters of the Last Sea are sweet. Superstitious (as are most men
of the sea), Lord Drinian* thinks the Sea People unlucky. As if to contradict
this suspicion, Lewis seems to make a great deal of the instant friendship[1] that
grows up between Lucy and the Sea Girl, a fish-herdess wandering alone with
her flock in the shallows of the Last Sea. Lucy is ever the figure of the person
who sees beyond what other people see to the possibilities of love and understanding.

(VDT 193–196, *188–191;* 202–203, *197–198.*)

---

[1] Friendship, for Lewis, was a gift; a spontaneous spark between strangers. If this recognition
of mutuality is acknowledged and given time to grow, it can develop into a real friendship. See
The Four Loves (New York: Harcourt Brace Jovanovich, 1960) pp. 87–127, esp. 96–97.

SEA SERPENT   A sea monster, which appears horrifying but acts stu-
pidly. Encountered by the *Dawn Treader* on its journey from Burnt Island* to
Deathwater Island,* it is attacked by Eustace and pushed off the boat by the

whole crew. The Sea Serpent is mentioned with the squid and the Kraken* as the three dangerous beasts of the deep that are feared by the Sea People.*

(VDT 96, *101;* 193, *188.*)
[*Mythology.*]

SECRET HILL   The expression "fire-stones of the Secret Hill*'' is found only in the British editions of LWW. In the heated exchange between the White Witch and Aslan, she alludes to the fact that the words of the Deep Magic* are deeply carved, like runes, into the fire-stones of the Secret Hill. No specific place is probably intended here, but Lewis may have used the term to evoke in the imaginations* of his British readers pictures of annual druidical rites throughout the British Isles in which the old year's fires were extinguished and the new fire was kindled at a sacred place, usually a low, round hill. The fire-stones were set in a permanent ring on the crown of the hill. No biblical allusion* is intended.[1]

(LWW *128.*)
[*World Ash Tree.*]

---

[1] Professor Thomas W. Craik comments that "the virtue of . . . 'fire-stones of the Secret Hill' is that [it is] suggestive and not precise. . . . [It] is not . . . an actual allusion (certainly neither to Hell or to Mount Sinai!), though to the Witch and to Aslan it evidently has meaning. But its suggestions are sinister, with a hint of (human?) sacrifice, and this is enough for Lewis's purpose. The depth of the letters, and the spear-image, reinforce the idea of an inescapable and deadly law." (Letter to author dated July 31, 1979.)

SECURITY   See *Comfort.*

SERPENT   See *Queen of Underland.*

SEVEN BROTHERS OF THE SHUDDERING WOOD   Red Dwarfs* who live among rocks and fir trees on the northern slopes of the mountains that border Narnia on the south. They are blacksmiths and armorers and work at an underground forge, where the blows cause the surrounding woods to shudder. Once they become convinced of Caspian's kingship, they give generous gifts of armor of the finest workmanship. They are also in attendance at the Great Council* and take active part in the War of Deliverance.*

(PC 70–72, *69–70;* 80, *76.*)
[*Geography, Narnian.*]

SEVEN FRIENDS OF NARNIA   They are Digory Kirke, Polly Plummer, Peter Pevensie, Lucy Pevensie, Edmund Pevensie, Eustace Clarence Scrubb, and Jill Pole.[1] These seven Sons of Adam* and Daughters of Eve are killed in a railroad accident in 1949. They are first called Friends of Narnia by Tirian,* who calls for their help in saving Narnia from its last great challenge. Tirian is somehow able to see through to our world, and as if in a dream* glimpses the seven friends. They in turn recognize Tirian as a Narnian and Eustace and Jill are dispatched to his aid.

(LB 42, *44;* 45 ff., *46 ff;* 183, *165.*)
[*Great Reunion.*]

---

[1] See *Susan Pevensie* for a discussion of her notable exception from this group.

SEVEN ISLES   A cluster of islands, and the third port of call of the *Dawn Treader.* First mentioned in Lucy's revery about past voyages in the Golden Age of Narnia,* they are the furthest limit of the special visionary powers of the Hermit of the Southern Marches.* The two western islands are given names: Muil,* the westernmost; and Brenn,* the capital city of which is Redhaven.* The other five are not named. When the elderly King Caspian sets out on his last voyage in order to seek Aslan's counsel, he intends to visit the Seven Isles.

(PC 107, *99.* VDT 18, *25.* SC 35, *42.* HHB 180, *158.*)
[*Geography, Narnian.*]

SEVEN NOBLE LORDS   Telmarine* lords, feared by Miraz* because of their friendship with Caspian IX.* They are Revilian,* Argoz,* and Mavramorn* (the Three Sleepers);* Octesian,* who met his end on Dragon Island*; Restimar,* transformed into a golden statue on Deathwater Island*; Rhoop,* the victim of the Dark Island;* and Bern,* who is made Duke of the Lone Islands.* Together they are sent by Miraz (who hopes to be rid of them) to explore for any lands that might exist beyond the Eastern Sea,* the end of the then-known world. They are the only Telmarine lords who are not afraid of the sea, but like all Telmarines they were forbidden by Miraz to learn any nautical skills. Thus they must buy a ship from Galma* and man it with Galmian sailors before they can begin their voyage. They have not returned by the time Caspian is told about them by Doctor Cornelius,* on the night that Prunaprismia* has a son. Caspian takes a coronation day oath* to seek for them and avenge their deaths; and the story of VDT is the record of how he fulfills this quest.*

(PC 56, *56.* VDT 16 passim, *23 passim.*)
[*Honor.*]

SEXISM   The issue of sexism in the *Chronicles* is more complex than might at first be supposed.[1] Although the books are filled with superficially sexist references, Lewis's insights into character often reveal a basic sympathy for the equality of women. This sympathy is especially apparent in the last four books (SC, HHB, MN, and LB), in which the female characters are much more realistically drawn than in the earlier books.[2] It is important to note that

---

although HHB was published after SC, it was actually written first; thus Aravis is the pivotal female character in Lewis's growing insight into feminine character.

In the first three books, Lucy especially shows bravery and courage,* but to Lewis's mind (and as Corin* remarks in HHB) these are still boys' qualities, not girls'. In LWW Susan and Lucy are not to be in the battle, not because women aren't brave enough, but because "battles are ugly when women fight." Mrs. Beaver* comments that it's "just like men" to be discussing swords when the tea is growing cold. Peter says to Susan, "Ladies first." All the children are crowned, but only Peter and Edmund are knighted; and only the girls are spoken of in terms of being sought after for marriage. Typical of the faithfulness and supportiveness that are traditionally expected of women, Lucy and Susan are faithful to Aslan in his Gethsemane; and in their compassion they endure the horror of the gore surrounding Aslan's corpse in order to honor* him.

In PC, Edmund says to Trumpkin* and Peter, "That's the worst of girls. They never can carry a map in their heads." Lucy retorts, "That's because our heads have something inside them." Although her reply shows her own self-confidence, it is a tacit admission of the basic truth of his statement. The girls also shudder at the bear-butchery task. Even the trees* are subject to sexism in these early books: the male hollies are referred to as dark, while their wives are "bright with berries." When King Peter kisses Trufflehunter,* Lewis quickly explains that this is "not a girlish thing," because such courtesy* is expected in Narnia. The Duke of Galma* hopes to marry his homely daughter to Caspian X, and not even the compassionate Lucy thinks to look past her freckles and her squint for inner worth.

With the introduction of Eustace, the subject of sexism becomes even more complex. His mother, Alberta Scrubb,* is a vegetarian, a progressive, and a feminist, and it is apparent that Lewis has no love for her. When Caspian gives Lucy his own fine cabin because she is a girl, Eustace complains that to do such a thing is really demeaning to girls. Of course his real motivation is selfish— he wants the fine cabin for himself. Lucy, for her part, has her own sexist opinion of men. "That's the worst of doing anything with boys," she says. "You're all such swaggering, bullying idiots." In the first of several inequalities between men's and women's weapons, Lucy uses a bow and arrow to fight the invisible enemies, while the men use swords; Lewis seems to want to distance Lucy from direct combat. When the Duffers* threaten Lucy in order to get her to undo the spell of invisibility,* she is the only one who behaves bravely. Her innate good sense cuts through to the practical heart of the matter, and the boys actually seem to be embarrassed at her courage and their cowardice.* But this suggests again that boys are supposed to be brave and girls are not. The Daughter of Ramandu* is never named, and even when she is Caspian's wife and Rilian's* mother she is called only the Queen. The company stands in her honor, "because they felt she was a great lady." This may be a sign of Lewis's inability to ascribe the ideal qualities of "greatness" to a specific woman (the same instinct that causes some men to idolize and idealize women in general, but to be dissatisfied with individual, human—and therefore imperfect—women.

With the introduction of Aravis, however, there is real change. In HHB, she flees from Calormen,* where women are chattel, to seek freedom in Narnia, where women are equal to men. Her instincts are always good, and it is the idea of marriage to the despicable Ahoshta Tarkaan* that prompts her escape. She refuses to be pushed around, and she will not accept the role of passive female (nor will her horse,* I Iwin). To Shasta's "Why, it's only a girl!" she bristles, "And what business is it of yours if I am *only* a girl?" She is "proud . . . hard . . . and true as steel," and she never once loses her head. In contrast to Lasaraleen,* the stereotypical fluttery female interested in clothes and men, Aravis has always been more interested in bows and arrows and horses and dogs* and swimming, considered boys' things by Lewis's generation. It is also in HHB that Lewis puts stock responses* to women in the mouths of fools: Rabadash* shows his complete misunderstanding of Aravis herself and women in general (and concocts a plot that leads to his own downfall) when he says ". . . it is well known that women are as changeable as weathercocks."

There is a subplot in HHB between the horses Hwin and Bree, in which Bree's condescension toward the mare shows him up as full of pride and vanity.* Corin, something of a sexist himself, gives implicit though patronizing praise for Lucy when he says that Lucy is ". . . as good as a man, or at any rate as good as a boy. Queen Susan is more like a grown-up lady."[3] When Lucy and Aravis meet, they like one another instantly and go off to talk about ". . . all the sort of things girls do talk about on such an occasion," which Lewis assumes to be clothes. This is a lapse in Lewis's newly nonsexist attitude. It is more likely that the girls would compare notes about battles and journeys, since that is what they have been involved in.

In SC the dichotomy is even stronger. Jill, the primary female character, is perhaps the most real of all the little girls in the *Chronicles*, and her actions are both brave and fearful, just as those of most little girls would be. But in the discussion of Experiment House,* Lewis mentions the Head* "who was, by the way, a woman," implying that the fact of her sex makes her even worse than a male Head. The Eustace of SC is improved but not totally reformed, and he echoes Edmund's comment about maps when he says, "It's an extraordinary thing about girls that they never know the point of the compass." Again, this may be intended as satire on Lewis's part, since Eustace doesn't know which direction is east any more than Jill does. Lewis adds parenthetically that Jill indeed does not know her compass points, but that this does not necessarily apply to all girls. He shows here a nice sensitivity toward his girl readers that is missing from the earlier books. As opposed to Lucy and Susan, who fought with bows and arrows only, Jill carries a knife and is glad of it. Indeed, she becomes more and more assertive as the story progresses. The quest* for Rilian is given to her personally by Aslan; and though Eustace tries to appropriate it for himself at the Parliament of Owls,* Jill takes it back for herself. When Eustace and Jill bow to the giant* king* and queen, Lewis remarks parenthetically that Jill has never learned to curtsey. (He considers this a lack on her part, which shows that he still strongly upholds at least the traditional formalities of sex roles.) Jill shows great awareness when she puts on an obsequious childishness to fool the giants, and Lewis comments that "girls do that kind of thing better than boys." Lewis may be suggesting that girls are naturally more deceitful than boys, but the meaning is not clear.

It is a sign of Rilian's enchantment that he fatuously pats Jill on the head and tells her that she will change her opinion about wife-bossed husbands when she is married herself. In a scene disappointing to many girl readers, Jill does not slay the Queen of Underland* but remains on the sidelines trying not to faint or cry. Although this is certainly a very real reaction, Eustace, Puddleglum, and Rilian are able to overcome their own distaste and do the deed. Rilian later says he's glad the witch was in her serpent form, because he would not have liked to slay a woman. The three men leave the witch's castle with drawn swords, and Jill with drawn knife; even in weapons Jill is creeping up to them in equality since Lucy's day, but she's not there yet. At the beating of the Gang,* Jill still has a unique weapon—a switch turned riding crop—while the boys use the flats of their swords.

Polly, in MN, is not the conventional turn-of-the-century girl. She has made a cave for herself with packing cases, is independently exploring her attic, and keeps treasures that include "a story she was writing." She is the first one into Andrew's* study, but Lewis lets women down again when he makes her attraction to pretty things and Andrew's appeal to her vanity the reasons for her transition* into the Wood between the Worlds.* Uncle Andrew, the evil* magician,* is also a blatant sexist. In defense of his amorality, he says that morality is for little boys and servants and women and people in general; later, when Digory's defense of basic justice and goodness gets through to his uncle, Andrew recovers with a perfect Bulverism*: You only say that because you were brought up among women and learned this natural morality from old wives' tales.

On the other hand, Lewis's stock responses are still operational. It is a sign of Andrew's cowardice that he sends a girl in his stead into the unknown. Lewis assumes that Polly's being a girl means that she would be especially interested in the clothing of the seated figures in the great hall of Charn.* When Polly hits the nail on the head by accusing Digory of covering his own desire to know the unknowable by pretending he is in the grip of an irresistible magic, Digory Bulverises her by attributing her remark to girlish narrowness. In a perfect circle of sexism and misunderstanding she replies, "how exactly like a man." At the First Council,* the Lady Raven is the only female invited. In the scene between the animals* and Andrew, Lewis lets slip that he conceives of his readership as male when he says ". . . no dog I ever knew . . . likes being called a Good Doggie . . . any more than *you* would like being called My Little Man" (my emphasis). Finally, Frank* puts Digory on Fledge's* back with a "rough heave," but places Polly as if she were delicate china. It is interesting to note that Polly never does fulfill the traditional female role, and we learn in LB that she has never married.

By the time of LB, Eustace has gained more respect for Jill's abilities, although Lewis still makes her carry a hunting knife, saying that there was no sword light enough for her to handle. Eustace, however, says that her skill with the bow is "about as good" as his, admitting that neither of them is that great. However, Jill succeeds in killing and preparing a rabbit, the first instance of hunting* by a woman in the *Chronicles*. She has certainly become self-sufficient, and she has at last learned her compass points, probably as a Girl Guide in England.* This time it is she who keeps the travelers on the path, and Tirian* puts her in the lead as the best guide of them all. She has come a long way from trying not to faint and cry, and is now brave enough to investigate the Stable* on her own, with knife drawn and ready. The men, however, still operate from their old sexist viewpoint: Eustace says that if she were a boy she'd have to be a knight* (implying that a girl can't receive such an honor); and Tirian says that if she were a boy she'd have to be whipped (implying that it is unmanly to whip a girl). She is still compassionate and supportive, however, and she saves Puzzle* from death* at the hands of Tirian. When Tirian tells Jill and Eustace that they must go home to avoid the bloody battle that will follow, Jill protests that they have not yet done what they came to do, and she does not shrink from danger. Although both children later admit that they are scared, Jill declares that she would "rather be killed fighting for Narnia than grow old and stupid at home."[4]

(LWW 104–105, *100–101;* 106, *101;* 123, *117;* 145 ff., *134 ff.,* 154–155, *142–143.* PC 114–115, *105;* 151, *136;* 167, *149.* VDT 25, *32;* 107, *111;* 116, *118;* 121–122, *123–124;* 153, *153.* SC 7, *16;* 23, *32;* 31, *39;* 43, *49;* 46, *53;* 71, *76;* 85–86, *89;* 94, *97;* 109–110, *111–112;* 138–139, *138;* 161, *158–159;* 173, *169;* 214–215, *204–205.* HHB 28, *33;* 34–37, *37–40;* 81, *76;* Chapter 8 passim; Chapter 9 passim; 131, *116–117;* 176, *154;* 205, *179.* MN 4, *12–13;* 13, *20;* 18, *23;* 25, *29;* 46 ff., *46 ff.;* 119, *111;* 130, *120;* 146, *135;* 184, 169. LB 54 ff., *55 ff.;* 118–119, *109–111;* 135, *123–124;* 161, *146;* 165, *150.*)

---

[1] Lewis felt that the basic distinction in nature is between that which engenders and that which is engendered; and that before God we are all feminine. "What is above and beyond all things is so masculine that we are all feminine in relation to it." *(That Hideous Strength* [New York: Macmillan Publishing Co., 1965; London: Pan Books, 1955] p. 316, *194.*)

[2] It must be said that in the second phase of the creative energy that produced the *Chronicles* —the phase that produced the last four books—Lewis's female characters, Jill and Polly, reflect a writer more in touch with the reality of women and therefore more willing to see them as free individuals, capable of exploding cultural strictures and stereotypes. This must be attributed to his growing correspondence with women readers, especially those seeking his advice in spiritual matters; to his firsthand relationships with female students and colleagues and with the wives of his male students and colleagues; and to his female friends, especially Pauline Baynes, Dorothy Sayers, Stella Aldwinckle, Ruth Pitter, Joy Davidman (later Lewis's wife), and Lady Dunbar of Hempriggs (Mrs. Moore's daughter Maureen, Lewis's "foster-sister," who is only eight years Lewis's junior and with whom he lived from late 1920 to the summer of 1941, the year of her marriage).

[3] This is also a comment on the difference between Lewis's conception of the values of adults* and children,* and a foreshadowing of Susan's later fall from grace.

[4] This comment smacks of ageism on Lewis's part, and indeed he did have trouble writing realistically about elderly men and women. See *Adults.*

SHADOW LANDS   See *Plato.*

SHAR   See *Darrin.*

SHASTA   The Calormene* name for Prince Cor, the lost son of King
Lune* of Archenland,* elder twin of Corin* Thunder-Fist,* unwilling companion, then friend, and finally husband of Aravis Tarkheena, and father of
Ram* the Great. His recovery of his identity as free-born son of a northern
king and his preparation to become the compassionate and just ruler of Archenland is the main story* in HHB. His becoming a horseman is a picture
of how much he has to learn to control himself and even push himself in order
to gain true freedom.* Bree, as an experienced horse, can teach him much in
this regard; but Bree's own blindnesses (his vanity and his reactions to his long
years of stifling himself in Calormen) aren't enough to form Shasta. Before he
is ready to become a king, the boy needs to meet Aravis and Hwin, to pass
through the fear* of the tombs and the trial of the Great Desert,* and finally
to be sent on by the Hermit* to experience Aslan both in the foggy night on
the pass and the bright morning of southern Narnia. Like Bree, Shasta has
picked up bad habits in Calormen and he knows little about the ways of free
people; his harsh upbringing leads him to expect nothing but ill-treatment and
duplicity from adults. But he does have an innate sense of faithfulness and
nobility, the foundation on which his character will be built.

From the first pages of HHB the reader knows of Shasta's longing to go
north, a sure sign, says Bree, of his northern heritage. When the two decide
to throw in their lot with each other, Bree begins Shasta's lessons in horsemanship.* The boy grows gradually more skilled and less sore. When the lions*
force the two horses and riders together, Shasta gives up hope of escaping
death* and also experiences the clarity such fearful circumstances often bring:
he notices everything about the other rider. Hearing a girl's voice, Shasta
exclaims in relief but also in a bit of sexist* arrogance, "Why, it's only a girl."
Aravis replies almost in kind and they begin their tumultuous relationship.
Shasta is quite dejected at Aravis's snub and tries to put on high-class airs,
which makes him look and feel more ridiculous. And he and she feel silently
indicted by their horses' ability to get along with one another.

When Aravis completes her story, Shasta is concerned about the maidservant she has abused, as anyone who had been similarly mistreated would be.
His concern also comes from his sense of fairness, a quality that will be tested
when he is sent on by the Hermit without rest to warn King Lune of Rabadash's* invasion. Bree makes many jokes at Shasta's expense when the horse
tells his story to Aravis and Hwin. The boy increasingly feels left out by the
exclusive conversations of Bree and Aravis. Shasta shows a fine conscience
when he calls stealing what Bree calls raiding, as earlier he was reluctant to
take from Bree's master's saddlebags.

Through Shasta, the reader feels the excitement of the sights and smells*
and sounds of Tashbaan.* He is solicitous for Aravis as they cross into the city,
but his concern is rebuffed by her arrogant assumption that she ought to be
borne into the city by soldiers and slaves. He doesn't cry long at the harsh blow
he receives from the soldier—this is treatment he is used to. The reader sees
the impressive Narnian men through Shasta's enthralled eyes. Mistaken for the
missing Corin, Shasta is caught in a double bind: he does not want to betray

Tied to a tree by the Calormenes and left to be killed by the followers of the false Aslan, Tirian is fed by three mice, two moles, and a rabbit. (LB 35-38, 38-40.)

his companions and so he is silent; but this silence betokens disrespect for King Edmund, whom he would very much like to impress. Significantly, Edmund is the first adult* Shasta admires. And for the first time in his life, people make much of him. This, and the comforts of their accommodations, lull him into forgetting how he can rejoin his companions. Out of a deeply rooted habit of suspicion of adults, he does not reveal his true identity. He has no idea of how free people behave, so he misjudges their character by assuming they will hate Aravis[1] because she is a Calormene woman, and kill him for overhearing their plans. And he is not able to recognize his twin when Corin arrives because he has never seen himself in a mirror. In answer to Corin's question, "Who are you?" Shasta replies that he's nobody of any consequence. This scene shows that he has much to learn about how valuable he is and what his identity, as a person providentially cared for and called to kingship, will be. He and his brother become instant friends.

At the tombs on the edge of the Great Desert, Shasta's fear causes him to imagine that Aravis and Bree have deserted him. This is the second misjudgment of character he has made. He is frightened by the thought of ghouls.* A cat comes along and leads him to a safer place, where he is able to sleep.[2] His dreams* are of his companions.

The next morning Shasta raids for his breakfast—he still feels a twinge of conscience at this—and has a refreshing swim. But Lewis comments that the good effect of the swim is wiped out by his mounting anxiety throughout the day. He experiences great relief when Aravis discharges the groom; and he envies the way she is able to swing up onto Hwin.

The journey across the desert[3] is felt by the reader primarily through Shasta. He is embarrassed by the fact that he cannot walk on the hot sand the way Aravis can, and he reproaches her. She says nothing but her prim look, meant or not, aggravates the boy. He has one of the loveliest moments of his life when he plunges into the pool of water that they discover. The sudden abatement of their trial and the comforts of the place prompt all four to rest more deeply than they ought.

As Chapter 10 begins, Lewis's focus is on Shasta; as the description of Archenland unfolds, the pronoun *he* in the sentence, "He could no longer make out Mount Pire," is given without an antecedent in the previous two pages. The freshness and greenness of the landscape is something that neither Aravis nor Shasta, raised in Calormen, had ever imagined could exist. When the lion roars behind them, Shasta recognizes him as the same one who had scared the four of them together weeks before. The trials of the desert crossing are beginning to take their toll even on Shasta's generous heart: he begins to blame events, fate, for being unfair to him. He doesn't dwell on this for long, however, because his selflessness moves him to try to aid Aravis and Hwin against the lion. When he can't get Bree to help, he drops to the ground, hurting himself; but he is heedless of his own pain as he runs back to confront the lion.

He no sooner sees the Hermit than he is given a new assignment: to run immediately to King Lune. Shasta experiences two reactions: his fatigue tells him he hasn't the strength to go on; and his lack of experience of the consequences of freedom[4] leads him to feel a violent conflict within himself—"he *writhed* inside"—over what he feels is cruel and unfair treatment. But the only thing he says aloud is to ask where the king is. Lewis means for his readers to cheer at the magnanimity Shasta shows.

In the eleventh chapter,[5] Shasta finds himself running out of sheer obedience—this is what Lewis means by saying that he has "nothing to think about and no plans to make: he [has] only to run and [this is] quite enough." He finds himself among King Lune's hunting party and alerts him to the danger from Rabadash. When Shasta mounts the horse they offer him, Lord Darrin* remarks on what a true horseman the boy is, a remark that pleases Shasta deeply—he has almost become the horseman Bree has tutored him to be. However, one vital element in his training has been omitted: how to use the reins and spurs to direct and motivate the horse. Soon the boy finds himself hopelessly lost in the fog, growing more and more sorry for himself: he feels that he is the most unfortunate person who has ever lived, that nothing goes right for him, that he is continually left behind, sent ahead, and left out. It is at this moment that he becomes aware of the Presence walking beside him. After he is helped over his fright, he obliges the Presence and tells his many sorrows. The Presence reveals that none of this has been bad luck or misfortune, but rather a providence,* and that He, the Large Voice, has been instrumental in every scene. More than the literal night is ended—Shasta's years of night in which he felt abused by Arsheesh,* unfulfilled longing for the north, and the frustration at what seems purposeless existence have ended in the revelation and the vision of the living and loving Person who has cared for and will always care for him.

Shasta finds himself in Narnia, the object of his quest,* not out of luck but because of providence. He meets his first Narnian Talking Beasts* and is treated to the hospitality* of the dwarfs.* When he is swept into the Narnian cohort that is on its way to help King Lune, he meets his brother Corin again and is properly introduced to King Edmund and Queen Lucy. Shasta's relationships begin to be repaired. He allows himself to be caught up in his brother's scheme to go against his father's orders and fight in the battle, although he would much rather be true to the implicit standard King Edmund sets for him. The fear of battle and his guilt make him feel as though he is in the wrong place. That he is knocked unconscious early in the fight probably keeps him from more serious injury. No sooner does he regain consciousness than he finds himself swept up again, this time into the joy* of his father, who discovers in him his lost son. And though he has many lessons to learn about court manners and about accepting his vocation to be king and the like, he has learned the great lesson of his life, the lesson of providence, of hope and of history*: Aslan "seems to be at the back of all the stories."

---

[1] That he thinks of her first is another instance of his growing consideration of her in all his plans—he is a thoughtful and loyal person.

[2] See *Aslan* for Shasta's experience with the cat and the lion.

[3] See *Great Desert* for commentary on the spiritual significance of this experience.

SHASTA

⁴ One application of this scene that Lewis sees for the spiritual life is that Shasta doesn't know what a vocation is: a call from God to obey at deeper and deeper levels of surrender until one's will is transformed into his will.

⁵ See *Aslan, Aslan's voice, Emperor-beyond-the-Sea, Holy Spirit,* and *Trinity* for discussion of the latter half of this chapter.

SHIFT   An ancient, clever, ugly ape¹ who lives by Caldron Pool* in an otherwise uninhabited area of Lantern Waste.* The name "Shift" is indicative of his manipulative personality: he is "shifty"—underhanded, sneaky, and a liar; and he has a great facility for "shifting" meaning—he redefines the meaning of freedom and Aslan to suit his purposes. He is completely selfish and totally corrupt, and he degenerates perceivably and rapidly from his first conception of Puzzle* as a false Aslan to his death* at the hands of Tash.* His relationship with Puzzle, which he calls a friendship, is really that of master and servant. Shift does not believe in anyone or anything but himself. As an ape, he looks like a man but isn't; in fact, he tries to pass himself off to the animals* as a wise old man.² At the Stable,* he is visibly gangster-like: he is dressed garishly, wears a paper crown, and calls himself "Lord Shift, the mouthpiece of Aslan." Although never as much in control of the deception as he thinks he is (Shift makes several Freudian slips along the lines of "I want —I mean, Aslan wants . . ."), as LB progresses he becomes an alcoholic and yields some power to Rishda.* By the time he gets to the evening assembly at the Stable, he has a hangover and it is no problem for Tirian* to toss the ape through the Door* to his death.

(HHB passim.)
[*Tashlan.*]

---

¹ The ape as figure of great evil has at least one antecedent: cf. "The Antichrist, the Ape" from John Daus, tr., *Bullinger's Hundred Sermons Upon the Apocalypse,* 1573.

² This is a twisted version of Lucy's fear in PC that men might still look like men but be wild inside. See *Dumb Beasts,* note 1.

SHIP   See *Leopard.*

SIGNS¹   Aslan gives Jill and Eustace four signs² by which he will guide them in their quest* for the lost Prince Rilian: (1) Eustace will immediately meet an old, dear friend, whom he is to greet at once; (2) the two must go north until they come to the Ruined City of the Ancient Giants*; (3) they will find there written instructions which they must carry out; and (4) they will know Rilian because he will be the first person to ask them to do anything in Aslan's name. Jill is instructed to remember the signs and believe them, because they will not be anything like what she expects them to be. She must repeat them day and night so that she will not forget them in the thick (in comparison to Aslan's country*) air of Narnia. She promises, but once in Narnia almost everything gets in the way of remembering the signs and she is continually tempted to give it all up. The comfort* and excitement of the trip to Narnia on Aslan's breath* distract her from the first sign; they fail immediately to recognize the Ruined City even when they are walking across it; they do walk right throu̇g̣ words "UNDER ME," but think they are deep trenches; when they do recog̣n̥ the fourth sign, they cannot believe they are meant to obey this madman. It is only due to the insistence of Puddleglum that any of the signs are remembered.

(SC passim.)
[*Earthquakes.*]

[1] The American edition capitalizes the word "Signs"; the British edition does not.
[2] Lewis virtually quotes Deuteronomy 6:418, and it is almost impossible to escape the connection between Jill's signs and the Ten Commandments of the Judaeo-Christian tradition.

SILENCE   Lewis frequently uses the aura of silence to denote the solemnity of a person or activity, and in so doing it often becomes a tool by which characters may face themselves. It is often the best answer to an overwhelmingly good or bad situation, one which no words can describe.[1] In LWW, Peter is silent at his commission to rule; and in PC all are silent for at least a minute at the sight of the treasures of Cair Paravel. There is deep silence between Caspian and Doctor Cornelius* at the revelation of the true history* of Narnia. After Aslan tells Lucy she will find him bigger the older she grows, she is so happy she does not want to speak. In VDT, everyone becomes silent at the departure of the *Dawn Treader,* perhaps because the real adventure* is to begin; Eustace is silent for a long time pondering what happened to him on Dragon Island*; the crew is silent in respect for the obvious greatness of Ramandu* and his Daughter*; there is silence after Reepicheep proclaims that the sweet water is a sign they are near the end of the world*; and the further east they sail, the more everyone is filled with joy* and excitement, "but not an excitement that made one talk." In SC, the "immense silence" of Aslan's country* reminds Jill of mountains; after the slaying of the Queen of Underland* they stand "staring at one another and panting without another word, for a long time." In HHB, Shasta's experience of the glorified Lion causes him to fall at its feet. "He couldn't say anything but then he didn't want to say anything, and he knew he needn't say anything." In MN, the Wood between the Worlds* is "the quietest wood you could possibly imagine." Charn,* on the other hand, is filled with a "dead, cold, empty" silence. At the creation of Narnia,* Frank* has frequently to call for silence to listen to the creation song: "Watchin' and listenin's the thing at present; not talking." At the selection of the pairs of Talking Beasts* from the Dumb Beasts,* there is complete silence for the first time since the creation began.

(LWW 126, *119.* PC 22, *28;* 51, *53;* 136, *124.* VDT 54, *61;* 86, *93;* 176, *173;* 199, *194;* 204, *198.* SC 10, *19;* 15, *24;* 25, *33;* 161, *158;* 199, *191.* HHB 144, *127;* 160, *140;* 193, *169;* 194, *170;* 197, *172.* MN 9, *17;* 29, *31;* 43, *43;* 98 ff., *93 ff.;* 115, *107;* 158, *146;* 164, *152;* 167, *154.* LB 28–29, *32;* 91–92, *85.*)

[1] "The stillness in which the mystics approach [God] is intent and alert—at the opposite pole from sleep or reverie. They are becoming like him. Silences in the physical world occur in empty places: but the ultimate Peace is silent through the very density of life. Saying is swallowed up in being." C. S. Lewis, *Miracles* (New York: Macmillan Publishing Co., 1978; London: Collins Fontana, 1960) p. 93, 97.

SILENUS   In Greek and Roman myth[...]gy,* the drunken attendant of Bacchus* who rides a donkey. He is an expert musician and a regular summer visitor to Narnia, and is of course absent during the Hundred Years of Winter.* In PC, he shows up with Bacchus at the third dance.* Old and enormously fat, he continually falls off his donkey and calls for refreshments—which seems to cause grapevines to grow luxuriantly and produce fruit.[1] Lucy sees a book entitled *The Life and Letters of Silenus* on Tumnus's* bookshelf.

(LWW 12, *19;* 13, *20.* PC 152, *137;* 192, *169.*)
[*Gods; Revelry; Wine.*]

---

[1] For the meaning of the cry, *Euan, Euan, euoi-oi-oi-oi,* see *Bacchus,* note 1.

SILVANS   In Greek and Roman mythology, woodland spirits. They are created (along with the Dryads,* Hamadryads,* wood people,* and gods* and goddesses of the wood) by Aslan's command to Narnia to awake.

(PC 184, *161.* MN 117, *109.*)
[*Trees; Tree-People.*]

SILVER CHAIR   Rilian is tied each night to a "curious silver chair"[1] in his apartments in Underland.* His first free act is to destroy the chair, and as it breaks under his sword "there comes from it a bright flash, a sound like small thunder, and . . . a loathsome smell."

(SC 141, *140;* 146–147, *145–146.*)

---

[1] See John D. Cox, "Epistemological Release in *The Silver Chair,*" in *The Longing for a Form,* Peter Schakel, ed. (Kent, Ohio: Kent State University Press, 1977) and (Minneapolis: Baker Book Publishing Co., 1979) pp. 162–163, 166.

SILVER SEA   The very last part of the Last Sea.* It is named for the white lily-like flowers whose indescribable fragrance, all-pervasive but not overpowering, fills the crew of the *Dawn Treader* with energy. Henceforth no one needs to eat or sleep. Another name by which this region was initially known is Lily Lake.

(VDT 204 ff., *198 ff.*)
[*Smells.*]

SILVER TREE   A tree* made of silver that grows from three silver half-crowns[1] that fall from Andrew Ketterley's* pocket into the rich Narnian soil. Along with the Golden Tree,* it grows inside the cage where Uncle Andrew is kept penned in.

(MN 132, *122;* 168, *155;* 171, *159.*)
[*Toffee Tree; Tree of Protection.*]

---

[1] A sixpence also falls from Uncle Andrew's pockets. Since no other trees are mentioned, it can be assumed that this silver coin was also one of the seeds of the Silver Tree.

SIRENS   See *Literary allusions.*

SLAVE TRADE   The appearance of the slave trade in Narnia always signals a decay in the social structure. Lewis comments that the worst part of being a slave is that one loses one's own will power. In VDT there is a thriving slave market at Narrowhaven,* in which children* and adults* are sold as impersonally numbered lots. Governor Gumpas,* who excuses the practice as an "economic necessity," is removed from office by Caspian and replaced with Lord Bern,* who abolishes the slave trade in the Lone Islands.* In HHB the Tarkaan* and Arsheesh* haggle over the selling price of Shasta, which implies that slavery is a common practice in Calormen.* Calormene slaves are treated very badly, as evidenced by the fact that Rabadash would think nothing of hanging an idle slave. Slavery is widespread in LB under the rule of the degenerate Calormenes, and even Talking Beasts* are harnessed for work. The animals* see that they are being sold into slavery, but Shift says they will be paid wages into Aslan's treasury.

(VDT 33 ff., *41 ff.* HHB 4–7, *14–16;* 107, *97;* 131, *117.* LB 30, *33.*)
[*Government; Joy; Pug.*]

SLEEP   Sleep (and its counterpart, waking) is a complex subject in the *Chronicles,* and operates on several different levels of meaning. In SC, Lewis offers a practical note* when he says, "The sleepier you are, the longer you take about getting to bed." Jill quickly forgets her sleepiness, however, when Glimfeather* takes her to the Parliament of Owls. And he offers a wonderfully realistic description of Shasta drifting off to sleep in the desert. Sleep may also be a gift of oblivion, such as the sleep given Lord Rhoop* after his years of nightmare on the Dark Island*; and the sleep given to Uncle Andrew* (the only gift he is able to receive), which is a temporary rest "from all the torments [he] has desired for [himself]." For the Three Sleepers,* sleep is an enchantment brought on by sacrilege. The apple* from the Tree of Protection* gives Mabel Kirke* her first "real, natural, gentle" drug-free sleep.

Beyond these meanings, however, there is the intimation that what we think of as wakefulness is only a dream,* and that there is another state in which we may be truly awake.[1] When Lucy first hears Aslan's voice* in LWW, she has "a beginning of vacation, waking up in the morning feeling."[2] There is a dreamlike quality to her first vision in PC, in which the trees* almost talk. In her second vision, she knows that the trees are not quite awake, but that she herself is "wider awake than anyone usually is." When Polly and Digory see the swirling vision of Aslan's glory in MN, they suddenly feel as though they have never "really been . . . alive or awake before." That this waking has to do with entrance into Aslan's country* is powerfully apparent in LB, when Jill and Eustace remember that Father Time,* whom they met as he lay dreaming in Underland,* is to wake on the day the world ends. Aslan adds mysteriously, "While he lay dreaming his name was Time. Now that he is awake he will have a new one." This new name is never revealed, but the implication is that time* itself is only a worldly dream. And if there was ever any doubt, at the end of LB Aslan fulfills Lucy's original feeling* back in LWW and tells the inhabitants of his country that now "the term is over: the holidays have begun. The dream is ended: this is the morning."

(LWW 65, *65.* PC 135, *122.* VDT 186, *182.* SC 41, *48.* HHB 129, *115.* MN 171, *158;* 178, *165;* 181, *167.* LB 150, *136;* 183, *165.*)

¹ See *Plato.*
² This is the first of many parallels Lewis makes between term-time* and sleep, and vacation time and waking. Lewis disliked schools,* and he compared life on earth to a finite series of lessons, and death* and entrance into heaven to the beginning of holidays and joy.*

SLINKEY   The only named fox in all of the *Chronicles.* He is on Rishda Tarkaan's* side, and dies at Eustace's hand in the Last Battle.*

(LB 118, *109.*)
[*Talking Beasts.*]

SMELLS   From the smell of fresh fish frying for the Beavers' lunch to the delicious smell of the garden* of the West, the smells of Narnia pervade the *Chronicles.* Smells often communicate visions and emotions: Lucy describes the smell that wafts in from the hills of Ramandu's Island* as "a dim, purple kind of smell"; and later, "the smell of the fruit and the wine* blew towards them like a promise of all happiness." The lilies of the Silver Sea* smell wild and lonely, and the sea itself smells tingling and exciting. A breeze from Aslan's country* bears both a smell and a music* that would break your heart if it could be spoken, but it is not sad.¹ Aslan himself—the transformed wooden horse in Jill's dream*—fills the room with "a smell of all sweet-smelling things there are." Along with all the wonderful smells, there are terrible smells: the "loathsome smell" of the disintegrating silver chair*; the sickeningly sweet smell of the Queen of Underland's* incense; the smells of unwashed dogs* and piles of garbage in the streets of Tashbaan*; and the smell of dead flesh that accompanies the approach of Tash.* The ordinary smells are wonderfully familiar: the "nice, honest, homely smell" of the Stable*; the fusty smell of the meeting room of the Parliament of Owls; the animal* smell of Aslan, who invites Bree to sniff him in friendship. Finally, there is the powerful and mystical smell of the Tree of Protection,* whose fragrance is "joy and life and health" to Narnians, but "death and horror and despair" to the White Witch.

(LWW 70, *70;* 159, *147.* PC 10, *17–18;* 205, *179–180;* 216, *190.* VDT 164, *161;* 166, *163;* 206, *201;* 211, *104.* SC 45, *51;* 100, *103;* 169, *165;* 180, *175.* HHB 49, *49;* 52, *52;* 125–126, *111–112;* 129, *115;* 160, *140;* 193, *169.* MN 156, *144;* 158, *147;* 173, *161;* 181, *167.* LB 80, *75;* 146, *134;* 178, *161.*)
[*Domesticity; Longing; Sounds; Tactile images.*]

¹ The enchanting power of smells—their ability to stir longing—is present in Lewis's earliest Christian work, from the sweetness of the Island in the West in *The Pilgrim's Regress* (Grand

Rapids: Wm. B. Eerdmans Publishing Co., 1958) p. 24, to "the scent of a flower we have not found" in his famous sermon, "The Weight of Glory," in *The Weight of Glory and Other Addresses* (Grand Rapids: Wm. B. Eerdmans Publishing Co., 1965) p. 5, and *Screwtape Proposes a Toast and Other Pieces* (London: Collins Fountain, 1977) p. 98.

SMOKING   Lewis makes several references to pipe smoking in the *Chronicles.* Trumpkin* enjoys smoking his pipe, and its tobacco is "fragrant," which implies Lewis's approval of the activity. The Red Dwarf* brothers Duffle* and Bricklethumb also take a pipe after dinner, and Poggin* (after first asking Jill's and Tirian's* permission) lights an after-breakfast pipe. Smoking is not limited to dwarfs; Marsh-Wiggles* smoke a dark blend (possibly mixed with mud) that is so heavy the smoke floats down instead of up. Master Rhince,* who worries that his tobacco won't last the trip, is the only human being in the *Chronicles* to smoke a pipe.

(PC 34, *40.* HHB 168, *148.* VDT 109, *112.* LB 77, *73.*)

SONGS   See *Music.*

SON OF ADAM, DAUGHTER OF EVE   Used interchangeably with the word human to identify human boys and girls. The use of these phrases by Lewis denotes the theological background against which the stories unfold, and his belief that man and woman have fallen from a primordial state of innocence. It is the only form of address Mr. Beaver* uses to introduce the children* to Mrs. Beaver,* and Aslan uses these titles almost exclusively in addressing the children. Tirian,* beholding Frank* and Helen* in Aslan's country,* feels awe in front of the Adam and Eve of his race.

(LWW 9, *16;* 68, *68;* 76, *76;* 78, *77;* 93, *91;* 104, *99–100;* 123, *177;* 126, *119;* 146, *135;* 148, *136;* 179, *165.* PC 50, *52;* 65, *64;* 211, *185.* SC 21, *31;* 35, *42;* 205, *196;* 212, *202;* 214, *204.* MN 145, *135.* LB 88, *81;* 179, *162;* 180, *162.*)
[*Hierarchy.*]

SOPESPIAN   A scheming Telmarine* Lord, counselor to Miraz,* and his Marshall of the Lists. He is hacked to death* by King Peter.

(PC 174 ff., *152 ff.,* 183, *161;* 189–190, *166–167.*)
[*Glozelle.*]

SORLOIS   See *Charn.*

SOUNDS   The sounds in the *Chronicles* are often evocative of whole bodies of experience. The plucking of Susan's bow string in PC brings back the old days more than anything that has yet happened, and "all the battles and hunts and feasts came rushing into [the children's] heads together." The sound of the long breakers on Ramandu's Island* is all-pervasive during the Dawn Treaders' stay. The dark, flat voice of the Warden of the Marches of

---

Underland* is a capsule version of the entire atmosphere of Underland. Sounds can also be treacherous and changeable. The Queen of Underland* tries to weave a spell with a monotonous thrumming on her lute that accompanies her sweet, quiet voice; the horns of Tashbaan* sound exciting to Shasta in the morning, but terrifying in the evening when he is shut outside the gates; and the "propputty-propputty"[1] sound of horse's hooves on a hard road sounds like "Thubbudy-thubbudy" on dry sand. The sound of the trumpet announcing the Narnian war-party is "clear, sharp, and valiant." Lewis contrasts it with the "huge and solemn" sound of the horns of Tashbaan, and the "gay and merry" sound of King Lune's* hunting horn. Here, with a simple literary device, Lewis distinguishes three entire experiences: forbidding Tashbaan, inviting Archenland,* and Narnia-at-arms.

(PC 25, 30. VDT 164, 162. SC 121, 122; 125, 126; 151, 149–150. HHB 49, 50; 81, 75; 148, 131; 169, 148.)
[Smells; Tactile images.]

---

[1] According to Professor Thomas W. Craik, Lewis may be alluding to the opening lines of Tennyson's "Northern Farmer (New Style)," in which the farmer is advising his son not to marry a girl without "proputty"—property, i.e., money:

Doesn't thou 'ear my 'orse's legs, as they canters awaäy?
Proputty, proputty, proputty—that's what I 'ears 'em saäy.
Proputty, proputty, proputty—Sam, thou's an ass for they paäins:
Theer's moor sense i' one o' is legs nor in all they braäins.

See Literary allusions.

SPARE OOM   Thought by Tumnus* to be the country from which Lucy came (the city being War Drobe). It is actually Professor Kirke's spare room,[1] which houses the wardrobe* through which Lucy and her sister and brothers get into Narnia.

(LWW 10–11, 16–17; 18–19, 25–26.)
[Transitions.]

---

[1] Tumnus's mishearing of Lucy is a clever fictional way for Lewis to show how words are really symbols. One other instance of this is the animals'* mishearing Aslan's statement in MN (119–120, 111) of "A Neevil" for "an evil." Lewis comments on this phenomenon in his seminal essay, "Bluspels and Flalansferes: A Semantic Nightmare" (Selected Literary Essays, Walter Hooper, ed. [London: Cambridge University Press, 1969] pp. 251–265).

SPEAR-HEAD   Narnia's guiding star,* the brightest in its northern night sky. It is brighter than our North or Pole Star.

(LB 58, 58.)
[Astronomy, Narnian.]

SPECTRES   Dreadful, terrifying ghosts,* summoned by the White Witch to the slaying of Aslan. As they leave the Stone Table,* they pass by the place where Lucy and Susan are hiding. The girls experience the Spectres as a cold

---

wind. Those Spectres remaining after the Witch's defeat by Aslan's army haunt the battlefield for awhile.

(LWW 132, *123;* 154, *143;* 180, *166.*)

SPIVVINS   A weaker boy persecuted by the Gang* at Experiment House,* whom Eustace defends (in some unrevealed circumstance) by not saying anything about him, even when tortured.

(SC 3, *12.*)
[*Autobiographical allusions.*]

SPLENDOUR HYALINE   The royal galleon of Narnia in its Golden Age,* it is modeled after a swan. It is used by Lucy and Susan in their visit to Terebinthia,* Galma,* the Seven Isles,* and the Lone Islands*; with Edmund along, it is the official vessel for the embassy to Tashbaan.* Luxuriously outfitted, it is nevertheless capable of being used in combat. Its silken sails and swanlike appearance may have suggested its name: *hyaline* is from the Greek *hyalinos,* which means "glassy" or "smooth."[1]

(PC 107, *99.* HHB 68–69, *65–66.*)
[*Dawn Treader; Literary allusions.*]

---

[1] Lewis may have had in mind a line from Milton's *Paradise Lost:* "On the cleer *Hyaline,* the Glassie Sea." (VII, 619.)

"SPOTTY" SORNER   See *Gang, the.*

SPRITES   Troublesome, terrifying, and hostile spiritual beings, present at the slaying of Aslan.

(LWW 148, *138.*)

SQUIRRELS   Flighty creatures, they are the message-bearers of the *Chronicles.* Squirrels bring news of Rilian's safety to the owls,* who are also messengers. Squirrels pour down from the trees* to help Jill, Eustace, Puddleglum, and Rilian out of the tunnel. The large red Pattertwig* is the only named squirrel in the *Chronicles.*

(SC 194, *187;* 203, *195.* PC 207, *182.*)
[*Animals; Talking Beasts.*]

STABLE   A hut with a thatched roof, located on Stable Hill, the site of the deception of Tashlan* in LB; Rishda* calls the Stable "the shrine of Tash.*" It is quite mysterious. Tirian walks around it and looks at it, and notes that the Stable Door* seems to lead "from nowhere to nowhere"; but when he looks through the cracks in the wall, the assembly area can be seen. He concludes rightly that the "the Stable seen from within and the Stable seen

---

from without are two different places." Digory adds later that "it's inside is bigger than its outside."[1] Finally, Lucy compares it implicitly to the stable at Bethlehem,[2] which also "had something inside it that was bigger than our whole world."

(LB 26, *29;* 38–39, *41–42;* 100 ff., *91 ff.;* 127, *117;* 136, *124;* 140, *127.*) [*Plato.*]

---

[1] Just like the garden* in which Digory first noted this phenomenon in MN.
[2] Lewis is likely to have first met this idea and image in Chesterton's *The Everlasting Man* (New York: Doubleday Image, 1955) Part Two, Chapter One, "The God in the Cave."

STANDARD See *Banner, standard, crown, coronet.*

STARS
The stars of Narnia are but actual beings, "glittering people with long hair like burning silver." They come into being at Aslan's song of creation, and shine and sing in "cold, tingling, silvery voices." Ramandu* was a star before the Golden Age of Narnia,* and he is refreshed by the fire-berries* that grow on the sun.* His Daughter,* Caspian's wife and Rilian's mother, has the blood of stars in her veins, which she passes on to the Narnian royal family. Coriakin* the magician* was once a star, but he is being punished for some unknown failure by being put in charge of the Duffers.* In an exchange between Ramandu and Eustace, we learn that what a star is made of and what a star is are two different things; the question of ingredients is far less important than the question of what kind of being a star is. The stars of Narnia look much larger than the stars of our world, because they are closer to their world than our stars are to our earth. The Centaurs* of Narnia can read the stars and make predictions based on their positions. According to Roonwit,* the stars never lie. At the End of Narnia,* Aslan calls the stars home with the sound of the horn* of the giant* Time,* and they fall to earth until the skies are empty and black.

(MN 99, *93–94;* 116, *108.* LWW 156–157, *145.* PC 45–46, *49.* VDT 138, *138;* 163, *161;* 170, *167.* SC 50, *56;* 197, *190.* LB 15, *19–20;* 150–151, *136–137.*)
[*Alambil; Aravir; Astronomy, Narnian; Creation of Narnia; Leopard; Reductionism; Tarva.*]

STATUES See *Castle of the White Witch; Credal elements.*

STOCK RESPONSES
Lewis felt very strongly, as did Plato,* that "the little human animal will not at first have the right responses. It must be trained to feel pleasure, liking, disgust, and hatred at those things which really are pleasant, likeable, disgusting, and hateful."[1] In the *Chronicles,* he wants to foster these stock responses in his readers. Digory's reiterated concern about Polly, about the sacredness of promises, about the wickedness of Mrs. Lefay,* about cruelty to animals* about courage* and cowardice* and honor* and

justice show how well-brought-up he is in Lewis's sense: he has all the right stock responses. Conversely, Uncle Andrew* becomes an evil* magician* and a shriveled human being by trampling on and inverting his stock responses. He ignores his oath* to his godmother, he learns magic in unimaginable ways from awful people; he disrespects his body and loses his health—and all for the sake of so-called "higher" knowledge.*

---

[1] Aristotle and St. Augustine held similar views. See C. S. Lewis, *The Abolition of Man* (New York: Macmillan Publishing Co., 1965) pp. 26–27.

STONEFOOT   A giant* summoned to battle by Roonwit* at the bidding of King Tirian.*

(LB 18, *22.*)

STONE KNIFE   An ancient stone knife, sharp as steel and evil-shaped. It is almost certainly the unseen knife being sharpened to kill Edmund, and it is used by the White Witch to slay Aslan. In the battle that follows, she goes after Peter with this knife, now designated for sacrificing the children. Later it appears on Aslan's Table,* enshrined as a holy relic. The third Lord, ignorant of its sacredness, tries to use the knife in his quarrel with his comrades; but the moment he touches it they all fall into an enchanted sleep.[1] The Daughter of Ramandu* then tells the voyagers that as long as the world lasts, the knife is to be kept in this place of honor, where each morning it catches the sun's first rays. Like the cross of Christ, this ugly instrument of Aslan's death* has become a revered symbol of the atonement.

(LWW 133, *124;* 152, *140;* 173, *160.* VDT 171–173, *169–170;* 177, *173.*) [*Literary allusions; Three Sleepers.*]

---

[1] Cf. the Dolorous Stroke, Lord Balyn's seizure of the spear that pierced Jesus' side in the Arthurian legend.

STONE TABLE   The great grim slab of grey stone, supported by four upright stones, upon which Aslan is sacrificed. It is carved all over with strange lines and figures that might be the letters of an unknown language, and which cause a curious feeling in onlookers. Its history is unknown, and it seems to have existed forever. According to the White Witch, it is the proper place for killing and the place where killing has always been done. Although its size is not mentioned it must be a low table, because the girls are able to kneel and still kiss Aslan's face as he lies on top of it. Unbeknownst to the White Witch, it was decreed before time* began that the table would crack when a willing and innocent victim was killed "in a traitor's stead"—exactly the circumstances of Aslan's self-sacrifice for Edmund's sake—and time would begin to run backwards. At the very moment the sun* comes up in Narnia, the table breaks in two with a deafening noise. By the time of PC, the Stone Table is in the heart of Aslan's How* (a mound erected over it) and the writing has all but worn away.

(LWW 76, 76; 121–122, 115; 131, 123; 133, 123; 154, 142; 158, 146; 160, 148. PC 89, 85.)
[Aslan's Table.]

STORIES   The seven books of the *Chronicles of Narnia* are testament to the fact that Lewis valued stories and storytelling as the best way to transmit values down through the generations. The difference in quality between the New Narnians and the Old Narnians (as personified by Miraz* and Prince Caspian)[2] is belief. Miraz thinks fairy tales are for children and to be outgrown, while for Caspian the old stories are his salvation. Because he has heard the old tales from his nurse* and had them verified by Doctor Cornelius,* he is able to return Narnia to its rightful state. Similarly, Tirian's* memory* of the old stories that told of mysterious children* who came to Narnia in times of crisis enables him to call on Aslan and the Seven Friends of Narnia* for help.

Storytelling plays a large part in Narnian life, and in Calormene* life as well. In fact, Calormene children are taught to tell stories just as English children are taught to write essays—and the stories are of course much more interesting. Aravis tells her own story in grand Calormene style. After supper at Cair Paravel, a blind poet comes forward to tell the story of the Horse and His Boy, which we are later told in HHB. It is possible that stories may become distorted, as the story of the Lion Aslan has become, in Calormen, the story of a lion-shaped demon. When Digory hears Aslan's "Well done," he knows that his victory over Jadis will be handed down in Narnia for a long time—indeed, Tirian asks Digory and Polly if the stories about their journey to the garden* were true.

The *Chronicles* themselves are really stories within stories within stories. The major motif of the first half of PC, for example, is Trumpkin's* recapitulation of Narnian history since the reign of King Miraz, within which Doctor Cornelius relates the history of the Telmarine* conquest. In VDT, the spell for refreshment of the spirit is really a story that is so engrossing the reader becomes part of it. On Ramandu's Island,* Caspian tells the Daughter of Ramandu* the story of Sleeping Beauty, which he must have been told by the Pevensie children.

An important aspect of storytelling in the *Chronicles* is the dislocation of the imagination* that it provokes. Caspian is excited when he hears that Eustace comes from a round world—he has often heard stories of such worlds and longed to live in them, but never believed they were real. The obvious inference here is to children who long to live in Narnia, but don't believe it is real. Just as Aslan tells Lucy that she will know him in her own world, but by another name, the implication is that it is indeed possible to live in Narnia, at least in spirit. In a lower key, Lewis points out the relativity of worldviews with the titles of the books* in Tumnus's* library, especially *Is Man A Myth?* Finally, Digory discovers with a shock that fairy tales about evil* magicians* are true when he encounters a modern magician, his Uncle Andrew* (who discounts the stories as "old wives' tales"). Similarly, Tirian's vision of the children suddenly makes the old stories seem real. Lewis tells the reader over

*It is Aslan's final coming. He bounds down the rainbow cliffs, a herald of power and glory. (*LB 182-183, *164.)*

and over again, in as many ways as he can, that the stories *are* true, that there
is both good and evil in the world, and that it is possible—given the spirit of
adventure* and faith—to do battle and win.

(PC 37–39, *42–43;* 66, *65–66.* VDT 20, *28;* 133, *135;* 174, *171;* 201, *196.*
SC 40, *46.* HHB 32 ff., *36 ff.* MN 24, *28;* 166, *154.* LB 16, *20;* 43, *40–41;*
46–47, *47;* 160–166, *146–150;* 175, *158.*)
[*Literary allusions; Mythology; Schools.*]

---

¹ See *Introduction.*
² And also, perhaps, between adults* and children.*

STORMNESS HEAD   The most prominent peak in the southern mountains of Narnia, so named because bad weather is signaled by clouds assem-
bling on its heights. The main pass to Narnia, Stormness Gap, skirts its western
flanks. King Lune* of Archenland* defeats Rabadash* here in 1014 N.Y. Later
Prince Corin* brings to law the renegade bear who has its den on the Narnian
side of the mountain.

(HHB 144, *127;* 176, *154;* 180–181, *158–159;* 216, *188.*)
[*Geography, Narnian; Lapsed Bear of Stormness.*]

STRAWBERRY   See *Fledge.*

SUN   The celestial orb of Narnia is a source of delight. In its mountains
grow the fire-flowers,* and the Birds of Morning* collect fire-berries* from
its valleys. To the voyagers on the *Dawn Treader,* the sun rising over the Last
Sea* looks twice or three times as large as the sun they are used to. At the End
of Narnia,* the sun is a dying star* and rises as a red giant, the moon rises
too close to the sun, which absorbs it, and both are extinguished by the giant*
Time.*

(LWW 105, *100.* VDT 178, *174;* 180, *176.* LB 156–157, *142–143.*)
[*Astronomy, Narnian.*]

SUNLESS SEA   See *Underland.*

SUSAN PEVENSIE   The second child and eldest daughter of Mr. and
Mrs. Pevensie*; she is known as Queen Susan the Gentle in the Golden Age
of Narnia,* and also Queen Susan of the Horn.* As a young, beautiful,
black-haired woman, she is so held hostage to her fears* and to her desire to
be thought mature and attractive that she is not included among those who are
allowed to enter Aslan's country.*¹ Her fall from grace seems sudden and, to
the extent that this appears so, shows an uncharacteristic lapse of style on
Lewis's part. However, a careful re-reading of her story shows that her fall is
much better prepared for than some critics think.

　　Susan's first two lines in LWW reveal a girl aspiring to adulthood: she calls
the professor "an old dear," and tells Eustace, "It's time you were in bed."
When Lucy returns from her first visit to Narnia, Susan uses more parental

phrases: "What on earth," "Don't be silly," and "Why, you goose." When in Narnia herself, she is always practical and sensible; her first suggestion is that they don coats for the wintry weather from the wardrobe,* and she is worried about food. She does not find Narnia safe or fun; and though she too believes that Tumnus* ought to be helped, she'd rather not get involved; she wishes they had never come into this country.

At the sound of Aslan's name* she has a numinous* experience (along with Peter and Lucy); but one of her concerns thereafter is how safe it is to know Aslan.[2] In her panic over their betrayal to the Witch by Edmund, she remonstrates with Mrs. Beaver* over packing a lunch—"fussing," as the she-beaver calls it. Susan receives a magical horn and a bow and arrows from Father Christmas* as her gift from Aslan. Her tension eases on her walk through a reviving Narnia, but when she sees Aslan, she is so overcome with awe that she pushes Peter forward. Aslan accommodates her need to do things by sending her off to prepare a feast. Like Lucy, her feeling that something awful is going to happen to Aslan keeps her awake; and the two agree to look for the Lion. Unlike Lucy, she worries that Aslan might be stealing away during the night and abandoning them to the power of the Witch. Her care for others triumphs over her self-centeredness as she accompanies Aslan in his agony and watches his mistreatment at the hands of the Witch and her forces. Becoming a little child again, she huddles with her sister. She tries to untie the Lion but cannot unfasten the knots. When the mice* come to her aid, she is repulsed; it takes Lucy to point out what they are really doing. At the sound of the crack of the Stone Table,* Susan is afraid to turn around until Lucy pulls her around. Like the risen Christ having to reassure his apostles that he is not a ghost,* Aslan breathes on her. Both sisters enjoy the romp with Aslan, but only Susan persists in asking what it all means. She is no longer enough of a simple child who can throw herself into whatever is happening; like an adult,* she has to know. But because she thinks it would be too awful for Edmund to know of Aslan's death on his behalf, she disagrees with Lucy, who thinks he should be told. LWW ends with the picture of the mature young woman, much sought after as a bride, but still disinclined to exertion in search of adventure*: it is her counsel that her brothers and sister give up the quest* for the White Stag.* In HHB, a story that takes place within the chronological confines of LWW, Susan is the most beautiful woman Shasta has ever seen. Rabadash's* desire to make her part of his harem is the catalyst for many of the events of HHB. When the Narnians ride to the aid of Archenland,* Shasta asks Prince Corin* where Susan is. His response, though coming from his sexism,* is revelatory: "She's not like Lucy, you know, who's as good as a man, or at any rate as good as a boy. Queen Susan is more like an ordinary grown-up lady. She doesn't ride to the wars, though she is an excellent archer." Whatever his other blindnesses, Corin senses her withdrawal from complete Narnian involvement.

In PC, Susan is the last of the four children to feel the pull into Narnia and it is quite unpleasant for her. After their arrival, her first plans (again) are about food, and she insists that Edmund and Lucy carry their shoes. She doesn't hesitate to say "I told you so" when the others regret they have eaten their few sandwiches too soon. When they reach the ruins of the castle, she recalls Cair Paravel "in a dreamy and rather sing-song voice." Since the only other person in Narnia with a sing-song voice is the Queen of Underland* and since it is a vocal quality Lewis did not like, it is perhaps the faintest premonition that all is not right with Susan. Her discovery of the jewelled chesspiece leads to the uncovering of the identity of this ruined place; as fond as she is of her memories,* she resists the "archeological excavation" every step of the way. A better side of her is revealed in her dislike of shooting at the Telmarines* and of defeating Trumpkin.* She especially hates killing anything, even the attacking bear. But her lack of patience shows in her grousing over the difficulties of their trek and over her sister's gift for seeing the implications of things (in this case, what it might be like if people in our world looked like people on the outside but inwardly were wild like the bear—an impractical thought, says Susan). Her second "I told you so" comes when she tells her companions that she knew all the time they'd become lost. When Susan gets tired, she becomes her most irritably adult; Lucy feels the full force of this galling quality. Susan grows increasingly grouchy, going even so far as to consider refusing to cooperate further until she gets the kind of respect Lucy is getting. But when they finally get to the other side of the gorge, Susan admits to her sister that she believed Lucy that Aslan was commanding them to go another way. She confesses that "deep down inside" she knew her sister to be right but that her fear, her desire to get out of the woods by the quickest route possible, and other motives which she does not or cannot name kept her from following Lucy's lead. (It is possible that her pride is offended by the thought that Aslan favors her little sister.)

After the first phase of dancing and feasting with Bacchus,* Silenus,* and the Maenads* subsides, Susan confides to Lucy that she would not have felt safe in the presence of all this wildness without Aslan at hand. As a girl moving into young womanhood, never an easy time, Susan is caught between the conflicting desires to be always a child and to be completely grown-up. Neither here nor there, the ecstatic side of life would be too much for her to deal with, were it not for Aslan in whose presence all revelry* has its place.

Susan accompanies her parents to America in the summer of 1942, and so is only in the background of VDT. Grown-ups think her "the pretty one of the family," an estimate that no doubt makes Lucy feel quite inferior. Her desire to behave as an adult seems to occupy the time she should be devoting to her studies, because her achievement seems to have waned. Lucy's temptation to say the spell that will make her surpassingly beautiful is significant as a way for the younger girl to compensate for feeling unfavorably compared with her sister. If Lucy had her way, a very plain and obviously jealous Susan would return from America at summer's end to discover that her ugly duckling of a sister had become a ravishing beauty. It is hard to escape the conclusion that Susan takes special pleasure in being compared with her sister.

In LB, Tirian* (remembering the history* of his country) asks about Queen Susan, and Peter explains that she is no longer a friend of Narnia. Eustace chimes in that she has no use for talk about Narnia and patronizes the others for their childishness, as she calls it. Jill adds that she is only interested in being grown-up. Polly completes the assessment (and echoes Lewis's own opinion on the matter[3]) with her observation that Susan is truly immature in wanting to grow up to a certain age and stay that way all the rest of her life. Peter changes the subject, although whether he does so out of kindness to Susan or from a desire to talk about something more interesting is not known. If the latter, he joins the rest in a rather unkind conversation, to be forgiven (if at all) only because they have been in Aslan's country for only a few minutes and their total acclimatization has not yet taken place.

---

[1] This is not to say, as some critics have maintained, that she is lost forever. Lewis intends only to explain how it is possible to reject the joy* that comes from being in Narnia and also to illustrate one way of doing so. It is a mistake to think that Susan was killed in the railway accident at the end of LB and that she has forever fallen from grace. It is to be assumed, rather, that as a woman of twenty-one who has just lost her entire family in a terrible crash, she will have much to work through; in the process, she might change to become truly the gentle person she has the potential for being. Lewis gives the impression of harsh and final judgment of Susan by the Seven Friends of Narnia,* an ungenerosity and superficiality he otherwise condemns in his other writings. See, for instance, his extended analysis of the difference between a Christian Miss Bates, a shrewish woman with many physical and character defects, and a secular Dick Firkin, whose handsomeness and affability make him a perfect candidate to promote toothpaste. It is unjust, said Lewis, to compare her almost fruitless struggle to transcend her defects with his lack of any sense that there is even any struggle in life in which transcendence is necessary (*Mere Christianity* [New York: Macmillan Publishing Co., 1960; London: Collins Fount, 1977] pp. 175 ff., *173 ff.*).

[2] This is a reflection of one of Lewis's main concerns. "I am a safety-first creature. Of all arguments against love none makes so strong an appeal to my nature as 'Careful! This might lead you to suffering,' " said Lewis in *The Four Loves* (New York: Harcourt Brace Jovanovich, 1960) p. 168. Lewis wanted to avoid pain and interference at all costs (see *Aslan,* note 63). Perhaps one of the reasons he is able to write so well of Susan's character is that he experienced her reluctances, fears, and desire to be thought adult in his own personality (for the last, see Lewis's autobiography, *Surprised by Joy* [New York: Harcourt Brace Jovanovich, 1955] pp. 67–68).

[3] In a letter dated August 1, 1953, Lewis tells a friend:

> . . . I . . . think there is lots to be said for being no longer young . . . it is just as well to be past the age when one expects or desires to attract the other sex. It's natural enough in our species, as in others, that the young birds show off their plumage—in the mating season. But the trouble in the modern world is that there is a tendency to rush all the birds on to that age as soon as possible and keep them there as late as possible, thus losing all the real value of the *other* parts of life in a senseless, pitiful attempt to prolong what, after all, is neither its wisest, happiest, or most innocent period. I suspect merely commercial motives are behind it all: for it is at the showing-off age that birds of both sexes have least sales-resistance!

From *Letters to an American Lady,* Clyde S. Kilby, ed. (Grand Rapids: Wm. B. Eerdmans Publishing Co., 1967) p. 19.

SWANWHITE   Queen of Narnia some time before[1] the Hundred Years of Winter.* Her beauty was so radiant that any pool she used as a mirror would reflect her face for a year and a day.

(LB 88, *82.*)
[*Magic.*]

---

[1] This is contradicted by Lewis's outline of Narnian history (PWD, p. 43), in which he states that Swanwhite was ruling in 1502 N.Y.

SWEET WATERS   See *Last Sea; Holy Spirit.*

TACTILE IMAGES   Lewis's use of tactile images in the *Chronicles* helps to make the children's* fabulous adventures* much more real. Lucy's transition* between Narnia and the wardrobe is marked by the feel on her skin of prickly fir branches turning into soft fur coats. SC is filled with such images: Jill's Narnian clothes are not only nice looking, but nice feeling; Glimfeather's* feathers "felt beautifully warm and soft"; the children's beds in the Marsh-Wiggle's* wig-wam are soft and warm in contrast to the cool, damp night air; and at Harfang* Jill's enjoyment of the giant* towels after her bath is especially sensual. Digory's bathe in the mountain stream in MN is compared with a sea-bathe, an autobiographical allusion.*

(LWW 39, *43;* SC 36–37, *43–44;* 43, *50;* 56, *62;* 98, *101;* 202, *194.* MN 154–155, *143.*)
[*Robes, royal; Smells; Sounds.*]

TALKING BEASTS   The animals* of Narnia who have been given the gift of speech* and dominion over the Dumb Beasts* by Aslan. They are not the same size as ordinary animals, the smaller ones being larger (talking mice,* for example, are two feet tall) and the larger ones being smaller. Their faces shine with intelligence. Although we may assume that Talking Beasts grow old and die (Mr. and Mrs. Beaver* are long dead and gone from Beaversdam* by the time of VDT), they are not shown to age, and the only death is that of the Bear in LB. Talking Beasts are present in every book of the *Chronicles.* [1]

Talking Beasts are created by Aslan from the ordinary animals. He goes among them and touches pairs of each animal by the sides of their noses; these animals instantly leave and follow him. In his commands to Narnia to awake, he commands them to "Be Talking Beasts." The animals know Aslan's name* intuitively, and pledge their obedience.* In return, Aslan gives them their world, their selves, and himself.

Although some are later corrupted (notably, Shift*), the Talking Beasts are originally innocent. Lewis implies this innocence by having them confuse even the sound of the words "an evil*" into "a Neevil." Their natural curiosity about Uncle Andrew* and the desire to exercise their newly made bodies moves them to pursue the fleeing elderly gentleman in a chase that is a deliberate reversal of an English fox hunt, with all the appropriate shouts. Some (with a degree of truth) think he is the "Neevil" Aslan is looking for.

Being a Talking Beast is both an honor* and a responsibility. When they gnaw through the ropes that bind Aslan to the Stone Table,* the mice are honored for their help by being transformed into Talking Beasts. Reepicheep takes himself quite seriously, and when Caspian slurs his mousehood he responds by reminding the King of his coronation oath* to be a good lord to the Talking Beasts of Narnia. Aslan warns the newly created Talking Beasts that they must abstain from their former wild ways[2] or have the gift of speech rescinded. When this does in fact happen to Ginger,* the other animals are terror-stricken. However, it is possible to be redeemed: the Lapsed Bear of Stormness,* who has gone wild, is reformed by Corin Thunder-Fist.*

The Talking Beasts are in many ways similar to humans; indeed they are anthropomorphized to a high degree. Reepicheep speaks of being in his "cradle" when the Dryad* spoke the verse over him. Mr. and Mrs. Beaver have, like all good beavers, built a dam; but they actually live in a house on top of the dam that has all the comforts of a cozy English home, and enjoy proper English meals. Bree and Hwin are personified to a greater degree than any other animals in the *Chronicles,* and are given the stature of fully developed characters. This allows us to see more deeply into the minds of Talking Beasts, and in so doing it becomes apparent that they retain their animal natures. Bree, who has been away from Narnia for so long, loves to roll in the grass but wonders if proper Narnian horses* have the freedom to roll. Even he is confused about where the line is drawn between the wild ways of animals and the responsibilities and dignity of Talking Beasts. Although they are so like humans, they still see life from the perspective of the specific animals they are. Thus Glimfeather* offers Jill a snack of bat, not realizing that little girls (unlike owls*) seldom, if ever, eat bats.

Cruelty to animals is abhorrent to Narnians (and to Lewis), and cruelty to Talking Animals is the worst of all. The evil side of the Calormene character is revealed by the way in which animals are treated in LB. The large animals have been pledged as dray horses, and the smaller animals have been sent to work in the mines. Tirian meets a talking horse who is both harnessed and whipped, at "Aslan's" orders. Although it is permitted to hunt Dumb Beasts for food (there are no vegetarians in Narnia), to eat a Talking Beast is akin to cannibalism. Eustace, Jill, and Puddleglum are horrified to discover, halfway through a meal, that they have been eating Talking Stag.[3]

Lewis uses the Talking Beasts as hieroglyphs, word-pictures that embody various human attributes (Reepicheep, for example, is a hieroglyph of courage). By using animals, Lewis can make graphic statements about the human condition that would be much more complicated to express in human terms. Like humans, Talking Beasts have continually to choose between right and wrong.* When confronted with the false Aslan, who is seductive and convincing, they are presented with a basic dilemma: should they follow him or not? The only animals to win through the crisis are the Lamb, the dogs,* the Bear, and the Boar. Each of these embodies qualities humans need when confronted with the same dilemma: innocence of belief (the Lamb), complete devotion (the dogs), honest befuddlement (the Bear), and tenacity of faith (the Boar). Finally, by portraying Talking Beasts that live in aid and friendship to human beings, Lewis reminds us that we are indeed part of the natural world, and not separate from it as modern science and technology* might have us believe.

(SC 111–112, *112–113. MN* 115–116, *106–108;* Chapter 10 passim.)
[*Creation of Narnia; Evil; Hierarchy; Hunting; Vivisection.*]

---

¹ To cite every reference to Talking Beasts is virtually impossible. Since many animals have their own entries, the only citations given are for material not otherwise covered.

² For a fuller discussion of wild ways, see *Dumb Beasts.*

³ Each reacts to this knowledge according to how long he or she has been in Narnia. Jill, a newcomer, is sorry for the animal and outraged at the cruelty of the giants*; Eustace, with one Narnian adventure under his belt and Reepicheep for his friend, says it is like murder; Puddleglum, a native Narnian, feels it as deeply as we would feel if we had eaten a baby.

TARKAAN   A Calormene great lord; the feminine diminutive is "Tarkheena." When Shasta meets Anradin,* the Tarkaan is wearing a chain-mail shirt and a silken turban with the spike of a helmet projecting through the middle. He carries a curving scimitar, a round brass-bossed shield, and a lance. His crimson beard is curled and gleaming with scented oil. Although he is a stranger, Arsheesh knows Anradin to be a Tarkaan by the gold arm-ring he wears. Tarkaans are accustomed to commanding groveling respect from their social inferiors. The origin of the word Tarkaan is not known, although phonetically it implies a "can of tar."

(HHB Chapter 3 passim.)
[*Ahoshta Tarkaan; Aravis; Axartha Tarkaan; Lasaraleen Tarkheena; Rishdi Tarkaan.*]

TARVA   One of two noble planets (the other is Alambil*) which every two hundred years pass within one degree of each other in the Narnian night sky. Doctor Cornelius* takes advantage of this heavenly event as a lesson in astronomy to speak to the young Prince Caspian out of earshot of Miraz's* spies. Glenstorm* the Centaur* interprets this event as a sign that the struggle to liberate Old Narnia from Telmarine* rule must begin. The Centaur surnames Tarva "The Lord of Victory."

(PC 43, *47;* 74, *72.*)
[*Astronomy, Narnian.*]

TASH   The chief god* of the Calormene* pantheon; he is called by worshipers "Tash the inexorable, the irresistible." He is a cruel, bloodthirsty god with a taste for human sacrifice. Vaguely man-shaped, Tash has a vulture's head, four arms, and twenty fingers that end in cruel, curving talons. A deathly smoke surrounds him and grass wilts under his step. His voice is the "clucking and screaming" of a "monstrous bird." Lewis derived the god's name from *tash* or *tache,* a Scottish dialectical word that means "blemish, stain, fault, or vice." Many Calormenes (with the notable exception of Emeth*) pay only lip-service to their god, and when he actually shows up at the Stable* they are terrified. He almost eats the atheist Ginger,* does eat the despicable Shift,* and is about to do something equally terrible to Rishda* when he is banished to his "own country" (presumably hell*) by one of the seven Kings and Queens* (presumably the High King Peter). While this seems to indicate that Lewis had Tash in mind (allegorically) as the devil, in HHB he is merely the antithesis of Aslan's qualities rather than of Aslan himself. The appearance of Tash in Narnia is perhaps the single most terrifying scene in the *Chronicles.*

(HHB 33, *37;* 38, *41;* 48, *49;* 102, *93;* 115, *103;* 154, *136.* LB 27, *30;* 31, *34;* 79, *74;* 80 ff., *75 ff.;* 115, *106;* 128, *117;* 132, *120–121;* 141–142, *129.*)
[*Tashlan.*]

TASHBAAN   The capital city of Calormen* and the seat of the Tisroc's* rule; its name is derived from the Calormene god* *Tash,* * and *baan.* [1] Tashbaan is located on an island in the middle of a broad river, and circles of buildings rise from the mean commercial district at the bottom, to the upper-class homes, to the Tisroc's palace at the very top. The city is crowded, filthy, and disordered. The only traffic rule is that "everyone who is less important has to get out of the way for everyone who is more important." There is garbage in streets, and the air is filled with the cooking smells of onions and garlic. Interestingly, from her vantage point in the garden* in LB, Lucy can see Tashbaan down below in the real Narnia: it is a great city. Thus Lewis must feel that there is something good[2] in the Calormene culture (as symbolized by its chief city) that allows it to pass into eternity.

(HHB Ch. 1, 4, 6. LB 181, *163.*)

---

[1] A Middle Eastern construction devised by Lewis, which he probably intends to mean "house of."

[2] Considering that storytelling, Aravis, and the noble Emeth* are the only features of Calormen culture of which Lewis approves, they may be its saving grace.

TASHLAN   The figure of Antichrist in LB and the personification of the lie that Shift* and the Calormenes* are telling to Narnia. The word is a combination of the names Tash* and Aslan. The name "Tashlan" is first spoken by the ape at the prompting of Rishda.* Lewis allows that some Narnians may have an "honest fear" of Tashlan that is not prompted by treachery; but Emeth,* the noble Calormene officer, is outraged by the equation of Tash, whom he loves, with Aslan, whom he hates.

(LB 101, *94;* 120, *111;* 128, *117;* 162, *146–147.*)
[*End of Narnia; Eschatology.*]

TECHNOLOGY   This term refers to the increasing separation of humanity from nature brought on, in Lewis's view, by the application of the scientific method to all aspects of human life. Narnia is a preindustrial, medieval world, but even there traces of technology can be seen. In LWW, the enchanted Edmund thinks vindictively how much better Narnia will be when he is king* and he can make "decent" roads, build his palace with a cinema, own a fleet of automobiles, and install a railway system.[1] This technological revery deflects him from repentance, and he escapes into power fantasies. Eustace, in VDT, is a perfect product of a technological society, and he sees all that is best in Narnia—that is, all that is natural—as primitive and second rate. He calls the *Dawn Treader* a "blasted boat," and says that in "civilized" countries "ships are so big that when you're inside you wouldn't know you were at sea at all." At the Land of the Duffers,* he is delighted to see the pump handle as a sign that he has come to a "civilized" society. Eustace's thought processes show how the separation and elevation of science above classical knowledge and religion can have the effect of narrowing thought. On Ramandu's Island,* Eustace remarks that on his world "a star* is a huge ball of flaming gas." Ramandu* corrects this assumption with the reply, "Even in your world . . . that is not what a star is but only what it is made of." It is this preoccupation with what things are made of—the sum of the parts as opposed to the appreciation of whole—that Lewis finds particularly abhorrent. The evil* people of the *Chronicles* are characterized by their exaggerated concern for the practical. He comments that witches "are not interested in things or people unless they can use them." At the sight of the growing Lamp-Post,* Uncle Andrew launches into an entrepreneurial ecstasy over the notion that "the commercial possibilities of this country are unbounded," and he plans to build a scrap-iron plantation and a health resort. In our world, Eustaces's parents Alberta* and Harold* Scrubb are enamored of the mundane aspects of life, and send their son to school* at Experiment House,* where the precepts of a technological age are preferred over the classics. In LB, the triumph of technology over nature leads to the end of Narnia.* Shift* intends to sell the Talking Beasts* and other animals* into slavery, and to use that income to build "roads and big cities and schools and offices and whips and muzzles and saddles and cages and kennels and prisons." Finally, in enslaving nature, the entire world is destroyed.

(LWW 87,*84.* VDT 31,*38;* 114,*116;* 180,*177.* MN 21,*26;* 72,*71;* 111–112, *102–103;* 125, *116.* LB 30, *33.*)
[*Ecology; Government; Reductionism; Slave trade.*]

---

[1] See C. S. Lewis, *The Great Divorce* (New York: Macmillan and Co., 1946) p. 75, in which a group of ghosts in purgatory are planning to take over Heaven and "dam the river, cut down the trees, kill the animals, build a mountain railway, and smooth out the horrible grass and moss and heather with asphalt."

TEEBETH   Site of a Calormene* conquest at which Bree and Alimash* fought on Calormen's side. Location unknown.

(HHB 41, *43.*)

TEHISHBAAN   A Calormene* city that lies west of the Great Desert.* It is the hometown of Emeth.*

(LB 161, *146.*)

TELMAR, TELMARINES   Telmar is a land far beyond the western mountains (the great western forest lies between Telmar and Lantern Waste*), from whence the Telmarines came into Narnia. The Telmarines, or New Narnians, are the offspring of marauding human pirates who blundered into Telmar in 460 N.Y.[1] through a cave—one of the last magic* connections between our world and that world. There they married native women, and in 1998 N.Y.[2] their fierce, proud descendents invaded a disordered Narnia and conquered it. The first Telmarine king* of Narnia was Caspian I,* and under his rule the Telmarines went about "[silencing] the beasts and the trees* and the fountains" and driving away the dwarfs* and fauns.* Throughout their rule Old Narnians must hide their identities, and the old stories* that tell the truth about Aslan and Old Narnia are largely forgotten and denigrated as "old wives' tales." The Telmarines' hatred of nature is complemented by their superstitious fears,* and they call the Great Woods* the Black Woods* because they imagine the woods to be filled with ghosts.* Captured by Caspian's army, the Telmarines make a fuss about wading a river because they are afraid of running water. At last all are compelled either to accept Aslan's restoration of Narnia or to go to a home back on earth that has been prepared by Aslan. Younger Telmarines want to stay on in Narnia, while the older ones are sulky and suspicious. That some Telmarines do stay is evidenced by the fact that Lord Rhoop,* in VDT, identifies himself as a "Telmarine of Narnia." Some Telmarines eventually do follow the Pevensie children* back through the door* in the air, and are deposited on a Pacific island.

(PC 29,*35;* 35,*41;* 42,*45;* 47,*50;* 50–51,*52–53;* 67,*66;* 204, *179.* VDT 161, *159.* HHB 180, *158.*)
[*Archenland; Calormen; Ecology; Government; Technology; Transitions; Imagination.*]

[1] PWD, p. 42. But see *Polly Plummer,* note 1.
[2] PWD, p. 43.

TEREBINTHIA   An island east of Galma* that Lucy remembers from voyages of the past. The island has one city, with some pirates in its population. There is sickness on Terebinthia when Caspian sails there on the *Dawn Treader.* Terebinthian slaves are aboard Pug's* ship. A rumored appearance of Aslan on the island moves Caspian to set out on his last journey to see the Lion face to face, and to ask his advice about who is to succeed him as king in Rilian's stead.

(PC 107, *99.* VDT 17–18, *25;* 36, *44.* SC 47, *54.*)
[*Geography, Narnian; Slave trade.*]

TERM-TIME   The time when school* is in session, especially the begin-ning of the school term, when children must return from their holidays or their vacations. In the *Chronicles,* term-time[1] is a metaphor for the unenjoyable seasons of life; thus the Pevensie children are fortunate to be whisked away to Narnia while on their way back to boarding school, of course only to be returned at the end of their adventure to face the summer term ahead of them. It is joy* indescribable to hear from Aslan at the end of LB, "The term is over: the holidays have begun."[2]

(PC 2, *11–12;* 216, *190.* LB 183, *165.*)

---

[1] In British schools, the Fall term is Michaelmas (from the Feast of St. Michael, September 29), the Winter term is Hilary (from the Feast of St. Hilary, January 13) or Lent term, the Spring term is the Easter Term, and the Summer term is Trinity Term (from the Feast of the Holy Trinity,* the first Sunday after Pentecost Sunday or Whitsun). Michaelmas Term now begins around the twelfth of October; and Easter and Trinity terms, named after moveable feasts, commence at the beginning of spring and of summer, respectively.

[2] See *Sleep* for a discussion of parallels between term-time and sleep, and vacation-time and waking.

THEODOLINDS   See *House of the Magician.*

THORNBUT   Guardian dwarf* to Prince Corin.* Appointed by King Lune* to keep Corin from entering battle, Thornbut sprains his ankle fighting with the prince in order to keep his charge.

(HHB 172–174; *151–153.*)
[*Corin Thunder-Fist.*]

THREE BULGY BEARS   Trufflehunter's* nearest neighbors, who live to the east of him in the northernmost part of Archenland.* Their behavior is a hieroglyph of the sort of personality, which though good-hearted, gives first place to food and habits of comfort. When they attend the Great Council,* the bears want to eat first and counsel later. However, they are not totally without ambition. When King Peter is to face Miraz* in single combat, they insist on their long-standing right to have one of their number be a Marshall of the Lists. King Peter appoints the oldest bear to this office even though, true to his nature, the bear is prone to sucking his paw and falling asleep. Later on, Caspian confirms the bear permanently in his hereditary office of Marshall of the Lists.

(PC 68, *67;* 80, *76;* 180, *157–158;* 183, *161;* 204, *179.*)
[*Talking Beasts.*]

THREE SLEEPERS   Argoz,* Revilian,* and Mavramorn,* three of the Seven Noble Lords* found in an enchanted sleep* on Ramandu's Island.* When they first arrive on the Island, sea-worn and exhausted, they come upon Aslan's Table* laden with food. There they begin to argue about what course of action they should take. Lewis's delineation of their responses to this dilemma reveals his care in distinguishing character through motivation. The first Lord, in his timidity and caution, is for returning to Narnia in the hope that Miraz* may have died. The second Lord, adventurer and idealist, is for risking all to find "the unpeopled world behind the sunrise." The third Lord, a here-and-now pragmatist, is for settling down on the island to live the rest of their days in peace. The second Lord, determined to convince his comrades of his viewpoint by violence if need be, reaches for the Stone Knife* on the table—certainly a sacreligious act, as the knife is a holy object. As a result, the three Lords fall into an enchanted sleep. When Caspian arrives—perhaps some seven years later—and tries to wake them, their trance-like responses once again reveal in cryptic form the basic dispositions they held in their arguments. Caspian learns that the three Lords' magic* sleep will be broken only after he has sailed to the World's End* and left there a willing person who will venture on into the Utter East,* never to return. Reepicheep, called to this endeavor from birth, is quick to volunteer. And ultimately the Lords are wakened from their sleep.

(VDT 163 ff., *161 ff.;* 186, *182;* 216, *210.*)

TIME   Time in Narnia and time in England* behave quite differently. Lewis speculated that time in other worlds might have "thicknesses and thin-nesses"[1] in addition to linearity; thus while time in England flows on in the usual manner, any number of years may have passed in Narnia in the same amount of "time." From its creation to the Last Battle,* Narnia has a total history* of 2555 Narnian years (N.Y.). The same amount of time in England spans only forty-nine earth-years, from 1900 to 1949. Furthermore, there is no direct correspondence: one earth year does not necessarily equal a corre-sponding number of Narnian years. Thus although the Pevensie children have been in Narnia long enough to grow to young adulthood, when they return through the wardrobe* to England almost no time has passed. On the other hand, as we are told in VDT, "If you went back to Narnia after spending a week here, you might find that a thousand Narnian years had passed, or only a day, or no time at all. You never know till you get there."

Even in our world time passes much more slowly for children* than it does for adults,* and this attitude is evident in the Narnian world of LWW, in which it is "always winter but Christmas never comes." To young children, each winter must sometimes seem like a hundred years. Also, there are different ways of experiencing time even among children. Digory and Polly experience the same two hours in different ways: Polly spends two long hours in bed without supper as punishment for coming home wet, while for Digory, waiting apprehensively for the return of Jadis, they drag on even longer—hours and hours pass by with each tick of the clock.

Discrepancies between earth time and Narnian time lead to other interest-ing speculations, especially Peter's observation in PC that the children's return to Narnia after so long (even though it was only a year in England it was 1303 years in Narnia) must be something like what it would be like for the Crusaders or ancient Britons to find themselves alive and well in the modern world.[2] In fact, the Old Narnians who have lived under Telmarine* rule have something of a hard time believing their own history, and it takes everyone a while to get used to the fact that these are the very same children who saved Narnia once before. While the Pevensies take a long time to understand that the ruins they find themselves in are Cair Paravel, the Narnians have a hard time understanding how these children can still *be* children. This distance in time is even greater for Tirian* and the Narnians in LB.

There are two timeless places in Narnia: the Wood between the Worlds,* which is almost outside of time; and Aslan's country,* which is eternal. The end of Narnia* also signals the end of time; and Aslan comments that Father Time's* name was time when he was sleeping (the same period that Narnia was awake and living), but now that Narnia was ended he would have a new name.

---

[1] C. S. Lewis, *The Great Divorce* (New York: Macmillan Publishing Co., 1946) pp. 128–129.
[2] See Lewis's *That Hideous Strength*, in which the self-same Merlin of King Arthur's day comes alive in modern England.

TIRIAN The last king of Narnia, the seventh in descent from King Rilian. In his early twenties, he is well-developed but with a scanty beard, blue eyes, and a "fearless, honest face." Although he has the nobility and honor* of all of the kings of Narnia, he cannot escape his country's overwhelming atmosphere of decadence and chaos. His emotions are not under control, and he swings from elation to depression to remorse to anger. He is first met at his hunting* cabin, where he has gone to escape the royal routine with his best friend, Jewel* the Unicorn.* In LB, Lewis is concerned with the eschatological themes of death,* judgment, heaven, and hell,* and so the characters are perhaps not as well-drawn as they might be. It is evident that Lewis would like us to see Tirian as the noble king in the face of the inevitable twilight of the gods, but this is not made as clear as it might be. Tirian seems to be out of touch with what is happening in his country, for he is not aware of the extent of Calormene* spying and the treachery and deception of Shift,* the ape. Excited by the news that Aslan is in Narnia, he is thrown into a rage by Roonwit's* statement that this is a lie. He spends much of the first part of LB in anger, which clouds his judgment and leads him and Jewel to murder two unsuspecting Calormene drivers.

Demoralized, he turns himself over to the Calormenes in expectation of justice from Aslan. He is again outraged at the misery of the Talking Beasts* and rages against the ape, but is knocked down and tied to a tree. The smaller Talking Beasts come to his aid, bringing food and drink. During his long, lonely night he recalls the history* of Narnia, and the children* that have always come to save the country in times of crisis. His first prayer to Aslan is seemingly ineffectual, but actually moves him to abandonment. Finally, when he wants nothing for himself, his prayer (though it changes nothing externally) changes him and gives him hope and strength. He calls out to the children,

---

and has visions of the Seven Friends of Narnia* (who, in turn, have a vision of him). When Jill and Eustace come to his aid, he is impressed with the fact that he is meeting people who figured in Narnia's earlier history.[1]

With Jill and Eustace, he is able to get himself under control, and is able to survive on a limited amount of sleep. With Jill in the lead, they free Jewel and a band of "honest" dwarfs,* who turn out to be renegades; the only honest dwarf in the group is Poggin,* who joins Tirian's forces. When Farsight* brings news of Roonwit's death and Cair Paravel's capture, Tirian prematurely pronounces the end of Narnia. However, he has not given up the fight, and the group moves inevitably toward the Last Battle.* Horrified at the vision of Tash* and the enormity of Shift's* plot, he reassures Jill that whatever or whoever is in the Stable,* they are still "between the paws of the true Aslan." At the sight of the Calormene soldiers about to attack the Boar, "something seemed to burn inside him," and he steps before the assembly. This is significant in light of Tirian's rather choleric character. It is difficult to determine whether Lewis means to approve of Tirian's imprudence at this point: he is certainly alluding to the stock response* of righteous wrath, but he has also mentioned earlier that Tirian behaves precipitously. Whatever his motives, Tirian throws Shift into the Stable, sends the mice* to release the horses,* and arranges his battle lines. At last in control, he reminds Eustace of the qualities of a true warrior, to "speak courteously and fight fiercely."

Tirian dies at the Last Battle,* although Lewis does not show his death in its physical manisfestation. Intending to show that death is a transition and not something to be feared, Lewis has Tirian come to his senses at the Door* and pull Rishda* inside with him. Thus it is apparent that Tirian has actually killed Rishda. Once inside the door, he is surprised to discover the Seven Friends of Narnia. He gradually awakens to the reality of his situation, and finds the freestanding door and frame quite unusual. He concludes that the Stable is two different places, depending on one's perspective. Tirian joins Lucy in mourning Narnia, with the metaphorical statement that "I have seen my mother's death."[2] The climax of Tirian's entry into Aslan's country* is his reunion with his dead father, Erlian,* which is perhaps the most genuinely emotional scene between an adult* and a child[3] in the *Chronicles.*

---

[1] See *Time.*

[2] Tirian considers Narnia his mother. Lewis comments about the rightness of a proper love for nature in *Miracles* (New York: Macmillan Publishing Co., 1978; London: Collins Fontana, 1960) pp. 66–67, 70–71.

[3] See *Autobiographical allusions.*

TISROC   The hereditary title of the kings of Calormen*; it is never mentioned without the obligatory "may-he-live-forever." Lewis probably derived "Tisroc" from "Nisroch," the Egyptian god in E. Nesbit's *The Story of the Amulet.*[1] His Middle Eastern–style palace is on the crest of the tallest hill in Tashbaan,* which it shares with the temple of Tash.* His garden runs down to the river. For a crown he wears a curious pointed cap, and his royal robes* are lavishly bejewelled and buttoned and tasseled. As befits the head of a superstitious culture, he wears a talisman, probably to ward off evil.* The Tisroc[2] in HHB is a very fat old man, and cruel: he has his third cook put to death for causing him slight indigestion; and he reproves Rabadash's* "cowardice*" with the statement that if the prince were not the Tisroc's son, his "life would be short and [his] death slow."[3] He is driven by the need for power, and tells his Grand Vizier, Ahoshta,* that "sleep is not refreshing, because I remember that Narnia is still free." Although his forces are defeated at Anvard,* the Calormene desire for victory lives on; in LB, the Calormene banner* of the last Tisroc flies for a time from the battlements of the captured Cair Paravel.

(HHB 5, *15;* 7, *16;* 48–49, *49;* 101–104, *92–94;* Chapter 8 passim. LB 29–30, *33;* 82, *77;* 91, *85.*)
[*Tarkaan.*]

---

[1] E. Nesbit, *The Story of the Amulet,* in collection with *Five Children and It* and *The Phoenix and the Amulet* (London: Octopus Books Ltd., 1979) p. 495.

[2] Always called "the Tisroc," never "Tisroc"; "the" is capitalized in the British edition of the *Chronicles,* lower-cased in the American edition.

[3] Compare this example of paternal cruelty with King Lune's* loving reproof of his son Corin's* rash courage, and with Lune's comparatively kind treatment of the would-be assassin Rabadash. See also *Adults.*

TOFFEE TREE   A tree about the size of an apple tree,* very dark-wooded, with whitish, papery leaves and date-like fruit. It grows overnight from one of Polly's nine toffees (all she and Digory have to eat on their journey to the garden* in the West), which Digory plants as an experiment. Lewis compares it to the herb called Honesty *(lunaria biennis),* because of its semitransparent pods and paper-like leaves.

(MN 151 ff., *140 ff.*)
[*Golden Tree; Silver Tree; Tree of Protection; Trees.*]

TOMBS, THE   See *Great Desert.*

TRADITION   See *Stories.*

TRAN   See *Darrin.*

TRANSCENDENCE   See *Greatness of God.*

TRANSITIONS   Human children* are called into Narnia in times of crisis, and only at Aslan's bidding or with his tacit permission. It is, however, possible to get in accidentally (like the Telmarines*) or by being attached to someone else (like Jadis and Uncle Andrew*). The transition from our world into Narnia and back again is accomplished in a number of ways. In PC, Lewis explains that the Telmarines first made their way from earth to Telmar through a cave, which is one of the last "magical places . . . one of the chinks or chasms between worlds." In LWW, the Pevensies go back and forth between England* and Narnia through the wardrobe.* Even though in Narnia they are Kings and Queens* and in England* they are still children, the transition is not abrupt. Lucy, for example, feels[1] the branches of the *fir* trees turning into *fur* coats, a transition that is sensual for her and visual for the reader. In PC Peter, Susan, Edmund, and Lucy are literally pulled by magic* from a train station in England right into Narnia. On the return trip, Aslan makes a door* in the air, which they and the Telmarines walk through. In VDT Lucy, Edmund, and Eustace enter Narnia through a painting of the *Dawn Treader:* first the picture looks real, then the wind blows, next noises are heard, then water splashes, and there they are on the real ship in Narnia. Their return to England is accomplished through another door, which Aslan makes in the sky. In SC, Aslan calls Jill and Eustace into Narnia through a doorway behind Experiment House.* As soon as they step through it, England disappears. On the return, Aslan leads the children and Caspian through the woods, where the wall of Experiment House suddenly appears before them. He makes a gap in the wall through which they can see everything they had left behind; and in this transitional place the Gang* can see them as well. In MN, most of the transitions are accomplished magically, via the magic rings.* But in the final return to England, there is no need to use them—it is the swirling vision of Aslan himself that sends Polly and Digory back. In LB, there is a very different transition. Tirian and the Seven Friends of Narnia actually appear to one another "as if in a dream,*" and Eustace and Jill simply appear before Tirian,* without explanation. The final transition is not from England to Narnia but from Narnia to the real Narnia, Aslan's country,* into which all the good creatures of Narnia enter through the Stable* Door. Once on the other side of the Door, they can see the end of Narnia.* And in the garden* of the west they can see that all that is real in Narnia and England is connected, and it is only necessary to walk in order to get from one place to another.

(LWW 5–7, *12–13;* 19–20, *26–27;* 24–25, *30–31;* 39, *43;* 49–51, *52–53;* 184–186, *169–171.* PC 2–3, *12;* 208ff., *183 ff.* VDT 6–8, *13–16;* 216, *210.* SC 9, *18;* 214–216, *204–206.* MN 14, *20;* 27–28, *30–31;* 36–37, *38–40;* 65–66, *64–65;* 90–91, *96;* 178–179, *165.* LB 125 passim, *115 passim.*)

---

[1] See *Tactile images.*

TREE OF PROTECTION   A tree* sown by Digory from the seed of the silver apple* of the garden* of the west. It grows on the bank of the Great River* near the Lamp-Post.* Its branches "cast a light rather than a shade," and it is filled with star-like silver apples. Its fragrance is breathtaking. When Digory buries the core from one of these apples outside the Ketterley house, a tree grows up overnight. It does not grow up to bear fully magical apples (because it is too far from the sound of Aslan's voice* and the touch of Narnia's air), but its apples are good and beautiful. Deep down inside, the tree is one with its Narnian parent and moves its limbs when Narnian winds blow. The tree is ultimately destroyed by a gale, and Digory has its wood made into a wardrobe*—the magic* wardrobe through which the Pevensie children are first transported to Narnia.

(MN 166, *154;* 172–173, *161;* 182, *168;* 184–185, *170–171.*)
[*Golden Tree; Silver Tree; Smells; Toffee Tree.*]

TREE-PEOPLE   Beings that are part tree, part human.[1] As trees* they look only vaguely human; but when some good magic* calls them to life, they look like leafy, branchy giants* and giantesses.[2] In PC they are first seen by Lucy; at Aslan's roar, they all look upon him, adore him, and dance* around him. Later, the awakened trees rush at the Telmarines.* Although not mentioned specifically, they are probably among the wild people, gods,* and goddesses who respond to Aslan's command to Narnia to awaken.

(PC 134, *122;* 151, *136;* 191, *167.* MN 117, *109.*)
[*Aslan's voice; Creation of Narnia; Dryads; Hamadryads; Silvans; Wood people.*]

---

[1] They are modeled on the woods at Helm's Deep in J. R. R. Tolkien's *The Lord of the Ring: The Two Towers* (Houghton Mifflin Co., 1965) pp. 146–147, 151. On the other hand, Tolkien's Treebeard is modeled on his friend C. S. Lewis. (See Humphrey Carpenter, *Tolkien* [New York: Houghton Mifflin, 1977] p. 194.)

[2] For a more detailed discussion of male and female trees, see *Dryads.*

TREES   The trees of Narnia are truly alive; at Aslan's command they become waking trees. Trees of Narnian countries include many species of English trees, such as oaks, hollies, beeches, silver birches, rowans, firs, pines, sweet chestnuts, and apple trees.* Most seem to be good—the Oak is present at the First Council*—but they are capable of wrongdoing. In LWW some trees are thought to be spies that would betray Aslan, and spirits of evil* trees and poisonous plants are at the slaying of Aslan. After LWW, however, there is no more mention of bad trees. In PC the Telmarines, who have no use for nature and pollute the rivers of Narnia, quarrel with the trees and are afraid to go into the Black Woods.* The trees Lucy sees are almost awake, and bow to Aslan. Trufflehunter* claims that if the trees would move against the Telmarines they would leave Narnia in a hurry, and they are eventually sent to aid Caspian against Miraz.* Trees attend Aslan's feast, where they eat earth and drink wine.* In LB, the sacred talking trees are felled by the Calormenes* in Lantern Waste.* At the End of Narnia,* the dragons* and dinosaurs destroy the forests.

(LWW 18, *25;* 63, *64;* 137, *127;* 148, *138;* 180, *166.* PC 76, *74;* 133, *121;* 151–152, *136;* 192, *168;* 206, *179.* HHB 133–135, *118–119.* MN 119, *111.* LB 16–17, *20–21;* 155, *140.*)
[*Dryads; Ecology; Hamadryads; Silvans; Technology; Tree-People; Wood people.*]

TRINITY   The central revealed mystery[1] of the Christian religion: Father, Son, and Spirit, three divine persons in one divine nature.[2] In the entire

Chronicles there is only one specific reference to the Trinity. For young readers it is perhaps only a slightly bewildering complication that they can pass over quickly. For older readers the allusion evokes a range of responses, from a wince at the rather heavy-handed allegorical insertion of the reference to a delighted recognition of part of the profoundest meaning of the mysterious fact of the Trinity.[3] This reference comes when Shasta, weary and alone, pours out his story to the Large Voice walking beside him in the foggy night. In answer to Shasta's question, "Who *are* you?" the Voice gives a three-fold "Myself" in three different tones of voice: (1) "very deep and low so that the earth shook"; (2) "loud and clear and gay"; and (3) an almost inaudible but also all-encompassing whisper. The first suggests the power and the greatness of God,* who in Narnia is represented by the Emperor-beyond-the-Sea.* The second reveals the Eternal Word and highlights his eternal youth and joy.* The third emphasizes the subtle yet all-pervasive activity of the Holy Spirit.*

This revelation removes Shasta's fear* of being devoured or of being in the presence of a ghost; the "new and different trembling" he now feels is the fear of God, properly so-called, the terror and delight that are the hallmarks of a genuine experience of the numinous* as Lewis sees it.

(HHB 160, *140*.)

---

[1] It is called a mystery, not with the connotation of being *kept* secret, but because human minds have very few handles by which to grasp it and because they are too small to comprehend it. The legend of St. Augustine and the Child explains this inadequacy thus: after a particularly successful morning of theologizing, this late fourth–early fifth century bishop of the coastal North African city of Hippo decided to rest his mind by walking along the seashore. There he saw a child working quite hard at an excavation in the sand. The boy then began to run between the sea and the hole, carrying tiny buckets of water to the hole. The theologian asked the child what he was doing. "I am trying to pour the sea into this hole," he answered. The bishop laughed aloud and told the boy how impossible this task was. The child responded, "So too is your boast that you have understood the meaning of the Trinity," and he disappeared, leaving a much humbled thinker.

[2] Each term in this definition is freighted with centuries of theologizing; it not the purpose of this *Companion to Narnia* to attempt to summarize trinitarian theology. For a brief but fine discussion, see Donald G. Bloesch, *Essentials of Evangelical Theology* (San Francisco: Harper & Row Publishers, 1978) Volume 1, pp. 35–37. For a veritable *Summa* of theology in 122 pages of the most economic and thoughtful prose this author has ever had the pleasure to read and reread, see John Courtney Murray, *The Problem of God* (New Haven: Yale University Press, 1962).

[3] See *Introduction*. Lewis was not so rash as to assume that he could understand or explain the Trinity. Chapters 2 and 4 of *Mere Christianity* (New York: Macmillan, 1960; London: Collins Fount, 1977) pp. 153, *149–150*, only serve to exploit the few avenues of understanding human minds have, that is, the mathematical, the philosophical, and the interpersonal. Answering the question of whether it matters to try to understand the inner workings of the Trinity, Lewis summarizes:

> It matters more than anything else in the world. The whole dance, or drama, or pattern of this three-Personal life is to be played out in each one of us: or (putting it the other way round) each one of us has got to enter that pattern, take his place in that dance. There is no other way to the happiness for which we were made.

TRUFFLEHUNTER   A talking badger with a large, friendly, intelligent face. His is the first Old Narnian voice Caspian hears when he regains consciousness. Older and kinder than either Trumpkin* or Nikabrik,* he begins the debate over Caspian's fate. He is the first to pledge fealty to the Prince, after restraining the suspicious Nikabrik from doing Caspian harm.

Trufflehunter is another of Lewis's solid, sensible and, above all, loyal characters.[1] He has a secure sense of self and so disdains the offer of armor from the Seven Brothers of the Shuddering Wood,* saying that he was created a beast and that if his claws and teeth cannot help him protect his skin, it is not worth saving. Learned as well as brave, Trufflehunter knows his place and defers to Doctor Cornelius* as a "learned man." His role in life is also clear to him: badgers, he tells Glenstorm,* have the duty to remember just as Centaurs* are meant to watch the signs* in heaven and earth. When Peter calls Trufflehunter the best of badgers, he explains that being a beast, he does not change; and being a badger, he holds on.

True to his nature, Trufflehunter tries literally "to badger" his companions into faithfulness and right conduct. He overrules the suggestion that ogres* and hags* be solicited to help fight Miraz,* because Aslan would disapprove of such rabble. Horrified at Nikabrik's blasphemous equation of Aslan's power with that of the Witch, Trufflehunter reminds the dwarf that she is the worst of all Narnia's enemies and counters Nikabrik's claim that she was good to the dwarfs by urging him to be faithful to his oath to Caspian. Likewise, he corrects Nikabrik's myopic vision of the battle by pointing out that all the creatures fought hard, not just the dwarfs.* Trufflehunter's faith in Aslan prompts him to urge Nikabrik and Doctor Cornelius to be patient in the certainty that Aslan will come to their rescue. Irritated by Nikabrik's reference to "a performing lion," he reminds him that Aslan did indeed come back to life. The argument between the good badger and the dwarf escalates until Nikabrik attacks Trufflehunter. Nikabrik killed, the badger is embraced and kissed by Peter. From then on he sits quite close to Peter and never takes his eyes from him —another indication of Trufflehunter's deep sense of loyalty.

When the Dryads,* Hamadryads,* and Silvans* come up behind Caspian's forces, it is Trufflehunter who identifies them. He is raised to the Most Noble Order of the Lion by Caspian, who will later (in VDT) ask him to select a king in his place. The white patches on Trufflehunter's cheeks are the last things Lucy sees in Narnia. He is among the blessed in the Great Reunion.*

(PC 61 ff., *61 ff.;* 78, *75;* 86, *81;* 89–92, *85–87;* 157 ff., *140 ff.;* 204, *178;* 209, *183;* 215–216, *189.* VDT 208, *202.* LB 178, *161.*)
[*Biblical allusions; Honor; Orders, chivalric; Talking Beasts.*]

---

[1] Consider the high praise Lewis has for Mr. Badger of Kenneth Grahame's *The Wind in the Willows* in OOW, p. 27.

TRUMPKIN   A Red Dwarf*; he is the Pevensie children's* D.L.F.* in PC, Caspian's Regent in VDT, and the old, deaf Lord Chancellor of SC. Trumpkin is a medium-sized dwarf, about three feet tall. Stocky and deep-chested, his immense beard and red whiskers of coarse red hair frame a beak-like nose and twinkling eyes. He is very brave, with hearty spirits and a droll humour. He[1] is characterized by his use of alliterative expletives, which include horns and halibuts, whistles and whirligigs, giants and junipers, bottles and battledores, bilge and beanstalks, cobbles and kettledrums, wraiths and wreckage, weights and watterbottles, and crows and crockery. It is he who tells the children the story of young Caspian, and his is the third voice that Caspian hears when he regains consciousness. Although as a dwarf and an Old Narnian he might be expected to believe in Aslan, for much of PC he is an agnostic. When Trufflehunter* says Aslan wouldn't care for Nikabrik's* desire to have the help of the blacker forces, Trumpkin says cheerily but contemptuously, "Oh, Aslan." He is also patronizingly skeptical about Trufflehunter's belief that the trees* would chase the Telmarines* out of Narnia, and attributes such talk to the imagination* of animals.* "Soup and celery" is his remark at Dr. Cornelius's* recommendation of a retreat to Aslan's How,* which Trumpkin considers to be "based on old wives' tales."[2] He is, however, brave and loyal. He complains of the loss of the two messengers from the army, but when Nikabrik refuses to go, he volunteers. He makes an act of obedience* similar to Jane Studdock's in *That Hideous Strength*[3] when he says, "You are my king. I know the difference between giving advice and taking orders. You've had my advice, now it's the time for orders." In this statement he shows the perfect qualities for a Lord Regent he is to become. Trumpkin is above all a realist; he doesn't believe anything unless he has seen it with his own eyes.[4] Even when Trumpkin finishes telling his story to the four children, he does not make the connection between them and help from Aslan. He is persuaded to believe in them only when he is bested at archery by Susan; and (like Bree in HHB) he believes in Aslan only when, face to face, the Lion (who likes the dwarf very much) grabs him in his mouth, tosses him into the air, catches him, and stands him up again. After the defeat of Miraz,* Caspian raises the dwarf to the Most Noble Order of the Lion. As Regent in VDT, Drinian* says Trumpkin is loyal as a badger and valiant as a mouse (a reference, of course, to Reepicheep). Caspian also names him to reward the Dawn Treaders upon their return to Narnia, and to head the committee to select a new king of Narnia in Caspian's place. In SC, Jill and Eustace meet the old, deaf Trumpkin, now Lord Regent for the aged King Caspian, and Glimfeather* attempts valiantly to shout loud enough for the old regent to hear their conversation. Trumpkin passes judgment into Aslan's country,* and is present at the Great Reunion.*

(PC passim. VDT 208–209, *202–203.* SC 39 ff., *39 ff.;* 208, *199.* LB 178, *161.*)

[*Humor; Orders, chivalric.*]

---

[1] The British edition prefers "it" as the pronoun; the American edition prefers "he."

[2] Andrew Ketterley* also pooh-poohs "old wives' tales," to his regret. See *Stories* for a discussion of Lewis's idea that it is precisely in such tales that the truth rests.

[3] C. S. Lewis, *That Hideous Strength* (New York: Macmillan Publishing Co., 1965).

[4] This seems to be a basic trait of dwarfs. It is taken to its extreme by the dwarfs at the Stable,* who only see what they want to see and can no longer see what is really there.

TUMNUS   A flute-playing faun* who is approaching middle age and becoming stout, he has the characteristics of his race: the legs of a goat, the upper body of a man, curly hair, and two little horns on his head. He is about the same height as Shasta, probably about four feet tall (the same height as a good-sized dwarf*). The origin of his name is not clear, although it is a Latin diminutive of some sort. It may be from *tumulus,* meaning "hill," as Tumnus lives in hilly country. He is the first Narnian that Lucy—and the reader—meets in LWW, and she politely calls him Mr. Tumnus. He invites her home for tea, thinking to turn her over to the White Witch as a Daughter of Eve; but he is too kind to do so, and is eventually arrested for treason and turned into a stone statue in the courtyard of the Castle of the White Witch.* Revived by Aslan, he and Lucy dance* together for joy. He is the first-named friend to be rewarded and honored at the coronation of the Kings and Queens,* and many years later returns to tell them of the sighting of the White Stag.* In HHB he is a loyal Narnian who hates every stone of Tashbaan.* It is his idea to stock the *Splendour Hyaline,* to fool Rabadash,* and escape. He enters into Aslan's country* at the judgment, and discloses to Lucy the mystery of the glory of the within-ness of the garden* and Narnia: "The farther up and farther in you go, the bigger everything gets."

(LWW 7, *14;* 11–12, *19;* 13, *21;* 16, *15;* 17, *24;* 37–38, *41–42;* 54, *55;* 93, *91;* 168, *156;* 179, *165.* HHB 59 ff., *57 ff.* LB 179–180, *162–164.*)
[*Books; Gods; Mythology.*]

TURKISH DELIGHT   Edmund's favorite confection. He unwittingly eats several pounds of the White Witch's enchanted Turkish Delight in LWW, and as a result he falls into her power.

(LWW 31, *35;* 33, *38.*)
[*Greed.*]

TWO BROTHERS OF BEAVERSDAM   Telmarine* Lords, rulers at Beaversdam* under Caspian IX.* They are last mentioned as being imprisoned by Miraz,* who falsely accuses them of madness.

(PC 56, *56.*)

TYRANNY   See *Government.*

ULYSSES   See *Literary allusions.*

UNCLE ANDREW   See *Andrew Ketterley.*

UNDERLAND   The generic term for all the territory that lies beneath Narnia. It is bordered at the top by the Marches; the Deep Realm is very much further down; and Bism,[1] the bottommost realm, is one thousand fathoms beneath them. The inhabitants of Underland, the Earthmen,* call the land above them Overworld or Upperworld, and refer to the people there as Updwellers. Underland is a dark, cavernous world, sad and quiet and held in enchantment by the Queen.* Mosses and tree*-like shapes grow in the tunnels, and dragon*- and bat-like creatures sleep, waiting to wake at the end of Narnia.* The capital city of Underland is a great seaport situated on the Pale Beaches, and all the outlets into Overworld are located on the other side of the Sunless Sea (except the escape tunnel that is dug directly under the site of the Great Snow Dance). The Earthmen,* who originally came from Bism, call Underland the Shallow Lands (which, in their view, it is). Bism, in contrast to Underland, is a bright land of molten rocks. A river of fire inhabited by salamanders* flows through Bism, and its banks are covered with fields and groves of a tropical brilliance. Edible gems of all sorts grow like fruits in Bism —rubies grow in bunches like grapes, diamonds like oranges. After the liberation of Underland by Rilian and the children,* the Narnians keep the entrance open. It becomes quite an attraction, and on hot summer days Narnians descend to the Sunless Sea with ships and lanterns to sail, and sing, and enjoy themselves.

(SC Chapters 10 through 14.)
[*Warden of the Marches of Underland.*]

---

[1] Appropriately, *bism* is an obsolete form of *abysm,* Greek for "bottomless pit."

UNICORN   A mythological beast with a single horn in the center of its head. It variously symbolizes purity, chastity, and even the word of God as brought by Jesus Christ. According to legend a Unicorn has the legs of a buck, the tail of a lion,* and the body and head of a horse,* although in art it is most often depicted as a white horse (as it is in the *Chronicles*). Also according to legend, it has a white body, a red head, and blue eyes; the horn is white at the bottom, black in the middle, and red at the end. It is fierce in battle. Unicorns are mentioned several times in the *Chronicles,* and the noble and delicate Jewel* is present throughout LB. In contrast to the classical description, Lewis's Unicorns have indigo blue horns.[1] One is present in the group that forms a half-circle around Aslan before Peter's first battle, and at least two are sent to rescue Edmund. Like horses, Unicorns carry smaller creatures into battle. They use their horns as weapons.

(LWW 122, *115;* 134, *125;* 166, *153;* 171, *158;* 174, *161.* LB 76, *72;* 87, *81;* 114, *105.*)
[*Centaur; Horses; Mythology.*]

---

[1] Lewis has his own wonderful vision of Unicorns. In *The Great Divorce* (New York: Macmillan Publishing Co., 1974) p. 58, he describes a herd of Unicorns: "twenty-seven hands high the smallest of them and white as swans but for the red gleam in eyes and nostrils and the flashing indigo of their horns."

UNIVERSALISM   The belief that all religions are basically the same and thus one is as good as another. Two scenes in the *Chronicles* raise in the mind of some older readers the question of whether or not C. S. Lewis was a universalist. Did he believe that all roads lead ultimately in the same direction: eternal happiness for everyone? Or did he favor Christianity over the other world religions and believe that it is possible for a person to choose to be eternally unhappy and therefore be in some kind of hell*?

In the first[1] of these scenes, after Aslan turns Rabadash* into an ass, the Lion declares that because the Calormene* prince has invoked his god* Tash,* any release that the prince will experience from this enchantment will take place in the temple of Tash. He warns Rabadash not to stray more than ten miles from this temple or he will return to the form of an ass forever—there will be no second chance. Though universalism can be viewed as a belief in any number of chances, this passage does not disabuse some readers of the notion that, since Lewis permits even one more chance, he is relativizing the traditional view that life before death is an unalterable experience—that "as a tree falls, so shall it lie."

As further and much clearer evidence of Lewis's universalism, some readers point to the dialogue between Aslan and the Calormene soldier Emeth* in LB.[2] Because Aslan accepts Emeth's devotion to Tash as devotion really paid to him, some say that Lewis is relativizing the necessity for a person to explicitly acknowledge Christ as Savior in order to be saved. But careful reading of the exchange between the Lion and the man reveals C. S. Lewis as a painstaking, ecumenical theologian.

Even from the terms by which Aslan addresses Emeth—"son," "child" (twice), and "beloved"—the reader can see that though Emeth has not known Aslan except as the lion-shaped demon that Calormenes believe to be the power behind Narnia, Aslan has known and loved Emeth. When Emeth tries to deflect the Lion's welcome[3] by reminding Aslan that he has been Tash's servant, Aslan tells him that he has drawn that service to himself. Emeth asks if Shift's lie about the identity of Tash and Aslan is really true. Lewis carefully uses the adverb "wrathfully" to describe Aslan's response and Lewis details the radical differences between Aslan and Calormen's chief god, even giving examples that are reminiscent of the prophet Ezekiel.[4] Aslan asks Emeth if he understands this explanation and Emeth's ambiguous reply suggests both that he does not comprehend (that is, *fully* understand) and that he intuits the *meaning* of what the Lion has said even if he doesn't grasp all the *facts.*[5] Emeth goes on to ask what has been the meaning of his lifelong pursuit of Tash.[6] Aslan responds, "Beloved, unless thy desire had been for me thou wouldst not have sought so long and so truly. For all find what they truly seek."[7]

These two scenes, then, need to be taken together with several others in order to answer the questions raised in the first paragraph of this entry. Recall the fact that when Aslan liberates Beruna* in PC, most of the inhabitants flee, though a few join his happy company.[8] And Aslan is able to do little with the recalcitrant Andrew Ketterley* in MN except to render the man benignly senile.[9] Aslan is able to do nothing for the renegade dwarfs* in LB.[10] So, far from being the universalist that some consider Lewis to be, Lewis is trying to avoid two extremes: on the one hand, the classic universalist position which takes so broad a view that the imperative to preach the Good News about the crucified and risen Jewish rabbi drops out altogether; and, on the other hand, the classic particularist belief that only the relatively few people in the history of our earth who have heard the Gospel and come to believe in Christ are destined to be eternally happy. Lewis believed that the goodness people find in the world religions finds its ultimate source in Christ and that every person will find complete fulfillment in Christ. He also believed that it is possible for a person to reject this fulfillment in whatever form it might come to that person.[11]

[1] HHB 211, *184*.

[2] LB 164–165, *148*.

[3] Since he knew it well, Lewis may be alluding here to George Herbert's poem, "Love," the remarkable dialogue between Love (Christ) and the reluctant soul.

[4] Ezekiel, chapter 18 (all).

[5] See *Introduction*.

[6] The "yes" of Emeth's further question in the American edition is a typographical error; it should read "yet."

[7] This is almost a direct quotation of the fictional George Macdonald's answer to Lewis in *The Great Divorce*, cited in *Aslan*, note 4.

[8] PC 195, *171*.

[9] MN 171, *158*.

[10] LB 146–148, *134–135*.

[11] For a further discussion of this complex matter, see *Mere Christianity* (New York: Macmillan Publishing Co., 1960; London: Collins Fount, 1977) about the incarnation of Christ having an effect on people who have never heard of him (p. 156, *163*) and people who may be unconscious carriers of Christ to other people (p. 163, *160*). See also *The Great Divorce* (New York: Macmillan Publishing Co., 1946) about George Macdonald's universalism and the complementarity of freedom and predestination (pp. 128–129). See also "Christian Apologetics" in *God in the Dock*, Walter Hooper, ed. (Grand Rapids: Wm. B. Eerdmans Publishing Co., 1970) pp. 89–103, esp. 102–103, for a discussion of Hinduism and Christianity, "thick" and "clear" religions, and this fine summary statement:

> . . . Though all salvation is through Jesus, we need not conclude that He cannot save those who have not explicitly accepted Him in this life. And it should (at least in my judgement) be made clear that we are not pronouncing all other religions to be totally false, but rather saying that in Christ whatever is true in all religions is consummated and perfected. But on the other hand, I think we must attack wherever we meet in it the nonsensical idea that mutually exclusive propositions about God can both be true. (p. 102.)

UPPER WORLD   See *Underland*.

URNUS   See *Fauns*.

USEFULNESS   See *Magic, magician; Technology*.

UTTER EAST   See *Aslan's country*.

UVILAS   One of the great Telmarine* Lords in the reign of Caspian IX.*
With Belisar,* he is "accidentally" killed by arrows at a hunting party arranged by the evil* Miraz.*

(PC 55–56, 56.)

VALLEY OF THE THOUSAND PERFUMES   See *Mezreel.*

VANITY   In Lewis's way of thinking, vanity—the desire to be loved beyond the limits God sets—is the chink in a person's armor that allows evil*
to enter in. In the *Chronicles,* pride and vanity are shown transmuted into
greed* and love of power. Because Lucy feels ill-favored in the comparison
everyone makes between her and Susan, she is tempted to know what her
friends really think about her and so she uses the spell in the magician's*
Book.* Andrew* is "vain as a peacock," and his wish for power caused him
to become a magician in the first place. Hwin discerns that Bree's vanity
prevents him from entering Narnia while his tail is in a shabby condition; Bree,
however, calls his vanity "proper respect for [him]self." It is Andrew's appeal
to Polly's vanity that brings her into his study; and Queen Jadis is so vain she
assumes that Uncle Andrew has seen a vision of her beauty and has sent the
children to Charn* to sue for her favor.

(VDT 129 ff., *131 ff.;* 171, *168.* HHB 190–191, *167.* MN 13, *20;* 65, *63;* 76,
74.)

VENGEANCE   See *Honor.*

VIOLENCE   One of the chief objections to the *Chronicles* is their violence. Lewis uses battle imagery to introduce Aslan in LWW, when Mr.
Beaver* says Aslan has "landed" and is "on the move." The hacking off of
the serpent's head makes a gruesome mess on the floor, and the description
of the battle at Anvard* is equally gruesome: horses* mauled by cats, one
giant* shot in the eye, men beheaded. The Last Battle* details the gore:
three Calormenes* shot by arrows, one pierced by Jewel,* one by Tirian's*

sword, the fox by Eustace's sword, the bull shot in the eye and gored in the side, three dogs* killed and one hobbled, and the quiet, helpless death* of the bear. Violence is also present in other, smaller ways: Puddleglum threatens the Earthman* with violence; the impact of each giant jumping in rage is likened to the falling of a bomb; and Shasta, mistaken for Prince Corin,* is promised his first suit of armor and a war horse for his next birthday. C. S. Lewis felt that life is violent, and to deny that would be wrong. He was a long-time reader of G.K. Chesterton, who anticipates Lewis's feelings in the essay "The Red Angel":[1]

> . . . a lady has written me an earnest letter saying that fairy tales ought not to be taught to children even if they are true. She says it is cruel to tell children fairy tales, because it frightens them. . . . All this kind of talk is based on that complete forgetting of what a child is like. . . . Exactly what the fairy tale does is this: it accustoms [the child] for a series of clear pictures to the idea that these limitless terrors have a limit, that these shapeless enemies have enemies, that these strong enemies of man have enemies in the knights of God, that there is something in the universe more mystical than darkness, and stronger than fear.

(LWW 64, 65. SC 70, 75; 159–169, 157–158; 173, 169. HHB 72, 68; 177 ff., 155 ff. LB 118–119, 109.)

---

[1] "The Red Angel" in *Tremendous Trifles* (New York: Dodd, Mead, 1909).

VIVISECTION   The practice of experimenting on living animals* in order to gain scientific, especially medical, knowledge. The problem of animal pain was one that Lewis pondered for at least a quarter century.[1] Cruelty to animals was for him a grave moral fault that led of necessity to the cheapening of human suffering. Thus Eustace would have become a vivisector (he liked to pin dead insects on a card) if he had not been changed in Narnia. Evidence of this change is seen in his confronting Carter,* a powerful student at Experiment House,* for having tortured a rabbit. What is potential in Eustace becomes actual in Andrew Ketterley,* whose cruel experiments with animals had caused him to fear and hate them. Thus he casually excuses his experiments with the magical dust on guinea pigs with the statement that they are his because he bought them; that's what they're for. He mocks Digory's implicit suggestion that he ought to have asked the guinea pigs' permission before he used them, and concludes, "No great wisdom can be reached without sacrifice." The only sacrifice he is prepared to make, however, is of Polly. For this disregard of the sacredness of life, he is punished by being the subject of the experiments of the newly created Talking Beasts.* The apex of cruelty to animals is seen in the White Witch's treatment of Strawberry, her reindeer, and Narnian Talking Beasts, and in the Calormenes'* flogging of talking horses* in LB. Vivisection is the very antithesis to proper Narnian relations with animals, talking and dumb.

(LWW 115, 108. VDT 1, 9. SC 3, 12. MN 23, 27; 87, 82; 128, 119. LB 22, 25.)
[*Curiosity; Fledge; Knowledge; Technology.*]

---

¹ An animal lover himself, Lewis insisted on getting beneath the emotional arguments on either side of the question. His basic position was that vivisection was a procedure to be used only in extreme circumstances. He summarizes it well: "If on grounds of our real, divinely ordained superiority [human life over animal life] a Christian pathologist thinks it right to vivisect, and does so with scrupulous care to avoid the least dram or scruple of unnecessary pain, in a trembling awe at the responsibility he assumes, and with a vivid sense of the high mode in which human life must be lived if it is to justify the sacrifices made for it, then (whether we agree with him or not) we can respect his point of view." From "Vivisection," p. 226, in *God in the Dock* (Grand Rapids: Wm. B. Eerdmans Publishing Co., 1970). See also "The Pains of Animals" in that volume. For more on this subject, see *The Problem of Pain* (New York: Macmillan Publishing Co., 1962) Chapter 9; *That Hideous Strength* (New York: Macmillan, 1965) passim; and *The Abolition of Man* (New York: Macmillan Publishing Co., 1965) pp. 81–82.

VOCATION   See *Kings, queens.*

WAND   The White Witch's wand is not specifically described; however, it is through her wand that she performs her magic.* Its destruction by Edmund turns the course of battle in favor of Aslan's forces.

(LWW 132, *123;* 173, *159;* 176, *162.*)
[*Sceptre.*]

WAR   See *Violence.*

WARDEN OF THE MARCHES OF UNDERLAND   The guardian of the borders ("marches") of Underland* (in this case, the "borders" would be the territory nearest the Overworld). As befits a citizen of a sunless land, he speaks with a flat voice in a tone as black as night. When he first meets Jill, Eustace, and Puddleglum, he is accompanied by a retinue of one hundred spear-carrying Earthmen.* A deadpan performer, he unwittingly makes a pun on his title when he commands the three to "March." To the consternation of the impatient Eustace, he continually repeats his stock phrase ("Many fall down, but few return . . ." and so on). It soon becomes apparent that this flat, rhythmic phrase is almost a password, and it allows the Warden to deliver the three travelers to the gnomes-in-waiting at the Queen's door.

(SC 121 ff., *122 ff.*)
[*Queen of Underland.*]

WARDROBE   The means by which the Pevensie children* first enter Narnia is a wardrobe in the house of Professor Kirke.* It is fashioned from the wood of the apple tree* that grew from the core of the apple of the Tree of Protection,* planted by the young Digory; and it apparently maintains an affinity with the land of its parent. It is three times the door to Narnia: once for Lucy alone, once for Lucy and Edmund, and once for all of the Pevensie children. Only Edmund is foolish enough to shut the door behind him, indicative of his future behavior in Narnia. The wardrobe is called "War Drobe" by Tumnus,* who thinks it is a city in Spare Oom.*[1]

(LW 5–7, *11–13;* 10–11, *16–17;* 18–19, *25–26;* 24–25, *29–30;* 49 ff., *52 ff.;* 185–186, *170.* PC 1, *11.* MN 184–185, *170–171.*)
[*Transitions.*]

---

[1] Lewis, when a child, had probably read E. Nesbit's story "The Aunt and Amabel," in which Amabel finds her way into a magic world via "Bigwardrobeinspareroom." (Roger Lancelyn Green and Walter Hooper, *C. S. Lewis: A Biography* [New York: Macmillan Publishing Co., 1974; London: Collins, 1974] p. 250, *250.*). See *Literary allusions.*

WAR OF DELIVERANCE   This term is first used in the Great Reunion* scene in LB to describe the civil war in Narnia which took place 250 years earlier, in 2303 N.Y. The story of this war is the chief burden of PC. Serious conflicts break out in the thirteenth year of the rule of the usurper Miraz,* who seems no more oppressive than any previous new Narnian (that is, Telmarine*) ruler of Narnia. Prince Caspian, won to the side of Old Narnia by the stories of his nurse* and Doctor Cornelius,* his tutor, leads the Old Narnians against the forces of Miraz with the help of Peter and Edmund. They and their sisters are brought into Narnia by the solemn winding of Susan's horn.* But Lucy and Susan do not fight; rather they accompany Aslan on a bacchanal.[1] As much is done to free Narnia from Telmarine tyranny by the return of dancing and celebration as by the actual combat. The two narrative strands join in the second battle of Beruna* in which the awakened trees* drive the forces of Miraz to complete surrender.

(PC passim. LB 179, *161.*)
[*Dance; Revelry; Violence.*]

WATER RAT   Obedient to what he thinks are Aslan's orders, he pilots a raft of logs made of talking trees* down the Great River* to the Calormene* merchants. When Jewel* and Tirian* hear this, they are frightened.

(LB 19, *23.*)
[*Talking Beasts.*]

WELL-WOMEN   See *Naiads.*

WEREWOLVES   Men who, by will or enchantment, are said to be able to turn into wolves. In LWW, werewolves are called to battle by the White

Witch; and some are glimpsed in the first months of the reign of the Kings and Queens.* In PC, Nikabrik's* unnamed friend has a dull, grey voice that causes Peter's flesh to creep. He is a ravenous, bloodthirsty, hateful beast who urges the hag* to call up the Witch and begin the magic.* He is killed while in the process of changing from man to wolf as he leaps on Caspian and bites him.

(LWW 132, *123;* 180, *166.* PC 160 ff., *143 ff.*)
[*Mythology.*]

WESTERN MARCH   The territorial border of which Edmund is Count. The word *march* means "boundary."

(PC 173, *152.*)
[*Geography, Narnian; Western Wilds.*]

WESTERN WILDS   An uncivilized country that forms part of the western border of Narnia. The Alp-like Western Mountains border a land of high green hills and forests, and hide a green valley. It is in this valley, with its blue lake, that the garden* on the high green hill houses the apple tree* that is so precious to Aslan. No Talking Beast* lives here; a hunter kills a dumb lion* here and discards its skin, which is later picked up and used by Shift* to represent the false Aslan.

(LWW 10, *17.* PC 42, *45;* 45, *48.* MN 143, *132;* 148, *138.* LB 6, *10;* 175–176, 158.)
[*Geography, Narnian; Hunting.*]

WHITE STAG   A beast, the quest* of great hunting* parties, who was said to grant wishes to his captors.[1] Tumnus reports that he has been seen at Lantern Waste.* The stag leads a group of Narnians, including the Kings and Queens,* on a difficult chase until only the four royal rulers are left in pursuit. They dismount and follow him into a thicket, where Susan loses her horn* and the children make the transition* back to England via the wardrobe.*

No physical description of the White Stag is given, but his extraordinary beauty may be inferred from the appearance of the unnamed stag that accompanies Duffle* in HHB. It is portrayed as a strong yet delicate creature with limpid eyes, a dappled coat, and slender, delicate legs.

(LWW 13, *20;* 182, *167.* PC 24, *30.* HHB 165, *145.*)

---

[1] Lewis, as a student of the Middle Ages, would know of the symbolism of the stag for Christ; but it is impossible to determine whether he intended an allusion here.

WHITE WITCH   As the White Witch of LWW, she is responsible for the Hundred Years of Winter* that falls on Narnia; as Jadis in MN, she is the possessor of the Deplorable Word.* The two are one and the same: characterizations of evil,* who cannot really be killed, but must be watched for and confronted over and over again. According to Mr. Beaver,* the White Witch is the offspring of a giant* and the demon Lilith.* She is bad through and through;[1] and she is especially villainous because she looks human, but has not a drop of human blood in her.[2]

When Lewis was writing LWW, he had not yet conceived of MN; thus, although he strives mightily to blend the two characterizations, there are loose ends and unanswered questions. At the end of MN, we are told that the Tree of Protection* will keep the witch out of Narnia as long as it flourishes; meanwhile, she has fled to the North, "growing stronger in dark magic.*" But by the time of LWW, she has managed not only to gain entrance into Narnia, but she has succeeded in gaining enough power over it to hold it in the enchantment of winter without end. This would imply that the Tree of Protection has either weakened, died, or been circumvented in some other way; or that Jadis has become such a master of the dark arts that she is able to overcome the Tree's effects. All this must remain speculation, however, because we are never told what happened. Another question that arises is how an inhuman witch became the last of a long line of kings* and queens of Charn,* when those kings and queens were all humans. Lewis's description of the royalty Digory and Polly encounter frozen in position at the great hall of Charn is meant quite obviously to show the progression of corruption that occurred in this line, from kindness to cruelty to despair to depravity, culminating in the most evil of all, Jadis herself. This corruption is only possible in human beings, as nonhumans (especially the combination of giant and demon) may be assumed to be bad from the start.

The White[3] Witch   She is the self-proclaimed Queen of Narnia, and she is determined to kill the Sons of Adam* and Daughters of Eve whose thrones, according to the prophecies,* are already waiting in Cair Paravel. She rides in a sleigh driven by a dwarf* and pulled by white reindeer, and she herself is dressed in white fur to her neck. She wears a gold crown and carries a gold wand.* Her face is deathly pale, and her mouth is crimson. Edmund thinks her beautiful[4] but stern. She has imposed winter without end on Narnia, and that world is blanketed with a white, killing snow. That she is evil is indisputable: she has no conscience and no scruples, and will do anything that is to her advantage. She entraps poor Edmund with the sweet seduction of Turkish Delight*; she turns Narnians into stone statues that decorate her courtyard; and she sends a pair of wolves to kill the beavers* and the children.* Her worst and most unforgiveable offense, of course, is her slaying of Aslan at the Stone Table,* during which she endeavors to drive him even deeper into despair by boasting that he has given her Narnia forever, lost his own life, and not saved Edmund after all. Here, however, she shows the vanity* that is in the end her undoing. She assumes that, like her, everyone else lacks a conscience and scruples—and if they do not, then they are fools. In believing she can control everything, she blinds herself to other possibilities. But her knowledge* only goes so far: she knows the Deep Magic,* but Aslan knows the Deeper Magic.* Her army consists of all the worst animals and most ghastly creatures of dreams* and nightmares, including bats, wolves, ghouls,* and hags.* Aslan's army, powered by the newly freed Narnians, overcomes these beastly apparitions and the Witch herself is killed by Aslan.[5]

Jadis Jadis is the Queen of Charn,* the last of a long line of kings* and queens, who desires to gain power not only over her own world, but over as many worlds as possible. Like the White Witch, she is pale and intense. Unlike the White Witch, who is a broadly-painted cardboard figure of wickedness, Jadis is more finely drawn. She wears extravagant royal robes,* bejewelled and embroidered and finer than those worn by any of the other queens in the great hall at Charn. She rules over a dead city, having overcome her sister (the former queen) with the ultimate weapon, the Deplorable Word, which she learned at great cost to herself.[6] Like the White Witch, she also deals in sweet seductions—the maddening verse on the pillar "causes" Digory to strike the golden bell,* and its sweet tone lets Jadis loose upon the world once more. In England,* Jadis is truly a vision. In that world she is larger than life, a vision of pure energy on the drab London pavement. Her power, which is sapped by the timeless air of the Wood between the Worlds,* is intensified in our world, and she is able to wrench an iron bar from the lamp-post* outside the Ketterley residence. That she is a figure of evil is indisputable (witness her selfish destruction of the innocent people of Charn; her merciless beating of Strawberry; her guided tour of the castle, in which she points out to Digory and Polly her favorite spots—the dungeons, the principle torture chambers, and the site of a great and arbitrary slaughter by her grandfather; and her knowledge* of the Deplorable Word; but she is also an occasion for laughter and the butt of jokes.[7] Her behavior at the lamp-post is outlandish and causes the onlookers to conclude that she is insane; Sarah* the maid finds it most exciting. The image of Jadis holding on to Jill's hair as they reenter the Wood between the Worlds is painful, but it also serves to make Jadis seem ridiculous and childish.

Perhaps her most frightening attribute is her desire to come into our world, and her assumption that magicians are the ruling class here as well as in Charn. Once she meets Uncle Andrew,* she ceases to notice Digory at all, and Lewis comments parenthetically that "most witches are like that. They are not interested in things or people unless they can use them; they are terribly practical." Finally, she is a symbol to Lewis of the inevitability of the chaos begun by the impersonal experimentation of our technological society.

(LWW passim. MN passim.)
[*Animals; Castle of the White Witch; Colney 'Atch; Fenris Ulf; Sexism; Technology; Vanity; Vivisection.*]

---

[1] See *Depravity.*

[2] For a discussion of the implications of looking human but being wild, see *Dumb Beasts,* note 1.

[3] The usual meaning of "white witch" as one who practices "white magic" (good magic in which the Devil is not invoked) is not the meaning Lewis intends. Here white is used as the color of death, the time of winter, when nothing can grow and good people are "frozen," prevented from overcoming the evil that holds them in thrall. The stage is thus set for the coming of spring and the rebirth of nature brought by Aslan. See *Aslan's country,* note 1.

---

[4] Similarly, Digory thinks Jadis the most beautiful woman he has seen, while Polly doesn't see her beauty at all. This is both an instance of Lewis's unconscious sexism*—the belief that women are jealous of the beauty of other women—and an ironic comment on the susceptibility of men to the physical beauty of women.

[5] It appears, however, that she does not really die. In PC, the hag* informs Doctor Cornelius* that the White Lady (her name for the Witch) is alive and may be called upon for help. Thus the Witch returns again and again, like evil itself.

[6] This is a parallel to Uncle Andrew, who ruined his health by becoming a magician ("One doesn't become a magician for nothing"). It is one of several intentional parallels that Lewis makes in order to impress upon the reader his belief that the quiet violations of natural law in the privacy of a scientist's laboratory are the same as, and lead to, the ultimate violations of the sacredness of life practiced by Jadis and other unscrupulous rulers.

[7] See *Humor.*

WILD FRESNEY   A Narnian wild herb that looks like wood sorrel[1] but tastes nicer when cooked, especially with a little butter and pepper.

(LB 76, 72.)

[1] The American edition of LB spells the word *wood sorel,* while the British edition spells it *wood sorrel.* The American edition may have misprinted the word, as Webster's Dictionary lists the correct spelling as *sorrel.*

WILD PEOPLE   See *Wood people.*

WILL   See *Joy.*

WIMBLEWEATHER   A small giant* known as Wimbleweather of Deadman's Hill. He is described as being brave as a lion* but not too clever, and is a member of Caspian's War Council. When he ruins a crucial battle by breaking out at the wrong time and place, he is so sorry that he begins to cry. His tears disturb the mice,* so he goes off to be by himself, but not before stepping on someone's tail. When Reepicheep's suggestion that he, as chief mouse, be one of the Marshalls of the Lists, the giant laughs, thus incurring the mouse's lasting scorn. He is a member of Edmund's parley, a Marshall of the Lists for Peter's single combat, and a major figure in the second battle of Beruna.*

(PC 80, 76; 173, 152; 183, 161; 190, 167.)

WINDING ARROW   An east-to-west swiftly flowing river. It is the northern boundary of the Great Desert* and has an unnamed south-to-north tributary.

(HHB 133–134, 118.)
[*Geography, Narnian.*]

WINE   The spirit of revelry* is alive in Narnia, and wine is an important part of celebration. Lucy's healing cordial* is probably an alcoholic beverage. In PC, a wine list includes thick wines, clear red wines, yellow wines, and green wines.[1] In VDT the crew of the *Dawn Treader* drinks the strong wine

of Archenland,* and in the Land of the Duffers* all but Eustace enjoy the mead served. The sailors award bottles of wine to the Duffers* who win the "boat races"; and Caspian calls for a round of grog to relax the crew after the escape from the Dark Island.* On Ramandu's Island,* Reepicheep drinks a toast to the Daughter of Ramandu.* In SC, supper at Cair Paravel* includes "all manner of wines and fruit drinks." At Harfang,* Puddleglum (who is fond of the rather strange alcoholic drink of the Marsh-Wiggles) drinks a salt-cellar full of giants'* liquor and becomes quite drunk. After the death of the Queen of Underland,* Rilian proposes that they refresh themselves and pledge health to one another with wine left over from their dinner. In HHB, Shasta's Calormene* meal includes a "white" wine that Lewis says is really yellow. In MN, Uncle Andrew's* weakness for brandy is one of many weaknesses. In LB, Roonwit* is offered a bowl of wine by Tirian,* and the small animals bring Tirian wine. He wishes ruefully that he had stocked the guard tower with a small cask of wine. The love of wine, however, reaches the point of excess in Shift, who becomes an alcoholic.

(PC 205, *180.* VDT 67, *74;* 124, *126;* 147, *147;* 161, *160;* 173, *170.* SC 40, *46;* 92 ff., *95 ff.;* 162, *159.* HHB 71, *68.* MN 74–77, *73–74.* LB 14, *18;* 36, *39;* 55, *56.*)

---

[1] Curiously, Lewis himself wasn't much of a wine drinker; he preferred beer or whiskey.

WOOD BETWEEN THE WORLDS[1]
The wood where Polly and Digory arrive after leaving Uncle Andrew's* study via the magic* rings.* Polly first calls it the Wood between the Worlds after Digory reasons that they are indeed between worlds. It is so dense and leafy that the light is green, the air is warm, and no sky can be seen. There is no sound of life or wind, and the wood is characterized by a feeling of timelessness. There are pools everywhere, and although they look deep they are really shallow. It is hard for the children to feel frightened in the wood, and at first it is difficult for them to remember who they are and where they've come from. They feel as if they have always been in the Wood.

Curiously, the Wood seems to affect people in varying ways, according to their innate goodness. When Digory and Polly return there from Charn,* the Wood seems "rich and warmer and more peaceful" by contrast. But Queen Jadis looks paler and far less beautiful in its atmosphere; in fact, the air seems to stifle her. The children lose their fear when they realize that they are stronger than she. Upon her return to the wood, Jadis becomes "deadly sick." Uncle Andrew is shivering there (probably with fear), but Strawberry seems to look and feel better.

(MN Chapter 3 passim; 66 ff., *65 ff.;* 95 ff., *90 ff.*)

---

[1] A name inspired by William Morris's novel, *The Wood Beyond the World* (New York: Ballantine Books, Inc., 1969). For an indication of Lewis's esteem for Morris, see OOW pp. 18–19 and *Selected Literary Essays,* Walter Hooper, ed. (London: Cambridge University Press, 1969) pp. 219–231.

WOOD PEOPLE   A general class that includes Dryads,* Hamadryads,* Silvans,* and Tree-people.* In PC they are called wood gods* and goddesses, and they are the awakened trees* that rush at the Telmarines.* They are certainly the wild people who emerge from the trees when Aslan commands Narnia to awake.

(PC 138–139, *126.* MN 117, *109.*)

WOOSES   Haunting spirits, present at the slaying of Aslan. The term may be of Lewis's own coining. It suggests both "ooze," that is, slime (*woose* is an older form of "ooze"), and the noise such a specter might make.

(LWW 148, *138.*)

WORLD ASH TREE   The expression "the trunk of the World Ash Tree" is found only in the American editions of LWW. According to the White Witch, the words of the Deep Magic* are written in at least three sacred places: on the Stone Table,* on the trunk of the World Ash Tree, and on the sceptre* of the Emperor-beyond-the-Sea.* These allusions are dense and somewhat imprecise.[1] The written words suggest *runes,* magical letters carved into stone or wood by many early North European cultures. The World Ash Tree is Yggdrasill, the great tree of Scandinavian mythology,* a symbol for existence. Its branches tower into the heavens, its trunk upholds the earth, and its three roots reach, respectively, into the realm of the dead, into the land of the giants,* and into the abode of the gods.* The holy fountain of fate, the Well of Urd, is under this third root; the council of the gods* is convened daily at this fountain. Nearby dwell the three maidens (the Nornir)—Past, Present, and Future (or Fate, Being, and Necessity): they rule the life of every person and the whole world.

(LWW 138.)
[*Secret Hill.*]

---

[1] No scholar the author has been able to consult has been able to pinpoint the allusion here. Dr. Hilde R.E. Davidson, author of the excellent *Gods and Myths of Northern Europe* (Harmondsworth, Middlesex: Penguin Books, 1964), makes the following observation in a letter to the author dated July 7, 1979:

> "It seems to me that when Lewis refers to the fire-stones and the Secret Hill he is simply being vague, with a background of burial mounds and hearths, where it would be natural to inscribe runes. He improved this in the American edition by a reference to runic letters on the trunk of the World Tree. I know of no reference to such letters, but the association of Tree and Spear could arise from the mention of Odin hanging on the Tree in *Hávamál,* pierced with a spear, and bending to pick up the runes. These are associated with destiny, and I think that this rather than justice would be behind the symbolism. Odin is not very concerned with justice, although Thor is, and this is an Odin image."

But Professor Thomas W. Craik does not think that Lewis's substitution in the American editions of LWW of "the trunk of the World Ash Tree" for "the fire-stones of the Secret Hill" is an improvement: "The World Ash Tree is, of course, monstrously and distractingly particular and irrelevant, and if Lewis requested or even approved this change I am surprised at him."(Letter to author dated July 31, 1979.)

As far as the author has been able to discover, there is no written record of Lewis's directives to make this change (or the Maugrim/Fenris Ulf* change or the rewriting of the ending of the Dark Island* chapter in VDT) in the American edition. It is to be assumed that he did authorize these changes—and, on that assumption, the author tends to agree with Professor Craik, preferring the vagueness of the druidic image to the specificity of the Scandinavian.

WORLD'S END[1]   A huge plain of utterly flat land, covered with short green grass. It intersects with the sky, which appears to be a bright blue, glasslike wall. It is located south of the place where Reepicheep goes over the last wave of the Silver Sea.* Here Edmund, Lucy, and Eustace meet the Lamb,* who is really Aslan.

(VDT 214, *207–208.*)
[*Geography, Narnian; Last Sea.*]

---

[1] This is not to be confused with one of the names of Ramandu's Island,* which is really only the beginning of the end of the world of Narnia.

WRAGGLE   The only named satyr* in all of the *Chronicles.* A traitor to the cause of Tirian,* he fights against him in the Last Battle,* and loses his life almost immediately when he is struck by one of Jill's arrows.

(LB 118, *109.*)
[*Mythology.*]

WRAITHS   Terrifying phantoms, present at the slaying of Aslan. The word is Scottish in origin and its use is another instance of Lewis's desire to evoke a "northern" atmosphere in his stories.

(LWW 148, *138.*)

WRONG   See *Right and wrong.*

ZALINDREH[1]   Site of a Calormene* battle in which Bree and his master Anradin* distinguished themselves. Bree likes to tell the story and gets the chance to at the victory celebration at Anvard.*

(HHB 41, *43;* 214, *186.*)

Spelled "*Zu*lindreh" in its first appearance in HHB and "*Za*lindreh" in its second appearance in the first edition and all subsequent editions. Given Lewis's affinity for the Arabic syllable *az* in his name-coining in HHB, "Zulindreh" seems to be a misprint.

ZARDEENAH   The moon goddess to whose service all Calormene maidens are dedicated until they marry; before their weddings they offer secret sacrifice to her. Also known as Lady of the Night.

(HHB 37, 39.)
[*Gods.*]

Appendix One

Chronology of the Composition and Publication of The Chronicles of Narnia
(together with Lewis's age, and certain other important essays, poems, and letters)

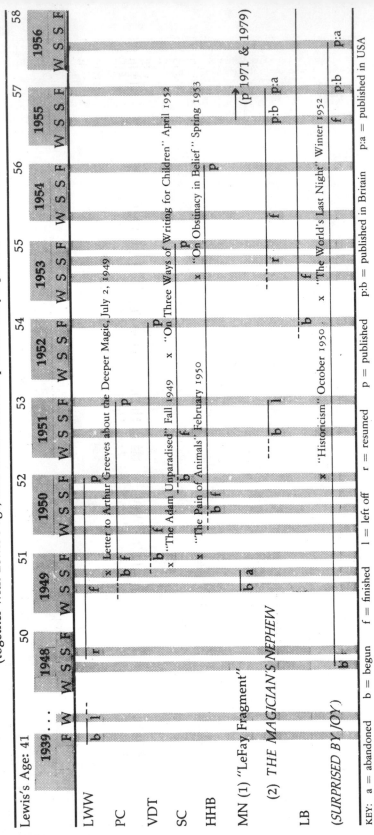

KEY: a = abandoned   b = begun   f = finished   l = left off   r = resumed   p = published   p:a = published in USA   p:b = published in Britain   x =   (p 1971 & 1979)

Appendix Two

List of Comparative Ages of Principal Characters in The Chronicles of Narnia
(all approximate; based on Lewis MS 51, published in PWD, pp. 41–44)

English people:

	MN	LWW	HHB	PC	VDT	SC	LB
Digory	12 in MN,	52 in LWW,					61 in LB
Polly	11 in MN,						60 in LB
Peter		13 in LWW,	27 in HHB,	14 in PC,			22 in LB
Susan		12 in LWW,	26 in HHB,	13 in PC,			21 in LB
Edmund		10 in LWW,	24 in HHB,	11 in PC,	12 in VDT,		19 in LB
Lucy		8 in LWW,[1]	22 in HHB,	9 in PC,	10 in VDT,		17 in LB
Eustace					9 in VDT,	9 in SC,	16 in LB
Jill						9 in SC,	16 in LB

Narnians:

	MN	LWW	HHB	PC	VDT	SC	LB
Caspian X				13 in PC,	16 in VDT,	66 in SC	
Rilian						31 in SC	

---

[1] LWW 41, 44, indicates that Edmund and Lucy are only a year apart in age. Since Lewis MS says that he was born in 1930 and she in 1932, they have to be slightly more than a year apart.

> *"Do you think I am trying to weave a spell? Perhaps I am; but remember your fairy tales. Spells are used for breaking enchantments as well as for inducing them."*
> —*C. S. Lewis, "The Weight of Glory"*

C. S. Lewis imbued *The Chronicles of Narnia* with a very special magic: opening any volume in the series, the reader is instantly transported to realms of adventure, delight, wisdom, and grace. Throughout these books, Lewis weaves spells that beguile or unbind the senses, so that we see the world of Narnia as someplace real and see, at the same time, the real world with fresh understanding. Now this monumental, illustrated *Companion* to the world-famous Narnia stories of C. S. Lewis—containing hundreds of indexed entries—is an indispensable handbook for all explorers of Narnia, Archenland, Underland, Calormen, and the other lands washed by enchanted seas.

From *Aslan*, the Great Lion of Narnia, to *Zardeenah*, the mysterious lady of the night, here are all the characters, events, places, and themes of Lewis's beloved *Chronicles of Narnia*. The Monopods, Northern Giants, Telmarines, Hollies, Dufflepuds, and Naiads who inhabit these wondrous realms are included, as are all geographical points from the Shuddering Wood to the Last Sea. *Companion to Narnia* omits no character: Prince Caspian, Lucy, Rilian, Reepicheep, the White Witch, Edmund, Susan, Puddleglum, Glenstorm, and Glimfeather—all are listed and defined in terms of their history, role, and significance.

Beginning anywhere—with a character, an object, an overview, a theme—readers can pursue a thread of inquiry as far as they wish with this simple-to-use, comprehensive system of cross-references. No matter how familiar you may be with the saga of Narnia, this magical *Companion* will lead you to a fuller understanding and appreciation of the treasures—hidden as well as overt—enriching these now-classic tales.

Paul Ford brings careful scholarship and contagious enthusiasm to his research. He examines classical, scriptural, and literary references; unearths the origins of crucial terms and concepts; and provides insight into the symbolic and thematic threads that amplify